Public Relations
Management

Public Relations Management

Jaishri Jethwaney

and

N N Sarkar

STERLING PUBLISHERS PRIVATE LIMITED

STERLING PUBLISHERS PRIVATE LIMITED
A-59, Okhla Industrial Area, Phase-II, New Delhi-110020.
Tel: 26387070, 26386209 Fax: 91-11-26383788
e-mail: mail@sterlingpublishers.com
www.sterlingpublishers.com

Public Relations Management
© 2009, Jaishri Jethwaney and N N Sarkar
ISBN 978 81 207 4611 4
Reprint 2010

All rights are reserved. No part of this publication may be reproduced, stored in a retrieval system or transmitted, in any form or by any means, mechanical, photocopying, recording or otherwise, without prior written permission of the original publisher.

PRINTED IN INDIA

Printed and Published by Sterling Publishers Pvt. Ltd., New Delhi-110 020.

Acknowledgments

Many faculty colleagues and professional friends have made this book possible. We would like to especially thank those peers who read various chapters of the book and offered valuable suggestions. Professor S Brahmachari, faculty in the Department of Advertising and Public Relations at the Indian Institute of Mass Communication (IIMC), Sanjay Meena and Tanushree deserve our special thanks for their constant help and support.

One of the authors viz. Dr. J Jethwaney who is a Professor and Course Director at the IIMC would like to make a special mention of Ms Stuti Kacker, Additional Secretary, GOI and Director IIMC for her unstinted support and understanding. The book could be completed in such a short time, because of the focus facilitated by the study leave granted to her.

Last but not the least we would like to acknowledge the support of our families who remain the reason for our achievements

The authors would welcome feedback from the readers.

NN Sarkar
Former Associate Professor IIMC
nnsarkar2000@yahoo.com

Dr. Jaishri Jethwaney
Professor and
Course *Director (Advertising& PR)*
Indian Institute of Mass Communication
jjethwaney@yahoo.com

May 2009
New Delhi

Preface

The book *Public Relations Management* comes as an extension of the book *Public Relations* by the same authors. The latter was last published in 2000, with several reprints later. Much has changed in the last decade or so in terms of media, matters and expectations.

Relevance of the book

The current century has witnessed a tremendous spurt in media and technology. What looked impossible just two decades ago, has become more than a reality in terms of connectivity with the world at large. Constant media exposure to matters—social, economic and political—has resulted in people demanding more accountability from those who govern them and also those in the marketplace. The new age media has brought about a paradigm shift about who really holds the power of the pen. Is it the mainstream media or the citizen journalists and bloggers, who spare no time in expressing their views on everything under the sun? If there are positive aspects about organizations reflected in various media through PR efforts, there is no denying that anyone who has been hurt in any which way in terms of quality or behaviour of an organization has the facility to write about his/her experience in a blog which is accessible to millions along with the "official" site. And this has made a difference to the organizations that have to be more vigilant than before. Those who are studying PR and those who practice PR have to understand the dynamics of the changing media matrix and acquire skills on how to handle various media. It is hoped that the book will provide lots of insights and hands on skills to both students and young practitioners in pursuing their job more efficiently and vigorously.

This time the book has been written in a textbook style with several citations and critical thinking exercises and questions at the end of each chapter.

Coverage and structure

The book has been structured in three parts. **Part I** "Understanding concepts, strategies and tools" provides the reader with a theoretical framework of PR along with a worldview of the profession for over a century or so. The segment moves on to discuss the relevance of PR to other management disciplines. The chapter, "Employee Communication" includes both the philosophy and hands-on-skills. The chapter has been embellished with various case studies to make the theory relevant to the practice of PR. The chapters, "The PR Process" and "Troika of Communication" delineate various steps in PR campaigning and a discussion on the need to bring about synergy in the three elements viz. medium, message and audience to achieve organizational goals. The chapters, "Media and its Relevance to PR" and "PR Writing" provide the reader with an overview of media, the future of media, and relevance of various media in PR and hands on skills in writing for various media to reach out to both internal and external publics. In the chapter the author shares tips on organizing media handling and media events.

Crises communication is considered the core of PR practice. Chapter 10, besides giving concepts has included a number of case studies that cover exploding crises, man-made crises and crises of corporate governance and terrorism, to quote a few.

Part II: "Understanding the technical aspects of PR" takes the reader through the technical part of PR, viz., the printing and production aspects that are so central to the day to day practice of PR.

Part III: "Understanding legalities and professional requirements" deals with various laws and ethical considerations in the profession and the future agenda for the profession.

Contents

Acknowledgments v

Preface vii

Part I
UNDERSTANDING CONCEPTS, STRATEGIES AND TOOLS

1. **Defining Public Relations** 3
   - What PR is; its various definitions, concepts and perceptions
   - What PR practitioners need to know to understand work requirements
   - PR in the global scenario: challenges and opportunities
   - Case study to make a link between concepts, practice and implementation

   Case study
   - *What Happened* by Scott McClellan

2. **Public Relations Theory** 26
   - The debate on the evolution and practice of PR in the last about a century and whether PR has theoretical underpinnings or is just a skill/craft
   - Various theories with arguments on their relevance and practice in PR
   - Case studies of corporates, civil society and NGO organizations on the use of strategies and their analyses

   Case studies
   - Save Narmada Crusade
   - The Nano ouster from West Bengal
   - Mc libel case: Examination of PR and the influence of activism
   - Case of French fries laced in beef tallow
   - Cola drinks and pesticides
   - Yamuna Pollution – Activism of NGOs
   - Averting the Nationalization of TISCO

3. Public Relations and Other Management Disciplines   45
- Communication flow process in an organization
- Various forms of communication within an organization
- Organizational communication and PR communication
- Interface of PR with various staff and line function departments

4. Media and its relevance to PR   55
- The changing media scenario, especially in the context of India
- Growth and expansion of various media
- The future of media and people's engagement with media.
- Trends and possibilities.

5. The PR Process   72
- The process through which PR works
- The various steps of PR planning and implementation
- Some case studies of PR programmes

Case studies
- Delhi government's PR
- Creating aware communities in disaster situations–a PR outreach programme in Tsunami hit Southern coastal India in 2004
- Economic recession—image impact on ICICI—salvaging it through strategic PR
- BSES 2002-07
- Social connect for inclusive development: Lead India and Teach India campaigns

6. PR Tools and Methods   91
- To introduce the role and scope of PR communication
- To discuss various tool/media used by PR in reaching out to various stakeholders
- To discuss the strengths and weaknesses of media
- To deliberate on the best strategies to make use of the media in an effective manner

Case study
- A crisis time study of DMRC

7. Troika of Communication—Message, Medium and Audience   120
- Attributes of media, message and audience
- The interdependence of the above three
- The use of strategy in synergizing the three to get the desired response

8. Employee Communication   134
- The definition of Internal audience
- The Communication needs of the Target Audience (TA)
- Various media to reach out to various employee echelons
- Case studies in Internal communication

Case studies
- Present the big picture : Dhabol project
- Create champions: Goodyear Tyres
- Reaching out to employees: LG
- When the going gets tough, the tough get going: NHPC
- GE
- FedEx
- Johnson & Johnson (J&J)
- Honeywell Aerospace

9. Public Relations Writing   145
- The role, scope and importance of PR writing
- Various kinds of PR writing
- Writing for the media – various genres
- Writing for internal audience
- Hands-on skills on writing for various target audience

Case study
- Available information about an accident

10. PR and Crisis Communication   159
- Definition of crisis
- Various kinds of crises
- Crisis communication plan and process
- Media handling during various kinds of crises

Case studies
- The Mumbai siege
- Babri masjid
- P&G
- Lies and politics
- Wrong representation of facts – A cause for war
- Case of moral turpitude – Phaneesh Murthy (2002-03)
- The TATA 'Nano' Story – the Singur Saga
- Satyam Computers – A case of a fraudulent company and poor corporate governance

11. PR in Marketing Mix   189
- The role of PR in the overall marketing mix
- PR support in brand building
- The need for synergy between marketing and PR to achieve marketing goals
- Case studies of brands that have used PR strategies and tactics to be successful

Case studies
- TUMS
- Microsoft
- Pierre Cardian
- Analgesic Drug
- Cooking oil
- The Hindustan Lever Limited (HLL) Experience
- ITC - Providing e-learning in the Indian hinterland
- Indian Farmers Fertilizer Cooperative Ltd. (IFFCO)
- Nike
- Subway
- VolksWagen's drivers wanted a PR campaign
- In-house models- a great PR triumph
- *Ghajini*

Part II

UNDERSTANDING THE TECHNICAL ASPECTS OF PR

12. Graphics as a Public Relations Tool   207
- Understanding the role of graphic as a PR tool
- Identifying the components of graphics
- Analysing the function of graphic components
- Learning the significance of design brief
- Explaining layout and design
- Studying the design principle

13. Understanding Type and Printing Processes   216
- Understand the letter form in terms of structure, face, style and function.
- Gain knowledge about font, family, readability and legibility
- Learn the use of pica scale for type measurement
- Prepare typesetting and copy for printing
- Learn about various printing processes and their features
- Understand the criteria for selection of a printing process

14. Printed Literature   235
- Understanding the role and scope of printed literature in PR activities
- Learning about the physical form of brochure and leaflet, their functions and design process
- Learning the use of newsletters as official periodicals
- Handling the distribution of these literatures

15. Web page Design   245
- To define web page designing and understand the functioning of the Internet along with its requirement
- To gain knowledge of connectivity between pages
- Learn the use of hypertext markup language for text, graphics and animation
- Design web pages based on medium's distinct characteristics
- To know about the various software available for web page editing and production

16. Understanding Multimedia   256
- Defining multimedia and its functions
- Understanding interactive and non-interactive multimedia
- Explain aesthetics and technicalities of each media content
- Know the various software available for developing a project
- Understand the assembly of pages using authoring tools

17. Corporate Identity for Image Build-Up   273
- Understand the concept of corporate identity and its role in image building
- Know the role of management and creative professionals in developing the physical forms of the identity
- Analyze the design brief, research and creative concepts
- Describe the creative process of an identity mark
- Handle the implementation of a corporate identity programme

Case studies
- Hindustan Lever Ltd (HLL)
- Vodafone
- Reliance
- Fever 104
- Indian
- Heritage Tea
- Coffeestop

Part III

UNDERSTANDING LEGALITIES AND PROFESSIONAL REQUIREMENTS

18. Public Relations – Laws and Ethics 289
- Various laws concerning the profession of PR
- Code of ethics propounded by professional bodies
- Case studies

Case studies
- The Elton John Defamation case
- How Mr. Swamy handled the defamation cases
- Nicole Kidman and Papparazi

19. PR: An Agenda for Tomorrow 302

Glossary 309

Index 315

Part I

UNDERSTANDING CONCEPTS, STRATEGIES AND TOOLS

1 Defining Public Relations

> **Chapter Objectives**
> - What PR is; its various definitions, concepts and perceptions
> - What PR practitioners need to know to understand work requirements
> - PR in the global scenario: challenges and opportunities
> - Case study to make a link between concepts, practice and implementation

Public relations since its inception has been a much talked about discipline, but not necessarily for the right reasons. Everyone uses PR, but criticize others for using it to gain undeserving mileage. The nineties has been particularly gainful for Indian PR practitioners. The liberalization of the economy brought in many multinational organizations in the country that in turn brought the PR culture. Since then public relations, has been viewed not as a window casing but an indispensable input in overall strategic management. The nomenclature may have changed from public relations to corporate communications, public affairs, corporate affairs and what have you, but the essence has remained the same.

Perceptions about public relations have however not changed drastically. More often these are not complimentary. In the USA, considered the cradle of PR, even after almost a century, PR professionals and professional bodies have to explain and justify the ethical basis of PR. The case study at the end of the chapter will bear this out.

In the first paragraph, a reference was made to the recognition of PR in India as a result of the opening of the Indian economy to overseas investment, which brought the PR culture, but the following comment from the former Prime Minister Narsimha Rao, the architect of liberalization in this country, makes an interesting reference point. Inaugurating the 15th All India Public Relations Conference on November 9, 1993, in New Delhi, he said of PR:

"You have the magic touch. You can make anyone believe that by using a small amount of hair oil you can get the hair to grow by one foot everyday, by taking some pills which one does not know whether they contain clay or anything else, one can become younger by twenty years within a short time. Now, this is the kind of conviction, a very genuine conviction, which you by your magic touch can bring to bear on the minds of people. What do I need more?"

If we were to analyze the above statement, it is sugar quoted, but subtly says that PR fiddles with truth! This is not very different from what Micheal Nauman, former senior editor of German newspaper *Der Spiegel* said. In his paper "The PR skeletons in democracy's closet", he remarked that the main task of PR in politics was to divert people's attention from serious problems and focus somewhere else—like the good looks of president's wife, the sexual moves of the opposition leader, or the wonderful tax cuts you are about to experience if you vote for that 'immaculately sun-tanned man on the billboard' in front of your house.

PR and propaganda

It is important that a clear distinction is made between public relations and propaganda. Described as an "instrument of politics, a power for social control", Goebbels felt the aim of propaganda was not necessarily to inform but influence; not necessarily to convert but to attract followers to keep them in line. The task of propaganda according to him was "to blanket every area of human activity so that the environment of the individual is changed to absorb the (Nazi) movement's world view." In propaganda, it is believed that one is free to distract or even falsely achieve the designated purpose. Public Relations, in contrast, recognizes the long-term responsibility, and aims at persuading and achieving mutual understanding and not coercing people to toe a particular line.

Defining PR

Founded in the USA in the first quarter of the last century, the term public relations essentially meant how a company was perceived by consumers and by the public at large. Over the years, its scope has come to include many publics such as employees, shareholders, future employees, bureaucracy, opinion makers, media, wholesellers, dealers, consumers, special interest groups, community and public at large.

Joy C Gorden in an analytical article " Interpreting definitions of PR: Self assessment and a symbolic interactionism-based alternative", writes that many definers of PR often describe the kinds of things PR practitioners do, what effect they think PR should have, and how they believe PR should be practiced responsibly.[1]

Baskin, Aonolf, and Lattimore define PR as a "management function that helps achieve organizational objectives, define philosophy, and facilitate organizational change. PR practitioners communicate with all relevant internal and external publics to develop relationships and to create consistency between organizational goals and societal expectations. PR practitioners develop, execute, and evaluate organizational programmes that promote the exchange of influence and understanding among an organization's constituent parts and publics."[2]

The British Institute of Public Relations describes Public Relations as "the deliberate, planned and sustained effort to establish and maintain mutual understanding between the organization and its various publics".

Crable and Vibbert describe PR as "the multi-phased function of communication management that is involved in researching, analyzing, affecting, and reevaluating the relationships between an organization and any aspect of its environment".[3]

Dr. Rex F. Harlow, a PR scholar and practitioner of long standing funded by the Foundation of PR Research and Education, collected scores of PR definitions and interacted with over 80 leading practitioners to develop the following definition:

"PR is a distinctive management discipline which helps establish and maintain mutual lines of communication, understanding, acceptance and cooperation between an organization and its publics; involves the management of problems or issues; helps management keep abreast of and effectively utilize change, serving as an early warning system to help anticipate trends; and uses research and sound ethical communication techniques as its principal tools."[4]

According to Grunig and Hunt, "PR is the management function which evaluates public attitudes, identifies the policies and procedures of an individual or an organization with the public interest, and plans and executes a programme of action to earn public understanding and acceptance".[5]

What Harwood I. Childs wrote in 1930s about public relations is almost timeless. Childs argued that the essence of public relations was *not the presentation of a point of view, or the art of tempering mental attitudes, or the development of cordial and profitable relations, but* **"to reconcile or adjust in the public interest those aspects of our personal corporate behaviour which have a social significance"**.

The Public Relations Society of America (PRSA) has defined 14 activities that are associated with PR: a) publicity, b) communication, c) public affairs, d) issues management, e) government relations, f) financial public relations, g) community relations, h) industry relations, i) minority relations, j) advertising, k) press agentry, l) promotion, m) media relations, n) propaganda.[6]

Coming to the brass tacks, let's see, what PR is supposed to do or achieve. PR has three major aims:

1. To change or neutralize hostile public opinion.
2. To crystallize unformed opinion.
3. To conserve positive public opinion.

Public relations constantly strives to:
- Start
- Lead
- Change
- Speed Up

It aims at starting a point of view, an opinion, a movement when none exists; it helps lead a movement, an argument; it aims at changing a negative environment, provide a stimuli; and speed up when issues get sluggish.

PR and public opinion

Public opinion, according to many experts works as the barometer of public relations. It provides the psychological environment in which organizations prosper or perish. Looking at the complexities of business, the growing heterogeneity of publics and the increasing expectations of consumers, public relations need not only work towards creating a favorable image of the organization but also what it stands for.

To cite an example, in 1988, when the VP Singh government was in saddle, a decision was taken to install Mahatma Gandhi's statue by removing one of the canopies at the India Gate to commemorate the 120th birth centenary of one of the greatest sons of India. The logic behind removing the canopy presumably was that Gandhi who was instrumental in removing the yoke of the British Raj could not be placed under the canopy built by the British! A famous artist was commissioned to make the bust. As the time of installation neared, Satish Gujral, famous artist and architect was the first to protest against the removal of the canopy. In an article carried by the *Times of India*, he questioned the logic of the government in removing the canopy. If the canopy reminded us of the British Raj, so did many other buildings including the Parliament House, the President House, argued he. 'History can't be changed', he reasoned. His simple logic however was that the canopy was a part of the overall design and planning and any tampering with it would be unfair to the landscaping of the entire area. After that scores of articles appeared in various newspapers. The issue almost became a national debate. There were two points of view, one against the removal of the canopy and the other for it. That the Mahatma must be honoured was a given. As public opinion gathered momentum, for years the statue remained in the studio till good sense prevailed and at last it was installed in the parliament premises. Many governments had changed in the meantime.

The example illustrates the role of public opinion and explains how a single person's conviction brought the issue in the public domain for discussion, making it an important national issue. Although spearheaded by one, like-minded people rallied around it

Professional PR people understand the intricacies of public opinion and not only keep a close watch on it but make, alter, and implement policies and programmes accordingly. Let's now analyze the basic issues that an effective PR practitioner needs to understand, assimilate and implement.

The core values and competencies of the organization

Each organization has certain core competencies, which may be unique to it. It could be the production processes, the product formulae, assembly line expertise, human resource, pricing structure and the like. It is very important for the public relations practitioner to understand the competencies and make use of the information suitably. Similarly, each organization has certain core values that it stands for. If the practitioner has an avid understanding of these, these come in handy while writing soft and hard stories on the corporation. To cite an example, many years ago, a national newspaper carried an interesting story about an organization run by a close-knit family. The story was about the Birla Group. It described some of the core values of the family. The story said that Birlas generally were teetotalers. [The exception was Late Shri Aditya Birla , who had unfortunately died in a plane crash]. The family at least till then had taken a decision, not to get into two industries, viz., hospitality and distillery. The logic was that when they don't drink why should they produce or serve liquor! If the company ran hotels, then it would be difficult not to allow serving liquor. That in no way meant that those they employed had to follow the family core values. The story however in clear terms reflected the personal value system of the Birla clan.

To identify various stakeholders/publics

In PR parlance the publics are generally segmented as internal and external. Broadly these would include the following:

The employees, their families, union leaders, both internal and outside supporters, shareholders which will include, financial institutions, local and overseas shareholders, banks, stock exchanges, agents etc, wholesellers, dealers, consumers, local and national governments, local and national administration, special interest groups, including various lobbies and professional groups, media, both regional and mainstream and last but not the least, the community.

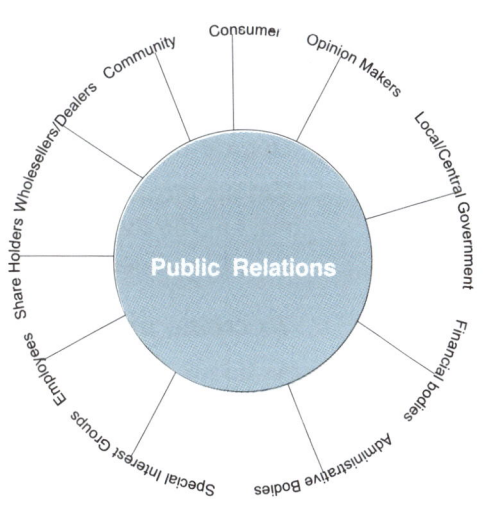

To understand the communication needs of various publics

Communication is a two way process between the sender and receiver of communication. The PR practitioner need to understand that both the sender and the receiver have communication requirements and obligations. An organization's basic communication need is to disseminate information about its activities to various target audience, work towards a positive image building for the organization. On the other hand, each target audience has or may have specific communication needs, which they would like to be fulfilled. To illustrate, the communication needs of employees invariably revolve around their welfare. The higher one goes in the hierarchy, the needs also include desire to acquire more knowledge, update one's skills and to be heard. On the other hand, wholesellers and retailers would have different communication needs. Their interest would be to know improvement in their commission structure, other incentives etc. The special interest groups would like to keep an eye on areas of public interest. In short, each constituent group would have communication needs as well as communication obligations.

In times of crisis, sharing information, listening to stakeholders about their fears and concerns become imperative. The chapter on Crises Communication has a number of case studies that touch this aspect.

Information is reckoned as power, but not if controlled—as believed earlier. Information in an age of instant connectivity becomes power when *it is shared* and *not when controlled*. Public relations, an important part of the overall information order must believe in sharing information.

Scanning Environment and keeping the organization abreast of the latest

An organization is an integral part of society. What happens in social, economic and political fronts have definite ramifications on the industry. It is imperative that PR professionals serve as antennae to the organization and keep a track of what is happening in the world outside. Media are good sources of mapping the happenings.

Decide on the best cost-effective media to reach out to publics

Various media have varying reach and accessibility. Public relations utilizes both mass media and interpersonal and social media to reach out to a disparate audience.

More about media will be discussed in the chapter: "PR Media and Tools".

To create distinct corporate identity for the organization

As no two human beings are alike, no two organizations can be similar. Corporate organizations spend a lot of money and resources to create a distinct niche for themselves. Creating corporate identity and managing the reputation of the organization is a very core function of Public Relations. The subject has been dealt with in great detail in the chapter on Corporate Identity.

In the context of PR, critics generally speak of "effective PR". For long PR practitioners have argued about the intangible character of their discipline, which they felt could not be measured. The latest thinking does not agree with that. The effectiveness of PR, it is argued, can be measured to precision vis-à-vis the objectives set for a PR programme both at micro and macro levels.

What is expected of PR? In other words what is the bottom line in PR? Is it one or all of the following:
- Dissemination of information
- Eliciting the trust of various stakeholders
- Increase in productivity
- Tinkling of cash registers
- Openness and integrity in relationships

Defining Public Relations

The chapter on PR and the Marketing Mix contains insights about a research conducted by the *Advertising Age Journal* which may be referred to gather insights on the thinking of marketing professionals on the subject.

How one goes about achieving effective PR? One can do so by addressing the following:

- Understanding the core values and competencies of the organization;
- By tracking issues and understanding the internal and external environment.
- By creating a distinct corporate identity for the organization;
- Helping in creating an environment of trust and understanding.

The first step

PR can't be top-bottom approach. The PR manager need to start with an avid understanding of the organization; its core competency, where it stands in competition, its uniqueness, its human resource capital, its perception in the minds of various stakeholders, what it has done besides the business, in touching lives

Brainstorm with a cross section of employees, viz. the top management, middle rung managers, the silent blue color workers, and the unions and understand what makes them feel proud or unhappy about the organization they work for. Understand the tangible and intangible characteristics of the organization, perform a dispassionate SWOT [Strengths, Weaknesses, Opportunities and Threats] on the organization. This could be a starting point in building communication initiatives for the organization.

After obtaining insights, the PR manager may consider mapping the perceptions of a cross section of external audience to understand where the organization stands in their scheme of things. A professional agency could be involved for the exercise. A thorough understanding will help the PR practitioner build an aura around the organization, create both hard and soft stories for various media.

A constant monitoring of the socio-economic and political scenario through media tracking is an important requirement in public relations.

PR-Global Trends, Challenges and Opportunities

Like any other social science discipline, public relations has continuously reoriented itself to suit changing times, changing environment and in gauging the complexity of the human mind. One thing however, has remained constant with the discipline, viz., *Relationship Building*. The last one decade or so has brought enough opportunities for public relations discipline to consolidate its position among various publics and stakeholders- be they government, industry, Market, NGO sector or people at large.

In more recent times, PR has suddenly found itself at the centre stage, being invited to lend support and advise on issues that traditionally did not fall in the ambit of its activities.

Some of the areas that have witnessed greater strategic influence of public relations include the following:

- Using public relations for brand building at the cost of advertising.
- PR advice on taking up issues that enhance public support for corporate governance, especially in the wake of growing scandals and scams in the corporate world.
- PR's putting media under the scanner as media's role in corporate coverage and handling crises has come under sharp focus.
- Public opinion consolidation by PR on issues concerning war, terrorism, and health et al.

The PR challenges in today's world, divided by rich and poor in economic terms, the 'haves' and the 'have nots' in media terms, the digital divide, religious bigotry, self-centredness of some nations, the terrorist threats and the growing impatience of people at large has to do with transparency, honesty and above all integrity of organizations, governments and individuals for whom PR is engaged.

The last few years have witnessed an unprecedented turmoil in societies, nations, and markets. The economic recession, wars, terrorist strikes, health issues, status of UN in a broader sense, the perils of a unipolar world and globalization *per se* have brought down trust levels among countries and individuals. Care management by governments, non-governmental sector and corporate sector especially in the wake of terrorist threats and wars on the one hand and health of teeming millions and the problem posed by AIDS, have necessitated reaching out to people who are affected and to communities at large. The world by and large stands united on these two areas, politics of various components notwithstanding.

PR is required for managing reputations, but are public relations professionals honest in reflecting facts or do they continue to remain busy in creating a world of make-believe is an issue that needs serious addressing.

In the following paragraphs, we shall discuss some of the above issues in terms of trends, challenges and opportunities.

PR in Brand Building

A significant trend visible in the last few years has been the use of public relations strategies in brand building, sometimes at the cost of advertising.

Famous authors Al Ries and Laura Ries in their book: *The Fall of Advertising & the Rise of PR* have brought smiles to many a PR professional while casting a sad spell on their counterparts in advertising. The authors argue that some of today's mega brands were born with publicity, not advertising. Advertising in their view lacks credibility, the crucial input in brand building. PR on the other hand helps build brand equity. They suggest that the 'big bang' approach advocated by advertising professionals should be abandoned in favor of slow build-up by third party endorsement in the media. The authors feel that advertising should follow only when brands have been established through publicity.[7]

In India an interesting trend was noticed when one of the top advertising agencies, viz. Mudra Communication hired a public relations consultancy, Perfect Relations to do its "image makeover" as reported in the media. It is all the more ironical when the agency has its own PR consultancy, Horizon. Justifying the decision AG Krishnamurthy, CMD of the agency said, "There is a knowledge vacuum in the industry, which we wanted to fill up. And we want to create awareness about the initiatives we have taken. We want people to know what we offer". [8]

The industry analysts feel that Mudra, which has always been a trendsetter, may prove to be a leader in this respect too. This clearly reflects changing times.[9]

In recent times the shift towards public relations has been vindicated in a Business to Business (B-to-B) marketing survey done by one of the top-notch global PR agency Edelman in the USA. According to the findings 38 per cent B-to-B marketing executives expected their budgets to be slashed, 44 per cent reported increase in their use of PR. 68 per cent respondents of the 300 surveyed said PR met or exceeded their expectations regarding ROI (Return on Investment). With economy in recession, companies are no longer thinking about broad-based marketing initiatives. There is a clear shift according to analysts from brand building to selling. The focus now is on ROI. The marketing effectiveness is now gauged on sales growth more than reputation.

According to an Industry Survey, 70 per cent of Fortune 500 companies spent in excess of $1 million on PR budgets in 1997, and 65 percent of these companies increased their public relations budgets in the past five years[10].

In a scenario where markets are becoming more competitive and pockets shrinking, the buyer is either waiting for better times to come or changing loyalties in favor of products that come with various goodies or buying generic products that suits their pocket. The latest Economic Survey in India also reflects a downtrend in the Fast Moving Consumer Goods (FMCG) sector.[11]

The companies on their part are trying hard to woo present buyers off competitive goods than exploring potential ones. The Cola and detergent wars are just a couple of cases in point This has required companies to be top-of-the line and work hard to innovate strategies. PR, hence has become an important part of the marketing mix. Customer Care Management and Relationship Marketing are the buzzwords.

It has been seen that in the area of products that are driven by technology, the organizations are focusing more on the experience of the products less on their "bells and whistles". Cell phones, DVDs, wireless telephones etc. fall in this category. Consumer Tech PR as it is called has been focusing on the changing expectations of consumers who are more interested to know what the *technology is going to do* for them and then *how technology works*. The revolution brought about by cell phones and the magic spelled by the SMS is a pointer in the direction. What a telephone could not do has been done by the mobile—providing a personal and emotional touch to communication. The publicity on the mobile has brought about an era of 'permission marketing' (that is, *I see it if I wish to*)

IT industry after an initial boom in the 90s to a terrible slump in the last few years is now seen making use of public relations techniques to surge back and there have been positive indicators.[12]

As public relations is people-driven, marketing, human resource and industrial relations departments are getting PR value addition in their strategies towards employees, shareholders, wholesellers, retailers and above all, consumers.

Corporate Governance

It is believed that the real differential among organizations revolves around their core philosophy and ideals of corporate governance. In recent times the Enron squabble has questioned the ethical governance of major corporate houses that have millions of shareholders. Closer home, Satyam Computer's fraudulent practices have been termed India's Enron. Case study may be referred in to in the chapter on Crises communication.

Some critics feel that a strong Investor Relations Executive could have alerted Enron's management early on the risks associated with the firm's aggressive accounting tactics. The Enron PR as reflected in the media reports was not responding to any queries from the media, saying they were busy on the routine work related to bankruptcy with "no time left over to speak to the press".[13] PR professionals are watching how Satyam PR is going to respond.

Public relations experts believe that Enron has been a textbook case of Crisis of Confidence. Learning quickly, some major companies like General Electrical (GE) and IBM have pledged greater disclosure so that shareholders and analysts have additional information. In their annual report, the IBM now provides information even on intellectual property income, the impact of gains and losses from investment, the effect of amortization of goodwill from acquisition, gains of sales in real estate and the performance of the IBM pension plan.[14]

PR works for organizations and individuals. The people in charge of PR are entrusted with the responsibility of managing the reputation of organizations and individuals. The biggest challenge for them is whether they are supporting honest causes in doing what they are asked to do? Are they fully informed by the board about corporate governance, in the first place? An honest reply would be in the negative in most circumstances, as the Satyam imbroglio has reflected. Unfortunately, the impression created by the likes of Enron, Anderson and Satyam and many more is that corporate management can't be trusted upon to deliver credible results. The audit firms they hire could possibly be pawns in their hand for some gratification. There are question marks on the auditing firm PWC in the Satyam case, though the auditing firm has denied any complicity in the matter. The financial analysts whose words are considered, as gospels of truth in stock market may not necessarily be the people of integrity. A lot of introspection and self-examination is the need of the hour to restore the dwindling confidence of millions of investors. For them it could be a matter of life and death.

Last year's Gallup Polls showed public confidence in big business at the lowest ebb since 1981. Some feel the current feeling about the market is unmatched since the 1929 stock market crash.

In an age when we have exclusive 24×7 news channels, special financial channels and Internet chat rooms, the irony is that organizations do and will remain in focus. There is a great public relations lesson in this—to be proactive instead of getting caught unawares.

Mergers, acquisitions and restructuring in an era of economic recession have fundamentally altered the relationship between employers and the employees. Many surveys indicate that massive layoffs have damaged the reputation of big companies. Added to this have been stories of the CEOs getting fat pay packets and perks, which at times could be 500 to 1000 times more than that of the lowest paid staff. In India also, in a conference organized by the Confederation of Indian Industries (CII) in late 2002, Naryana Murthy of Infosys questioned the logic and ethics of such practices even among companies that were making profits. Paul Argenti and Janis Forman authors of the book *Corporate Communication* point out the prevalence of this phenomenon everywhere. The popular press, according to him is "beating up on business with a new generation of muckrakers".[15]

A recent survey in the USA indicates that because of a general mistrust of business among people at large, there is a trend among chief executives putting public relations directly under their charge to closely monitor this aspect. Some analysts have predicted top level seats for PR people at board level to facilitate decisions that are based on public opinion monitoring

Given the environment, corporations will have to enter an era of transparency and openness. At the World Economic Forum held in 2002, CEOs of 36 countries issued an unprecedented document called "Global Corporate Citizenship: The Leadership Challenge of CEOs and Brands" exhorting business leaders around the world to improve their mark on society and their relationship with their stakeholders.

Some critics place blame on media, arguing that a single line of negative coverage about a company may send stocks plummeting. There is however, another point of view that the blame does not lie with the media but the fact that trust at all levels has eroded not only in private but also public institutions and opinion makers engaged in governance. The controversy about 'match-fixing', especially among traditional rivals refuses to die (especially when India and Pakistan are pitched against each other). The March 2004 series of five one-day matches between India and Pakistan were being openly talked of as 'fixed', two wins each and one draw.

In the context of global companies, it is felt that they will have to work out public relations strategies especially in developing countries in the wake of a general outcry against globalization. These companies will have to make themselves more relevant to the local needs and ethos and run campaigns to educate people on how their being in these countries has made a difference in employment generation, development and revenue sharing. Pepsi did a good campaign on this aspect in India. Enron's Dhabol power project failed to get people's empathy because of their poor public relations approach. Kentucky's inept handling of the hygiene issue was a PR failure. McDonald on the other hand has been going great guns at least in this country. Its decision not to use beef products to respect the sensitivity of the majority population was well received. When the controversy in the USA over using beef tallow in French fries ended in a legal suit, McDonald in India, just to play safe once again announced that it never used it here. They printed it on the paper mat placed on the tray to ensure that it reached the right target audience. When animal activist Maneka Gandhi wrote to Mercedes Benz not to use leather for car seats in India as it is tantamount to cruelty against animals, the company immediately decided to heed the advice to avoid being in a controversy.

The market prognosis indicates that Industry Analysts' surveys, once a mainstay of top technical companies, will become commonplace for various other brands due to technology explosion and the emergence of e-commerce. How are Industry analysts (IA) different from stock market analysts? An Industry Analyst is a third party objective source that continuously watches, examines forecasts, and scrutinizes the marketplace. An Industry Analyst helps an organization identify market niches, offer competitive analysis, recommends strategic partnerships and help break through the clutter in the marketplace. According to *Houston Business Journal*, unlike a stock market analyst an IA avoids stock price analysis. An IA's findings help in validating a company's values and critiques business practices. He serves as a thought leader who lends an essential element of credibility.

Another visible trend is the increasing use of online surveys by companies to get a close check on the public nerve. Some companies have made use of their websites and e-mails to get quick feedback on their new products, pricing and consumer experience etc.

Media Watch

PR generally under the media microscope for an alleged 'manipulation of minds', has for a change now put media under a scanner. Media have been and would always remain important conduits for PR to reach out to its constituent publics with information that readers perceive credible. However, a research study released by International Public Relations Association (IPRA) that has members from over 90 countries reflects rampant corruption among journalists. "Cash for editorial" and other unethical practices both in print and broadcast media are commonplace in many countries. 242 public relations professionals from 54 countries participated in an e-mail survey through a questionnaire. The typical activities seen by the study include:

1. A corporate organization or public relations firm also employs a journalist in full time employment with a newspaper either openly or secretly. In Eastern Europe, Africa and Middle East, 27 per cent respondents said it happened "often" or "all the time".

2. An advertising agency sends out press releases to a publication's media department in order to put pressure on the editor to use material from the

advertiser. In central and south America 47 per cent respondents said it happened all the time.

More than 63 per cent journalists in Eastern Europe according to respondents in these countries accepted bribe for exchange of coverage. As a part of IPRA's recently launched Campaign for Media Transparency (CMT), Alasdair Southerland, past president of IPRA and co-chairman of the CMT cited among corrupt practices, editors and journalists asking for inducement to publish news releases or feature items in exchange of paid advertisements elsewhere in the publication. Advertisements disguised as editorials, material appearing through influence or payment by a third party and publications asking for payment not to publish certain stories.

The Institute of Public Relations in USA is supporting IPRA through the development and publication of a biennial International index of bribery and the media. IPRA on its part will encourage media houses all over to sign the IPRA Charter on Media Transparency, which is about to be released.[16]

Ironically while the IPRA findings were making rounds, *Times of India*, the leader among English newspapers in India decided to charge for news that aimed at building brands. There have been adverse reactions from the media, which the publication has not taken to kindly, but has defended its position. *India Today*, a weekly magazine in its editorial, "Sacred Space: If the media sells news columns, what is the need for advertisements?" expressed fear of truth being an easy casualty, if papers started charging for stories. How would the reader differentiate between news that has been bought and that, which has not been, asked the paper? The publication argued that advertisers were interested in media because they proved to be vehicles to reach out to their buyers, because media offered circulation and eyeballs. The journalists were expected to pursue the path of truth fearlessly so that the market executives get attracted to advertising on the strength of these values. The publication's logic was that such news was limited to the lifestyle section. To this the *India Today* retorted, " It is like being somewhat pregnant".[17]

Times of India in an article "Compete, don't Carp: copy cats shouldn't point fingers" presented the logic of their decision but criticized the opponents for copying their paper in design, style and coverage. The argument of the paper was that it had not started a trend of planting plugs to make money; rather it had taken the cover off those who misused news columns for personal favours. "We have given the competition a future shock; woken up to the entertainment revolution".

On the professional front, the PR industry launched Public Relations Consultants Association of India (PRCAI) in December 2001, an umbrella body representing many public relations firms. This is besides the Public Relations Society of India (PRSI) that has more than 30 chapters and a membership running into thousands.

It is hoped that these professional bodies would spearhead the issue of media transparency in India. The movement if it gets consolidated will go a long way in creating mutually trusting and interdependent roles for the media and public relations.

Public Opinion Consolidation

The world seems to be sitting on a volcano ready to explode any time. Every utterance by spokespersons of governments and other organizations have an instant display of public approval or disapproval. Public opinion is regarded as the barometer of public relations. Public relations professionals have to keep a constant vigil on public opinion and advise their organizations accordingly.

One has seen in the present times (before the US onslaught on Iraq), millions of people joining in solidarity marches; tens of thousands consolidating anti-war opinion through the Internet cutting across nationalities, castes, colors, creeds and religions. Over one million telephone and fax lines were jammed in the USA by anti-war groups to make their point in the age of Information. The traditional mass media like newspapers, television and radio in the USA and Britain however, toed the government line, without engaging in a dispassionate and independent analysis of the situation. Many critics have blamed the American media for being an ally of the government in an unjustified war on Iraq, covertly waged on the plea of finding the Weapons of Mass Destruction (WMDs), that have not been found despite turning the whole country to a virtual rubble and killing or maiming thousands of innocent citizens including women and children. On the other hand many analysts considered taking hundreds of embedded journalists to cover the war, a public relations triumph. From the Pentagon's point of view this was publicized as a 'part of its larger embrace of an information society'.

Embedded journalism has been a part of the war reporting for long. Ernie Pyle wrote stories of America's soldiers in World War II and the heavily televised Vietnam War of the 1960s.

One school of thought believes that what comes through the pen or mike of a reporter is what is informed to him by the military general who looks after the safety and comfort of the journalist which may not really be what really happened, while the other school feels that journalists who are on live coverage have a mind of their own and they don't mind taking risks while reporting at the time of pitched battles. Although journalists have been patronized as long as one can remember and they have written stories in line with the spokesperson, but it was not an 'accepted practice', until recently. Now it is projected as facilitation by the sponsors. Some military training schools have begun training journalists in war reporting.

Placing reporters on the front lines with the US military in Iraq has been a public relations success, according to Professor Robert Pritchard from the Ball State University Journalism school. "The embedded reporter programme stands to dramatically improve the credibility of the individual soldier, sailor, airman, marine and coast guardsman," Pritchard said. "It also improves the credibility of the military with the media and public". The US government placed 600 print and broadcast reporters to provide 'real time television, radio and website report'.[18]

It may be a 'PR coup' from the government's point of view, but pictures don't lie. The live coverage of unopposed US armor racing through the desert, images from video and some television channels, other than British and American (AL Jazeera especially) of dead civilians and soldiers, wailing women and children, blood and gore all around, called the bluff of embedded journalists. Martin Turner, one of the embedded journalists in a panel interview during the American Forum on 21 April 2003 said, " In an era where we have 24 hour news, where... it's required to get news out as quickly as possible, then the danger is that people leap to conclusions, they report things that turn out not to be true, and you just have to be honest and say that that is what happened quite often in the coverage of this war. And I don't think anybody should be surprised about it. It is what goes with the territory".[19]

On asking if the citizenry was well informed, given the extent of coverage, he said, "well, I think they certainly had a selection of impressions, a wide range of media that they could go to, but I think they had to a lot of work on their own to get an accurate impression about what was going on".[20]

Facilitating media in times of crisis is a normal practice. It suits the media facilitators to impose their point of view. However, it is the responsibility of the scribes to ensure that their stories have more than one point of view. It is hoped that serious researchers will analyze the loads of media coverage based on embedded journalists' dispatches and draw lessons that can be learnt for the future.

Pictures of an American soldier posing with a heap of naked Iraqi prisoners of war and an unidentified American soldier urinating on an Iraqi prisoner and some other pictures of British soldiers torturing Iraqi soldiers made way in the mainstream media all over the world. Despite the quick denial and talk about an alleged manipulation of images by government spokespersons in Britain and *The Daily Mirror* publishing an apology on the front page: 'An apology. We were hoaxed', the pictures did enough damage to both the governments, especially George Bush and Tony Blaire to allow any room for damage control.

Sensing the damage done by the candid pictures and a growing anti-US feeling in the Arab world, US Prez Bush using the public relations strategy appealed to the Arab world on 5 May 2004 on the US-backed Al Hurra station, expressing his sorrow over the abuse of Iraqi prisoners. He said the actions of some soldiers did not represent "the America that I know. The actions of these few people do not reflect the hearts of American people".[21]

According to a news report, many editors and reporters of 'Al Sabah', a US-funded publication that the US calls a model for journalism in West Asia, walked out saying "we thought the Americans were here to create a free media". Editor-in Chief Ismael Zayer said, "Instead, we were being suffocated". [22]

British and American media in general have received flak from all over the world for being partisan in covering the war.

America's onslaught on Iraq had its repercussions on the markets as well. As most of the European countries especially France and Germany made no bones about their strong condemnation of war, public opinion build-up was on boycotting American goods. "No more American Coca-Cola or Budweiser, no Marlboro, no American Whisky or even American Express cards, a growing number of restaurants in Germany are taking everything American off their menus to protest the Iraq war," reported Erik Kiirschbaum, from Berlin. In retaliation to France's criticism, some US restaurants renamed french-fries to 'Freedom Fries'.[23]

Thanks to seamless media, the outcry against war was reflected all over. Analysts have seen a great role played by the Internet in consolidating world opinion. People of various nationalities, race, religion and creed participated in Internet chats and in registering their protest against the war.

Keeping in view the public opinion sensitivity, many companies used their discretion and desisted from releasing advertisements in news channels despite the increasing TRPs brought by the Iraq war coverage.

To understand the anxieties of the people, governments will have to fully grasp the trends of public opinion, which would include what people are thinking, what their hopes, expectations and susceptibilities are.

Crisis Communication

Crisis communication, always an important part of public relations activities, is becoming all the more important. A literature review indicates that at least in the developed world especially in the USA post 9/11, any definition of crisis and a disaster management plan includes terrorist attack and bioterrorism. The terrorist attacks according to some analysts have brought about a paradigm shift in defining villains and victims. A case in point is of United Airlines whose airplanes were used by the terrorists to create havoc. The company did a masterly job in quickly realizing that it could not handle the situation with the same crisis approach, as it would take for a crash of its jets. So rather than be the centre of information and handle matters on its own, it reached out to American Airlines and they worked together, deciding to let the government be the information clearing house on the events.

9/11 provided many lessons in communication. Public opinion as always determined what was and what was not right.

Red Cross that has an impeccable reputation learnt its lesson painfully on communication. Red Cross collected nearly $1 billion from the people; many of them dropped $10 and 20 bills in the buckets piled up at various places to help the 9/11 victims. Originally it had planned to do with the money as it does with other donations to dedicate a certain amount to a specific disaster. The balance is put in the national disaster fund. When there was no information on how the money was being sent to the victims and no information was made public, people felt cheated. The complaints grew so loud that the Congress asked a number of charitable organizations to explain their practices and the Red Cross had to part company with its CEO. There was no intent to mislead or cheat the public, only a lack of clear communication. When the issue came for postmortem, the Red Cross felt that their messages had to be "brief and brilliant". From the very beginning so much was changing so rapidly, that at times their messages contradicted each other

Care Management

Health care PR has become a genre by itself and has grown manifold especially in the wake of the AIDS scare. One can see campaigns all over the world reaching out to various categories of population—both high risk and caregivers. In the US, health care PR was the number one growth sector in the last couple of years. Many pharmaceutical companies have been releasing public relations campaigns to reflect their community work and at times disseminating information about various breakthroughs in AIDS regimen. Cipla launched one such campaign, bringing home the point that though life does not remain the same, one has to find reasons to be happy and live for someone.

There are at least 25 top notch Health PR firms in the US engaged in this niche area. To deduce the volume of work one may note that, the overall billing in this sector was more than $4.10 billion with the top most agency in this field: Fleishman-Hillard doing a business of over $60 million during 2002.[24]

Care management and dissemination of information would in time grow both in the developed and the developing world. It is unfortunate that despite so many years of information dissemination, a majority of people are still ignorant about the spread of AIDS. Any strategy on AIDS hence will have to address connecting with communities and opinion makers.

In India various state and central health ministries in disseminating information on various health issues, including AIDS spend a lot of money. However, unlike the USA there probably are no specialist agencies in health care communication in the country to undertake the mammoth task. More often advertising agencies pitch for health accounts and get away with them, without much knowledge of the bio-medical, epidemiological and social sciences issues.

South Africa that has more than four million people afflicted with HIV or AIDS, challenged the World Trade Organization (WTO) policies which allow members to buy products from only certain countries instead of markets from which drugs could be bought cheap. Due to tremendous public pressure and various cases in South African courts, drug prices have come down and there is preferential pricing for poor nations.

An average person may have no idea about the working of the WTO but thanks to media stories spearheaded by activists, a lot of people feel concerned about whether or not multinational companies have undue influence over its policies.[25]

As the public relations sector tries to keep up with the fast paced health care environment to get business in a competitive marketplace, one has witnessed PR campaigns cutting across geographical boundaries and partnering to become large multinational agencies, especially in pharmaceutical sectors.

The sheer volume of health information generated from advances in medical technology including the tremendous growth in the biotechnology sector has given a spurt to health care PR.

Concerns about genetically modified foods, accusations on fast food companies in making children obese and more recently the story of worms in Cadburys chocolates and pesticides in Colas are other issues that have witnessed employment of judicious public relations strategies in containing adverse public opinion in recent times.

CASE STUDY

The recently published book *What Happened* by Scott McClellan has jabbed the hornets' nest about the ethical base of Public Relations. The following case study would be interesting from two perspectives:

a) That not much has changed about perception on PR, being 'oh not so clean a profession' and b) the role of professional bodies to respond to criticism instantly.

McClellan, the former Press Secretary of George W Bush criticized the Bush administration in his 2008 memoir *What Happened*. In the book, he has accused Bush of "self-deception" and of maintaining a "permanent campaign approach" to governing rather than making the best choices. McClellan stopped short of saying that the president purposely lied about his reasons for invading Iraq, writing that the administration was not "employing out-and-out deception" to make the case for war in 2002, though he did assert the administration relied on an aggressive "political propaganda campaign" instead of truth to sell the Iraq war. His book was also critical of the press corps for being too accepting of the administration's perspective on the issue and of Condoleezza Rice for being "too accommodating" and overly careful about protecting her own reputation.

Here is an excerpt from the book:

"The most powerful leader in the world had called upon me to speak on his behalf and help restore credibility he lost amid the failure to find weapons of mass destruction in Iraq. So I stood at the White house briefing room podium in front of the glare of the klieg lights for the better part of two weeks and publicly exonerated two of the senior-most aides in the White House: Karl Rove and Scooter Libby.

There was one problem. It was not true.

I had unknowingly passed along false information. And five of the highest ranking officials in the administration were involved in my doing so: Rove, Libby, the vice President, the President's chief of staff, and the President himself"

The Bush administration responded through press secretary Dana Perino, who said, "Scott, we now know, is disgruntled about his experience at the White House. We are puzzled. It is sad. This is not the Scott we knew." Reactions from other Republicans were also similar expressing confusion, surprise and sadness.

McClellan responded by stating that he was inclined to give the Administration the "benefit of the doubt", and did not fully appreciate the circumstances until after leaving the "White House bubble."

On CBS News 1 June 2008 Sunday Morning, Legal Analyst Andrew Cohen offered his opinion on the book, which almost became a commentary on the profession of PR per se. Here is the reproduction:

"The Flak Over Flacks"

"There is nothing funny about this past week's revelations that former White House Press Secretary Scott McClellan lied to the American people about certain vital policy decisions within the Bush Administration.

It's a confession, which supports the worst suspicions that millions of Americans have about the current leadership in Washington.

But in every tragic drama comes a moment of comedic Zen. And in *L'Affair McClellan*, that has come from the public relations community, where some now wonder whether the former flack violated the "ethics" of his craft.

Apparently, an industry the very essence of which is to try to convince people that a turkey is really an eagle has a rule that condemns lying. The Public Relations Society of America states: "We adhere to the highest standards of accuracy and truth in advancing the interests of those we represent..." This clause strikes me as if the Burglars Association of America had as its creed "Thou Shalt Not Steal."

Show me a PR person who is "accurate" and "truthful," and I'll show you a PR person who is unemployed.

The reason companies or governments hire oodles of PR people is because PR people are trained to be slickly untruthful or half-truthful. Misinformation and disinformation are the coin of the realm, and it has nothing to do with being a Democrat or a Republican. So McClellan is a liar. Big deal. Thomas Jefferson was a liar, and so was Franklin Roosevelt. John Kennedy lied and so did Richard Nixon.

During the time it took me to write this essay I'll bet dozens of PR people blatantly lied to their audiences, despite the presence of proclamations declaring that they should not.

You can't try to convince someone that a milk cow is really a racehorse without lying. You can't build a profession based on deceit and spin, then create "ethics" rules that call for honesty, and *then* criticize McClellan.

He did what his predecessors had done and what his successors are doing and will continue to do until no one listens to them anymore from the podium. It's as American as Apple Pie and indictments - as book deals, and perjury.

And that's the truth."[26]

The Public Relations Society of America (PRSA) responded to the CBS story challenging Public Relations without losing time through the following letter. The industry response was mixed on the rebuttal.

Dear Mr. Cohen,

Regarding your commentary on today's "CBS Sunday Morning," the Board of Directors of the Public Relations Society of America finds it imperative to affirm the professionalism of public relations practitioners and to take exception with what we regard as a misguided opinion. The **PRSA Member Code of Ethics** to which all members pledge, embodies a strict set of guidelines defining ethical and professional practice in public relations. Professionals who meet the Code's standards stand in stark contrast to the simplistic, erroneous characterization of the profession you presented.

Contrary to baseless assertions, truth and accuracy are the bread and butter of the public relations profession. In a business where success hinges on critical relationships built over many years with clients, journalists and a Web 2.0-empowered public, one's credibility is the singular badge of viability. All professionals, including attorneys, accountants and physicians, aspire to ethical standards, and public relations professionals are no different, always striving for the ideal.

For public relations professionals, engaging diverse and often skeptical audiences requires top-flight skills in communications, creativity and even persuasion, but a trust once lost cannot be regained. Unemployment, contrary to your opinion, is reserved for the professional who has lost his or her credibility.

Building upon a foundation of integrity, implementation of those professional skills can also yield some very positive and powerful outcomes. Spreading the word about available health services has gotten thousands of infants immunized. Uncovering facts about post-9/11 air quality has helped scores of New York children unravel the mystery of a high incidence of asthma. Creating programmes that engage veterans has helped them make the personal and professional transition to civilian life.

Curiously, you also assert that lying is no big deal. To the public relations professional, that is far from the truth. To "try to convince people a turkey is really an eagle" would leave true professionals eating crow, if they could eat at all.

Very truly yours,
Jeffrey Julin, APR
Chair and CEO, PRSA

> The entire story appeared on the PRSA website, attracting comments and observations from a number of people, including some PR professionals. A few samples of such responses:
>
> **Dan Keeney, APR** said:
>
> "While I appreciate the sentiment expressed, I can't help but feel that this organization's knee jerk defensive response to criticism of the profession leaves something to be desired. Instead of a defensive response of, "You're wrong, we are good people," it might be more valuable to be OPEN to such critiques. The reason PRSA was created in the first place was because WE in the PROFESSION were worried about unprofessional practitioners tainting our credibility. So instead of attacking the critic, maybe we should welcome the criticism as an opportunity to explain this organization's role in encouraging professionalism and opening dialogue. I'm constantly amazed that we as a profession fail to follow our own fundamental advice so often."
>
> **Deanna Harms** said:
>
> "All too often we PR "pros" are like those in the movie "Iron Man"– routinely holding press conferences to disseminate misinformation and counseling our clients to "stick to message" when in fact we should be urging them to speak the truth, to say, "I am the Iron Man." We each need to look at our own practice of PR – and clean house if needed. Mr. Cohen's challenge can benefit our profession if it leads to greater scrutiny and accountability. We need both"
>
> **Pamela Maize Harris, PhD** said:
>
> "Thank you for your response to Mr. Cohen's CBS appearance. I'm hoping that PRSA will request equal time on CBS to rebut and address Mr. Cohen's opinions. This would allow the dialog to continue and provide opportunity for us to share with CBS's audience a different view from Mr. Cohen's."

What are the lessons for PR professionals?

Being in a profession that deals with people, perceptions, attitudes, controversies, disasters, PR will always attract strong opinion, including criticism and appreciation, depending on where it is coming from.

Many scholars have reckoned the role of PR as of image build up. It is immediately deduced by critics that means fair and foul may be used for creating the "desired image", and this goes against the reputation of the profession.

The various traditional interpretations of PR include, "controlling minds" of publics, responding to publics and achieving mutually beneficial relationships among all publics and "correspond to the manipulative, service and transactional models of PR".[27] This premise will always bring PR the criticism.

To conclude, amidst threats of terrorism, wars, diseases, death, mayhem, scandals, scourge, dishonesty, and lack of integrity, communication will become all the more crucial. Public relations has had a tough going right from inception to prove its intentions, because it is required to be a 'deliberate, planned and sustained' effort at communication. Hence when a spokesperson promotes a point of view, defends an argument, or conceals information/facts, doubts will always be raised and aspersions will continue to be cast. That is the *fait accompli* of the discipline. Public Relations will continue to go through the litmus test, every time the governments, organizations and individuals are placed in the dock in the court of public opinion.

Summary

This chapter has focused on public relations as an indispensable management discipline. We looked at various definitions of public relations propounded by experts over the last one century or so. We discussed what a public relations practitioner ought to know to pursue the job efficiently. We looked at the changing expectations from public relations, given the globalization of markets and target audience. We discussed the new areas that public relations is asked to lend support to such as care management, corporate governance et al. The chapter ended with a case study that looked at concepts vis-à-vis implementation and interpretation of public relations.

Critical thinking exercise

Critically study various definitions included in the chapter and analyze how PR has been defined over the years by different scholars. Based on your understanding, make a working definition of PR that amalgamates the essence of various definitions.

Questions

Q.1 What in your view is the role and scope of PR in management. Delineate its various functions.

Q.2 "Propaganda has nothing to do with PR?" Write your answer arguing for or against the statement.

Q.3 What role does public opinion play in the application of PR in various spheres? Illustrate with examples.

Endnotes

[1] Joy C Gorden, "Interpreting definitions of PR: Self assessment and a symbolic interactionism-based alternative", *PR Review* 23 [1] 57-66, Spring 97.

[2] Otis W Baskin, Croig E. Aronoff, and Dan Lattimore, *Public Relations: The Profession and the Practice*, 4th ed. Dunuque: Brown & Benchmark, 1997, p.5.

[3] Richard E. Crable and Steven l. Vibbert, *PR as Communication Management*, Edina, Mn: Bellwether Press, 1986, p5.

[4] Rex F. Harlow, "Building a PR definition", *PR Review*, 2, 1976, p. 36.

[5] James E Grunig and Todd Hunt, *Managing Public Relations*, New York: Holt, Rinehart and Winston, 1984, p.7
[6] www.prsa.org
[7] Al Ries and Laura Ries, *The Fall of Advertising and Rise of PR*, New York: Harper Collins, 2000
[8] *Economic Times*, September 19, 2002
[9] Ibid.
[10] Nichol & Co. NY
[11] The Economic Survey (released in February 2003).
[12] *PR Quarterly*, Summer 2001.
[13] *PR Week*, March 11 2002.
[14] Ibid.
[15] *PR Week*, March 4 2002.
[16] www.Media4Exchange, (February 2003)
[17] *India Today*, March 3 2003
[18] www.bsu.edu/news by Marc Ransford, Media Relations Manager.
[19] www.soc.american.edu/main.
[20] Embedded Journalists: 'Is truth the first casualty of war? www.soc.american.edu/main
[21] As reported in *The Times of India, Indian Express, Asia Age* and other newspapers in the month of May 2004.
[22] *The Indian Express*, 6 May 2004
[23] *Economic Times*, 27 March 2003
[24] *PR Week*, June 2002
[25] Dougals G Pinkham, *PR Quarterly*, Vol. 46, No. 2 2001
[26] Legal Analyst Andrew Cohen in CBS News 1 June 2008
[27] Doug Newsom, Judy Van Slyke Turk and Dean Kruckeberg, *This is PR*, Thomson Asia Pvt Ltd. (2000) p. 27.

2 Public Relations Theory

Chapter objectives
- The debate on the evolution and practice of PR in the last about a century and whether PR has theoretical underpinnings or is just a skill/craft
- Various theories with arguments on their relevance and practice in PR
- Case studies of corporates, civil society and NGO organizations on the use of strategies and their analyses

Much to the consternation of PR professionals, it is often believed by critics and a section of the media that there is nothing more to PR than media relations. They often refer to the fire-fighting function of PR in times of crises as – obliquely assigning only craft function to public relations. They feel that PR is one sided and manipulative in favour of the client/organization. The profession of PR, in fact has faced these allegations right from its inception during the early part of last century, when the co-founders of PR, viz. Ledbetter Ivy Lee and Edward Burney began to practice it.

In retrospect, Edward Bernays in his books "*Crystallizing Public Opinion* and *Propaganda*" argued about why and how the practice of PR should be based on theories and methods of the social sciences. Ivy Ledbetter Lee, a journalist turned PR practitioner, felt that the analysis in practice was largely based on case-by-case application of certain basic principles such as the need for openness and for doing good works to receive favourable publicity. His contemporary, Bernays on the other hand proposed that PR could develop as an applied social science on its own strength. He argued that psychological and sociological insights help in gathering and interpreting data about PR, its needs and preferences.

Four decades later, Edward J Robinson in his book "Communication and PR" did the same. In the Nineties, authors Hugh M. Culbertson *et al* felt that far more practitioners talked about theory and research rather than use it. [1]

Grunig and Hunt argue that such a process is essential if PR has to became a two-way communication that Bernays saw as essential in establishing a "mutually supportive relationship between client and public." [2]

Some academics and researchers emphasize publicity writing and techniques as published by IVY L. Lee, while others emphasize behavioural science theory as advocated by Bernays to be the core of the discipline of PR as practiced by professionals over the last one century.

The craft approach to PR education according to Botan and Hazleton does not help in producing the unique body of theoretical knowledge necessary for the development and advancement of a profession. They argue that as engineering as a profession is derived from physics and other natural sciences rather than construction trades, and as medicine was practiced in barbershops until it was linked to the science of biology and chemistry, so we have to look towards humanistic and empirical tradition of social sciences to develop a PR theory.[3]

James E. Grunig argues that the prevailing worldview sees PR as "persuasive and manipulative". As a replacement, he has proposed a symmetrical view of Public Relations that looks at the purpose of PR as managing conflict and promoting understanding.[4]

According to editors of the book, *Public Relations Theory*, a functional analysis of theory considers at least four goals. First, theories may be seen to perform a descriptive function. They help provide a vocabulary for studying and talking about PR. Secondly, theories aim at promoting understanding. In addition to telling us what PR is, (definition) a theory may tell us why PR exists (understanding). Thirdly, prediction and control are also useful criteria for assessing and comparing theories. Prediction refers to the ability of theories to anticipate the future value of concepts from current or past observations of those concepts or related concepts. Control refers to the ability of theorists to systematically intervene and influence outcomes predicted by theory.[5] Finally, there is this heuristic function of theory. The heuristic function of theory refers to the tendency to generate research and additional theory.

Grunig is of the view that PR is a nascent scholarly field although practiced for nearly a century. There could be many social theories applicable to PR, but it is more difficult to think of a PR theory (one that is not borrowed from any other discipline). The practice of PR also, feels Grunig, is fragmented because the practitioners don't apply a common set of skills or a common body of knowledge.

The practice of PR according to Kuhn is guided by one single "mindset"—that defines PR as the use of communication to "manipulate" publics for the benefit of the organization.[6]

Persuasion, feel analysts, is a safer word to replace "manipulation". The changing of the word, however, does not change the mindset, argue many critics. Interestingly, many practitioners feel convinced that the "manipulation" helps the publics as well.

Summing up the argument, Grunig writes: "Roughly described, the dominant mindset defines public relations as the manipulation of public behaviour for the benefit of the manipulated publics as well as the sponsoring organizations. It also suggests the relevance of some obvious communication theories, most notably, theories of attitudes and persuasion". He refers to this mindset as the *asymmetrical model of public relations* against which he suggests an alternative, which he calls the *symmetrical model of public relations*, which has a different set of presuppositions and calls for a different kind of theory [7]

J M Grunig's Model of Symmetrical Public Relations

Explaining symmetrical PR, Grunig explains that the term may be new, but "allusions to the concept can be found throughout the history of Public Relations – specially in the works of Ive Lee and Edward Bernays in the last century and John Hill, Scot and Cutlip, more recently". From the symmetrical theories of communication emerge the following presuppositions, according to the author of this model:

Communication leads to understanding

We communicate to facilitate understanding among people and such other systems as organizations, publics, or societies. Persuasion of one person or system by one person or system is less desirable.

From the systems theory, emerge four more presuppositions:

Holism

Systems consist of sub-systems and supra-systems. The whole is greater than the sum of its parts, and each part of the system affects every other part.

Interdependence

Although systems have boundaries that separate them from their environment, systems in the environment cross that boundary and "interpenetrate" the system.

Open system

The organization is open to the interpenetrating systems and freely exchanges information with those systems.

Moving equilibrium

Systems strive towards equilibrium with other systems although they seldom achieve it. The desired equilibrium state constantly moves as the environment changes. Systems may attempt to establish equilibrium by controlling other systems, by constantly adapting themselves to other systems, or by making mutual cooperative adjustments. In the symmetrical approach to public relations, cooperative and mutual adjustments are preferred to control and adaptations.

Some more presuppositions, according to Grunig would include:

Equality

People should be treated as equals and respected as fellow human beings. Anyone, regardless of education or background may provide valuable input into an organization.

Autonomy

People are more innovative, constructive and self-fulfilled when they have autonomy to influence their own behaviour, rather than having it controlled by others.

Innovations

New ideas and flexible thinking should be stressed rather than tradition and efficiency.

Decentralization of management

Management should be collective. Managers should coordinate rather than dictate. Decentralization increases autonomy, employee satisfaction, and innovation.

Conflict resolution

Conflict should be resolved through negotiation and communication and not through force, manipulation, coercion, or violence.

Interest group liberalism

Interest group liberalism views the political system as the mechanism for open competition among interest groups. Interest group liberalism looks to citizens groups to "champion interests of ordinary people against unresponsive government and corporate structure."

Analyzing Grunig's theory, Greg Leichty in his scholarly article "The Limits of Collaboration"[8] writes that the worldview of symmetrical PR, is typically contrasted with the paradigm of two-way asymmetric PR. Where the former calls for cooperation, the later model emphasizes manipulating the attitudes and behaviours of publics for the benefit of the organization. The asymmetric PR or the persuasive paradigm is said to opt for a win-lose perspective in which one party's gain is necessarily matched by another party's loss. However, Leichty disputes the claim that two-way symmetric or collaborative PR is always possible.

Case studies documenting collaborative PR in conflict situations are rather hard to find compared to case studies in which a more confrontational approach has prevailed. Larissa Grunig's study of 31 organizations studied revealed that practically none of them had used two-way symmetrical PR when dealing with activist groups. Ironically, however, the strategy did not work favourably for any of the organizations studied. Collaborative PR, argued Larissa Grunig would have been more appropriate because of involvement of a variety of publics, whose interests may not always be similar, addressing the concerns of one public may have the effect of causing concern or alienating another important public.[9]

Richard Ice analyzed this phenomenon in the Bhopal gas tragedy in 1984. In the immediate aftermath of the incident, the Union Carbide emphasized that the Bhopal plant was similar to plants in the USA in terms of its construction and operational procedures. The strategy was intended to deny that the company placed a lower value on the lives of Indian workers and citizens than it did on American Workers. [10]

However when the workers in the USA expressed their concern questioning, if the standards were similar, were they also exposed to similar catastrophe, the company had to use caution to avoid a boomerang.

Marcia Prior-Miller believes that PR is an inherently organizational form of communication. Contemporary organization theory has its roots in a number of social scientific disciplines. Researchers in PR use more than one perspective to explain relationships. Several writers including Cutlip and Center have noted that research in PR may draw on as many as 10 or more different research traditions. [11]

Sriramesh, K. and Enxi, Liu in their paper "Public Relations Practices and Socio-economic Factors: A Case Study of Different Organizational Types in Shanghai" presented at the annual meeting of the International Communication Association, in New York City, NY, bring about interesting insights about the use of PR model by various kinds of organizations.

The West has influenced Shanghai, one of the first Chinese ports, opened to Western traders, since the Opium War of 1840. This study investigates the nature of public relations practices among a sample of different types of organizations in this cosmopolitan city that is "leading China's explosive economic growth." Due to its history and an increase in the influx of foreigners to the city especially in the 1920s and 1930s, it became one of the most cosmopolitan cities in China, thus bringing the influence of the practice of PR.

The team studied the pattern in 23 organizations that included, government agencies, non-profit, and corporations—domestic and multinational. The personal influence model was found to be the most prevalent model in all the organizations based on personal networking ("Guanxi") due to China's relation-centric culture. Relationship with the media was less valued particularly amongst government agencies and state owned enterprises. Contrary to published literature, share the authors, the public information model was least used by government agencies and non-profit organizations in the sample. Multinational Corporations however practiced the two-way asymmetrical or symmetrical model more often than domestic organizations.

The "Lun zi pai bei" system (valuing seniority over performance or qualifications), which has not been discussed at all in PR literature contend the authors, reflected that heads of PR departments of government agencies often had no education or even background in public relations. As a result, railway workers and even chefs were asked to head public relations departments in Shanghai.[12]

The practice of a PR job being handled by non-PR professionals is quite commonplace in India, especially in the government, when young bureaucrats are asked to handle PR for the government, at the district level and in public sector enterprises, where it is common to find engineers and marketing professional heading PR departments. There has not been any known empirical study in India on this aspect of PR functioning and the impact on organizational communication with various stakeholders.

Organizational theories

Contemporary organizational theory is rooted in a number of social scientific disciplines. Researchers point out four theoretical frameworks within Sociology viz., Symbolic Interactionism, Exchange Theory, Conflict Theory, and Structural-Functional Theory. Drawing on these frameworks, analysts have sought to understand behaviours of individuals in organizations, structures of organizations and networks in and between organizations.

Let's look at the four theories more closely that are said to have relationship in the Practice.

Symbolic Interactionism

Symbolic Interactionism, with its genesis in behaviourism grew out of some of the earliest efforts of sociologists to understand the interactions among people and the impact of their interaction on society.[13]

Symbolic interactionism proposes that social reality is what people think it is. This would mean that social phenomena are in a constant state of negotiation. Hence, organizations would be what people believe them to be. They are the products of social interaction.

Social psychologists have found symbolic interactionism a useful perspective for fully understanding intra-organizational dimensions and processes i.e., how people behave in relation to organizations and the impact that organizational patterns and structures have on individual behaviours.

Wilson and Stryker have explored the role of this perspective in building corporate identity for organizations. Symbolic interactionism can be used to explore now those symbols to become statements of strategic choice.[14]

The more an organizational symbol is associated with organizational reality, the greater will be the expectation of that reality when the symbol alone is presented.[15]

Exchange Theory

The theory posited by key theorists Peter M. Blau, George C. Homans and Richard M. Emerson is the basic proposition that social structures result from social exchanges between individuals.[16]

The perspective of this theory assumes that people form and sustain relationships when they believe that the "rewards" from those relationships would be greater than the "costs" involved. When translated to organizational behaviour, it can be assumed that organizational communication will occur or fail to occur when inputs and outputs are not in balance and organizational change will result from continually negotiating inputs and outputs. Hence organizational management will both be reactive and proactive in such organizations. Therefore proposition from the exchange theory in the context of an organization might include the following:

1. When the organizations find that they are able to retain experienced and brilliant people at low salaries and low positions, they would continue to offer low remunerations.
2. When organizations get a feedback that indicates practitioners apply and accept placement in positions without greater rewards, the more likely they would continue to offer low salaries to experienced individuals.
3. When such organizations continue to reap profits, they are likely to continue with the pattern explained above.
4. When the practitioners depend more on organization for job tenure, the greater will be the organization authority over practitioners.

Conflict Theory

This theory assumes that conflict is the basis and the product of social interchange. The theory emerged from the writings of Karl Marx, Georg Simmel, Ralf Dahrendorf, and L A Coser.[17]

Conflict theory is based on the premise that conflict is an inevitable part of social interaction. This happens because of the competing goals and values of individuals and organizations. In other words every activity has both positive and negative aspects and changes occur as a result.

Structural- Functional Theory

This theory assumes that people's social interactions are determined by the larger social order and that interactions serve to maintain that order rather than people setting the rules for their social interactions and acting to shape and mould the social order to suit their meaning. Talcott Parson, Robert Merton, and Peter Blan propounded the theory among others.[18] Because of these assumptions, the theory has been an important sociological perspective for understanding of complex organizations. However, the perspective has been little used in the study of communications in organizations, particularly mass communication.

Analysts feel that a careful analysis of these four theories will enable public relations researchers to build connections between theories and practice of PR.

Carl Burton examines public relations as an applied social science based on communication. PR uses communication to create and maintain relationships between an organization and its various publics. Hence Public Relations as an instance of applied communication can be studied using theoretic and research tools, believes Burton. [19]

According to Hawes: "the social scientists primary task is to explain all manner of human behaviour. Such explanations are referred to as theories". To illustrate, when a practitioner offers an explanation for why a PR effort failed or succeeded, he is taking a first step in propounding a theory. Hence the general explanation and skills used over the years can be construed as rudimentary theories.[20]

Theory development is based on research. How things work or should work are tested, results are used to modify the formulations with which the process started.

According to Kaplan when we develop a theory by reaching out for knowledge bit by bit, using each existing bit as a lead to the next bit, we are engaged in theory development by extension.[21]

Similarly when we develop theory through a deeper understanding of existing knowledge, we are engaged in theory development by intention. After a certain path of development by ways, viz., extension and intention, a situation develops which requires taking a large leap outside step-to-step approaches. Kuhn refers to this phenomenon as scientific revolution. He illustrates his point by referring to Einstein's theory of relativity as an example of scientific revolution from the physical sciences.[22]

Accepting PR as an applied social science based on communication however, would have several implications on professionalism, practitioners, scholars and ethics, feel analysts.

Pavlok and Salman noted that the lack of a systematic body of knowledge is particularly significant as its major impedimenta in the development of PR as from 'practice' to a profession. Journalism also forms a part of the same category. Due to a lack of an underlying systematized body of theory and knowledge which practitioners draw for their work.[23] However, it is a fact that theory does not develop automatically out of a large body of practical research. Many analysts believe that PR has gone through a rich experience, but has not embraced the theory development process. Hence, if an applied social science approach is taken, PR is capable of developing a body of theoretic knowledge that meets the needs and distinguishes the practice of PR from the craft of communications techniques.

Case studies on use of various theoretical models in pursuance of a Public Relations goal

In an age of global markets, many multinational companies use public relations techniques to reach out to various cross-cultural markets. Many scholars feel that activists should not be considered confrontationists in the true sense, because it is through their efforts, the organizations are forced to look at issues, they may not have considered necessary or important. These more often are issues that address the concerns of one or more stakeholders.

Defining activism: Dewey (1972) defines activists as "a group whose members face a similar problem, recognize that the problem exists and organizes to do something about it". Gruning and Hunt (1984) argue that there are three stages in the evaluation of publics. In the first, called the latent stage, the public does not recognize the problem even if it is there. In the second stage, it becomes aware. In the final stage, which is the active stage, the public recognizes the problem and organizes to do something about the problem. Therefore from the public relations perspective, the most suitable stage to intervene is the second stage when the public becomes aware of the problem. Before they decide on a possible confrontational action, it is important to arrest the problem through suitable public relations strategy.

Defining activist public, Grunig (1992) says, "is a group of two or more individuals, who organize in order to influence another public or publics, through action that may include education, compromise, persuasion, persuasive tactics or force."

Anderson (1992) defines activists groups as "strategic publics, because they constrain an organization's ability to accomplish its goals and mission".

Minzberg (1983) feels that activists more often work as pressure groups that are "based on confrontation, not cooperation. They assume that the organizations must be forced to change against their will". If the organizations bother to find the perceptions of such publics beforehand, the problem may not escalate into pressure groupism.

According to Lesley (1992) there are five kinds of activists groups, who have to be tackled according to their type:

a) the sincere group that has "clear purpose that frankly reflects their rights or interests"

b) The "do-gooders", a group that is comfortable and effluent. They seek an outlet for their purposefulness in helping others or in making things "fit their theories of life".

c) The "social engineers" who consider themselves intellectually and morally the "cream of society and are intent on imposing their superior judgement on to the entire human system."

d) This group has the attitude of "holier than thou". They tend to feel that they have a special role to play as they are ordained by some superior order to impose it on others.

e) The "anti's" who are against everything under the sun. They are constantly dissatisfied with their lives and the world.

Lesley suggests public relations practitioners to be sensitive to the psyche of the people that comprise the above mentioned variant groups.

CASE STUDY

Save Narmada Crusade

Activist groups often use public relations tactics, calling it "media advocacy". Such groups bank a great deal on research and data so that they use these in pressurizing the organization directly and through media. As per the theory of Agenda Setting, the media lends a sort of legitimization and confers status on the individuals involved in the activism.

Medha Patkar, a social activist, who was on constant media radar during the Sardar Sarovar agitation, became internationally known for her crusade. She was able to exert influence because of the acquired status, for which media can partly take credit. She, as a part of strategy roped in Booker Prize winning author Arundhati Roy that further consolidated the position of the activist group, Narmada Bachao Andolan (Save Narmada Crusade). The media interviews of the activists, the imagery, the tears, the fasting, all became engrained in public memory.

The World Bank that had partly funded the project has become very cautious while funding large scale hydro projects and insists that the borrowers adopt a fool proof communication strategy with locals, those whose land would be purchased, the activists and the media.

The Nano ouster from West Bengal

Mamata Banerjee of Trinamool Congress took a confrontationist posture and ensured the ouster of Tatas from Singur in 2008. This meant a loss of atleast Rs. 500 crores to the company that had begun work on manufacturing the "Nano" car that is said to be cheapest in the world, in a communist-led government in West Bengal. For her it was a win-lose situation with no scope for any dialogue. Ratan Tata, chairman of the group after leaving the state; lock, stock and barrel issued an open letter as an advertisement in many newspapers, expressing his angst. The case story may be referred to in the chapter on "Crises Communication".

Oil Sector Strike

When officers of the entire oil sector struck work in January 2009 in India, demanding the implementation of revised pay scales, the government refused to be bogged down, it felt that it was not expected of officers to strike work, as that would mean hampering supply of essential commodities across the country. The central government was in no mood to bow down to the confrontationist attitude of thousands of officers. The government threatened to invoke the necessary Act which would mean dismissal and arrests for many. All the officers reported back for work unconditionally.

On the other hand, when the truck operators, that are in the unorganized sector, struck work around the same time, they were difficult to handle when compared with the oil sector officers, who were governed by the disciplinary rules, besides awareness on their part about the legal aspects of strike.

Mc libel case: Examination of PR and the Influence of Activism

McDonald's spend nearly $ 2 Billion annually on advertising and brand promotion. The world's best-known fast food giant has also been in the public gaze constantly, more often than not for wrong reasons. When confronted with pressure groups, it does not hesitate to take them on, often through legal action, in which the company has been able to get apologies from its critics to avoid legal proceedings. The situation however was different when it got embroiled in a long legal battle with Greenpeace, an activist group with a whopping 3.3 million members in 22 countries. Greenpeace has often been in the media glare for drawing the attention of the policy makers on environmental issues.

In 1986, London Greenpeace brought out a six-page pamphlet entitled: *"What's wrong with McDonald's? Everything they don't want you to know"*.

The leaflet criticized the company and accused it for many issues, such as starvation in the third world countries, use of children in advertising, being cruel to animals, serving unhealthy food that caused cancer of the breast and bowels and heart ailments, and, poor working conditions for its employees.

At the end of the leaflet, the group advocated that consumers boycott McDonald's.

Timeline of the events in the McLibel action:

1982: Dave Morris joined the group
1988: Helen Steel joined the group
1986: The leaflet "What's wrong with McDonald's" was produced.
1989-91: McDonald's employed seven private investigators to infiltrate the group
9/20/90: McDonald's served libel writs over the leaflet asking for an apology. The group was given two hours of free Legal Aid, but it refused to apologize.
6/28/94: After 12 preliminary hearings and four years of appeals, the trial started. The McDonald's barrister predicted the trial would last 3-4 weeks. The trial took place in Court 35 of the Royal Courts of Justice, London. McDonald's successfully argued that the case was too complex for a jury, thus Mr. Justice Bell would decide the case.
6/30/94: Day three. Evidence started.
8/23/96: McDonald's, in a publicity stunt, gave 500 pounds to Charlie's Play Centre, a children's charity.
8/94: McDonald's initiated settlement negotiations by flying over two McDonald's vice presidents. Since Greenpeace was unwilling to negotiate, McDonald's mirrored the "non-nice" behaviour by sending out it own leaflets, in an attempt to discredit Morris and Steel.
2/16/96: McSpotlight, an Internet site was launched.
6/28/96: Second anniversary of the trial.
11/1/96: Day 292. McLibel became the longest trial in English history.
12/13/96: Day 313. End of hearing.
6/19/97: Judgement day. [24]

In the verdict Justice Bell held that Greenpeace had not proved that McDonald's products caused heart diseases, cancer and food poisoning. The Court did hold it against McDonald's that it did exploit children through misleading ads; it indeed was cruel to animals and paid low wages.

According to analysts, the strategy used in the Mclibel case by Greenpeace was extreme, unilateral and reflected its intolerance for compromise. This was termed as the "Zero-sum" approach of the Game theory. The basic premise of the Game theory holds that conflict of interest can be modeled as games of strategy. The participants, viz., the organization and the activist group are seen as "players" in the game. There are two classes of game, the "Zero sum" and "Non-zero sum".

In the former, the pay offs to the player is any outcome adds up to a zero, i.e., when one player wins, the other has to lose. In non-zero sum, the game is dominated by mixed motives, with each side playing with a strong sense of self-interest, but is motivated to cooperate to a limited extent, in order to maximize very different benefits from each other.[25]

In the case of Greenpeace and McDonald, both the parties exemplified through their action; both refused to cede any points. Greenpeace used flamboyant symbols in celebrating the second anniversary of the trial by inviting media and public, who were fed with a cake in the shape of Ronald McDonald's face.

Analysts believe that McDonald made a number of mistakes in pursuing the case. The first mistake was the "legal vendetta" against two Greenpeace activists, viz. Steel and Morris. The company "jumped the gun" in protecting its image/reputation. It had no idea of public perception after they received the Greenpeace pamphlets against it.

The company also failed to do an environment scanning on Greenpeace to know the size, the power, the clout of the NGO locally, nationally and globally and its credibility.

McDonald used asymmetrical method to disseminate information on the eve of the trial through 3,00,000 pamphlets that called the activists liars, as a way of discrediting them. The strategy backfired as no research was conducted on the activists, who had earned a great reputation for themselves.

The protest campaign was activated in 24 countries, McSpotlight an Internet site was launched in 1996, which is an online library that provides over 10,000 files, original leaflet, full transcript of the trial and other campaign material.

The legal suit cost McDonald $16 million, which in turn also resulted in a lot of adverse publicity for the company. McDonald's UK president defending it said, "This is about reputation".[26]

Case of French fries laced in beef tallow

McDonald's was involved in a spat with a Hindu group a few years ago that challenged its contention that its French fries did not contain any meat or animal oil content. When a research laboratory confirmed that the French fries were polished with beef tallow, the company went in for an out of court settlement worth a few million dollars that the group was asked to use in community welfare. Fearing a backlash in India, McDonald's went in for a damage control campaign claiming that in India the company did not use beef products at all and the French fries were cent per cent vegetarian. For a long time, the restaurants used paper mats that reflected a collage of newspaper clippings that had published Mc Donald's stand that it never used beef products or animal oil in its products. In some select restaurants in India, one can see a metallic plate hung at a prominent place behind the counter with the inscription that McDonald's India does not use beef or beef products. The perceptions were managed just on time and there was no issue later.

Cola drinks and pesticides

The Centre for Science and Environment (CSE) is a non-governmental organization that has raised issues about environment for over three decades in India. The publication *Down to Earth* continues to raise important issues and advocates policy intervention. It has been a kind of a trendsetter. Its first protagonist was late Mr. Vinod Aggarwal, a journalist by profession. The CSE has been in focus for taking on big companies including multinationals like the Coca-Cola and PepsiCo. CSE was the first to bring the issue of pesticides in Coca-Cola in the public gaze in India in 2003. A lot of furore resulted when the CSE findings of pesticide content much above the permissible limits was published in media. The Parliament also had to appoint a committee to go into the issue.

The CSE claimed to have analyzed samples at its laboratories from 12 major soft drinks that were sold in and around the capital and found that all of them contained residues of four extremely toxic pesticides and insecticides—Lindane, DDT, Malathion and Chlorpyrifos.

"In all the samples tested, the levels of pesticide residue far exceeded the maximum permissible total pesticide limit of 0.0005 mg per liter in water used as food, set down by the European Economic Commission (EEC)," said Sunita Narain, Director of the CSE at a press conference convened to announce the findings.[27]

A media channel around that time covered a clip reflecting farmers in Uttar Pradesh using Coca-Cola and Pepsi as pesticides in their fields as against the regular pesticides. They seemed happy that in less than half the cost of purchasing pesticides, the colas were performing the same function. The clip had an interview with a farmer on this. The camera panned to show empty bottles of both the brands lying in the field.[28] Both the companies used long perception management campaigns to allay the fears of consumers. While Coke used celebrities from cinema, PepsiCo's CEO Bakshi appeared in the commercial, assuring people about the safety of the drink.

Both the companies however have used silence as a strategy, in not responding to popular yoga guru Baba Ramdev openly criticizing the multinational giants in spoiling the health of people. He is said to be taking pledges from youngsters to not consume aerated drinks. The marketing people may not be talking publicly to avoid a backlash from the seer, but agree that it has made a difference in their sales.

Yamuna Pollution – Activism of NGOs

The CSE has been very vocal on the pollution issue of river Yamuna that is the lifeline of millions of people. In 2007, the NGO brought out a book entitled: *"Faecal Attraction: relationship between rich man's shit and poor man's water"*. A lot of pre-publicity was arranged for the book in mainstream media. Copies of the book were also sent to people who mattered, including the organization in charge of water treatment and supply in the capital city of Delhi, viz., the Jal Board, the Chief Minister of Delhi and the Environment Minister in the central cabinet and well known policy makers and activists. A function was organized to formally release the book, which attracted hundreds of people who mattered in the city, including of course the Chief Minster and the Environment Minister. The CSE head Sunita Narain introduced the book, speaking from a podium. Her passion and raw energy were too visible to be ignored.

The book cover has the picture of a toilet commode on it. If we were to analyze, the NGO used the imagery to bring home the point that the sewage from urban homes may not necessarily go to sewage treatment plants (STPs) but back to the river through open drains that are not connected to any STP. The content of the book interestingly in most parts has only government data, a bit of interpretation here and there. It does not give a workable solution to the issue so forcefully raised.

It is not uncommon for many activist groups to raise issues, when they may have no solutions to offer.

The book release was also accompanied by screening of a short documentary on the subject. The amateur video, seemingly shot by CSE staffers, used rhetoric and smart use of one liners/bytes from people to bring home the point. Sample some of these:

Question: "What do you do with your shit?"

Answers: " No idea"; "I take it out every morning"; "I do nothing, everything happens automatically"; " Shit is converted into gas".

Question: "Where does the water go?"

Answers: "Don't know"; "from river to sea"; "It goes back to Yamuna".

A trailer of the video posted on NGO's site, has drawn quite a few comments from the viewers. Sample two of these:

"so..... this wonderful video only offers the problem, not the solution. What the f#*^ is this solution. Make a video about that. There are a ton of videos documenting India's problems, but not many offer any solutions. This video is just another in the same stupid line"

"I think it a great one. It shows the awareness (or lack of it) of water issue in India. Out of so many people not many could answer where do they get the water from and where it goes back".[29]

The event created a lot of hype in the media, besides instant selling of books and film DVDs at the release function.

The issue of Yamuna Pollution has been in the Court with a number of public interest litigations (PILs) by several civil society organizations. There are many NGOs working on the issue, but CSE with its innovative and activist communication strategy has been able to bring the issue in the public domain more forcefully than many others. It has also been able to garner appreciation for its crusade from far and wide. On the other hand, the organization in charge has not really used a proactive stance to talk of the problem per se, the reasons behind the pollution and why it is not in a position to meet the deadlines of cleaning Yamuna.

The problem when dispassionately analyzed can be seen as multi-disciplinary that needs action by many organizations, strong civil society support, besides a robust political will. Being a part of the government, the Delhi Jal Board (DJB) obviously is not in a position to defend its stand vis-à-vis the government or speak candidly in the Court.

Delhi has thousands of unauthorized colonies that exist without a sewage system. The human waste obviously goes back to the river through open drains. Many of these colonies get "regularized" from time to time as election largesse from the party in power against the expectation of votes. Once the colonies are regularized, the sewage line has to be provided to them. The entire length and breadth of the sewage line for these colonies runs in to thousands of kilometers, the construction of which obviously is time consuming. On the other hand some sewage lines have become clogged and non-functional as they are very old and need repair. All this and more is being addressed by the Yamuna Action Plan II. Educating the media, and reaching out to the communities is an important task to handle, especially when media keeps writing negative and at times sensational stories based on its "investigation" or on NGO input, without realizing that it is a Herculean task for the DJB to complete it in the stipulated time schedule. The apex court's intervention about deadlines for completion of works, which may not always be feasible, given various factors, including delays, and bureaucratic red tape, among other things.

In India, it is not commonplace to take cudgels with the media, even if organizations, especially in the public sector feel that the former has been unfair or has gone overboard without appreciating its perspective. The case of Yamuna pollution is no different.

Averting the Nationalization of TISCO

Tata Iron and Steel Company Limited (TISCO), the largest steel company in the private sector was on the verge of being taken over by the Janata government, a coalition of parties that formed the government in 1977, being the first non-Congress government. George Fernandez, the socialist leader was the minister in charge of Industry. He successfully sent back Coca-Cola and IBM around that time.

TISCO had a turnover of Rs. 23,000 million; it had 75,000 employees and over five lakh shareholders at that time of possible nationalization.

The government apparently had no reason except to achieve political mileage. TISCO had long been a respected company for its vision, technical competence and welfare activities. It commanded great brand equity among its various stakeholders and people in general.

The company undertook an integrated communication approach that included lobbying, advocacy and public relations to reach out to various stakeholders with its point of view. The stakeholders the communication programme targeted included shareholders, employees, trade, opinion makers, government, politicians, bureaucrats and general public.

Myths vs. Reality

	Government attitude	TISCO's stand
1.	Pre-conceived notion: Big business means exploitation	Large business does not exploit
2.	Prejudice: Big business hinders national progress in a socialistic economy	Big business helps national, industrial and economic progress
3.	Suspicion: The company fills its coffers	The company contributes immensely to labour welfare and community development
4.	Belief: Take over or controlling TISCO's operations is necessary	Controlling or taking over of TISCO's operations is against national interest.

Broad strategy

The basic objective behind the 360-degree communication campaign was to stop the government from taking over TISCO by influencing the thinking of different target groups through various media and well thought out strategies.

The campaign was not overtly critical of the government, but at the same time put the company's point of view forcefully and succinctly in various media that included print and television. It organized conferences and seminars to enlist the support of the industry, by subtly reflecting the working of TISCO and its contribution in nation building. In its shareholder communication, it kept them informed of the developments and company's stand.

The company created a number of awareness programmes for the employees, which covered various operational activities through audio-visual means.

The company termed advocacy and lobbying as the "non-public media" that "formed the main thrust of TISCO's programme. Chairman of TISCO, JRD Tata, one of the highly respected business leaders in India, sent a memorandum to the concerned ministry, following up with personal letters to the members of parliament, highlighting TISCO's contribution in the national, industrial and social fields.

Third party endorsement through editorial support was constantly maintained. Letters to editors from friends and general public were organized to be sent, and journalists were taken for facility visits to the TISCO factory in Jameshdpur. Regular meetings with senior correspondents and various editors were arranged

> in three metros viz., Delhi, Mumbai and Calcutta to keep them posted and enlist their support. The media persons were also mailed company literature during the campaign period.
>
> JRD Tata during his visits abroad spoke to media about India, its industrial progress and government's role in the development, indirectly contributing to a perception of Tata's being a company that contributed to nation building.
>
> Before the government could make its stand clear, though the tirade stopped thanks to the superb communication strategy of the Tatas, the government fell, and the Congress led government bounced back and with that the concept of nationalizing big businesses also died down.[30]
>
> When we analyze the strategy of TISCO, it was non-confrontationist with the government, but persuasive enough using various tools, both formal and informal, to make its stand clear based on facts and figures. At the same time, it made it a point to communicate that private sector was as much engaged in nation building as the public sector.

It is important for PR practitioners and academics to work in conjunction to build a body of knowledge based on some of the theories discussed in the chapter with the actual practice of PR. It is hoped that some of the case studies discussed above would leave some food for thought.

Summary

In this chapter we looked at the evolution of certain public relations theories. We looked at the role of communication in an organization and how the application of certain models can be made use of to fulfill public relations goals. A few case studies have been included to analyze whether the models made use of in certain cases brought about the desired results. Similarly, some other case studies where some inference of use of theories can be made have been included in the chapter.

Critical thinking exercise

Study various case studies reflected above. Make a connection with various theories to create an understanding about their use in campaigns aimed at interfacing with stakeholders in normal as well as critical times.

Surf the Internet and evolve an understanding about Yamuna pollution and varying perspectives, viz. government's civil society and media's. Suggest a strategy based on symmetrical PR theory on behalf of the Yamuna Action Plan.

Questions

Q.1 Trace the evolution of PR using various models in communication.

Q.2 What is Grunig's Symmetrical model? How is it different from the asymmetrical model? Discuss.

Q.3 Analyze Mclibel case and suggest an alternate strategy that in your view would have been more suitable to McDonald's image.

Endnotes

[1] Hugh M. Gulbertson, Dennis W.Jeffers, Denta Besser Stove, Martin Terrell, *Social, Political and Economic Contexts in PR: Theory and Cases* (LEA: New Jersey 1993).

[2] JE Grunig, T Hunt, *Managing Public Relations* (NY: Holt, Rinehart and Winston, 1984), pp. 4-11.

[3] Carl H. Botan and Vincent Hazleton Jr., *Public Relation Theory*, eds, 1989) (New Jersey, Lawrence Erlabum Associates, Publishers)

[4] JE Grunig, T Hunt, *Managing Public Relations* (NY: Holt, Rinehart and Winston, 1984)

[5] Carl H. Botan and Vincent Hazleton Jr., *Public Relation Theory*, eds, 1989 (New Jersey, Lawrence Erlabum Associates, Publishers)

[6] T S Kuhn, *The Structure of ScientificRevolutions* (Chicago; University of Chicago Press, 1970)

[7] James E. Grunig, "Symmetrical Presuppositions as a Framework for PR Theory" Ibid. no. pp. 17-44.

[8] *PR Review* [23(1) – pp. 47-55]

[9] Larissa A. Grunig, "Activism and Organizational Response: Contemporary Cases of Collective Behaviour", paper presented at the meeting of the Association for Education in Journalism and mass communication, (Norman, OK, August, 1986).

[10] Richard Ice, "The Corporate Publics and Rhetorical Strategies: The Case of Union Carbide's Bhopal Crisis", *Management Communications Quarterly* 4, 1991, pp. 34- 62.

[11] Scot M. Cutlip, Allen H. Center and Glen M. Broom, *Effective Public Relations*, Seventh ed. 1994 (Prentice Hall: NJ)

[12] http://www.allacademic.com.

[13] J.H. Turner, *The Structure of Sociological Theory*, 3rd ed. (Homewood, IL: Dorsey Press, 1982).

[14] J. Wilson, *Social Theory* (Englewood Cliffs, NJ: Prentice-Hall, 1983), S. Stryker, "Symbolic Interactionism: Themes and Variations", in M. Rosenberg & RH Turner (Eds.), *Social Psychological Perspective* (New York: Basic Books, 1981), pp. 3-29.

[15] Ibid.

[16] P.M. Blau, *Exchange and Power in Social Life* (New York: Wiley, 1964) P.M. Blau, "Interaction: Social Exchange", in D.L. Sills (Ed.) *International Encyclopedia of Social Sciences* (vol.7, 77. 452 – 458C New York; Macmillan, 1968); G. C. Homans, *Social behaviour; Its elementary forms*. (New York: Harcourt Brace Jovan ouch, 1974); R.M. Emerson, *Exchange theory*, parts I & II. In J. Berger, M. Zelditch, and A. B. Anderson (Eds.), *Sociological Theories in Progress* (Vol.4) (Boston: Houghton – Mifflin, 1972).

[17] Karl Marx, *Karl Marx and Frederick Engels: Selected works in three volumes*. Prepared by the Institute of Marxism and Leninism under the Central Committee of the CPSU (Moscow: Progressive Publishers, 1969), G Simmel, *Conflict in Industrial Society* (K. H, Wollf. Trans) R Dahrendarf, *Class and Class Conflict in Industrial Society* (London: Routledge & Kegan Paul, 1959), L A Croser, *The Functions of Social Conflict* (Giencoe I L: The Free Press, 1956).

[18] T Parson, *The Structure of Social Action* (2nd ed.) (Glencoe:IL: The Free Press, 1948); R K Merton, *Social Theory and Social Structure* (revised and enlarged edition) (New York: The Free Press, 1968); PM Blau, *Inequality and Heterogeneity: A Primitive Theory of Social Structure* (New York: The Free Press, 1977).

[19] Carl. H. Burton, "Theory Development in PR'" In Carl H Burton & Vincent Hazelton, Jr. (Eds) *Public Relations Theory* (Hillside: NJ: LEA, 19890, pp. 99-110).

[20] L C Hawes, *Pragmatics of Analoguing: The Theory and Model Construction in Communication* (Reading. AA: Adison Wesley, 1975)

[21] A Kaplan, *The Conduct of Inquiry: Methodology for Behavioural Sciences* (New York: Chandler Publishing, 1964).

[22] T S Kuhan, *The structure of Scientific Revolution*, 2nd ed. enlarged (Chicago: University of Chicago press, 1970).

[23] J V Palvik and C T Salman, *Theoretic Approaches in Public Relations Research*, (Public Relations Research and Education), Vol. 1, no. 2, pp. 39-49.
[24] http://iml.jou.ufl.edu/projects/Fall99/Westbrook/litrev.htm
[25] A. Coleman, *Game Theory and Experimental Games*, 1982 (Oxford: Pergamon)
[26] http://iml.jou.ufl.edu/projects/Fall99/Westbrook/litrev.htm
[27] http://www.indiaresource.org
[28] www.youtube
[29] www.cseindia.com
[30] Adapted from the case study that was published in volume II of PR Case studies, brought out by the India Foundation for Education and Research, 1992.

3 Public Relations and Other Management Disciplines

Chapter objectives
- Communication flow process in an organization
- Various forms of communication within an organization
- Organizational communication and PR communication
- Interface of PR with various staff and line function departments

To facilitate smooth flow of work, the internal structure of the organization calls for the creation of various specialist departments. Depending on the role and functions of individual departments, their jobs are referred to as *line* or *staff* functions. Engineering, assembly, production and marketing are in the *line* category. Finance, Human Resource Development, Company Secretariat and Public Relations are in the category of *staff* functions. The line departments are engaged in the core business of production, assembly, development and marketing. They however, need the support and assistance of staff officers in the form of plans, advice and suggestions. In the context of the military, the staff officers present studies of various possibilities, and based on these the line staff take action. There is generally a watertight compartmentalization of line and staff functions in military. In the corporate context however, especially in problem solving areas, staff executives work in close collaboration with line managers to make decisions.

There is no model to suggest where public relations fits in the hierarchy of management. In fact, various organizations have different public relations setups. Many examples suggest that that the PR hierarchy depends on the circumstances that went in to the creation of the public relations department. In some organizations, public relations outfit is created, when it is faced with a crisis situation. The department continues to function because the management feels that it did a fairly good job. In other organizations, the public relations departments are created as a deliberate choice. The objectives in this case are well defined. Here, the hierarchy of the public relations head is also decided keeping in view the overall corporate objectives and the expectations from the department. Let's define first what is expected of the public relations department before we discuss their interface with various management disciplines.

In a recent survey of PR, 100 employers revealed that knowledge of PR theory was placed last in terms of importance in the list of 11 competencies. Interestingly an understanding of business principles came second last. A majority of respondents felt writing skills and an understanding of media relations is most important. [1]

The integrated perspective of management communication comprise the following:
- Information sharing
- Responsiveness
- Reliability

The challenges before professional communicators toady are diverse and many such as globalization, proliferation of media, multiple competition and a seamless market, among others.

Understanding Organization

Various Concepts

An organization is seen by experts as a dynamic system in which individuals are engaged in collective efforts to achieve set goals. Organization is a word that has emerged from organizing—an attempt to bring order out of chaos, or establish organizations/entities in which purposeful and orderly activities take place.

Objectivists' define an organization as a concrete thing which has physicality, that has a structure with definite boundaries. The term organization implies that something tangible binds people, relationships and goals together. Some critics refer to this definition as the "Container approach" which looks upon an organization as a basket with all elements placed in it.

The subjectivist's approach looks at an organization as jobs and activities that people perform. In other words an organization in this approach, is seen as a series of interactions and transactions in which people engage. The behaviour of the people, hence, is very important in making the organization as it is perceived by the outside world.

Kinds of organization communication

Organizational communication takes various forms and dimensions. Some forms are discussed below:
- Vertical/upward flow of communication
- Horizontal information flow
- Informal information flow

Vertical/upward flow of communication

Upward information flow helps managers to gather important inputs from junior level employees about what is going on at the shop floor or within the department. The insights gathered help in quick problem solving. It however goes without saying that effective managers must gather a cross section of views to facilitate better understanding and avoid bias. Many organizations place idea boxes to invite feedback and to find innovative ways of problem solving. This helps reticent employees share their ideas. This also facilitates managers to coordinate tasks and responsibilities. For example, the construction department may send an e-mail or memo to the PR department about a possible delay in reaching a target, so that the departments plan the PR event accordingly.

Horizontal information flow

This kind of information flow implies that communication flows between and among various line and staff functional departments either laterally or diagonally. Many companies inform all the departments through Intranet about all that is happening in various departments and in some cases various country offices in a global environment. For instance, Sun Microsystems uses a worldwide network to link thousands of its employees in various countries situated in different time zones.[2]

Informal information flow

Every organization has an informal information flow that almost runs parallel to the formal flow. Many experts believe that the informal information flow, also known as grapevine often is more powerful and more effective than the formal, also know as "official" information flow. Organizations who have tried to quash the grapevine have not really succeeded in the effort. Hence prudence lies in recognizing the existence of grapevine and making use of the same to gather management intelligence and also vital areas of concern among employees.

In crisis times, the grapevine becomes very active, which could be detrimental to the interests of the organization. Therefore, it is important to keep a close eye on the grapevine so that appropriate communication can be used to quash misperceptions, if any.

Some companies provide a toll free number, wherein the employees can call anonymously with any issues or concerns [Ombudsperson]. This works efficiently in tapping grapevine or gossip mongering.[3]

PR communication

The foremost job of PR is to manage the reputation of the organization among various stakeholders such as employees, shareholders, policy makers, dealers, special interest groups, media and public at large. It is important that any piece of communication that passes through PR hands must clear the following tests:

- It should be truthful/factual
- It should stand legal scrutiny
- It should stand any ethical/moral scrutiny

If one were to define the concept of PR in practice, according to Cutlip et al, "Public Relations is the management function which evaluates public attitudes, identifies the policies and procedures of an individual or an organization with the public interest, and plans and executes a programme of action to earn public understanding and acceptance".[4]

Understand the organization

To achieve the above, the first and foremost job of a public relations department is to understand the organization closely enough to be able to make communication policies and decisions. In fact, public relations professionals need to develop the organization they work for as their "beat", the same way journalists specialize in their beat in a media office. Public relations practitioners are supposed to be experts in the area of communication, but they work for a vast array of specialized industries, which may range from space technology to petrochemicals, from missiles to pharmaceuticals, from textiles to thermal projects. The companies may be in consumer goods to infrastructure development. Hence it is very necessary for them to understand the core competence of the organization they work for. Also, since information from the company has to be conveyed to various publics who may not always be interested in the technical part, the public relations professionals will have to understand all the technical jargon and processes so that these are de-jargoned in common man's language for clarity and better understanding.

Change is the only constant, therefore it is imperative that the PR manager becomes a change agent, a facilitator of change in an organization. The following exercise will help understand and focus on change goals:
- Ask yourself what are the primary challenges facing the organization?
- What are the driving forces for change?
- How does the management tend to respond to environmental signals?
- To what extent is there a shared understanding of agreement on the need to change?

Corporate Visioning

The public relations department should ideally be involved in the corporate visioning exercise of the organization. Given the extraordinary exposure of people *per se,* corporations today are less known for what they produce than what they stand for. The public relations department hence has to keep in touch with the latest management thinking within the organization as also keep a constant watch on the latest trends in this direction. All the information sifted from the environment hence must be brought within the organization and percolated down to various management echelons as required. The PR department must work as an antenna to an organization—bringing in the information that is crucial, within the organization and sending out information to various stakeholders from the organization. This two-way process must be taken on a continuous basis.

Defining publics

Defining and understanding various publics of the organization is a major responsibility of the public relations department. Each target group would have specific communication needs, which the professionals must understand and fulfill. The chapter, "Troika of Communication" has dealt in detail with the subject and the interdependence of the three viz. message, medium and audience.

Creating corporate identity

Creating a distinct identity for the organization and building corporate reputation also falls in the arena of public relations. In fact, this is a long drawn exercise and should not be dismissed in a hurry. Professional help from advertising agencies specializing in corporate identity programmes may be taken to build a corporate personality for the organization. The corporate identity would broadly encompass, the logo, the masthead, the lettering style, the house color, and the mission statement, among other things. Effective top management spend a lot of time, effort and resources in building a suitable identity for the organization. Many corporate houses have gone in for a change of identity because it was felt that the old identity was either not relevant anymore or did not convey the core competence and philosophy of the company.

About a decade ago Air India went in for a fresh exercise. This, among other inputs, meant change of logo from the archer with a bow to Sun and a new color scheme. This led to the repainting of the entire fleet. However, they soon realized that the changed identity did not bring about the "desired response" so they reverted to the old one. This was probably because of bad judgement and lack of research among a host of other mistakes on the part of the team in charge of the exercise, both from within and outside the organization. On the other hand, Britannia, a company, which was long known as part of a bakery industry, was able to provide a new thrust and positioning to itself with the change of corporate identity. The color scheme and mission statement were not only changed, a vigorous advertising campaign reinforced the change in the minds of consumers. *Swasth Khao, Tan Man Jagao* [Eat healthy, think better] recapitulated the ethos of the Indian psyche.

Building bridges of understanding within the organization

Although PR is supposed to be the voice of the management, it must strive to remain neutral and exclusive of the various echelons of management and staff. It's a tough job, but not unachievable. Every organization has a place for organizational communication as discussed above, the public relations communication is not in competition with it. Both must complement each other. Professional PR practitioners use a variety of tools to achieve synergy among various management areas. The chapter "PR Tools and Methods" discusses in detail about various tools to choose from available at the disposal of a public relations professional.

Media Relations

Traditionally, media relations expend a lot of PR time. Media serves as a very important conduit between an organization and its various publics. PR mileage in media lend credibility and visibility to organizations. Therefore it is important for PR practitioners to not only understand media, their functioning, requirements and susceptibilities, but also how to handle them professionally. Chapter 4, "Media and its relevance to PR" deals with the subject in detail.

Having said all this, it must be understood that public relations can't exist in a vacuum. In order to achieve the corporate goals, it is important that the public relations department works in close association with various management disciplines within the organization. In the following paragraphs, we shall have a look at PR interface with various management disciplines.

PR's interface with other management disciplines

Not many in the management echelons believe that any special academic or professional training is required to be a communication specialist. Many tend to believe that any one who could not fit anywhere can easily be brought to the communication department. More often than not the departments within an organization also strongly feel that PR should report to them first and obtain their consent before making use of information. However, keeping in view the functions detailed above, the ideal situation is that the PR manager report directly to the top management. Cutlip et al argue that "an organization's public reputation derives in substantial part from the behaviour of its senior officials". Therefore, PR is "inescapably tied, by nature and necessity, to the management function".[5]

The varying perceptions are a cause of occasional friction between PR and other departments. This is unfortunate, since each function of the PR needs the support and cooperation of the other departments for the smooth discharge of organizational functions. In this context, let us see PR's interface with major line and staff departments.

Marketing

Marketing is all about products and people. As they reach out to the consumer, marketing people feel that they are also in the business of public relations! The major area of conflict is advertising and publicity, especially product and institutional advertising. In non-profit organizations, the cause of friction is the allocation of funds, raising funds and reaching out to a variety of publics with educational messages.

Let's take an example from advertising. An institutional advertising campaign for a corporate sector company to enhance the goodwill of the organization would need the expertise of an advertising agency, but as the primary aim is to push not the product but the company, it will be a function of the PR department. Conversely, publicity about products and services aimed to increase sales or use is a part of the marketing function, but because public relations professionals are trained in the field and are more skilled at writing and placing publicity, the function is generally a part of their purview. Unless, however, there is integration in communication, both PR and marketing are bound to go different ways. This at times gives wrong signals to various stakeholders. Let's look at a hypothetical case—a company has launched a new product in the market, and a vigorous advertising campaign is on to woo the consumers, but on the other hand the public relations department is issuing press releases about some other aspects of the company which appear in the newspapers which also carry the product ad without a special reference to the newly launched product. The two communications will be seen to be at variance by the readers. These have to be integrated because the aim of both advertising and public relations in a broader sense is the acceptance of the organization and its products in the market place.

Law

In times of crises, especially in cases of alleged libel or slander lawsuits top management seeks legal aid to get out of the mess. In such times, it generally refuses to speak to the media because the counsel may have advised them to keep quiet.

Ivy lee, considered the father of public relations, felt very strongly about this. He stated,"I have seen more situations where the public ought to understand, and where the public would sympathize with", he remarked, "spoiled by the intervention of the lawyer than in any other way. Whenever a lawyer starts to talk to the public, he shuts out the light".

Close cooperation between public relations and law is the requirement of the current times. Safety, environment, health and resettlement are some of the issues that occupy the minds of the corporate managers. With increasing expectation and awareness among employees, specialist groups and lobbies, public relations may have to respond to their queries through media intervention. While dealing with the issues in print and through other channels of communication, it is very necessary that while taking care of the legal aspects, the human touch is not lost sight of in aiming at achieving the PR mileage.

Personnel, HRD, Industrial Relations

As both the PR and personnel departments deal with employees, the risk of friction between the two is high. The employees are governed by certain policies, procedures and codes of conduct. Reaching on time, performing the assigned work and receiving a salary – are these all that the employees and the management expect from each other? With time, the roles and expectations of management and employees have also been redefined. The management is increasingly aware that a motivated employee is an asset. An employee is also an ambassador of goodwill. If the relationships are stifling within an organization, these inevitably have their echo externally. Who should communicate to the employees? The answer is, both Personnel and PR, each having its area defined. While information relating to policies, procedures, welfare activities and trade union negotiation are HR functions, writing hard and soft stories about the organization, the achievements of some employees, and other human-interest stories are a part of the PR arena. Close cooperation between PR and HR brings about better understanding and respect among employees and serves as a morale booster for them.

Infosys recruitment ads often include an Infosys employee, whose job profile is assayed to attract people with similar aspirations. Such ads not only attract the right talent, they also achieve a PR mileage for the company in introducing an employee and his profile that the employee seems to enjoy and is proud of.

Once Gas Authority of India, a public sector company advertised for opening in its PR/Corporate Communication department. The visual had a picture of a group of smiling people of various age groups with painted faces. The picture obviously included existing employees in the department. Through this visual strategy, the ad communicated about the potential joy of working in a creative department! It surely boosted the morale of people working in the company.

Finance

With an increasing number of organizations going public, the number of shareholders is also multiplying. Besides shareholders, the financial community, stock exchanges, the financial press forms an important "Public" for the public relations department. The requirements of all these publics are specific; hence the communication packages designed for them should have the expertise of the finance department and the language and presentation skills of the public relations department.

The finance department has to be made aware of the value and objectives of PR activities. Expenditure on PR, advertising and publicity is still considered by many finance experts as dispensable. Whenever there is a financial crunch, the victims more often than not are the PR and advertising departments. The finance officers are trained budget slashers. At times, they just do it for the sake of doing it.

To quote a real life situation, a PR manager while putting up the annual PR budget for a year, detailed the various media heads for which the funds were required. The individual appropriations were based on the manager's vast experience in the field. Against the medium of corporate film, she had indicated Rs.2,25,000 for a 12-15 minute documentary. When she received a copy of the approved budget, among other slashes, the appropriation against the corporate film was indicated as Rs.1,91,275. She was bewildered as to how the Finance Department had arrived at that figure and that too an odd one when no one in that department was probably familiar with the film medium! After much hunting, she was informed that due to economisation, some of the media in the PR proposal had received a 15 per cent cut, hence the odd figure. That incident however made her wiser for the next time. All her calculations thereafter had a suitable escalation, with the expectation that some cut was inevitable, if it had to come through the finance mill. To her utter surprise, she ended up with more 'real' funds in future, though finance duly inflicted its cuts into her 20 per cent escalation in the proposed appropriation without ever knowing her mind!

Production

PR normally speaks about products, people and the organization through its various communications in the appropriate media from time to time. In order to write stories in the employees' house journal and communicate through other channels, it is imperative that a PR person regularly visit project sites and shop floors to gather both hard and soft stories for various media. The PR manager must have an eye to catch the right story and a nose for the news value of various events within and outside the organization. He/she should see the human effort involved, the drama, the risks, and the fun, almost anything that will engage the readers' interest. The raw materials for PR stories are real life incidents. The PR person must understand the reader's pysche and also how to give the story a human angle. He/she should also highlight the marvels of the human spirit against all odds.

The PR person has to be motivated before being able to motivate and influence others. Besides knowing the product attributes of the organization one belongs to, one must gather data about the competitors' products and activities. Information, in fact, is oxygen for an effective PR practitioner. For motivating employees in the production line, PR can play a complementary role with the production chief by working out incentives, covering human interest features, highlighting news about the employees who excel in meeting targets or who bring about innovations on the production floor. A continuous dialogue with the chief of the production will provide enough material for making the internal media interesting and employee-oriented.

How to control rift and synergise

Ideally, an organization should have a PR committee comprising heads of departments of all staff and line functions with the PR person as the member secretary to aim at centralized communication. The committee should meet periodically say once a week or a fortnight and discuss areas where PR could be put to use. The PR manager can bring proposals, discuss the thrust areas and work out programmes aimed at different publics. Sub-delegation or attendance by proxy should be discouraged. The chief executive officer should also once in a while be invited to participate in the deliberations to lend greater weight and seriousness to the discussions. Such meetings will synergise the work of various departments with the PR department.

The annual programme both at the macro and micro levels should ideally be presented through a written proposal accompanied by slides, charts and pilot films (if possible) to the Board of Directors not only to make the top management aware of the thrust areas but to make them appreciate the role and dimensions of public relations in shaping and giving a definite corporate personality to the organization.

Summary

In this chapter we discussed communication in an organizational perspective, the various kinds of communications forms, organizational communication and PR communication. We discussed the role and scope of communication within and between departments to achieve organizational goals. Line and staff functions of management were discussed. The positioning of PR in the management hierarchy was deliberated upon. PR's interface with various line and staff functions was discussed and causes of friction as well as synergy were discussed.

Critical thinking exercise

Visit the website of two competing brands and study how the organizations connect with their various stakeholders and more importantly how they respond to the concerns of their various stakeholders.

Questions

Q.1 Describe organizational communication and how it is different from PR communication, providing relevant examples.

Q.2 What are the various points of PR interface with various management disciplines? Discuss.

Endnotes

[1] Charles Moncur, "Embracing PR theory: an opportunity for practitioners?", *Journal of Communication Management*, Volume: 10, Number: 1, 2006, pp: 95-9, Emerald Group Publishing Limited.

[2] John V. Thill & Courtland L. Bove'e, *Excellence in Business Communication*, fourth edition, Prentice Hall, NJ, 1998

[3] Carol Haymowitz, "Spread the word: Gossip is good", *Wall Street Journal*, 4 November 1988, B1.

[4] Scot M. Cutlip, Allen H. Center & Glen M. Broom, " Effective Public Relations", Prentice Hall, NJ, 1994, p. 3.

[5] Ibid, p. 59.

4 Media and its relevance to PR

Chapter objectives
- The changing media scenario, especially in the context of India
- Growth and expansion of various media
- The future of media and people's engagement with media
- Trends and possibilities

The media scene in India is both intriguing and mind-boggling. There are so many media available that one is not able to keep a track on how many new channels are starting in a month! India is the only country where the print media is growing despite the proliferation of electronic media. Media consumers have increased tremendously in the last one-decade.

The media have made penetration far and wide. It seems a kind of poetic justice. There was a time when PR persons were chasing media for coverage. It was a great achievement to get a 10 second coverage in one of the two bulletins that DD carried, until the revolution brought by satellite television and the onset of dozens of 24x7 news channels. It is now media's turn to chase PR people for bytes! The 24x7 news channels, and a number of business channels have changed it all. Are PR people having the last laugh? Yes and no both.

Yes, because, they have more media to choose from; they can manage their organization's name floating constantly. They can reach out to their constituent publics instantly and far and wide. No, because it would now mean; being on ones toes constantly, to cultivate the articulation; choosing the right media, especially in times of adversity. It also means that PR professionals have to be on a constant vigil and have a greater share of media tracking. It also means more availability, hence more preparedness. It also means mentoring a large number of scribes. It can be seen as a challenge or an opportunity.

Most of the public relations mileage is achieved through the media. Hence it is important that media practitioners constantly update their knowledge about media and gather necessary insights. PR practitioners need to understand a lot of things about media.

First, the latest insights on media industry:

The Changing Media Scene in India

Growth and Expansion

The growth of Indian media and entertainment industry has been phenomenal as per the FICCI Powerhouse Cooper (FICCI-PWC) Report 2008. In 2007, the entertainment and media industry recorded a growth of 17 per cent over the previous year, which incidentally was higher than the projected 15 per cent. The industry reached the size of Rs. 513 billion in 2007, recording a cumulative growth of 19 per cent on an overall basis.

The advertising industry reflected a growth of 22 per cent over the previous year. It contributed an estimated Rs. 196 billion in 2007 as compared to Rs. 161 billion in 2006. Although different segments of the industry grew at different rates, the tiniest segment in the industry — online advertising recorded the highest growth.

The segment grew at a whopping 69 per cent from 2006, albeit from a low base of Rs. 1.6 billion to Rs. 2.7 billion in 2007. Its share in the overall advertising pie grew to 1.4 per cent. The other high growth segment was Out-of Home (OOH) at 25 per cent. The media grew to an estimated Rs. 12.5 billion in 2007, up from Rs. 10 billion in 2006.

The radio industry also made impressive growth of 24 per cent over the previous year and is estimated at Rs. 6.2 billion in 2007, up from Rs. 5 billion in 2006.

The television industry was the other industry that recorded a growth higher than the overall growth of the industry in 2007. It recorded a growth of 18 per cent over the previous year and is estimated at Rs. 226 billion in 2007, up from a substantially large base of Rs. 191 billion in 2006.

Print media also recorded a growth of 16 per cent over the year 2006 and is estimated at Rs. 149 billion in 2007, up from Rs. 128 billion in 2006.

The following figures will provide a bird's eye view of the growth in the last four years:

Indian Entertainment & Media industry[1]

(Rs. In Billion)

Industry	2004	2005	2006	2007	CAGR 2004-07
Television % Change	128.7	158.5 (23%)	191.9 (21%)	225.9 (18%)	19%
Filmed entertainment % Change	59.9	68.1 (14%)	84.5 (24%)	96.0 (14%)	14%
Print media % Change	97.8	109.5 (12%)	128.0 (17%)	149.0 (16%)	15%
Radio % Change	2.4	3.2 (33%)	5.0 (56%)	6.2 (2.4%)	37%
Music % Change	6.7	7.0 (4%)	7.2 (3%)	7.3 (1%)	3%
Animation, gaming & VFX (% Change)	-	-	10.5	13.0 (24%)	-
Out-of-home (OOH) advertising % Change	8.5	9.0 (6%)	10.0 (11%)	12.5 (25%)	14%
Online advertising % Change	0.6	1.0 (67%)	1.6 (60%)	2.7 (69%)	65%
Total E&M Industry	3.4.6	356.3 (17%)	438.0 (23%)	512.6 (17%)	19%

[1] Source: The Entertainment & Media Industry-Sustaining Growth Report 2008 FICCI Powerhouse Cooper

Indian Advertising Industry[1]

(Rs. In Billion)

Media	2004	2005	2006	2007	CAGR 2004-07
Television advertising	48.0	54.5	66.2	80.0	
% Change		14%	21%	21%	20%
% Share	42%	42%	41%	41%	-1%
Print Advertising	54.4	62.7	78.0	94.0	
% Change		15%	24%	21%	20%
% Share	48%	48%	49%	48%	0%
Radio advertising	2.4	3.2	5.0	6.2	37%
% Change		(33%)	(56%)	(2.4%)	
% Share					
Out-of-home (OOH) advertising	8.5	9.0	10.0	12.5	
% Change		6%	11%	25%	14%
% Share	7.5%	6.9%	6.2%	6.4%	-5%
On-line advertising	0.6	1.0	1.6	2.7	
% Change		67%	60%	69%	65%
% Share	0.5%	0.8%	1.0%	1.4%	38%
Total advertising	**113.9**	**130.4**	**160.8**	**196.4**	**20%**

1 Source: The Entertainment & Media Industry-Sustaining Growth Report 2008 FICCI Powerhouse Cooper

The size of the industry is estimated by FICCI-PWC at Rs. 513 billion in 2007 and is projected to grow at 18% CAGR for the next 5 years to reach Rs. 1.157 trillion in 2012. TV homes are projected to increase from 115 million in 2007 to 132 million by 2012. DTH homes are projected to increase from 4 million in 2007 to 25 million by 2012.

Cable homes are projected to grow from 70 million in 2007 to 90 million by 2012. Overall, the C&S homes will constitute 68% and DTH 19% of total TV homes.

As on May 2008 more than 65 news channels are operational and numbers continue to soar. Now the PR practitioner has the choice to select from all kinds of news channels — language and genre wise including national, regional and city specific channels. The sustenance of media is basically driven by advertising revenue, which is over Rs.800 crore.

If we were to look at the sociology of the television industry, the ownership rests with all kinds of interests, including foreign holding companies, joint ventures, politicians, builders, businessmen, NGOs, religious trusts.

The government of India issued policy guidelines for downlink of television channels in November 2005, which provide that "no person/entity shall downlink a channel that has been registered with the Ministry of Information and Broadcasting. All the programmes of satellite television channels, transmitted/re-transmitted through cable network are required to adhere to the programme code and advertising code prescribed under the cable YV Networks (Regulation) Act 1995 and the rules framed thereunder." [1]

Programme content

The content of the programmes has drastically changed over a period of time. The cut-throat competition among competing brands has made programmers take up issues and use treatment that leaves much to be desired. It is widely believed that channels will go to any extent to attract eyeballs and raise TRPs.

Sting operations, sensational stories a huge dose of non-news input in news channels, frivolous issues, and stereotyping of gender, religion and politics; to name a few, rule the roost and most channels have much to answer for.

The breaking news syndrome has lost its value, as everything seems to be breaking news, leading a scholar to comment that when channels reflect something for the first time, it is breaking news for them, literally!

Citizen journalists and stringers are playing an important role in providing content. Accountability, checking facts and biases however, are issues that need to be addressed. User Generated Content (UGC) is fast occupying space both on national and local television channels. This has lent voice not only to common people, but political adversaries and market competitors to their advantage, which is not a healthy sign.

Print media

The world over, particularly in developed western countries, access to print media is on the decline, but the Indian print media industry is booming and projected to grow by 14% over the next five years reaching Rs. 281 billion in 2012 from Rs. 149 billion in 2007. The newspaper industry constitutes 86% of the total market while the rest belongs to magazines.

Trends in print media

One has witnessed a changing ownership pattern in the print media. There has been an increasing big business approach in the print media. The government of India has opened up the news sector for FDI up to 26 per cent. There are indications of its further escalating. In the non-news sector, the limit has been enhanced to 100 per cent from the previous limit of 74 per cent.

When the country witnessed a proliferation of electronic media, many pundits forecasted doom for the print media. The newspapers however, took on the challenge and proved all prophecies wrong. Not only has print media survived, but it has also rediscovered itself. One has seen increased circulation and also surging ad revenue in print media. However, there is no gainsaying the fact that there has been an increasing trivialization of content. It is widely believed that most news channels depend on the morning newspaper stories to decide their coverage for the day! Similarly, the print media looks at the last edition of news bulletins to ensure that their stories are not a repetition of what the audience have watched a day before, but that they contain insightful content.

Revenue earning is the most important consideration for the media in general and print media is no exception. One has seen a vanishing line between advertisements and news: Advertorial content is written for promotional schemes like private equity. *Medianet*, initiated by the *Times of India*, charge money for personal and corporate news published on certain pages.

Earlier editors of newspapers were a respected lot. They were considered the soul of a newspaper. But the increasing commercialization has witnessed the virtual demise of the editor. Instead of the editor, now we find managing editors, or marketwise editors. The regional newspapers attract more readers.

Trivialization of issues, concerns and human matters

If connectivity is the one reality, too much of the same and triviality is the other reality. Sample this: *"I think I may need a bathroom break. Is this possible?"* was the close up of a piece of paper with the caption - *"US president George W Bush writes a note to secretary of State Condoleezza Rice during a Security Council meeting on Wednesday"* (Circa 2005). As to how many newspapers and channels carried this story globally, there may be no empirical data available, but many Indian mainstream newspapers went berserk on the story.

Bollywood influence on news media

When the UPA government steered through the confidence vote in India on 22 July 2008, some channels like Aaj Tak and NDTV had the animation ready for the breaking news. It had the PM's caricature with the caption "Singh is King", obviously taken from the movie by this name, that was being promoted around the same time. *The Economic Times* in its political theatre column, taking cue from the television caption from previous evening, said "Sting, not Singh, is King", when stories about MPs being bought for votes, surfaced in the media.

Media fragmentation

India in the middle of the year 2008, has more than 65 news channels, and the number is increasing by the day. Switch to any channel, you would be lucky to be able to watch the programme straightaway, chances are that when you surf between channels, you end up watching more ads. When the audience is getting fragmented, how is it that the clients are advertising on all and sundry channels?

Media agencies claim that they are buying more ad time for their clients across various channels and programme genres, only to get the same audience numbers in an increasingly fragmented viewership scenario. Despite the fact that viewership has increased over the years and the penetration of Cable and Satellite (C&S) has increased, the benefit is not accruing to the advertiser. Advertisers, according to industry buzz are buying more spots to deliver to the same audience, so they end up paying more.

Once, the peak programme Television Rating Points (TRPs) used to range between 10 and 12; in 2008- it was at four to five on an average. There was only one audience measurement agency called the TAM, now there is another called AMA [Audience Measurement Analytics Ltd. (e-MAP)]. According to the agency, even the well-watched IPL cricket series on Set Max (August 2008) did not garner more than 4.2 ratings.

The Beijing Olympics opening ceremony was watched by around 1.8 Crore Indians, it however delivered a rating of 4.6 according to e-MAP. The closing ceremony was watched by 3 Crore Indians, which attracted the highest rating in any sporting event and other programmes, but there is no comparison with earlier viewership rating points any longer.[2]

Radio

Radio that can have a reach to almost cent percent geographical area and population, unfortunately took a dip, but is trying to pace up, albeit at a slow but steady speed.

There has been a tremendous network growth of All India Radio (AIR). In 1947, AIR had a network of six stations and 18 transmitters. It reaches 205 per cent geographical area and 11 per cent population. Now AIR has 223 broadcasting centres covering 91.42 per cent geographical area and 99.13 per cent population. However, figures and percentages can be dicey, because, reach is not equivalent to access; access, not equivalent to comprehension and comprehension does not necessarily ensure credibility. The fact of the matter is that the radio audience has drastically decreased over the years.

After liberalization of the radio sector, private FM players are playing a key role in the return of the Radio. Currently, more than 150 FM channels are operational and industry estimates that in the next five years India will have more than 800 FM channels. The Telecom Regulatory Authority of India (TRAI) has recommended to the government to allow news on private FM channels.

Infrastructure licensing and renting has been extended to many private FM players in various parts of the country.

As of now the FM channels are entertainment driven and generally cater to the young and mobile population.

New media

Internet has changed the world for the common person. It has changed the way people perceive the world. Instant connectivity, bonding with people one has never met and may never meet, is the reality of times. There has been a growing penetration of Internet in India. As per industry trends the Internet was accessed by 250 million urban population in 2007, out of which 32 million are active users and 46 million claimed users. Around 65 million users are computer literate and 77 million are English knowing.[3]

The cell revolution

Mobile telephony is seen as the fourth screen. From games to Internet connectivity, from commercial messages, to social messages, not to forget astrology connect, you name it and you have it on the mobile. The latest additions are video and animation clips. Very soon there will be television on cell. For the purpose of cellular services, the country is divided into 19 telecom circles areas and four metro service areas for Cellular Mobile Telephone Service (CMTS) as well as United Access Services (UAS). As per June 2006 government data, there are over 78.48 million cellular subscribers and the number is growing at the rate of more than a million per month.[4]

What are lessons for PR professionals?

The media scene is changing at a very great speed, so it is important to keep a constant watch, draw lessons, understand the changing trends in media and prepare media material keeping in view the technological changes, content style changes to suit media's needs. What will be the media scene like in the coming decade or so? Let us take a look.

The future of media and people's connect with them

"The farther away the future, the better it looks" is an age-old adage, but when said for media, it defies all logic.

The technology age of the 20th century that brought about the telegraph, the telephone, the camera, later the radio, the talkie, the television, satellite and the Internet have not only changed the world forever, but also the way the human species think or are engineered to think through media stimuli. If the last century was of technology, the current one will be of super technology and instant connectivity. We always marvelled at the speed of human thought and often felt that no supercomputer could ever match it. We have been proved wrong in our lifetime, as technology has surpassed the speed of thought.

Better connectivity, affordability, speed and interactivity will be the hallmark of the coming two decades on the one hand and responsibility, innovation, human concern and accountability will be demanded from the media on the other.

Media undoubtedly will be on the public opinion radar more than ever and constantly.

The journey in the last one century

Information was always reckoned as power and will continue to be so. However the tables have now turned in favour of media consumers. As the trends reflect, it will now be the people's turn to be empowered, as media will be more and more people-centric. Media probably will have no choice but to take up issues concerning the common man, to survive in a highly competitive world with fleeting viewer/reader loyalties.

There is no gainsaying the fact that it is mass media that have truly globalised the human race — creating a seamless world that transcends artificial barriers of geography and economic, political and social divide. Media have empowered people like nothing else. The Internet provides the knowledge of the entire world at the touch of a button.

Media have ensured unlimited entertainment at a cheaper cost to anyone who has the necessary gadgetry. Media, especially the Internet, has created a world community that bonds together, especially in critical times—as many events in the world have reflected, the 9/11, the Tsunami, the London bombing, the Katrina waves, the Iraq war, the Afghanistan war, the 26/11 Mumbai siege by the terrorists, to name a few. In a spilt minute, public opinion is made and spread globally. In a subtle manner, media have helped create a more humane world as more and more individuals and communities extend support and help to their far flung brethren in trying times.

Convergence

Convergence is the key word and will continue to be so, as the copy of one of the ads for a mobile phone suggests, "Browse for beauty. Surf for serenity. The power of the web is always with you. With the Internet, e-mail, video and a 2 mega pixel camera in your pocket. Inspiration is where you find it. Meet the new………..." this is still fine as everything is related to communication. Imagine a Micro wave-TV! Whirlpool's concept microwave has a flat-screen television in the front and tiny cameras inside so that you can see what's cooking and watch your favorite programme on television at the same time.

The increasing convergence will blur artificial barriers among various media/gadgets. This will reflect on the potential of new audience base, innovative media content and packaging, and greater reader/viewer involvement.

Internet

There will be an increasingly greater spread of the Internet that will be accessed by poor and aspiring communities in remote areas in developing countries.

In order to reach out to these disparate audiences media will mostly be e-enabled in future. The websites of corporate sector ventures will be a researcher's delight. Consumers will be courted, wooed and indulged through consumer friendly schemes and sharing of information through websites.

> A silent revolution has already started in some rural hamlets of India. Referred to as Knowledge Centres (KCs), some of the spirited national and international NGOs are opening Internet centres by providing technology, know-how and training to village youth who are bringing about a quiet, knowledge revolution by accessing information on health, agriculture, livestock etc. via the Internet. The requisite software translates the information in the regional language. MS Swaminathan Research Institute (MSSRF) in collaboration with a British NGO, One World South Asia, has created a software "Open Access Knowledge" which translates information in six languages. It is amazing to see how school dropouts, young men and housewives are joining the Knowledge Centres and making use of the information in their day-to-day life. MSSRF, founded by one of the greatest agricultural scientists of the country, trains youngsters free of cost and allows them to make use of their resources in some select villages in Tamil Nadu and Pondicherry. The MSSRF team visits various villages, discusses the need for a Knowledge Centre with village heads, and if they agree, sets up the KC at a place provided by the village. The community is required to maintain the KC, including bearing the cost of telephone. The experiment is bearing fruit in no uncertain terms.

Cyber crimes

Technology and its spread has brought with it new challenges. Cyber crimes have surpassed drug trafficking in terms of turnover, according to a report released by the US Government. More than $100 billion worth of cheating was reported every year. Gambling, porn, copyright violations and political dissidence are a click away. Shooting through candid mobile phones and making MMS has become crude reality. Surprisingly, Indians are credited to use the medium more than their counterparts anywhere, according to a media report.

Future television

The future television may progress from phone-in programmes to interactive programmes with anchors in television studios and viewers sitting before their camera-enabled computers participating in talk shows.

Power of people

Bloggers will occupy greater space and become a challenge to traditional journalists. Google and Yahoo have been inviting people to join the blog space and make an earning. *The Washington Times* includes blogs in its paper. So, instead of stringers appointed by newspapers and channels, people will volunteer with reportage for the media on a larger scale. Bloggers and Citizen Journalists can already be seen reporting in a host of news channels in India. There is a lesson in this for organizations, as consumers and advocates would be occupying more and more blog space to give vent to their feelings against companies on issues they are crusading against. The organizations need to track blogs to track issues that concern people about it.

Pharmaceutical companies are already feeling the heat, as millions of sites have people writing about various issues including the alleged lack of research and development in major pharmaceutical companies who many believe are making profit and spending more money on executive salaries and promotional activities than research and development (R&D).

> Launched in the beginning of the current millennium, blogs, according to analysts have reshaped the web, rudely shaken up journalism from its one-upmanship and arrogance, impacted policies and enabled millions of people to voice their concerns and connect with them. UGC will rule the roost in times to come.
>
> There are millions of blogs on the net and other media space. With so many versions of news and views on blog space, "reality" will be all the more confusing!

The Right to Information Act (RTI) has been a boon for many. Information that was difficult to access from government offices, is now surfacing easily. The other reality is that RTI, that is supposed to empower people in seeking information from government offices, despite honourable intentions on the part of the Government, may become an easy handle for bidders to play havoc with the bidding process, if they lose the contract. This may end up not only in delaying developmental projects but many public sector bids may get involved in litigations.

> A case in point is of a public utility organization that invited international bids for improving the water distribution and maintenance of the capital city. A number of litigations have already been filed questioning the intention of the Board in selecting one of the bidders that has allegedly been favoured. An article written by an Indian, teaching in Italy to this effect was carried by one of the mainstream newspapers. When the so called "independent" point of view is carried by media, there are chances that people are misled. Involvement of 'neutral' stakeholders is one of the tactics employed in a highly competitive world. Media unfortunately lends legitimacy to issues when it publishes or broadcasts them.

Social networking sites

Of the 32 million active Internet users, one-third is formed by young men, followed by collegiate users at 21% in 30 cities across India. 14% school children use the Internet. 11% working women and 6% non-working women also surf the net.

Some of the popular social networking sites include Orkut from the Google stable, myspace.com from Fox network owned by Rupert Murdock, Facebook, a privately held company by Palo Alto in California and the latest craze Twitter. Among the desi versions, BigAdda.com is from the Reliance group, brijj.com, fropper.com, Apnacircle.com and ibibo.com are by young entrepreneurs from India.[5]

As millions of youngsters are hooked on to these social networking sites, marketers are seriously considering the use of these portals for promotion of brands. Many employers and headhunters are using social networking sites like Linkedin.com for finding the right people for the job market. The medium is going to grow with time and will be a money-spinner for the organizations concerned.

The flip side

On the flip side, the media proliferation has allowed enough room for increasing consumerism within media. To be first with the news has become an obsession with the media industry so much so that one feels a trivialization of human concerns and dignity. This will only increase with time.

Media intrusiveness is going to be a harsh reality. People's engagement with media will increase. An average person will depend more and more on media for information on all counts, which may unfortunately mean more government, or commercial control on the minds of the people. With so much information from all directions, thinking will probably take a back seat — the world will be more full of information junkies than original thinkers.

Invasion of people's privacy through spy cameras, CCTV, mobiles, hidden microphones in a larger measure is expected. In probability, offices may ask for frisking of visitors/contractors before allowing entry. People may go back to discuss issues verbally, in person rather than through e-mail or phone, to guard against official surveillance and phone bugging. Suspicion and mistrust levels will go up. More laws and enactments are expected in this regard.

Media is a tool—a technology driven channel, which will reach the highest levels of sophistication and connectivity, but the issue of its impact on the human mind, relationships, sensitivity and susceptibility will be in focus.

Too much of the same thing

Researchers have often spoken about media suffering from a collective mind—it is manifest more than ever before. Media have lent legitimacy to non-issues. Media trial begins much before the issues are judged by judicial courts.

Page three kind of reportage will only increase. Newspapers will enhance the paid coverage and include a lot of trivia. Taste one such news item in a leading newspaper "imagine a week that included Diwali, Eid, Halloween and cricket... the four national religions... on the upside, and bomb blasts on the down. Shall we just call it an extremely swinging time—swinging from one extreme to the other". Since when has Halloween become an Indian obsession? To trivialize human suffering relating to bomb blasts on the eve of Diwali and Eid and calling it 'swinging times' speaks volumes about the insensitivity of the reporter. [6]

The umpteen quotes that commercial papers now have on everything from nuclear science to sexuality of Indian women, from Ashiwariya's break-up with Salman Khan to her marrying Abhishek Bachchan, Musharaf's haveli in Purani Delhi to Mahinder Singh Dhoni's hair style, from Sonia Gandhi's "irrelevance" to her "coming of age". These invariably are from people who frequent page three, many of whom should rather be behind the news rather than becoming news themselves. For a change, it is the college youth whose quotes are included. They seem to know or atleast have a point of view on everything under the sun, or so believe the media. Do they represent the real India; there are no prizes for guessing!

Media and social responsibility

From the era of muckraking a century ago to hidden cameras, where will the media stop? Sting operations were not considered decent until recently, but have become a norm now. A certain private school of journalism has started imparting training in sting operations! On the flip side if you see the extent of corruption and compromise of one's professional ethics, one feels, the sting operations may be able to instill some kind of scare at least in those in whom the public has placed its trust—those occupying public offices.

There are bizarre strategic alliances. When economy airliner Air Deccan was launched a few years ago, it had NDTV as its media partner. It seemed funny, but NDTV was painted in bold colours on both sides of the aircraft. If media enters into partnership with the corporate world, what kind of coverage can one expect, both in normal and adverse times from the "partner media house"?

Ethics and media will be distant cousins. Media spying will surpass corporate spying. It is already there in some measures and will only increase with time.

Reality shows

The underdog, the weak and the meek will always rule the hearts of Indian respondents, emotional outbursts and hysteria of participants and judges' verdict, notwithstanding.

There will be more and more reality shows until people understand the commercialization and the exploitation behind these.

> For instance, one reality show claimed over 50 lakh responses through the Short Message Service (SMS). Each such SMS costs Rs. 6 to the sender, the money earned by the mobile operator and the show collected in a single opportunity worked to 50,000,00 x 6 = Rs. 3 crores in a couple of days. There are more than half a dozen

> reality shows going on at any given time running their programmes two to three times a week. On a rough calculation the money involved is something as the following:
>
> 6 programmes x 2 shows per week = 48 programmes per month X 12 months = 576 shows X 50,000 respondents per show = 28,80,00,00 audience x Rs. 6/- per response = 1, 72, 800000. So approximately, 1800 crores worth of audience money is squeezed every year.

Beating trumpets

Promoting media channels and newspapers will take gigantic proportion—from branding of channels/newspapers to branding of individual programmes will be the order of the day. 'Exclusive', 'new', 'only by this newspaper/channel', 'the first one to report' though may not have much relevance for the audience, as after a split- minute glory, the news is on every channel, but the trend will not recede. "Is your news full of holes, click here for the full story" kind of blurbs will appear automatically on the PC.

Charging for editorial and reportage space- the 'Media net' kind of arrangements will be commonplace.

Media are trying to reposition themselves- as messiah of the underdog, responsible social crusaders- they will continue to do. Some varieties in this may emerge which will account for brand differentials for various competing media.

The paid communication

Advertising, predict many, may not be seen the way it is now- distinct, bold and pervasive, but shall take the surrogate route in a big measure through product endorsement in the entertainment media. From reading news bulletins to 'home delivery' of pizzas by actors, news media will play actively along with the entertainment media.

Advertising will come a full circle- from the original route of endorsement in films and soap operas back to the surrogate route to avoid watchers' axe.

There will be more sales promotion, point of purchase communication, web advertising instead of traditional routes to advertising. The share of print advertising will go down. Television and radio by and by will move over to the endorsement route.

On the structural side, the advertising industry will witness the death of the traditional full service agency. With media planning and buying function taken away from it, soon, strategy and creative functions will also be outsourced. The 15% commission from the media will become irrelevant, much to the consternation of the ad professionals. Agencies will redefine themselves by undertaking various below-the line activities.

Media and politics

The relationship between politics and media defies any conclusive definition- it at best is intriguing.

The whole notion of media in a liberal democracy was to strengthen democracy on the one hand and provide space to media to grow and work as a watch dog of democracy. The critical issue that emerges in this context is that with increasing growth of media monopolies and cross-media ownership, are we creating appropriate mechanism for independent and fair decision making or are media engineering control of minds by subtly but definitely substituting citizens with consumers.

If politics has an agenda, so have the media

Democracy and media are like twin sisters, each complementing the other, yet no debate can be conclusive about their true relationship and dependence. There has always been a love and hate relationship between politics and media, although some scholars firmly believe that both cross-fertilize each other.

Both institutions draw their supposed power from public- politics from the power of the people that elect representatives to political institutions and media from the eyeballs they are able to generate through entertainment programmes, coverage of events, personalities and ideas. Power in politics is inherent, but for media it is 'assumed' and acquired. Some analysts put both, politics and media as "Power" institutions.

The engagement of politics with media and media with politics will not go away too soon, it will be redefined.

Media traditionally have had the power to scare the mighty especially corporate honchos and politicians. A certain threat perception has always been felt. It has started to change and may change completely in two decades. Sample two incidents, one a live coverage and the other a talk show anchored by one of the powerful anchors, Karan Thapar.

> In a popular news channel, a commissioner was being grilled about a riot in a politically sensitive district in a live news bulletin. While he was being questioned, the video coverage was also shown on the spilt screen. The commissioner chided the anchor for showing a file coverage, which had no connection with the immediate situation calling it misleading. The channel could not edit it, because the programme was live.
>
> In the other case Ms. Jayalalitha, Chief Minister of Tamil Nadu also brook no nonsense when made uncomfortable with the verbal salvo of her host in a live show. She retorted that it was he who had been requesting her for a long time to come for the show, was it to humiliate her on issues he already had made up his mind on. "What if I walk out of your programme?" she asked Karan Thapar.[7]

With so much media space and time available, the perceived power of the media and *'you can't take cudgels with the media'* has mercifully changed and will continue to do so.

The future – a decade from now

Net will closely bond with varying communities, like-minded people across the world. The governments and powerful world bodies will have to listen to the collective voice of world community. The Indian vision and philosophy of *Vasudhev Kutumbkam* (World is one family) will not remain a metaphor but soon be recognized and appreciated in full measure. The world community will be more introspective than it is now and media will play a great part in the oneness process- Asia, especially India would be the hub of 'thinking beyond the physical' realm. .

Continuing with the trend, people will engage with media more and more-stretching time for all kinds of media in the course of a day. In other words, media will become all pervasive. The increasing involvement with media and technology however will create a sense of fear about our minds being controlled by technology, a scenario projected by the film Matrix.

The world may be uni-polar or bi-polar with varying political structures, but there will always be multiple cultures and diverse engagements with media. Whether we shall have global media structures, segmented structures or both, the biggest fear of the globe will stem from the political ideologies, marketing strategies and cultural diversities.

The last one-decade or so has reflected the stage-managing of media by subversive forces in various countries. Media, despite its love for reflecting the bold and not so beautiful reality will do some introspection and strike a balance in coverage.[8]

Summary

In this chapter we looked at the all pervasiveness of media, the changing media content and the expectations from public relations. The 24X7 channels have changed the concept of news completely. We looked at the growth and expansion of media in India. We addressed the issue of future of media given the fast pace with which the technology is changing. The changing expectations of people and the merging of markets have also influenced the content of media during the last decade or so.

Critical thinking exercise

Study the local media in your town/city (newspapers in the regional language, regional and cable channels) and critically analyze the content in terms of similarity or difference.

Questions

Q. 1 What are the major trends in India media in the last one decade or so? Discuss with examples.

Q.2 Study the future trends enlisted in the chapter and make your prognosis of more changes in future. Give your answer with logic behind your thinking.

Q. 3. Visit some social networking sites like the Facebook, My space.cm, Orkut etc. and study the issues that concern the youth of today. Do you think these sites can be used for connecting with the youth on issues concerning them?

Endnotes

[1] Source: The Entertainment & Media Industry – Sustaining Growth Report 2008, FICCI Powerhouse Cooper

[2] Source: The Entertainment & Media Industry – Sustaining Growth Report 2008 FICCI Powerhouse Cooper

[3] India 2007 – A Reference Manual, Publication Division, Ministry of Information & Broadcasting, p. 629.

[4] *The Hindustan Times*, 4 September 2008.

[5] *Pitch*, Volume v, Issue 4, February 2008, 5th Pitch-Madison Advertising Outlook, quoting *Source iCube Report*, 2007, pp. 70-73.

[6] *India 2007*, Publication Division, Ministry of Information and Broadcasting.

[7] *Pitch*, Volume v, Issue 11, September 2008, p. 130

[8] *Times of India*, October 2005.

[9] In the programme Devil's Advocate, the CNN IBN reversed the process on the eve of the news year i.e., 2009, it was this time former I&B Minister Arun Jaitely interviewing Karan Thapar. While talking on the issue of his intimidating style of extracting a "yes" or "no" answer, quoting an expert Karan Thapar said, there could be only four replies to a question, "yes", "no", " don't know", "can't say", which can be easily veered around to two that's why he insists on only "yes" or "no".

[10] The futuristic trends in media is based on the paper "Media 2025", read by Dr. Jaishri Jethwaney, at IIMC, during the International Public Relations Festival and 27th PR Conference in New Delhi in November 2006

5 The PR Process

Chapter objectives
- The process through which PR works
- The various steps of PR planning and implementation
- Some case studies of PR programmes

Public relations is often described as a "Fire Fighting" discipline. Whenever any organization is faced with a crisis, the busiest department probably is none other than the Public Relations department. There is, however, more to Public Relations than salvaging damage and image building. In this chapter we shall look at PR as a proactive communication management discipline in an organization. The chapter on Crisis Communication has provided a wider perspective on the PR process in critical times.

PR practitioners have long spoken about the intangible character of their discipline, which in their view cannot be measured easily. This is partly ascribed to the lack of enough body of scientific knowledge—as a common frame of reference—to the practice of managing and counseling in public relations or for that matter, public affairs. According to many practitioners and academics in the field, more research is needed to build a body of knowledge and gain credibility about this indispensable discipline, which unfortunately is reckoned as spin doctoring by critics.

How often do we in Public Relations look at secondary data or do formative research before starting on a project? This is in contrast to other scientific disciplines like engineering or medicine, which are based on time-tested procedures. However, the good news is that the laid back attitude is now changing. Mapping the audience before a PR campaign and post testing the campaign have become essential ingredients of any Public Relations plan. Some of the questions raised within the organizations that employ public relations are: What has the public relations department or consultancy contributed to the aims of the corporation or non-profit organization during the past one year? Was it worth it? Are they properly staffed?

When do we need a specific PR programme? Is PR a proactive or just a reactive activity? Do we make two kinds of PR programmes—one as a routine function to create an organization where there is free flow of information and another for critical times? These are some of the concerns a Public Relations practitioner must address. Whatever the kind of programme undertaken, it is essential for a practitioner to put the team through a six-pronged scrutiny.

The Six Pointers

- WHY – Why are we communicating?
  This will help define the objectives of a particular programme/campaign.
- WHO – Who are we trying to reach out to?
  This will help define the target audience.
- WHAT – What is to be said to gain the desired change?
  This will work out the key communication proposition.
- WHERE – Where do we disseminate our message so that it reaches the desired target audience?
  This will help select the media vehicles.
- HOW – What is the best route and the best strategy to reach our target audience?
  This will define the strategy of an action-oriented programme.
- WHEN – When is the "right" time to launch the programme to achieve the desired response?
  This will help in working out the timetable, in other words, the scheduling and frequency of our messages.

Besides the five Ws and one H, a lesson drawn from journalism books, two other inputs would be included, viz., budgeting and evaluation of the programme.

The advertising specialists generally follow the planning cycle while launching a campaign. Evolved by one of the reputed advertising agencies, viz., J. Walter Thompson, and known as the T-PLAN, most of the modern day campaigns adapt the cycle to ensure the programme is on the right track. It is felt that Public Relations can also learn from this. The plan when adapted to public relations practice should ideally address five basic questions.

The diagram below indicates the cycle a campaign should ideally undergo.[1]

Planning Cycle

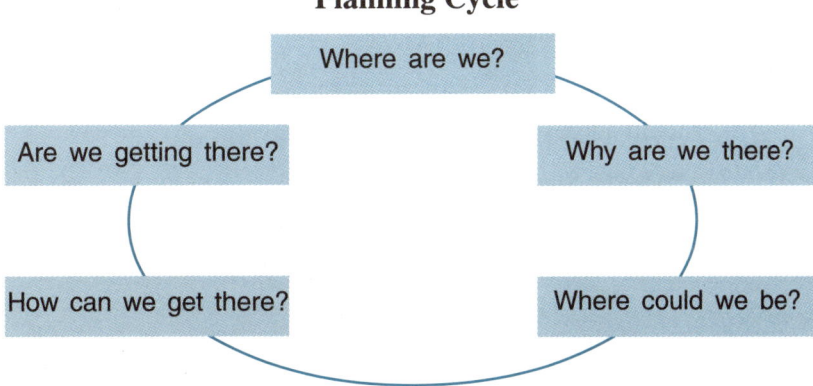

The five questions

1. Where are we in the minds of the target audience?

It is imperative to have insights about the target audience we are trying to reach out to. Are they familiar or unfamiliar about the issue at hand? Are there misperceptions or pre-conceived notions about the issue? Mapping the perception of the desired target audience hence becomes the first priority before taking up a campaign.

2. Where are we in the environment?

This should answer the current positioning of the organization in the market/environment. What kind of goodwill or equity does the organization have? This is very important especially when a damage salvage campaign is launched. In the chapter on crisis communication, case studies of Tata's withdrawal from West Bengal, Jet Airline's crisis situation emerging from firing its employees and Satyam Computers' fraudulent practices may be referred to, for understanding the concepts better.

3. Why are we here?

Analyse reasons for the current market standing or the lack of it; reasons for poor image, media's perceptions about the organization, stakeholders' perceptions and the possible reasons for the existing image. Perception mapping, media content analysis and constant probing would provide enough cues to a PR practitioner for working on an appropriate campaign .

4. Where do we go from here?

Determine not just "where it is desirable to be"? But also "where we can possibly be"? Once this is worked upon, establish the goals to work on the communication objectives.

5. How do we get there?

"How to" is the most challenging part in a communication plan? The team has to work out the strategy to achieve the desired goals and the intended route to reach them.

Strategy

Strategy must cover both the media to be selected and the communication plan and should address the following:

1. Media Strategy:
- Which media are most suitable to reach out to the desired publics fast and at the lowest cost per opportunity?
- Which media are considered more credible?
- Which media would prove more impactful on the audience?

2. Creative strategy:

- What is the problem?
- What is the role of public relations in solving the problem?
- Who are we talking to?
- What is the desired key response we are aiming at?

In brass tacks the route of a Public Relations campaign would be as follows:

Problem definition

This first step is to define the problem and why it is a problem. There are various kinds of problems for which public relations solutions are increasingly sought. The problem could be growing absenteeism in an organization, drug use/smoking at workplace, political interference in union activities of an organization, exodus of the core human resource to competition, critical media, activities of special interest groups that jeopardize or sully the image of the organization, lack of confidence of the shareholders and a host of other areas.

When defining the problem, it is easy to rely on gut feeling or inference, but these rarely help in the long run. Problem definition must begin with listening to the views of concerned stakeholders. According to celebrated communication expert Wilbur Schramm, feedback is a powerful tool. When it does not exist or is delayed or feeble, then the situation engenders doubt and concern in the communicator, and frustration and hostility in the audience. In fact, research is one method of structuring symptomatic "listening" into the communication process.

Research is a means to an end. The formative research helps diagnose the problem. Research can both be informal and exploratory, and formal.

Informal research techniques:

Informal methods, according to practitioners, still dominate public relations research despite the availability of highly developed social science methods. Some of the informal methods include the following:

1. By personal contact

In order to size up people's awareness about the concerned issue and map their perceptions, opinion seekers move about freely and informally to gather information by talking to a cross-section of target audience.

2. Through gatekeepers

A variant to personal contact is the use of key informants. It involves identifying leaders, opinion makers and experts. They could be editors, reporters, teachers, taxi drivers, postmen, village headmen, restaurant waiters, and in the Indian context even *paanwallahs* (vendors) and *naais* (village barbers) have been great source of gathering the "pulse" of the critical stakeholders, especially before elections. In-depth interviews with them often provide the researchers rare insights about the response of the desired public. In fact, during public opinion surveys during elections, these gatekeepers tend to pass on almost accurate information due to their interaction with the public on a continuous basis. In the context of organizations, rival union leaders and a cross-section of "friendly" insiders provide useful information about the line of thinking of important publics especially in critical times.

3. Through mail analysis

Companies in product line receive tremendous amount of mail from their consumers, all of which are not complimentary. A periodic analysis of letters can reveal areas of disfavour, and lack of information. This would help identify areas of ill-will or problem relationships. President John F. Kennedy called for every fiftieth letter coming to the White House, a practice he picked up from President Franklin D. Roosevelt. The weekly reports on the mail helped him read the pulse of public opinion and a brief summary of such letters was permanently recorded to track public concerns.

Ford Motors once launched "We Listen Better" campaign, which brought them thousands of letters.

After the third victory in a row for Ms Shiela Dikshit of Congress (I) in Delhi Assembly election held in November 2008, termed as a hat-trick by the media, *Times of India*, published a "report card" of the Chief Minister (CM), of programmes undertaken by the government in the last ten years, that were citizen friendly and others that needed attention. It exhorted the public to send in their concerns through e-mail to the publication, which it intended to sift and forward to the CM.[2]

A customer who complains is always better than the thousands who walk away silently, opines Janelle Barlow, from University of California at Berkley. She suggests "next time you are confronted by complaining customers, don't go red-in-the-face, say thank you instead". When a customer complains, she reasons out, she has had faith in the company's product, she cares. Most of the times, the companies blow the chance, others don't respond.[3]

4. Through field reports

Organizations generally have agents, field officers and marketing officers stationed at various places. They send their periodical field reports. The Department of Field Publicity of the Ministry of Information and Broadcasting have a bevy of field publicity officers who visit the nook and cranny of the country to disseminate information on various issues of public concern and the achievements of the Government. They have "talking points", a brief given to them about the particular issue they have to touch upon. The "talking points" vary from time to time. The field officers submit their reports, which also have the informal feedback from the area visited. These reports can provide a wealth of information about the concerns of the people to the government.

5. Through Focus groups

Focus groups are identified keeping in view the aims of the research. In this technique, the sample is subjected to deep probing with a view not only to seek information about *what* is being said but also *why* it is being said.

6. Media Content analysis

One of the important areas of public relations activity is to scan the environment, which includes a content analysis of media reporting. Press clippings and broadcast monitor reports have long been used for content analysis. They however indicate what is being printed and broadcast and not what is being read. An analysis of media, nonethless, does indicate issues of public concern and agenda setting by the media.

Formal Research Methods:

Formal research methods include, benchmark studies, communications audits, social audits, community/opinion studies, attitude/opinion studies and survey of social issues.

Besides, a lot of syndicated research is available about communities, media and media habits of the people, at a certain price, which the public relations practitioners must have access to.

In a nutshell, public relations needs research on people's attitudes, organizational's image, political and social issues, and media perception about its policies and achievements. The research has to be undertaken as a planning tool and not as an afterthought. Organizational objectives should outline the scope of the research. Research that is not specific but vague achieves little. The practitioner must determine the most relevant information for decision to direct the study. Research assumptions/hypothesis must be worked out carefully. While designing research one must address questions such as: Is the design rigid or flexible? Can the study accommodate the unexpected? Answers to these would help select cost efficient research options. Research is a tool, which should complement experience and judgement and not replace it.

Planning

Having defined the problem through research and based on expert adjustments and recommendations, the practitioner now would be in a position to precisely define the target audience and communication objectives. Now the stage is set to develop the most appropriate mix of public relations campaign elements. These will include the following:

- The potentially suitable and effective persuasive propositions
- The message packages that have the greatest impact
- The most efficient media vehicles
- The most suitable evaluation methods, besides
- The campaign timetable, and
- The budget

Having worked on this, the practitioner can present it to the management for approval. When an outside consultancy is involved, they often first hold a discussion with the public relations practitioner on whose brief they have worked, before presenting the plan to the client's management.

1. Message-package production

Having taken the management's approval and after making necessary modifications and adaptations, if need be, the stage is now set for message-package production. Experts within and outside the organization are commissioned to write/produce the chosen message package. The choice would be from the array of expertise available in the field of internal and external media.

2. Channel-media preparation

The drill now would be to set up the channels through which the selected messages will reach the members of the constituent public. This may simply mean making media bookings or may entail organizing activities like major openings/event management, conferences, celebrity appearances etc. The choice of media could be complex—from mass media to personal channels and at times special promotional media. For details, refer, Chapter 7.

Communication

The job is still not accomplished. It involves thorough communications management. The professional public relations practitioner will have to ensure that the proposed message package reaches the target audience. Merely sending press releases may not be enough. The PR department/consultancy has to follow up with concerned media to ensure the receipt of press release at various ends on time, keep a personal contact with the scribe or news editor to ensure publication. In short, the aim is to be sure that wherever possible the communication involved in committing the message package to the channel is received and attended to by the target audience to obtain a response and to produce a communicative transaction.

The experts must ensure that the communication thus designed achieves the following:

- It must be seen/read/listened to
- It must be assimilated
- It must be believed
- It must be remembered
- It must be acted upon

Ray Eldon suggests a four-pronged guideline for developing a message. First, determine *what people think about the issue*, the message would be worthless if, you don't know what people's perceptions about the issue are. Second, *establish what the problem really is*. Problem identification and research will answer this. Third, *establish the desired image you wish to achieve*. Finally *choose the most suitable communication proposition and media* to say what you want to say to bring about the desired change in the outlook of the target audience. To be acceptable, the communication has to be credible in context, clear, consistent and compatible with the receiver's value system.[4]

Monitoring and evaluation:

Evaluation helps in quantifying the public relation process. In other words, the exercise will reflect whether the objectives of the campaign were achieved. For long drawn programmes, it is advisable to conduct a mid-term appraisal so that adjustments, if any, can be made before carrying on with the exercise.

According to experts, the exercise has to be circular. If post campaigns reflect that the problem is not solved to the management's satisfaction, the professional may have to go back to the beginning of the exercise. However, it is also a fact that there generally is not enough data available on which to base a confident assessment of impact. Many evaluations become exercises in rationalizations. However, this does not mean that the professional gives up the need for a rigorous evaluation in the interest of professional development and achieving credibility.

Let's take the example of evaluation of a company's house journal. Let's see what the evaluation should ideally aim at.

Reach: To evaluate what percentage of employees received the publication on a timely basis?

Exposure and recall: How well did employees recall important issues covered in the publication?

Credibility: In case of some specific issues, were the views of both the management and employees taken? Did the employees consider the journal trustworthy?

Understanding: Did the readers understand company's position on important and critical issues, which may concern the employees, themselves?

Readability: Were the employees able to comprehend the contents without difficulty?

The evaluation can be through a questionnaire, interview or electronic mail.

Public relations practitioners need to follow the PR process broadly. No two programmes or campaigns can be the same. The above can provide basic guidelines which need to be adapted/modified and adjusted depending on the aims of the given programme.

CASE STUDIES

Delhi government's PR

The Congress (I) has been in the saddle for 10 years in Delhi. The verdict was out in the November 2008 elections and this time again it was Congress (I). Despite mounting recession, demolitions, BRT corridor, terrorist attacks and Batla House encounter that invited allegations against the government, the going was smooth for the party. Many ascribed this largely to the participative mode of governance of the party. Delhi government's Bhagidari (Partnership) scheme is said to be responsible for connecting the government with its governance on various issues that touch the lives of common man.

The Consumer Connect Initiative of the government—Bhagidari, is an initiative taken by the Delhi government by partnering with Delhites through various Resident Welfare Associations (RWAs) in solving issues proactively. Some of the initiatives include the following:

Solid waste management: In many colonies, RWAs have come forward to partner with the municipal corporation in improving garbage management

Rainwater harvesting: The Delhi Jal Board offers technical expertise and also partly finances the rainwater harvesting undertaken by organizations and residential colonies. The government also rewards successful schemes.

Development of community parks: More than 500 parks have been adopted by RWAs for upkeep and cleanliness

Greenery and plantation: School children through various schools and NGOs have been active in this scheme in increasing the green cover of Delhi.

Water distribution and management: Water councils comprising representatives from civic agencies and the community at large have been constituted in colonies of Delhi which have been facing water crisis. RWAs have also been authorized to collect water bills by signing an undertaking with DJB.

Public education: Public education on various issues of concern like use of plastic, fire-crackers, saving the Yamuna, have been very successful through community involvement

Improving the reach of services: Neighbourhood watch services in collaboration with RWAs and the Delhi police, and the verification of antecedents of servants and drivers have been initiated in many colonies.

Care for senior citizens: Smart identity cards for multiple use, help with old age pension and dedicated children groups for care of senior citizens have been initiated.

Women empowerment: More than 4 lakh women from the disadvantaged class have benefitted from the Stree Shakti scheme which covers intervention in areas of health, literacy and income generation. 'Ladli' is a scheme for empowering the girl child by supporting her education.

Gender resource centre: Forty five gender centres in collaboration with the NGO sector have been made operational which provide single window information about facilities to women. Some of these centres have been providing skill development in photography, videography, information and communication technology, driving, plumbing etc.

School welfare committees: Seven hundred school welfare committees have been set up to improve the management of government schools in Delhi.

Industrial estate association: These associations have been formed for proper development and maintenance of industrial estates.

Rural citizen groups: With support from the government, these groups have contributed to the upkeep of village schools, ponds, sports centres, roads, drains and community centres.

Implementing the Right to Information (RTI): The government in consultation with citizen councils has formulated guidelines for the enforcement of RTI.

Social audit of public services: Independent agencies have taken up social auditing to provide feedback on levels of public satisfaction with services provided.

'My Delhi, I Care' fund: Under this scheme, citizens participate in upkeep and protection of their own habitat through partnership with the government.

Sanjha prayas: Working with slum dwellers, the scheme aims at identifying their issues and developing action plans to improve the quality of services in their settlements.

Aapki rasoi: In collaboration with business and corporate houses the Delhi government has initiated its "hunger free Delhi" campaign. Under this, the companies as a part of their CSR are encouraged to adopt a site for providing a square meal to the destitute.[5]

Creating aware communities in disaster situations–a PR outreach programme in Tsunami hit Southern coastal India in 2004

Two international NGOs came up with a Community Outreach programme on communication to empower communities that suffered during the Tsunami in 2004 in India.

Community participation, in effect, was aimed at reflecting 'voices and choices' of the community and thereby developing the human organizational and management capacity to solve problems to sustain improvement. In terms of Disaster Preparedness, a proactive approach was sought from the proposed programme.

The goals behind community preparedness were broadly the following:
1. People can be a source of useful ideas.
2. People can help adopt inputs coming from outside.
3. Communities can set examples for others to replicate success stories.
4. Communities can be involved in the decision-making process.

Field Visit

A field visit was made in February 2005 to gather insights on issues referred to above and map peoples' perceptions in three villages, namely, Nagapattinum (Akkaraipettai); Pondicherry (Periyakalapet, and Veerampatinam) and on national highway Chennai-Pondicherry (Pattipulum Kuppam) and to conduct a communication audit for a possible media campaign in the near future.[6]

The field visit enabled the visiting team to articulate issues that needed addressing, people's perceptions on various issues and the possible of role of communication media in reaching out to communities and enabling them to overcome the trauma and get on with life.

A year later

Realizing the importance and role of community involvement in carrying on the task further and empowering them for future disasters, One World South Asia, in association with Plan International (India) introduced the concept of building communication opportunities for community communicators on how information could be converted into knowledge and how knowledge could be shared with communities through various media tools, viz. radio, comics, photography, written communication and Internet and to groom some from among the communities as Change Agents, who would eventually become Community Knowledge leaders.

The capacity building workshops were initiated in the month of November 2005 with selected children and youth of Sirkali, Dindigul, Kanchipuram, Marakanam. The blocks were chosen from the coastal areas of Tamil Nadu and Pondicherry. During this process, around 500 children have been trained in communication through various media tools on various issues identified by them in their communities with a wider canvas of life-cycle approach.

The week long training modules in various areas gave them intensive understanding on the development issues; how visual media like comics and photography can communicate, especially on issues that concern communities.

During the training workshops, community communicators were introduced to ICTs like radio and Internet and how the process of using radio and Internet enhances the communication opportunities among grassroots communities on development issues.

The participants were also exposed to the community software developed by One World South Asia, open ENRICH and how they could share the local/global contents among the communities. Experts were drawn from various areas of communication specialization to anchor various modules in the said workshop.

During this process, they learnt why community voices were important; how they could be recorded and transcribed; how radio could in turn be used to address issues such as these. With the concept of situational analysis, the participants were exposed to the process of understanding issues (where they were, why they were there, and what lied ahead).

The workshop included input on the potential of local folk media in communicating with communities. *Vello pattu* a folk form prevalent in Pondicherry, based on storytelling to a gathered audience was used as pedagogy for that module. The participants learnt it and delivered a sterling performance weaving in the Tsunami story.

In Pondicherry, during the radio training, the young participants were enabled to speak with the Union Minister for Information & Broadcasting in Delhi on 12

November, that incidentally is celebrated as the Public Broadcasting Day in India as on this day in 1947, the father of the Nation, Mahatma Gandhi spoke to the public through All India Radio (AIR).

Participants from Pondicherry who probably had never spoken Hindi, sang Gandhiji's favourite prayer *Raghupati Raghav Raja Ram, Patita Pavan Sita Ram* that was broadcast live from AIR Pondicherry, thus symbolizing the power of radio in reaching out to a large audience.

The concept and importance of Community Knowledge Centres was introduced and how the knowledge could be collected, collated and disseminated through various media tools and through community software solutions; and how communities were connected and empowered through the whole process.

This exercise was aimed at creating an environment for the Right to Information and Knowledge through the vibrant Grassroots Media and to bring in the synergy among grassroots and mainstream media. This effort has visibly ignited the spark within the young community communicators, thus empowering them to think and act for their own development and for the communities to which they belong.

During the orientation programme, various stages of disaster management were discussed, such as (a) Pre-disaster; (b) Disaster and (c) Post-disaster (long term planning) and the need for making disaster management committees in villages.

After every module, the participants were given simulations and role-plays to ensure learning of various communication tools.

In the workshops that aimed at participative planning and programming, the following critical insights emerged:

What can communities do in times of natural disasters?

- Need assessment capacity of possible dangers
- Awareness creation
- Motivate people
- Educate people on disasters
- Engage in decision making in corrective measures
- Attend to the injured
- Perform last rites of the dead
- Provide food and shelter to victims
- Save property and providing for its security
- Identify safe places for stop-gap arrangement
- Compassion, care, especially for women and children
- Help authorities in rehabilitation efforts

Use of Communication in Critical Times

- Preparedness
- Spokesperson
- Local media
- Mass media
- Post Trauma Stress Handling
- Survivor stories
- Preparing communities to use the power of media

The workshop delegates were asked to provide their input on planning and preparation required to face disasters. The following input emerged from the expert team:

1. A Disaster Management Committee (DMC), comprising the youth, panchayat representative and an opinion maker from within the village to be made.
2. Terms of Reference of the DMC should be worked out.
3. Information on possible kinds of disasters should be shared with the community.
4. Seasonality of possible disasters, if any should be prepared and a tentative calendar could be maintained.
5. Being prepared in advance whether or not disasters occur.

Participants' input on disaster management after learning the concepts:

A list of do's and don'ts suggested by them

- Constructing houses away from the seashore.
- Prevent sand dunes.
- Plant trees near shores.
- Convince the government to create a wall along the coast.
- Check on rumours.
- Names of Disaster committees to be made available to everybody with their telephone numbers. The lists can be pasted on walls, temples and other prominent places.
- Safe places should be identified in advance so that the entire village should know in advance where they have to run for safety.
- Planning could be done according to the availability of safe shelters nearby.
- Disaster committees should use various modes of communication like public address system, loudspeakers from places of worship, schools, cable television, mobiles, word-of-mouth so that the public could be addressed with no loss of time.

- The building owners/authorities should be informed in advance so that they are prepared to provide shelter to the community.
- The names of the NGOs, government persons and volunteers should be pasted on the walls and made available at prominent places so that they can be contacted in case of an emergency.
- All valuables could be kept in one place, maybe in a box, so that at the time of disaster, these could be picked up fast and could be shifted to possible safety places. (In fact, a box/bag containing a change of clothes, first-aid kit, money/chequebook, valuables, contact number/address of a relation need to be always kept ready per person for any eventuality).
- Mock drills could be practiced every three months so that people could be prepared well in advance for the real exercise at the time of disaster.
- Youth to join the volunteer team so that they could later join the DMC.
- Pool resources every month, to meet needs at the time of disaster. Otherwise, this money would be available at the end of year for some community welfare scheme.
- Review the committee's performance after two years and change the members.
- Skills could be built on alternative jobs so that at the time of disaster, these skills could be utilised for taking up an alternate livelihood.
- Micro-credit societies could be formed wherever not available, so that money is available at the time of disaster.

When actual disaster strikes, the DMC needs to meet immediately and designate work to volunteers as decided in the plan. The plan is:

- ✓ Evacuating people,
- ✓ Opening emergency call centres,
- ✓ Helping people move to many places,
- ✓ Provision of food and water,
- ✓ Getting in touch with the medical community for attending to the injured,
- ✓ Making a list of dead/injured,
    Arranging proper burial of dead,
- ✓ Networking with NGOs and other bodies.
- ✓ Social audit with community interventions to make a list of issues to be taken up immediately.
- ✓ Calling clinical psychologists/psychiatrists for trauma counselling.
- ✓ Communicating important notices to the community using various media including public addressing system/radio/cable for immediate interface with the community.
- ✓ Check gossip mongering by providing immediate facts and figures.

Economic recession—image impact on ICICI—salvaging it through strategic PR

As soon as the news of the crashing of banking behemoths in the USA poured in, whispers about ICICI bank also surfaced, sending panic waves among depositors and investors in October 2008. A Google search on ICICI brought in 99,200 responses in .28 seconds on 22 October. Sample one of the inputs on a blog: "Right from the past few years......... to be exact 3 years, I have been worried about this ICICI bank, India. They have been aggressive in their strategies, and investments. And today, I read that they have lost considerably in the UK, USA bankruptcy cases. Has anyone got some more information about this?"

Weekly journal *Business World* reported: 'ICICI Bank, India's biggest bank said on Tuesday that rumors being repeatedly circulated about its financial strength were baseless and malicious, saying that the bank had a strong capital position."

As per media reports, the bank lodged a formal FIR with the Mumbai police which set out to investigate a 'bear cartel' of brokers who were indulging in a smear campaign against the bank through SMS, and e-mail asking people to withdraw their deposits from the Bank.[7]

As soon as the problem surfaced, the bank management did not evade but agreed that it has been a victim of rumours repeatedly circulated in certain centres regarding the financial strength of the Bank. It's CEO stated that the rumours were baseless and malicious. Mr. Kamath, appeared in many news channels assuring stakeholders that the bank was extremely healthy and had ample capital. In its effort of damage control, the then Joint MD, Chandra Kochar who later took over as the CEO, also joined in interfacing with the media.

The Bank roped in cine actor Shahrukh Khan, who reinforced his trust in ICICI talking about "trust" and "faith". "ICICI bank. It's a smart choice. Take my word for it", endorsed Shahrukh in a TV ad. He further said he had his money in ICICI bank and would continue to have it there.

In an in-depth study of the banking sector under the caption "Agony Time Marketing", Ashley Coutnho argued that the global turmoil was threatening to boil over, a liquidity crunch affecting the Indian banks as well. It was important that banks brought back the good old plank of faith and trust as ICICI bank did. Their earlier *"Mein hoon naa"* could not have worked in troubled times when the bank's stock plummeted to a 52 week low in the second week of October 2008.[8]

During the Great Economic Depression of the 1920s and 1930s, the banks in the US created ads that spoke of safety and security, the tone was one of assurance and the visuals of the banks' monolith edifices served as imagery of the stable and unshakeable. The author recollected the ads of Indian banks in the 1960s and 1970s that "chose to dwell on the bankable nature of banks—banks routinely highlighted the better returns they offered on savings and the element of bank deposits being safe was never far from the surface". Later, with the growth of retail banking and easy consumer credits, safety and trust took a backseat, as these were taken for granted, the banks then shifted to the 'value-added' advantages of banking with them. Is it not time to go back to the good old positioning of trust and faith (?), argued the author. [9]

To arrest gossip mongering and an overactive grapevine, the Bank in an unprecedented move sent SMSs to its customers requesting them not to believe any rumours surrounding the Bank with the message "your deposits with the ICICI Bank are safe. Your bank is well capitalized with good liquidity. Please don't listen to baseless rumors. Happy festive season". The bank simultaneously issued print ads to highlight its strong liquidity. One of the ads had the text:

"At the end of the day, truth and trust have no equal." In the body text it spoke of the rumors about the bank. Sharing the facts, the ad touched the following areas, viz., sound banking system, healthy capital, large net worth and strong credit rating, in various subheads, to support its claims through robust data and testimonials.[10]

BSES 2002-07

BSES Rajdhani Power limited is a Reliance Anil Ambani group Company distributing electricity in Delhi. The company suffered rough weather in the beginning, when it was a kind of paradigm shift from a government distribution to a private company distribution of power. Utility services have always attracted political interference. The company, at the same time, was also fighting to gain credibility with its own employees (the same people who worked for the inefficient Delhi Electric Supply Undertaking (DESU) and were not used to the private sector work culture, also created hurdles for the management). The company used BPO services to attend to customer complaints about faulty meters, exaggerated bills and power cuts. This was very different from the earlier system of calling up the local DESU office in various localities to solve the problems instantly. It was not an uncommon practice when unscrupulous consumers in league with DESU employees would tamper with their meters to pay less. All this changed when the reins went in to the hands of a private player.

The company improved the billing process, made the bill clearance offices computerized. In order to reach out to its customers, it used the route of printed literature which was freely available at its bill clearance offices.

After completing five years, a booklet was widely distributed through the Residents' Welfare Associations (RWAs) in various colonies. The booklet had an interesting caption:

"Sometimes, you can witness change. And yet, not see it happen. BSES 2002-07"
The booklet has pictures in black and white depicting how it was like before and also provided an explanation of change after BSES Rajdhani took over. How things were earlier is written in black text and the change, in white text (in reverse).

Sample the following:

"Not too long back, the noise of gensets was a familiar sight in Delhi markets.

Just a few years back, gensets emitting foul fumes were unavoidable in every bazaar and market in Delhi. Today, they are a rare sight, an indicator of reduced power cuts.

Delhites were used to the incessant clicks of the fridge stabilizer and shrinking of the TV picture thanks to low voltage.

Voltage fluctuation, once the bane of Delhi's power supply, now seems a distant memory.

In those days you didn't have to wait for an occasion to have a candle lit dinner.

Since 2002 BSES has been revamping Delhi's power distribution system. Over Rs. 3,000 crores have since been invested towards upgrading the entire distribution system including.......

When did all this fade away?

When did people stop taking half-day leave to stand in unending queues to pay power bills?

When did all this change, you wonder.

And then you realize, when you are too close to change, you often don't see it "happening..."

Social connect for inclusive development

Mainstream newspaper *The Times of India* has pioneered many interesting campaigns from time to time involving people at large. The group launched the **Lead India** and the **Teach India campaigns** in 2008. The former invited people from various strata to participate in the *Lead India campaign*, involving people to vote for the favourite candidate who had the potential to lead in the area of his/her profession/choice. The *Teach India campaign* invited civil society to participate in making India literate.

The Teach India campaign

It's not just a campaign, it is aimed at being a movement and it has become one, going by the response.

Years ago the famous campaign "Each one teach one" won many accolades and awards, but the campaign was not considered successful. Analysts feel that it was too good to be true! The campaign invited people to ask for a free kit for teaching. So overwhelming was the response that the agency in charge could not cope up with the response, and a great idea died an instant death!

A campaign may have a great idea, but the important question is, can it be implemented.

"What a great idea, Sir ji" the Idea cellular campaign of a rural school through the Idea connection with Abhiskek Bachchan as the protagonist, has all the ingredients of emotion, drama and success in a 60 second plot, but is it achievable?

> The Teach India campaign is said to have 90% response from people who are supporting a cause for the first time as per TOI revelation. The publication also shared that in the first 11 days it received a response from over 55,000 people. Interestingly, employed people have responded more than retired people and students, which, according to TOI, has brought forward a new category of people that can be tapped for social initiatives. Engineers form the largest segment from various cities. Traditionally women have preferred teaching jobs, but in case of this campaign women have not come forward as much as men have.

Summary

In this chapter we looked at the PR process and various stages in the planning cycle. We deliberated on different steps for planning and implementing a PR programme. The case studies encompassed various sectors including government, corporate sector, besides initiatives from a media house.

Critical thinking exercise

Pick a PR campaign launched by the national, local government or by an organization and critically analyze them based on the parameters of the PR planning process you have learned from this chapter.

Questions

Q.1 Describe Planning Cycle in a campaign and its various components.

Q.2 Discuss the various forms of formal and informal research techniques used before mounting a PR Campaign.

Q.3 Study in detail all the case studies given in the chapter and make a PR plan for your city on one of the following campaign themes:

- Caring for the girl child.
- Education for all.
- Exhorting citizens to make use of the "Right to Information" to improve governance in their locality.

Endnotes

[1] Jaishri Jethwaney and Shruti Jain, *Advertising Management*, 2006 (OUP:New Delhi)

[2] *The Times of India*, 10-11 December 2008.

[3] As quoted by Dibyendu Ganguly "Complain with me", *Times of India, Brand Equity*, 22 July 2008.

[4] Ray Eldon Hiebert, *Precision Public Relations*, 1988 (Longman Publishing Group:US)

[5] *Times of India*, 3 August 2008

[6] One of the authors, Dr. J Jethwaney was a member of the team that strategised the entire programme and made the field visits along with other team members both immediately after the Tsunami struck and a year later to see the impact of the community initiative undertaken by the NGOs.

[7] *Business World*, 30th September 2008

[8] Ashley Coutnho, "Agony Time Marketing", *Times of India, Brand Equity*, 30 October 2008.

[9] Ibid.

[10] Various newspapers like, *The Hindustan Times, The Economic Times* and others carried ads for more than two weeks at a stretch, October-November 2008.

6 PR Tools and Methods

Chapter objectives
- To introduce the role and scope of PR communication
- To discuss various tool/media used by PR in reaching out to various stakeholders
- To discuss the strengths and weaknesses of media
- To deliberate on the best strategies to make use of the media in an effective manner

The traditional definition of an organization is that it is a self-contained entity made up of specialist departments, each adept in its area of activity, and it competes with other similar organizations with one objective—maximizing sales and earning profit. This definition has long been replaced. A modern organization is a living entity, with a skin that is porous. Its objectives and activities reflect the society in which it operates. Business life is characterized by interdependence rather than independence.

The organic approach to management recognizes that the health of an individual department or "organ" will influence the general health of the whole organization. Profit may be the bottom line and no doubt remains the lifeblood of the organization, but equally, the communication system is its nervous system.

Besides planning, organizing and achieving, management is also about information and communication. The major PR communication tasks in an organization include the following:

1. Processing of information from the environment

Scanning environment is one of the very important functions of an organization. The information gathered facilitates goal setting and decision-making about various aspects like production attributes, diversification and strategic planning among others. Keeping a vigil on competitor's activities and products is an important aspect of market surveillance. All the information thus gathered is studied, sifted, processed and made to percolate to different internal departments. Getting information from the environment is primarily a communication activity.

2. Identification of 'publics'

The second stage, after processing information, is to identify the outside "publics" and accommodate information in the communication messages designed for various publics.

There can also be a situation where an organization has just one client and still cannot do without communication. Let us take the example of a company which produces fighter planes. The client for them obviously would be the airforce or the government of that country. In order to "sell" the product, it must bring out literature detailing its attributes, make prototypes, arrange trial flights and communicate other information before the deal can be finalized.

3. Building internal environment

Employees are the life and soul of an organization. Reaching out to this internal audience is an important responsibility of the communication department of a corporation.

Within the organization, it is necessary to establish an attitudinal environment for effective communication. Supervision is the task of a few members within an organization. Interpersonal communication is required to achieve the goals of the department. In any given organization, we never have a situation when everyone is satisfied. Some are unhappy for various reasons. Among various reasons, some experience job dissatisfaction. This situation could arise due to two reasons. In some cases, an employee may think that he does not have enough information to do the job. In other cases, interpersonal relations among the unit's members may be poor. Job satisfaction is a very complex area. People enjoy or dislike their jobs for various reasons. Such dissatisfactions can be removed through effective communication.

As discussed earlier in the chapter, some employees have the supervisory role of controlling others as part of the hierarchical system within an organization. Such people are referred to as managers or leaders. Communication in the organizational context involves an attempt by the leader to establish open relationships with subordinates. This helps the leader receive and transmit information. Effective managerial communication, however, is often subjective, reflecting the personality and traits of the leader.

4. Establishing a corporate face of the organization

All organizations communicate with the outside world, some through deliberate and planned effort by using various communication tools, others may not communicate formally, but by their very existence, they communicate through their products, services, policies and programmes, without formally using any communication tools.

The above paragraphs may lead you to question the positioning or role of PR. Communication after all, is intrinsic to all kinds of jobs like production, processing, packaging or marketing, so how does PR specifically contribute to organizational communication? The answer is, communication is not the business of the public relations department alone. Public relations is the process through which an environment can be created for effective communication.

PR is often referred to as the top management function. The responsibility of communicating with different publics ultimately rests with the top management. PR aids and advises on how to go about the act of communication. It helps decide what to communicate, to whom, and through which channels, and most importantly how to communicate so that the response is in the mutual interest of the management and the employees.

We have all heard of the expression "from the horse's mouth". The horse in the organizational context is the top man, the ultimate source of information, who cannot get away by saying "I do not know". In crises or volatile situations, the press frequently seeks the comment of the top man. If the crisis is political, the opposition seeks the Prime Minister's statement. All this is in the interest of getting credible information.

PR is a link between the management and its various publics. Of all the forms of communication, interpersonal communication probably is the best. It is also referred to as face-to-face communication. Ideal it may be, but such communication is not possible under all circumstances. Organizations at times are very large, multi-locational, multi-directional conglomerates, employing millions of employees with different languages and specializations. Hence it is imperative that the public relations department creates the right channels to reach out to the varied constituent publics. It is the responsibility of the public relations department to understand the communication requirements of these publics, select channels and prepare relevant communication messages and evaluate their efficacy and impact from time to time.

Media relations can be both proactive and reactive. By the former it is meant that a PR practitioner plans to get his organization's news covered by the media as a planned effort. At other times, he may have to react to certain press coverage, which the organization feels is not based on facts and has earned negative publicity in the minds of the readers. React he must, but not till he is fully convinced that the story is malicious or derogatory or unflattering to his company. Also when he reacts, he should have facts and data to back up his organization's point of view. In this situation, he may have to issue a rejoinder clarifying the management's point of view or meet the concerned correspondent or news editor, or organize a press conference for the top management to address, depending on the extent of damage caused due to irresponsible reporting.

Let us now discuss the various tools or media available to PR both for internal and external communication, and the methods to utilize them. First, the external communication tools:

External Media

1. Mass Media

The Press, TV, radio, films, documentaries, outdoor (hoardings and posters) among others comprise mass media. The mass media constitute a nation's public information system, a process in which PR plays an important role. With the coming of the worldwide web, the physical barriers of borders and nationalities have suddenly given way to a seamless world where people connect with each other on issues that interest them.

a) The Press

Referred to as the *Fourth Estate*, the press wields enormous power and clout in a society. It plays a significant role in the life of an organization, enabling it to reach out to various categories of external publics. The press, in fact, puts the "third party endorsement" on the activities of an organization. The source of news coverage and editorial content about different organizations in a newspaper can both be known and unknown. If used properly, the press can play a complementary role, but if mishandled, or when PR is in the hands of immature practitioners, inept handling could lead to damaging the image of the organization.

Media relations, in fact is the proverbial acid test for PR practitioners. Many a PR person has been fired for mishandling the press. To make PR and the press complement each other is challenging, but not an impossible task. The news is created by the work of the organization, which in turn is articulated by people authorized to do so. How faithful the news coverage is, depends on the power of articulation. The problem arises when organizations want news reported in a manner which is favourable to them and which will promote their objectives and will not cause them trouble, whereas the news media want news that will interest their readers. Martin Nobon, a Washington reporter, once remarked that a reporter had a "vested interest in chaos". Sensationalism, juicy copy, and newsworthy personalities rather than news, occupy the minds of a great number of journalists. A PR practitioner, on the other hand, has a vested interest in projecting his organization in a favourable light. Let us admit that a PR practitioner is a paid advocate to influence the minds of the people. He cannot, however, get away by giving false versions or concocting things. In this age of information, a PR practitioner is just one source of information. A good scribe will not submit his copy based on just the official source. He will collect different versions and juxtapose them with the official version.

In order to utilize a powerful medium like the press, it is very important for a PR practitioner to understand the press scene, the content of different publications, their dynamics and the functioning of the press, and establish working relations with the concerned reporters, news editors etc.

The relationship between PR and press is of mutual interdependence. With the changing market scenario and the growing importance of the capital market, coverage of the industry is a necessary component of newspapers.

In order to be credible, it is important to be knowledgeable. The first step, which a PR person should take, is to acquaint himself fully with the organization he is working for. To begin with, he should develop his own organization as his "beat" just as journalists work on their assigned beat.

The PR person need not be conversant with the technical aspects of the company he is engaged but, even if the organization is technical in nature like those producing scientific, chemical or precision products his being a communication expert will help the organization in putting across the most technical information in the common man's language through the media. And the media appreciate contributions of this nature.

Press relations can't be built overnight. It is a continuous process. To be successful in this respect, a PR person must go beyond the "press release relationship." Press briefings and informal meets help develop a lasting relationship. Writing press releases is an art. Later in the chapter we shall take up the subject of media writing.

The Government of India has a network of information officers in its Press Information Bureau (PIB). Headed by the Principal Information Officer, the information officers are attached to various ministries. Their job is to provide information to the press relating to the policies and performances of their ministries and the viewpoints of the legislature on different issues through their ministries. PR practitioners working in the public sector and in government-funded organizations can utilize the services of the PIB to reach the nooks and corners of the country through their vast network.

b) Television

The advent of television has been a watershed in the world of communication. A force to reckon with, television has a great scope as a publicity medium. A channel which allows the use of the printed word, the spoken word, pictures in motion, colour, music, animation, and sound effects, all blended in one message. Being an intimate mass medium, TV has great communication potential for a PR person.

Until the end of the eighties, the country had to make do with one television channel—the Doordarshan, which was fully funded and operated by the government. Everything changed after the first Gulf War, that brought the war theatre through satellite communication into the living rooms of people all over the world. Today, television reaches people's homes through a variety of means, viz., terrestrial, DTH (Direct to Home through a personal dish) or via cable operators. There are several operators. Viewing television being free at one point of time, is not so any more. From a two hour transmission, to hundreds of channels beaming 24X7 programmes, people could not have asked for more. People have to shell out payments depending on how many channels they subscribe to. As brought out in the chapter Media and PR, at the latest count we in India have 65 news channels, which, all put together have just about 7% viewership, but despite that, more and more channels are being added to the stable. News channels like newspapers are powerful media of moulding public opinion on issues of social, political and economic nature. They set an agenda for debates in the public domain. Various kinds of entrepreneurs are getting in the media business—big business houses, realty sector, politicians, religious outfits and what have you. Besides the mainstream news channels, there are about half a dozen business channels that are doing good business.

From the perspective of a PR professional, the proliferation of news channels can either be seen as a problem or an opportunity. When the news is bad, it gets repeated time and again during a day making the life of a PR professional miserable, but when the going is good, organizations are able to garner tremendous amount of positive publicity.

There are certain ground rules which, if followed, can get enormous publicity for an organization through this medium. The starting point is to understand the working of various TV channels available and their programme content, and then to decide dispassionately what aspects of the company are newsworthy. As TV is a visual medium, the subject has to be colourful and action-oriented. A dull meeting, a panel discussion or a laboratory discovery (unless it has movement) is not subject for making TV news releases.

A new release will not be accepted if it is too sales oriented or looks and sounds like a commercial. The best approach is to make an informational clip, which has news values for the viewer. The name of the organization should appear incidentally. Non-profit organizations stand a better chance of getting coverage for their activities due to the nature of their work.

Ideally, a news release should not exceed 90 seconds. The story should be arranged in such a manner that, if the news editor wants to reduce length, he should ideally clip the least important portion at the end of the story. In other words, the most important news should be arranged in the beginning and the less important in descending order. There was a time when television studios accepted only professional U-matic, 3/4 inches tapes and not half-inch unprofessional tapes or 16 mm and 35mm spools. With the availability of digital equipment, things have become easier. Now in a day and time when TV channels are accepting footage from mobile phones, it is not difficult for a PR professional to arrange for a videographer at a nominal cost.

After the film footage is shot, the edited version need not have a voice cast, music, etc., One can send an edited clip with a written script indicating the visual input in the film alongside to enable the newsreader to lend his/her voice.

On special occasions, say a landmark, a VIP visit, or a crisis situation like an accident, a fire, or sabotage, the TV team may approach the PR person to allow shooting. Professionalism demands that after verifying the identities and authority letters of the TV station, the PR practitioner should facilitate coverage by providing access to the place, information and management's viewpoint, should the coverage be after a crisis situation.

Proactive PR demands that a PR practitioner should plan in advance the occasions which demand sending news releases to TV stations. A list of good video producers with comparative rates should be kept handy for use as and when the occasion arises. Another way could be to get a list of stringers working for TV stations or private companies providing news-clips to TV. They have more or less fixed rates. If a PR person has footage in store, such companies or stringers could be approached for preparing news releases from the file shots. Appreciating the news value and after checking with concerned programme producers, they prepare clips and charge the TV stations as per their approved rates. PR people in such circumstances don't have to spend any additional money. All that is required is right networking contacts and timelines.

c) Radio

Radio, like television, can be a close ally of a PR practitioner. In India, radio has the capacity to cover more than 95 per cent of the population. However, the reach has been consistently going down due to a variety of reasons. Analysts enumerate the following reasons for poor reach of radio, which has come down to about 24% on all-India basis:

- Low per capita ownership of radio sets.
- Lack of power connection, or, power cuts in villages.
- Preference for television over radio.
- Poor content quality.

However, the FM stations have improved the access, especially in metros and small towns. A mobile medium, the radio receiver has a flexibility which no other medium can match. Even through it is a mass medium, radio possesses the qualities of direct personal touch as it uses the spoken word for the most part to convey its message.

How can radio be used as a PR medium? News bulletins are broadcast over the radio at fixed intervals throughout the day, both on national and local frequencies. Organizations can use the medium by sending press releases relating their performance and development. All India Radio's code, however, rules out the mention of the name of a private company in a news bulletin or newsreel. News is selected for broadcast based on its newsworthiness to the listeners. While there are a number of FM Radios in the private sector, they have not been given the permission to broadcast news. The issue is under consideration of the Central Government.

It is ironical that in an age and day when there are over 65 television news channels through satellite communication in the private sector in India, that also include international equity in some, the government seems hesitant in allowing news broadcast to FM radio players.

Abhilaksh Rekhi in an article "The National Rural Employment Guarantee Act (NREGA), Gram Panchayats and Community Radio: exploring structural linkages to strengthen access and transparency", explores the possibility of using community radio for implementation of NREGA in the truest sense. The act will cover over six lakh villages, and by connecting the people through community radio, the government can ensure access to information, transparency and accountability. The community radio, the author argues "holds tremendous potential as a tool of empowerment to conscientise and build capacities for communities and enable them to become active participants in the scheme's implementation".[1]

A radio news release should be written in radio style so that an announcer can use it without much editing.

Besides news, AIR has a number of programmes pertaining to industry, current affairs and panel discussions which can be befittingly utilized by a PR practitioner. A PR practitioner should be an avid radio listener to get a grasp of the style and to identify programmes which will be suitable for his organization. He should also identify the concerned producers.

d) Film/Video

The film, first the silent and then the talkies in the earlier part of this century, represents one of the most significant landmarks in the development of mass communication. The shift in our dependence from words to pictures has made all the difference to the way we think and perceive things.

Film/documentaries can be made on formats like 35 mm, 16 mm and video. As a PR practitioner, one does not need to be an expert film-maker, but should necessarily have a working knowledge of the medium. This will help one decide the line of approach, the format, the treatment and, of course, the budgeting and appropriation of funds, etc.

Making films on celluloid in 35 mm or 16 mm format promises excellent results, but it is cumbersome, time-consuming and expensive. Unless the film is to be viewed by a very large audience in a theatre, video can easily replace celluloid. Video equipment has the advantage of playing back the image immediately. It does not need processing as in the case of film. It is also possible to re-shoot on the same film if the results are not satisfactory. Synchronized sound is possible with every video recorder and if necessary different sound tracks can be superimposed on a sound track in different languages or dialects. A videotape can be redone by adding fresh coverage or by replacing some shots in order to update the programme. Video has the easy choice of computer-backed special effects.

In the last two decades or so there have been many generations of video equipment—from the Low Band to High Band, Beta Chem to the latest being the state-of-the-art digital cameras and equipment. The cost of film also varies depending on the kind of equipment used.

Video has its disadvantages too. The equipment is delicate and susceptible to moisture. Videotapes used to get jammed or damaged with repeated use. As compared to film, the videotape had a smaller life. All this is history now, as the spools and videotapes have been replaced by high quality DVDs and CDs.

As a PR practitioner, one should be acquainted with the equipment and studio to know about the options offered by, and capabilities of the medium. A couple of visits to a video studio are all that is required to gain a working knowledge of the medium.

A CD or DVD can be used for communicating with a variety of publics like employees, shareholders, specially invited audiences or the general public during exhibitions etc. One can make news clips, documentaries or films to reach out to specific publics as the occasion demands.

The release function of the video can be an excellent time for sending it to electronic media news channels. In order that these are accepted by the channel, Scot Cutlip et al recommend the following, quoting a New York based VNR maker:

"Don't mix natural sound with voice-over narration; don't overuse stills as a substitute for action video, don't place titles of "supers" on the video news segment. The information may be provided separately so that channels can insert titles in their regular fonts and styles. Don't use fancy special effects and repetitive dissolves not ordinarily used in news packages; don't put your reporter on the screen." [2]

d) Outdoor

Outdoor communication has done to the environment and landscaping what no other medium has. It is impossible to ignore the loud messages staring at one from large billboards, hoardings and posters as soon as one steps out of home. As the day graduates to dusk, some of the large cities turn into a virtual kaleidoscope of colour, fantasy and imagery with neon signs blinking at passers by. Environmentalists all over the world have been crying themselves hoarse about the damage to the landscape, but outdoor medium is here to stay. Generally used as a secondary or complementary medium, outdoor has a great potential as a reminder medium. Its strength lies in being a mass medium with 24-hours exposure. Outdoor creates a larger than life feeling with high penetration.

However, it has its drawbacks too. One has to restrict oneself to short, simple messages. High blowing winds cause damage to the boards, rain and storm can result in short circuiting of neon signs. It is not possible to gauge its impact per exposure opportunity on the audience. The biggest criticism, however, is that it obliterates the natural beauty of the environment.

As a PR medium, it rotates the audience to maximize audience delivery. It also promises graphic flexibility. Compared to other mass media, outdoor works out cheaper. In fact, if we see in the Indian context, wall writing or painting on the wall, which costs next to nothing, and pasting of paper posters can serve as an excellent publicity medium.[3]

There has not been much research to know how effective the medium is, yet appreciating the flexibility and cost-effectiveness of the medium, outdoor publicity is much in demand. The price of hoarding sites, which are let out generally on a monthly and yearly basis, varies, depending on location, flow of traffic, positioning vis-à-vis traffic signals, etc.

The government of India has a full-fledged Outdoor Publicity Department, which uses the medium for disseminating information about its policies, programmes and various social marketing issues.

Selective media

Selective media are those media that are decided upon keeping in view the identifiable target audience. The audience can be employees, shareholders, wholesalers, consumers, opinion-makers and also some sections of the public at large. Let us discuss some of these media. As the nomenclature signifies, in selective media, one has a fairly good idea about the target audience that are being reaced.

Channel for employee communication

This probably is the only branch of public relations in which the PR practitioner has complete control. Internal communication often requires designing and producing media material which may include a whole range of employee magazines, films, AVs, instruction materials, safety manuals, corporate identity manuals, bulletin boards etc.

What medium is best for which message and vice versa are eternal questions that haunt professional communicators.

Marshal McLuhan, the Canadian scholar and author of the oft-quoted book *The Medium is the message: An inventory of Effects* created quite a few ripples when he said that the form used for a communication is communication in itself. [4] To illustrate, in times of a national crisis, if a TV station announces that the Head of the Government will address the nation on TV at such and such time, the audience would assume that some important or critical message is forthcoming. In another case, if an employee receives a letter from the President of his company, even before opening the envelope, he would expect some important communication, because it has arrived through mail.

Many scholars, however, do not agree with McLuhan's theory. They argue that a medium may be a just a tip off about the quality and nature of the message but is not surely all the message. Access to a medium does not necessarily mean that the message has in reality reached the target audience. To illustrate, many subscribe to a newspaper but not all the people read all of what is published therein.

While creating channels of internal communication, a PR practitioner has to weigh the pros and cons of all the media individually and collectively keeping in view the demographic profile of the employees while not losing track of their psychographic profiles. According to expert view, the effectiveness of internal public relations largely depends on:

- Candid/Open management
- Recognition by management of the value and importance of employee communication.

Cutlip et al propose the following seven conditions for achieving an effective working relationship:

1. Confidence and trust between employer and employees.
2. Candid information flowing freely up, down, and sideways.
3. Satisfying status and participation for each person.
4. Continuity of work without strife.
5. Healthy surroundings.
6. Success for the enterprise.
7. Optimism about the future.[5]

The range of media for internal communications is immense but not all media are used by all the organizations. It depends on how much importance the organizations give to Public Relations, locations of the its projects and the interest the PR team takes in the activity.

Let us have a look at some of the popular media for internal communication.

Induction Literature/Information kiosks

For the new staff, the story of the organization, its core philosophy, values and ethos need to be communicated. How the organization works, its hierarchical structure, the decision-making process, its various product range, locations etc. can be explained in an introductory booklet. With technological advances, one may make an interactive CD-ROM/DVD or set up electronic information kiosk, which function at the touch of a finger.

House journal

Known by various nomenclatures as news bulletin, news magazine, employee newsletter, a house journal or magazine, as commonly referred to, is a means of reaching a particular set of publics with certain written material at a particular periodicity.

There are no hard and fast rules as to what it should contain. In fact, the content depends on the overall environment of the organization. The house journal of an open company will have a two-way flow of communication between management and employees, while a look at the house journal of a closed company will reflect one-way communication. In other words, it would be top-down flow of communication from management to employees.

A PR practitioner should be careful to follow a conscious policy and formulate objectives when planning to publish a house journal. The practitioner must bear in mind that communication is a means and not an end. A house journal, if carefully produced, serves as an important link between the management and its various employees.

A house journal can cover topics in a number of areas. The mailing list may encompass employees, distributors, agents, opinion-makers and other external publics. Larger companies can have separate journals for internal and external publics. The bottom line for a house journal is that it must satisfy the needs and interests of its readers. A house journal, in fact, is about people, their interests, their hopes, and their aspirations. It must satisfy their inquisitive minds. It should attempt to answer all by creating a healthy forum for expression of thought and vision of the management and employees. Human interest should be the governing principle for stories. Too many uninteresting figures and technical details are unlikely to interest readers.

The PR person is ideally the editor of the house journal. For publishing a house journal, let us consider the following steps:

- **Planning:** Develop a concept that serves the company best. The decision about size, format and periodicity may be taken after a brainstorming session with the team and the management. The popular formats are tabloid and magazine. While getting the management's approval, a format presentation should ideally include suggested titles, masthead design, some page dummies, suggested quality of paper and an indication of the expenditure envisaged.

- **Organizing:** Organizing is all about putting together a network. Once the management's approval has been taken, the PR practitioner must set about organizing staff to get going with the job. The shorter the frequency, the greater the need for staff. Depending on the size of the PR department at the corporate office and availability of PR staff at projects, proper networking for news gathering should be made. In the absence of regular staff, it is advisable to develop a band of "freelance writers" from within the organization. It is a great feeling to see one's name in print. The employees will like the idea. Discretion, however, should be used in selecting the right people for the job. The immediate step is to work out a strict schedule for collection, writing of stories, production and printing.
- **Publishing:** A professional PR practitioner plans several issues ahead in addition to the one being worked on. As an editor, the PR practitioner must inculcate the habit of reaching out to people and places. It is not possible to write interesting editorials, cover stories and human interest write-ups while sitting glued to the corporate seat. Every good house journal should have a definite "personality" and that is the responsibility of the editor. In order to bring out the publication on time, one should involve as few management hierarchies as possible for the clearance of text/copy.
- **Distribution:** A journal loses its value if it does not reach the targeted public on time. The quickest and most economical means possible must be selected to reach out to the readers. Some organizations distribute the journal at the place of work, while others mail it to employees' homes. The obvious advantage of the latter means is that the potential reader is relaxed at home and can read the journal leisurely. Also, family members can have access to the publication.

A PR practitioner must appreciate the importance of feedback. In order to make the publication popular, it is necessary to make it reader oriented. Organized feedback through a questionnaire survey could be undertaken to examine the extent to which employees are satisfied with the publication. It needs to be remembered that the shorter the questionnaire, the better would be the chances of receiving the response. In fact, a one-page questionnaire should suffice.

Closed-circuit television

Closed-circuit or in-house TV is a good medium of linking up a scattered audience. Cable TV has further cemented the bond of fellow feeling in corporate townships. The medium is cost-effective, if there is personal involvement. Looking at the multi-dimensional impact of the audio-visual medium with a captive audience, it can work wonders, if ingenuity is used. Visuals within an organization can be used to train, inform, motivate, and entertain.

Some of the leading organizations—to name a few, National Thermal Power Corporation, Steel Authority of India, Tobacco Company, have been using video magazines for employee communication. The contents include management's point of view on various issues; company performance, welfare measures, human-interest stories, community PR glimpses, etc. However, video magazines have not replaced printed house journals. They complement each other.

Idea Boxes

Idea Boxes are placed at vantage points for employees to place their ideas in for improving systems, working, or even complaints. When sifted and analysed closely, the medium helps in tracking employee perceptions on various issues, areas of their concerns and sharing of innovations etc.

Shop-floor discussions

Interpersonal communication, also referred to as the eyeball to eyeball communication probably is the best form of communication but not always feasible. However, at shop floors it can easily be organized to facilitate staff to speak their mind to higher echelons in hierarchy. During such discussions it is easy to gather the feedback to various points of views of both the management and employees.

Bulletin boards

A bulletin board in an organizational context can be described as a stage for a continuous flow of news and messages concerning employees. They can be seen at shop floors of organizations in various formats and sizes. Sometimes they are vertical, at other times horizontal or square. In some organizations they are drab-looking plain boards, while in others they are fancy, of cork surface with a good teak, walnut or stainless steel frame. Papers are stuck on to the board with pins; if it is metallic, then with little magnets. The messages stuck on the boards have more or less a fixed life. Professional PR departments take pains in designing and preparing an interesting layout for their bulletin board.

Before we discuss what it contains, let us analyze the objectives of bulletin boards. Every office has a system of interacting with its employees on official matters. Circulars and memos are an essential part of the life of an average employee. Most of the circulars and memos that have relevance for a large number of employees are on issues concerning job, welfare activities, change in policies, etc. These have also to be displayed on notice boards besides being circulated individually, if required. Apart from personnel news, bulletin boards have become a sought after medium by production heads/PR practitioners motivating employees to reach production targets. Giving shift wise production details on the bulletin boards also encourages competition among different shifts.

Bulletin boards at times also serve as an unofficial grapevine and centre for corporate intelligence/observation. While going in or coming out of the shop floor, employees tend to gather around the bulletin boards to read the latest information. While being there, they also exchange views on a number of critical issues with their peer group and it is here that the group stimuli are at their peak. A lot of important information can be collected from these places for a healthy employer-employee relationship, especially in times of industrial unrest or other volatile situations.

Visits by management

The companies which have their projects/factories at many locations, must ensure that management from the headquarters visit various units, speak to employees so that they don't have the feeling of management remoteness. Similarly, it should also be ensured that a cross section of employees from units also visits headquarters to see the functioning to avoid any gaps in communication.

Clubs and Societies

In order to encourage fraternity that cut across official hierarchies, it is important that employees socialize and share common interests through sports clubs, literary societies etc. This helps build personal rapport and respect among managers and workers for each other as human beings.

Media for External Communication

Annual reports

Not long ago, annual reports were drab-looking journals without much thought given to their presentation. Not any more. Annual reports have come to be recognized as an important PR tool for corporate communication. With more and more organizations going public, you need a large quantity of annual reports to be sent to shareholders. Although the PR department of a company does not have a direct responsibility of preparing the balance-sheet and statements of accounts, it does advise the management on the overall approach of the Report, the theme of the Chairman's statement and on the format and presentation of the Report.

Apart from registered shareholders, there are other segments of the financial public whose interest are required to be addressed while providing information through the Annual Report, such as:

a) The investing community in general, the potential shareholders, who are on the lookout for investment opportunities in a suitable company.
b) The banks, financial institutions etc.
c) The financial press.
d) The business community in general.

As a PR practitioner, you must invite a professional advertising/designing agency to handle the assignment. The profile of the company during the year under review can be befittingly projected in the Director's report which can have diagrams, pie charts, and pictures of developmental activities of the company.

Care should be taken to choose a printer who has the expertise in printing annual reports. As bringing out annual reports is a statutory requirement and it should be published before the annual general meeting, a strict time schedule must be worked out with the printer. In fact most of the annual reports have to come out at the same time, hence one must select a printer who has the capacity to undertake and deliver the job on time. One should plan to the minutest detail. As the annual report contains the balance sheet, be careful about proofreading. It is advisable to get the final proofs cleared from the Company secretariat department, which has prepared the manuscript and the statement of accounts. Bloomers are visible only when finally printed. So let the concerned executives carefully go through the printed copy before allowing it to be distributed.

Printed literature

It is rare that an organization, whether in the product or the service line, does not need publicity literature to promote its products and activities. In fact, printed literature can be segmented into various classifications such as brochures, leaflets, booklets, direct mail etc. All have the same objective, that is, to inform or persuade the audience about an idea or a service. Let us examine some of these.

Brochure

A brochure is a multi-panel publication that conveys information usually on a single subject. A brochure is also called a pamphlet, a flyer or a folder. A booklet serves much the same purpose as a brochure except that it has more pages that may be stapled together rather than folded.

Organizations need brochures and booklets for a variety of reasons—to explain a new programme, a process, a product, a new building or plant, or a laboratory, to ask for donations, or to sell a product by describing its virtues. Such publications are reasonably inexpensive, relatively fast to produce, and are attractive to read, if prepared carefully.

Although as a PR practitioner you will have the services of a professional designer or a professional agency to go about the job, it is important to know the basics in order to be able to guide the production.

The first step is to identify the aim of the brochure. In other words, what problem it is meant to solve, and what information it is supposed to disseminate to the target audience.

Copy or the text is the most important part of the brochure. It is not possible to write long copy because of the size of the brochure. Identify the person who will write the copy. The person can be from within the organization or from an advertising agency/PR firm. The copy writer must be given the right brief to be able to develop the text. Pictures, graphs must also be selected carefully to go with the copy.

A brochure has an overall size with fold configuration like four panel, six panel, eight panel and so on. In deciding on the number of folds, remember that the ease of reader's comprehension is important. Brochures need to be folded in such a manner that they can be easily opened and read from one panel to another.

Other Publicity and Promotional Literature

In the face of tough competition in the marketplace, where similar products vie with each other, it is necessary to promote products and services continuously. Consumer durables and capital goods need a large amount of support literature in contrast with small items like chocolates, candy bars or ice-creams. With modern retailing techniques, products have to really sell themselves. This has led to aggressive publicity at the point of purchase or retail outlets. As a PR person in charge of publicity, you will have to decide on the kind of promotional activities including literature. Some of the options are:

- Stickers, posters, labels to serve as reminder.
- Racks or bins for display of products.
- Identification on the pack and/or elsewhere of current sales promotional activity.
- Provision of any necessary leaflets, catalogues etc. to assist the customer's decision to buy.

Direct mail

Direct mail in some circumstances is the most powerful and certainly the most cost-effective method of publicity. It uses the postal service to deliver messages to a selected target audience. In fact, it is also called selective marketing technique.

The receiver of the direct mail literature is generally invited to send for further information and/or to request for some kind of home visit for the company to provide a demonstration or to furnish further details of the product being offered. Hotel chains, investment agents, etc., use it as a means of keeping in touch with their regular clients.

Direct mail is both a selective and a flexible medium, which makes it cost-effective. It is selective because it is addressed to those and only those people whom an organization wants to reach. It is flexible because the number of letters you mail can be increased or reduced according to the capacity of the sales force to cope with enquiries. Direct mail can be a friendly and personal medium of reaching out to a specific target audience.

Direct mail has its limitations too. If it is to be effective, one has to carefully make a list of the target audience. Compiling a good list usually entails a great deal of research and keeping it up to date, calls for concerted effort.

Whatever is sent in direct mail—a brochure, or a small sample of the product—should be accompanied by a letter addressed to the recipient by his/her name, outlining the benefits likely to be of interest specifically to that reader. The material has to be designed and copy written in such a manner as to create an instant rapport with the recipient.

Exhibitions

Exhibitions cover a very diverse series of events, ranging from major international trade fairs to small local activities organized for a neighbourhood community. An exhibition can be general in nature or specific. You must be aware of the India

International Trade Fair, which is organized every year by the Trade Fair Authority of India (TFAI) at Pragati Maidan in New Delhi. The fair begins on November 14 every year for a period of two weeks. Among the participants are various Indian states, some foreign countries, and public and private sector companies. On display are products and activities through various communication media. Trade talks are also held between countries and different companies. The TFAI also organizes exhibitions and fairs on specific themes from time to time, like engineering goods fair, electronics exhibition, sports goods fair, textile fair and automobile fair to name a few.

The TATA group introduced its Nano model in 2008 at one such fair. So much was the craze among the general public to see the Nano, that there was a traffic jam for hours together, on all major roads in Delhi.

If handled properly, exhibitions can be a very powerful medium of communication. The medium helps publicize the image of a country, a state or a company to an interested captive audience. It becomes a meeting place for existing customers and potential customers and can identify new sales areas/outlets. New products can be introduced and the feedback of the customer can be had instantly. It also helps assess the performance of the competitors in terms of products, services and presentation.

Exhibitions and fairs can also help in booking orders.

In fact, products can be exhibited and demonstrated in a relaxed atmosphere. The prospective customers are generally in a "buying mood".

The main difficulties with exhibitions, however, are to establish clearly:
a) How many people of the "right" type visited the exhibition;
b) How many visited and what was the effect of their visit;
c) Was it worth the cost?

Exhibitions are an expensive medium. The costs include expenditure towards space, designing, construction of stall, delivery, withdrawal of exhibits and hospitality etc. Hence, it becomes necessary to plan it well to obtain substantial returns in terms of exposure.

Open days

An "Open day" is a great PR tool to build rapport with the community/neighbourhood where the plant is located. It is also a traditional way of building pride and morale among employees and their families. The PR department invariably organizes visits of employees' families and of the community at large to the plant to see the product manufacturing and other facets of the plant on a few days in a year which are referred to as "open days". Such visits are accompanied by hospitality by the plant owners.

It is important, however, to make suitable arrangements to receive visitors. This entails not only provision of trained guides but also hospitality etc.

It is usual in many industry-conducted tours to provide refreshments to visitors at the end of the tour. If however, the factory is situated out of town, and it has taken long for the visitors to reach there, it is advisable to offer refreshments on arrival. Factories producing eatables generally not only offer the visitors their items in refreshments but may also present gift packs, for example, a chocolate, a biscuit or a stationery producing factory can present its products which surely will be appreciated by the visitors and help in creating goodwill.

The Delhi Milk Scheme, when it was set up, organized open houses for school children. The children were offered flavoured milk on their visit. Similarly, Coca Cola organized such visits many years ago. The visitors besides being served with its various aerated drinks, were also given mementoes of bottle openers and trays with the "Coca Cola" logo imprinted on them for remembrance.

In fact, open houses and tours of the plant should be geared to a wide range of audiences, from plant neighbours, elected representatives to parliament and legislative assemblies.

Special events

Special events are the most visible component of a community relations programme. The events however must be well chosen. The special events should reinforce key messages that a company is communicating to its target audience.

Special events can range from participating in a community related activity to sponsoring a national or international event. The ITC, one of the leading corporate sector organizations in India, organized yearly music concerts as "ITC Sangeet Sammelan" for quite some time. Besides providing a forum for upcoming artistes, it honoured veterans and famous artistes. Free entry passes were distributed to the community through their outlets. The programmes became so popular that music lovers look forward to such events.

In planning special events, large or small, it is important to have a management structure that is ultimately responsible for the event, and make timely decisions. The event itself needs publicity for better response from the target audience.

Organizing a special event can be cumbersome and time consuming. In order to make it a success, the event has to be planned to the minutest detail. A checklist would include the following:

- Deciding on the objective
- Date, time, venue
- List of the celebrities and the guest of honour if one is to be invited
- List of invitees including the media
- Programme details
- Organizers/volunteers with specific and clear cut duties
- Background material, press kit
- Transportation
- Hospitality
- VIP security, if required
- Inform the local administration, police, and ambulance for any emergency
- Work out entry, and exit routes, parking etc.
- Take stock of the event after it is over.

Media Characteristics

Each medium is endowed with unique capabilities and distinctive characteristics in terms of technical, physical and aspirational values. Each medium has varying reach, accessibility and credibility with people at large. A medium does not ensure equal reach among its routine target audience, as the interest levels, availability of time, the preoccupation of the target audience at various parts of the day and environmental factors affect media usage. To illustrate, a person may be an avid watcher of television serials, but has some interest in sports. It is quite likely that when his favourite team is playing, he may watch a sports channel against his general habit of watching serials. A war may drastically change the television watching habits of an average person, who may stay glued to news channels against his general habit of watching news only once or twice a day. Even within the same genre, the choice of channel may vary at such times. For example, after the 9/11 attack in the USA, a study conducted in India reflected a preference for CNN among those viewers who normally watched Indian news channels.[6] The reason obviously was that CNN is an American Channel and the tragedy occurred in the USA, so the audience presumably thought what the channel provided was swift and most authentic.

In short, all media work successfully at some point of time for various brands. According to Marshall MacLuhan space and time are not the most useful dimensions for classifying media. He categorized media as 'Hot' and 'Cool'. Radio and newspapers according to his classification were 'hot' media which he believed were active, aggressive, crammed with information. A 'cool' medium like television according to MacLuhan must be activated and participated in by the viewer to "suck out information and meaning." [7]

The real difference between print and electronic media according to Bogart starts at the point where the message is physically presented to readers or viewers and where the attrition of interest sets in. A medium that "flows in time begins with a higher probability of dominating the senses on behalf of a given measure than does a static medium in which the printed word is scanned and assimilated selectively." [8]

In the following tables an effort has been made to provide the relative strengths and weaknesses of each medium keeping in view its inherent characteristics. When one analyses, one may find the strength of one medium may be other medium's weakness. To illustrate, newspapers have a better shelf life and can be read at leisure and referred to when required, hence its strength. This becomes a "weakness" for television and radio as once you miss a programme or even a part of it, you can't rewind or refer back. To stretch the argument further, news coming via newspapers is often stale, if the television and radio covered the story in its evening bulletin.

Media are very significant vehicles for PR departments to spread their message to a wide audience. Therefore, a lot of consideration about the relative strengths and weaknesses of various media, their reach, what kind of audience access, which kind of media, what kinds of brands were bought by what kind of media users, their demographic segments; frequency of readership; extent of duplication between publications; exposure of cinema, radio, television and the extent of duplication need to be understood by the PR practitioner when deciding on media options.[9]

Print Media

Press

Strengths	Weaknesses
Message received at home in a relaxed atmosphere.	Suffers from literacy barrier.
The readers look forward to receiving their newspaper.	Low shelf life as newspapers become stale in a day.
The urge to seek news gives the newspaper a better position to be trusted.	Lacks drama and emotion.
Reading a newspaper becomes a matter of habit, hence one can achieve regular attention value.	Demonstration of product features not effective.
Can cope with detailed coverage.	Overtaken by television in speed.
Written word has greater credibility.	Lacks empathetic readership.
Messages carry urgency	'Bad' news is often considered 'good' news.
Can be read at leisure.	What is of reader's interest is decided by the newspapers.
High on national coverage.	Average time devoted to newspaper reading is very low, hence developmental news does not stand much chance of being seen carefully.

Local/ regional newspapers

Strengths	Weaknesses
Strong reader loyalty.	Small circulation.
Local coverage.	Potential to be biased.
Regional flexibility.	Generally poor readership data.

Magazines

Strengths	Weaknesses
• Selective readership.	• High production cost.
• High shelf value.	• Long copy and cancellation dates.
• Create a bond and empathy with the readers.	• Expensive advertising medium.
• High on style, design and colour.	• High printing costs.

Television

Strengths	Weaknesses
• Reaches a wide audience.	• Expensive for time and production.
• Sight, sound and colour creates dramatic possibilities.	• Bad quality, transmission problem and poor anchors may put the viewers off.
• Larger than life image.	• Too much viewing bad for the eyes.
• Achieves viewers' empathy.	• Tends to make people "home birds" and unsocial.
• High on credibility.	• Too much viewing can have an adverse effect on impressionable minds.
• Wide choice of channels without incurring extra cost.	• Depiction of too much sex and violence can have an adverse impact on young audience.
• A family medium.	• Transient messages.

Radio

Strengths	Weaknesses
• Wide coverage.	• Suffers from apathetic listeners.
• High Opportunity to Listen (OTL) among listeners.	• Audience intentionally use it as "audio wallpaper".
• Advertising inexpensive as compared with TV and press.	• TV preferred over radio, if there is a choice.
• Long broadcasting hours.	• Speed of broadcast (short lead time).
• High impact and immediacy.	• Not a very interactive medium.
• If a transistor is used it becomes a mobile medium.	• Not very innovative.

Cinema

Strengths	Weaknesses
• Impact of big screen with sound, movement and colour.	• TV has eroded the cinema audience base.
• Attracts young crowd.	• Slow build up of audience.
• Theater viewing is a socializing event.	• Attendance is low and infrequent.
• Selective local advertising coverage possible which can gain immediate impact.	• Commercials shown either at the beginning or during the interval, when high attendance is not ensured.

Outdoor (posters, billboards/hoarding)

Strengths	Weaknesses
• High coverage and OTS.	• High printing cost of posters unless used on large scale.
• Large-sized billboards give larger than life image.	• Suffers poor audience research.
• Sites can be booked very flexibly.	• Environmentalists' crusade as they spoil the landscape.
• Can create drama with colours and size.	• High blowing winds often damage the boards and lead to accidents.
• Twenty-four hour projection.	• Short-circuiting possible in monsoons.
• Good reminder medium.	• Only small messages possible.
• A community medium.	• They distract attention of drivers.[10]

New Media; Internet

Strengths	Weaknesses
• Global networking.	• Low access.
• Seamless coverage.	• Information overload.
• No hierarchical setup for access of information.	• Banner ad recall not very high.
• High interactivity.	• Low on research hence not a favourite medium with media planners.
• By and large a free-to-access medium.	• Message spill over to unrequired territories.
• Instant connectivity.	• Not a medium to suit all demographic profiles.
• A storehouse of knowledge.	• Requires time commitment.
• Online marketing.	

Mobile phones and SMS

Strengths	Weaknesses
• A communication revolution.	• Nuisance value.
• Reach not dependent on location.	• Intrusion in privacy.
• Reaching the right target audience (TA).	• A possible health hazard.
• Permission marketing possible.	• Literacy barrier.
• Emotional connotation.	
• An all pervasive medium.	

Employee communication media

(House magazines, video magazines, bulletin boards et al)

Strengths	Weaknesses
• High planning.	• Controlled media.
• Pre-test possible.	• Management interference on content.
• Reaching the right TA.	• Enjoys less credibility.
• Emotional connect–family feeling	• Requires balance in coverage to avoid annoying any section of employees whose views are not included, especially unions.
• Helps build personal connect.	• Requires sensitive handling in times of crises.
• Motivates employees.	• Receivers often take such media for granted as often it is provided *gratis*.
• Participative.	• Generally wanting in keeping within the time schedules.
• Feedback possible.	• Often expensive.

While taking the decision on the choice of media, PR will have to consider the following:
a) Most effective media
b) Most efficient media
c) Most credible media

Some organizations have full-fledged PR departments to handle internal communication; others depend on outside expertise in designing and producing house journals, video magazines and bulletin boards for employee communication. As mass media, especially when paid time and space is required, professional agencies are commissioned to handle the communication.

Media Relations

Media relations form the most basic activity of public relations. Media relations, in fact, take a good part of the practitioner's working day and are exacting in demand. Some of the tools for maintaining effective media relations are organizing press conferences, holding press briefings and arranging press visits or facility tours for media men. Let us discuss these one by one.

Press conference

As a PR practitioner, you will be solely responsible for organizing press conferences from time to time. A press conference is generally used as an occasion for the release of news simultaneously to all media, provided the subject is newsworthy.

When should a press conference be organized? The answer is—not very frequently. Do not fall for the temptation of calling a press conference, if the subject does not demand a discussion between your organization's spokesperson and the media. In such a case, a press release will do the job. If however, your organization has to announce a major policy, speak about a labour-management rift, or launch a product that requires demonstration—things that would suggest the need for a face-to-face dialogue and not a one-side statement—then call a press conference.

Consider the following carefully before holding a press conference:

- A decision about the spokesperson who will address the press conference. Remember, the PR person himself should never address a press conference. It should ideally be the head of the organization or department.
- Prepare a press kit, which would ideally contain a press backgrounder, a news release or releases, pictures, literature about the organization, a writing pad and a pen or pencil.
- Make the list of invitees from the media carefully. The list should comprise those who cover your organization.
- Decide a venue, which is suitable for the media persons to reach.
- Make arrangements for the transport of media persons from a convenient place to the venue and for the return journey.
- Decide on the timing. It should neither be too early nor too late in the day. The conference should end at such a time that the media persons are able to get back to their place of work to file the story on time.

Arrange hospitality

A PR person, in effect is the MC (Master of Ceremonies) in a press conference. He is in complete control of the press conference from beginning to end. After the chief spokesperson and the media persons have taken their seats, introduce yourself and then introduce the spokesperson who will be addressing the conference. After a brief address by the spokesperson on the subject matter, the podium is thrown open to the media persons to ask questions.

Set a time frame for the press conference to continue. Depending on the occasion, the ideal duration should be between 45 minutes and one hour. When the time is nearing completion, you can announce that there is time for, say, two questions or so.

Normally, after setting the conference in motion, take a seat and do not intervene, but at times you may have to interject to rescue the spokesperson who may have been pushed into a corner by a reporter's question.

Establish a personal rapport with mediapersons. This cannot be achieved in a day but requires concerted efforts over a period of time. Press conferences should not be the only occasion you meet them. It serves your cause better if you have a friendly press.

Press briefings

Press briefings are different from press conferences in that they are informal and do not require elaborate arrangements. Press briefings can be both proactive and reactive. By proactive, it is meant that certain clarifications or points are required to be given after a crisis situation. In this case, some media persons are invited for press briefings.

In case of critical issues, besides an informal briefing by the spokesperson, a written statement is also handed over to avoid misquotation.

In case of reactive press briefings, a pressman seeks an audience with the chief spokesperson for seeking certain clarifications or to find out his point of view before filing the story. Similarly the spokesperson may have been misquoted, and he invites media persons for clarification.

Press tours/facility visits

In press tours or facility visits, much of the exercise is similar to organizing a press conference. More elaborate arrangements are however required to be made as it may involve transporting the press party a long distance. The occasion could be a landmark achieved, or the commissioning of a project, or a crisis situation, like an accident. Both occasions need careful planning and organization of the visit.

While inviting a reporter to join your press tour, it is always advisable to write to the editor or chief of the bureau of different newspapers. In normal circumstances, sufficient notice must be given, because the concerned reporter may have to be spared for a number of days from the place of work.

The PR person needs to consider the following carefully before organizing a press trip:

- List of media men
- Suitable travel arrangements
- Accommodation at site
- Briefing press party at site
- Background information
- Facilitating information flow from media persons to their respective offices
- Hospitality

It is necessary that a responsible representative of the organization accompanies the press party and personally supervises travel/hospitality arrangements.

Keep the programme as compressed as possible. Don't leave much free time by engaging the party in various activities. When a press party visits a project, it is not uncommon for disgruntled elements within the company to pass on information, which may or may not be true. Guard against that. Similarly, it is not uncommon for some media people to look for the "other side of the story" from unauthorized sources. It may not always be possible to stop that, but one can try to ensure that the purpose for which the press trip was organized is achieved.

Except when the press has gone there to cover a crisis situation, the filing of the story has to be instant, set an embargo after discussing with the members of the party about the day the story would appear. Just a day or two in advance, send a soft reminder to all, so that the story appears on the same day. If there is a communication gap, resulting in a newspaper carrying the story before the embargo date, then the story gets "killed" by others as it would lose the value. The very purpose of the press visit would be defeated, besides losing on the purpose and resources.

CASE STUDY

A crisis time study of DMRC

The impact of running the organization efficiently and partnering with media in the saga of development

Delhi Metro is one government organization that has been able to project itself positively among various stakeholders. The organization however has worked very hard in cultivating a niche for itself. Communication has been used as a strategic tool in achieving great brand equity. This was more than evident, when in an accident two people were killed and some 10 injured due to a possible mechanical failure at one of the sites in Delhi in October 2008. Delhi Metro's PR department was on an overdrive to interface with various stakeholders, including media about what had happened, what was the action plan etc. The organization did not get any negative report in any media. It was a factual reporting without any exaggerations or speculation or raising doubts on the intent of the organization.

Sample the following two dispatches in one mainstream newspapers and a wire agency:

"Two dead, 30 injured after Delhi Metro flyover collapses"
October 19, 2008

New Delhi: At least two people were killed and 30 injured when part of an under-construction flyover of the Delhi Metro collapsed here Sunday morning, officials said.

The accident—for the first time in the decade-old history of Delhi Metro—occurred at around 7 a.m. in Laxmi Nagar locality of East Delhi when a launcher machine joining prefabricated, heavy concrete structures between two pillars lost control, leading to a part of the flyover coming down, a Delhi Metro Rail Corporation (DMRC) official said.

A Blue line bus plying on route number 39, a crane of the construction company, one truck and a few cars were trapped under the debris of the flyover.

"There were about 15 people inside the bus when the crane and construction materials came crashing on the bus. The front portion of the bus was trapped due to which the driver was killed," Dipak, the helper of the Blueline bus, told IANS.

Rescue operations are on and all the injured have been shifted to hospitals.

"This has happened for the first time in the decade-old history of Delhi Metro. We are asking AFCONS (the private construction company in-charge of the segment) about the technical failure," said Vijay Anand, Director, Delhi Metro.

"We have ordered a high level enquiry into the incident," Anand told reporters.

Delhi Finance Minister A.K. Walia, who reached the accident site, said: "Eight people were rushed to my nursing home (close to the accident site) a little after 7 a.m. At least three people were later referred to bigger hospitals."

Walia said the Delhi Metro has to furnish a detailed report about the mishap and his government would take further action.

Delhi Metro, the modern mass transport system in the capital, ferries over 7,00,000 passengers daily over a network of 65 km. Work is on to construct another 125 km of metro network before the 2010 Commonwealth Games.[11]

"Two killed as Delhi Metro flyover collapses"
19 Oct 2008, 1400 hrs IST, TIMES NEWS NETWORK & AGENCIES

The driver of a Blueline bus and a labourer died and 10 people were injured when a girder launcher and a part of the under-construction overhead Metro line between Lakshmi Nagar and Nirman Bhavan in East Delhi collapsed and fell on passing vehicles on Vikas Marg at 7.05am on Sunday. The accident occurred when workers were lifting a 400-tonne concrete span of the bridge with the help of a crane. According to eyewitnesses, the launcher, which was launched on top of the newly constructed girder, collapsed along with a 34-metre-long span comprising 10 segments of the bridge on top of the Blueline, two cars and two trailers. Delhi Metro Rail Corporation has ordered an inquiry into the incident and has asked IIT-Delhi to depute a structural engineer who would conduct the probe along with the DMRC design chief and a representative of the foreign consultancy working on the project along with DMRC.

The dead are 28-year-old Surender Kumar, who was driving the Blueline and 25-year-old labourer Chhotte Lal. The injured have been taken to Lok Nayak Hospital, Hedgewar Hospital and the MCD Hospital in Karkardooma.

Of the injured two are said to be in a critical condition, one person had to undergo amputation of both legs and another person underwent an amputation of one leg. "It is a big shock to us. We are taking it seriously and we are for an independent high-level inquiry," DMRC spokesman Anuj Dayal said. Delhi Metro has also announced Rs. 5 lakh compensation for the family of Surender Kumar who lost his life in the incident while the injured will be given Rs. 50,000 besides all help in medical treatment.

Dayal said the Delhi Metro has seized the records of AFCONS, the company which is undertaking the construction, to ascertain the cause of the accident. "Prima facie, it appears that some mechanical items of the launcher had given up. We will also investigate about the safety inspection of the launchers done by the company," he said.

Delhi Police spokesman Rajan Bhagat said 10 people were injured in the accident.[12]

Summary

In this chapter we defined various tools or channels of PR communication and their management from the PR perspective.

There are various media available to a PR practitioner to reach out to a disparate set of publics an organization has to deal with from time to time. Broadly, the publics of a company comprise the employees, the shareholders, the dealers, the stockists, the customers, the government, the media, the Special Interest Groups and the public at large. For reaching out to the public, one needs to use mass media like TV, radio and films. Through the medium of house journals, we can reach both internal and external publics. In order to promote the products or the services of a company, various types of promotional literature like brochure, point of purchase material and direct mail can be made use of. Through exhibitions, trade fairs, special events and open houses, one can attract people to appreciate an organization's activities. The products can be demonstrated, and the activities can be shown through working models to attract attention. Media relations form an important part of PR activities. In fact, it is through the media that public relations can reach out to a large audience without spending much.

Critical thinking exercise

Follow news about an organization in a critical time and analyze at least four newspapers and four news channels to understand the stand/bias of various media against or in favour of that organization. Discuss within your peer group to analyse the reasons for particular media coverage.

Questions

Q.1 What in your view are the various PR communication tasks in an organization? Elaborate.

Q.2 Discuss various media to reach out to the internal publics and the reasons behind using such media.

Q.3 Choose any three media to reach out to the external target audience and discuss their relative strengths and weaknesses.

Endnotes

[1] Abhilaksh Rekhi, "The National Rural Employment Guarantee Act (NREGA): Gram Panchayats and Community Radio", *Communicator*, vol. Xxxx, no. 2 July-December 2005, pp. 39-43.

[2] Scot M. Cutlip, Allen H. Center and Glen M. Broom, *Effective Public Relations*, 7th ed. 1994 (Prentice-Hall: NJ) p. 297.

[3] Jaishri Jethwaney and Shruti Jain, *Advertising Management*, 2006 (OUP: New Delhi)

[4] Marshal McLuhan and Quentin Fiore, coordinated by Jerme Agel, "Medium is the Message", 2000 (Random House: Ginko Press)

[5] Scot M. Cutlip, Allen H. Center and Glen M. Broom, *Effective Public Relations*, 7th ed. 1994 (Prentice-Hall: NJ) p. 261.

[6] Jaishri Jethwaney "Terrorist attack in the US-an IIMC media study 2001", *Communicator*, Vol. No. January-June 2003. (*Communicator* is a journal of the Indian Institute of Mass Communication, New Delhi, India)

[7] As quoted by Leo Bogart in *Strategy in Advertising*, Second ed. (Illinois: NTC Business Books, 1986), pp 121-150.

[8] Ibid. 4 above.

[9] Jaishri Jethwaney and Shruti Jain, *Advertising Management*, 2006 (OUP: ND), pp.291

[10] The Supreme Court ordered the removal of roadside hoardings in Delhi in its ruling of November 97. The Municipal Corporation of Delhi issued a notice of 48 hours to advertisers on 24 November to remove unauthorized hoardings or face seizure. Supreme Court's order came in the wake of increasing instances of road accidents, specifically after one of the worst bus accidents in which 28 school children died when the driver, driving rashly plunged the bus into the river Yamuna on 17 November, 1797. Quoting an advertiser, the *Times of India* wrote, "Accidents take place because drivers drive rashly and not because they get distracted by hoardings", *Times of India*, New Delhi, 23 November 1997, p. 1. Also see *Express Newsline* of *Indian Express*, 24 November1997.

[11] www.samachaar.in

[12] 19 Oct 2008, 1400 hrs IST, TIMES NEWS NETWORK & AGENCIES

7 Troika of Communication—Message, Medium and Audience

> **Chapter objectives**
> - Attributes of media, message and audience
> - The interdependence of the above three
> - The use of strategy in synergizing the three to get the desired response

Effective Public Relations is dependent on three elements, viz., Message, Media and Audience. The three elements, in fact, form the trinity and part of the overall communication strategy, which in turn is linked specifically to campaign objectives. The campaign manager needs to address the following:

- *Who will change* (specific category of target audience)?

  What are going to be the specific themes and appeals to get the target audience to yield (persuasive propositions)? and
- *Where to advertise to reach out to the target audience* (media channels)?

In the following paragraphs we will discuss the elements in greater detail.

The Message

Effective communication depends a great deal on a well thought out purpose of message followed by clarity of words. It is important that the words are creatively used to attract attention and build the necessary emotional crescendo.

A message can be worked out under various situations and circumstances. It can be deliberate, planned, proactive, involuntary, spontaneous or reactive. A message might have been sent quickly to pre-empt a possible action or in response to another message. A message has at its inception, reasons and emotions and individual or group perceptions. It could be clear or vague, relevant or out of context. It may be deliberately designed to educate or confuse, soothe frayed tempers or enrage an audience. The tone of the message is as important as the factual content. If it is said orally, it is important to know who says and how he says it. A body gesture and gesticulation may send signals, which may be unintended. The recipients of the message may read "between the lines" or "take it with a pinch of salt".

The context in which a message is received, contemplated and interpreted may not match the intention of the sender. A message that is appropriate at the time it is sent may not remain appropriate when it arrives. In an emotionally surcharged atmosphere, the voice of reason may not be listened to. It may rather ignite passions.

Coding of messages is an integral part of a message. It has to be acceptable to the channel concerned, e.g., sound waves, electronic signals or the print medium. The code must match the needs and characteristics of the target group and be easy to understand and assimilate. To illustrate, news about a mishap or accident in a factory can be sent through a press release for mass communication, but to inform the employees through the written word will be seen as a cold and callous act. They must be informed interpersonally and fast.

The Satyam Computers imbroglio in January 2009 sent shock waves within and outside the country. The government regulator talked tough at the right time and the concerned minister appeared on various news channels to assure stakeholders of appropriate action without losing time. Chairman HDFC Bank, Deepak Parekh commenting on the act said, "Unprecedented, timely, done in quick time. This had to be done before clients turn away and investors dump the stock. New directors should be announced asap".[1]

The government acted quickly under speculation that the CEO Mr. R Raju may have fled the country. The media commented that by booking the former chairman of Satyam and his brother for non-bailable offences under the Indian Penal Code, which could put them behind bars for several years, and by superceding the board, the government sought to ensure that papers were not tampered with while restoring investor confidence and protecting the interests of over 50,000 employees of the beleaguered IT firm.[2]

Talking tough with violators at a time of grievous economic recession sends the right signals to the market. Infosys CEO Gopalakrishnan commented, "It's a good sign that if corporate governance breaks down, the government will step in. This act will restore confidence among investors, customers and employees".[3]

As if on cue, the realty sector also felt the tremors as analysts and consultancy firms had been hinting at some of the accounting practices of the major realty sector organizations that could mislead investors. As per media reports, senior board members of a number of real estate companies quit prompting speculation that suspect accounting policies in the sector could have triggered the exits.

In this case, those concerned were not communicated with specifically, but the stimuli provided by the environment resulted in the action.

Designing messages

When we talk of designing messages in PR, it is not just writing good language or coining catchy slogans. "The enunciation of ideas, the propounding of truth, the statement of fact, the expression of emotion are not communication", points out S.Watson Dunn, "there must be perception as well. Until the delivery is made to another mind, nothing at all has happened. To have great poets, there must be great audiences too".[4]

In other words, the key factors while developing a strategy must include the following:
- Clearly defined target audience
- Clear, precise, quantifiable communication objectives;
- Communication element considered most appropriate to the target audience.

The creative strategy, among others, will include selection of appropriate media/channels and persuasive proposition.

A persuasive message is usually an attempt to get the reader/listener to associate a plan with a motive or value. A motive is the element a communicator feels is a strong value for the receiver of the message.

There is a strong relationship between beliefs, plans and values. In other words, what value our message promises against our wanting to change an existing perception of the receiver has to be clear in the message delivered. To illustrate, if there is a growing menace of pick pocketing in a city, one of the messages could be, "Help us help street children, else you find street walking not without danger". The appeal is fear and the value promised is safety. Or it could be, "Society is responsible for creating street children. Let us help them in finding their lost childhood". The appeal is survival and the promised value is altruism/self-esteem.

The choice of persuasive propositions/themes and appeals is almost limitless. But there are common themes revolving round the theory of the "Hierarchy of needs" propounded by Abraham Maslow. He believed that human beings progress up the hierarchy of needs—moving from physiological needs like food and water, to safety, love and belongingness, esteem and finally to self-actualization—once one's needs have been satisfied at a lower level. Based on the theory, some of the appeals can be as follows.

The themes

Themes resonating with survival needs
Fear, anger, curiosity, disgust, stability, uncertainty, trust, security, scapegoating, intimidation, economic, integrity, freedom (to... or from...)

Themes to resonate with love and belongingness
Identification, tradition, sense of fairness, sympathy, patriotism, determination, solidarity, humour, nationalism, involvement, religion, majority bandwagon, familiarity

Themes to resonate with esteem needs
Progress, sense of responsibility, status quo, community pride

Themes to resonate with self-actualization needs
Participation, sacrifice

Maslow's "hierarchy of needs" model, though generally relied upon by creative writers, does not cover all aspects of human experience and to that extent is limited.

Many communication practitioners follow the human-interest approach developed from the print media for over 200 years. The concept embraces the belief that there are some topics, which always will have a fascination for human beings, no matter what the level of rationality, education or intelligence of the target audience. The Human Interest Formula developed by Merrill Goddard (Hearst) is something like this:

• Love (Sentimentality)	• Evil doing (Crime, scandal, dissipation etc.)
• Hate	• Morality
• Vanity	• Fear
• Selfishness (Self interest, self-indulgence)	• Ambition (Love of power, desire to excel, Fashion in vogue)
• Immortality (Including long life)	• Curiosity (Mystery)
• Heroism (Bravery, adventure, self-denial)	• Inventiveness/Science (Craving for knowledge to reduce uncertainty, anxiety)
• Veneration (Reverence for customs, tradition and great men)	• Amusement (Recreation, sports, contests, games)

The human-interest approach is invariably used by the media as themes for gaining a larger audience/readership. For the professional communicator, the task is more complex. He has to use some or many of these characteristics to develop a persuasive proposition that will not only attract or receive attention but which all energize the members of the target public to yield to the proposition.

The target audience will, however, yield only if they can allay their concern about the potential risk of adopting a new behaviour or changing their perception about an existing belief, viz.,
a) Social risk (is it socially acceptable to those whose opinions he cares about?)
b) Psychological risk (will this yield its promised benefit—one of the needs?)
c) Physical risk (could his decision be harmful to the people he cares for?)[5]

Because the audience varies in needs and motives, it is necessary to develop multiple messages for use in personal communication. Let us take the example of AIDS. For high-risk groups like sex workers, people leading promiscuous lives, people addicted to drugs and blood donors, the message must persuade them to take the AIDS screening test. But for, say, the youth, the message has to be designed with a view to educating them about the causes of getting AIDS and how the risk could be minimized. AIDS awareness being a global mass communication programme, the local social, cultural ethos, religious susceptibilities, customs etc. have to be kept in view while designing messages. In an open society like the United States, graphic and explicit advertising is a popular mass communication style. A newspaper ad in 1987 depicted the spilled contents of a woman's purse, including a comb, lipstick, and condoms, and offered the bold warning "Don't go out without your rubbers".

On the other hand, a poster in Trinidad sought to sell the idea of monogamy rather than active but safe sex. The poster showed a man and a woman on a park bench looking happy, with the headline "You are safer with one partner. Avoid AIDS".

In India, a print ad in early 1990s had a visual of popular film actress Pooja Bhatt (known for her upfront attitude) with the headline "Love life, not death". The punch line was "AIDS is closer than you think". Looking at the choice of the media, the ad was subtle and aimed at flippant college-going youngsters of the metros. The target audience, in this case, was expected to know about the deadly syndrome. The message was meant as a reinforcement.

Indian AIDS campaign has undergone a sea change in the last about two decades. The syndrome has attracted tremendous stigma against people living with HIV and AIDS. Shabana Azmi, a noted actor and social worker was roped in a popular television commercial (TVC) in which she was shown visiting a hospital ward which had children living with HIV and AIDS. She was shown hugging a child and said. *"Aise pyar badta hai.* AIDS *nahin"*. She explained the various ways in which one can get infected by HIV and AIDS.

Mainstream filmmakers used the theme in two path breaking films, viz. "Phir Milenge" and "My brother Nikhil", which depicted widespread ignorance leading to stigma and weak laws and social support system against people living with HIV and AIDS.

Much later the campaign "Bindas Bol" won many national and international accolades. Thanks to the efforts put in by many organizations and the NGO sector, people are openly talking about issues relating to HIV and AIDS.

As a PR practitioner, one may or may not go in for institutional or corporate advertising very often, but would need appealing stories for the enormous writing one needs to handle, including ghost writing. For example, if you edit a house journal or bring out a video magazine for employee's communication, human-interest stories will more often decide how popular the journal or video magazine will be. The PR manager may like to look for popular angles in stories in the most mundane, day to day activities of employees.

Some industries have chronic problems of absenteeism, slow work tactics, unmotivated employees, use of drugs, and now the latest menace of AIDS. All these issues can be taken up using persuasive propositions aimed at informing, educating and communicating for a change in existing perceptions and behaviour patterns of the target audience.

The Global Economic recession of 2008 which is seen as the worst in the last 100 years, has seen employees getting pink slips without notice, the salary of employees is being reduced and many perks are being withdrawn. If the management thinks the employees will understand on their own or appreciate what the management is doing, it is expecting the impossible. It is important for various management bodies to discuss the issue with employee associations and unions before they learn about the management decisions through the media. Sample the following front page story from the leading economic paper in India, *The Economic Times*:

"Auto majors slash travel and perks, freeze fresh hiring: Tata, M&M, Renault act Tough to ride out storm".

The story had the following highlights:

Five day a week work: Force Motors, Kirloskar Oil engines, Bharat Forge, Thyssen Krupp Industries, Kirloskar Brothers (Dewas plant).

No salary for management staff for the sixth day: Kirloskar Oil Engines.

Removal of trainees and probationary technicians: Bharat Forge.

No new cars for promotes, VPs: Bharat Forge.

Air travel only for GMs and above, and only in economy class: Thyssen Krupp Industries, Kirloskar Brothers.

No luxury taxies, hire Tata Indica on emergency: Kirloskar Brothers.

No guest entertainment, no foreign travel, limited fuel bill: Kirloskar Brothers.

No electricity after 6 pm.: Tata Yazaki.

The story was ascribed to "sources" within the various companies. It was however, not clear whether the sources were from among the management or the affected parties, the employees.[6]

On the same page was a box item "Jet Airways goes for 25% pay cut".

How to package a message and what to include always remains the most difficult task for communicators. The information will need to address the following:

- Communication habits of the proposed target audience
- Persuasive "resonance" impact variables of the various types of message packages.
- Production demands in terms of cost, time and management.
- Production talent availability – writers, graphics, in-house availability of resources, production houses.

Some available message package options:

- **Print**

Circulars, handbills, brochures, information kits, annual reports, submissions, newspapers/newsletters, news releases, press kits, news features, magazine features, fact sheets, photographs, newspaper advertisements.

- **Audio Visuals**

Slide-sound presentations, multi-vision, filmstrips, multimedia display, static display, audiotronic displays [electronic puppetry].

- **Radio**

News releases, news tapes, "promo" announcements, special broadcasts, radio plays, theme music, jingles/songs, interactive radio programmes.

- **Television**

News film, news releases, current affairs, interviews, talk shows, guest appearances, teleconferencing, special broadcasts, public service announcements, satellite hookups.

- **Video**

Videotape presentation, corporate news shows, corporate briefings, training presentations. Employee communication news tracks, etc.

- **Films**

Instructional short films, documentary films, etc.

Media

Whether one agrees or not with McLuhan's thesis that the *medium is the message* or not, the importance of the medium in effective communication is too well known to need emphasizing.

When we talk of the medium or various media in public relations, it is not just the selection of the media vis-à-vis the target audience but much more.

The medium or channel is determined as much by the nature of the message as by the target group. One medium may not be appropriate for a lengthy piece of information, while another may not be suitable for speedy communication. It is also a fact that all media may not be available at the given time, or at a price one is willing to afford. A channel may refuse to transmit a certain message. A publisher may refuse the advertisement of a rival publication. Others may not mind.

Here is an interesting classic case study. *The Times of India* and the *Hindustan Times*, one a multi-edition publication and the other the largest selling daily from the capital, keep fighting an interesting duel. *The Hindustan Times*, campaign once asked, "Can you think of Delhi without the *Hindustan Times*?". *The Times of India* responded with "Graduate to T.O.I.". The climax was when one of the magazines of *The Times of India* group printed half-page ads of the rival daily paper on the same page, *The Hindustan Times* advertisement on top screaming, "Can you think of Delhi without *The Hindustan Times*"? In addition, *The Times of India* ad below it counseling, as if in reply, "Graduate to the Times". That was not all, a later campaign of the Times was headlined "Delhi is more than monuments" with "Graduate to the Times" taking the place of the signature line. *The Hindustan Times* retorted; "We sell more because we tell more".

The nature of the message also strongly conditions channel choice. Good news announcing profits through a newsletter to the shareholders may be an accepted method, but to ease out an important office bearer or to announce a policy, which would have some ramifications, had better be done at a meeting. It will also depend on who is saying it and who is the affected party. Russi Mody who was the uncrowned king of the corporate sector until sacked by TISCO, probably felt humiliated when he walked out of the 12 March 1993 board meeting, refusing to discuss his retirement from the company. He felt, the company, having used his services for 54 years, owed him the right to decide how and when he would lay down his mantle, instead of them resorting to boardroom intrigues to get rid of him.

Depending on the target audience, internal and external and the nature of communication, the channels are decided. They will range from interpersonal or selective to mass media. The case study of Nano Exit from West Bengal may be referred to in Chapter 10. Ratan Tata, the generally reticent person decided to issue an open letter in the media through paid space in which he poured out his angst, not sparing the people he thought were responsible for the Tata Ouster.

In this age of information, the media world is complex and all pervasive. It has to cut across territorial boundaries, thanks to satellite communication. We no longer have local or national issues in a broader sense. Anything happening in any part of the world has wider ramifications all over. The Gulf War was equally a tele-war. The enormity of the vast array of media makes the planning process complicated and at times awesome. As a PR practitioner one needs to consider Media attributes, objectives, strategies and requirements, keeping in view the target audience analysis.

Let us take these issues one by one.

Media attributes

Each medium has certain characteristics, which are unique to it. Each medium has strengths and weaknesses. Hence it is important to understand the media thoroughly before making a choice. Chapter 6 details various attributes of media and the strengths and weaknesses of each media.

The PR practitioner needs to utilize one or all media at different times in pursuance of his job requirements. The objectives of individual programmes/campaigns however will decide the selection of media, besides the availability of funds.

Media objectives

Media objectives are positive statements of what is to be achieved against a certain programme. It should ideally answer the following questions plus other considerations unique to the particular situations. Objectives tell us what will be done and not how it will be accomplished.

Who is to be reached?

The target audience for each communication, whether goodwill or paid, must be identified precisely in terms of primary and secondary audience. If advertising is used in PR for an institutional or social marketing campaign—when the sponsor has complete hold over the message and visual in the space/time purchased—the prospects are commonly defined in terms of socio-economic characteristics (age, sex, education, race, family size, income etc). The other means of defining the target audience are "psychographics" or lifestyle characteristics. If more than one target audience is proposed, then the relative importance (weight) of each needs to be established.

What is to be accomplished?

It needs to be precisely identified whether we are trying to inform, educate or reinforce.

When does the message appear?

This goal establishes the proper timetable for message occurrence. The decision about the time is very crucial to the success of the message. For a deliberate or proactive message, there is a well thought out strategy; but in times of crisis or reactive situations, the media are insistent, hence it is necessary that a communication vacuum is avoided by sending a rejoinder or the management's point of view immediately.

Where does the message appear?

This will also depend on the requirement vis-à-vis target audience to be reached. Some of the considerations will include the need for national, regional, local support, problem areas, competitors, adversary activities, message testing and population density (city, suburban, rural etc).

How much?

Depending on the situation, some messages may need single time exposure or media reach. At other times, information has to be supplemented as and when new facts come to light or when the media are investigating. In case of institutional advertising and paid campaigns advertising weight goals need to be defined in terms of reach and frequently during flight or on a monthly basis.

Media strategy

When we talk of strategy, what we have in view is the art of placing the major elements of the proposed programme and projecting and directing the thrust areas so as to control as far as possible the preferred place, time and conditions considered most likely to achieve the set objectives.

Media requirements

The raw material or the lifeblood for media is information. They cannot survive unless there is information, more information and better or unique information. As a PR practitioner, one needs to understand and appreciate the urge of the media to seek information, probe and investigate stories to get the "punch" or to satiate readers' requirements. This is an area, which needs better understanding between the sources of news and news creators.

As a part of their job of environment scanning, PR practitioners must pick up the thrust of each medium and the way it presents news. This helps while writing stories for general circulation to the media or when given to a particular medium as an exclusive story.

The stories get treatment in different newspapers and other media according to the characteristics of the media. A regular newspaper and a financial newspaper will use a press release issued after the annual general meeting of the shareholders of a company differently. A regular newspaper may just dismiss the story in a few lines telling about the profit and loss situation, while a financial newspaper will detail the story because the readers of financial newspaper have different requirements. At other times, in case of an event of national importance or a tragedy, when newspapers gather news from a number of sources, the treatment differs from one newspaper/medium to another.

For instance, when the Satyam Computers fraud surfaced, the financial papers invariably had banner headlines, but not the mainstream newspapers.

In short, the PR practitioner, without losing sight of his media objective, should also keep in view the individual requirements of the media for effective communication.

Some of the decision choices facing the communicator will boil down to the following:

What combination of channels or media will be:
a) most effective
b) most efficient

In other words, in getting your target audience to attend to your message package, what is going to be involved in lining them up and who is going to do it—the in-house professionals or an outside consultancy? In fact the message packages and media are so closely linked up that often the decision can't be taken in isolation of each other. Some of the channels and media options are as follows:

- **Personal**

Interviews, discussions, canvassing, business luncheons.

- **Group**

Briefings, seminars, conferences, workshops, symposiums, public meetings, conventions, dinners, community information centres, information kiosks, special events, parades, official openings, street theatre, competitions, art shows, guided tours, concerts, special camps, crusades, film festivals, Internet chat groups.

- **Helping channels**

Political parties, church/religious organizations, trade associations, commercial sponsors, paid workers.

- **Mass**

Press, radio, television, direct mail, sporting events, exhibitions, regional fairs, trade fairs, theatres, bill boards, video vans, point-of-sale displays.

- **Special promotionals**

Neon signs, skywriting, "give aways", car stickers, coasters, key chains, T-Shirts, ashtrays, matches, pencils, pens, balloons, souvenirs, cufflinks, banners, buntings, etc.

Audience

Target audience also referred to as "Public" in PR parlance is not a faceless mass of people. The expression denotes a specific group and seldom the entire population even while a country is going to the polls. The publics of different organizations will vary depending on what they produce, sell or service. The average organization will have the following publics: employees, stockholders, communities, the press/media, government, customers (industrial, wholesalers or retailers, purchasers and consumers) and the people who are interested in the fortunes of the company, the industry or the personnel.

Simple it may seem, but their behaviour is very complex and has a direct bearing on the success or even existence of the organization.

As a PR practitioner, one has to understand the communication behaviour of the varied publics for effective communication. The challenge in fact is to reduce uncertainty about how to communicate effectively with this chosen target audience. It is probably the trickiest of assignments because one has to deal with the "inner-state" of the people, the target public, their attitudes, their ideological predispositions, their values and different feelings that go on in their minds. One-time research hence never suffices. It has to be a continuous process. Accuracy in knowing the minds of the people towards a particular issue, product or service may not be possible to achieve, but some guidelines are available to help a PR practitioner to work out ways to reduce that continual uncertainty.

In research terms, the central question faced is, "How do members of our target publics get their data about their world—and how to go about making sense of the data?"

To answer this question, we need reliable information about,

- Who are the members of our target publics and where are they?
- How do they get their information about the world per se?
- What are their inner dispositions about the issue the researcher is trying to tackle?
- What is their existing attitude about the organization and the individual product about which the researcher is trying to gather information?

In order to get to the above, we need basically two different sets of information about the target publics, viz., their *communication habits* and their *communication behaviour*.

The following checklist will help build an accurate picture of the members of the target audience:

a) The size of the target public
b) Where they are located
c) Their language usage
d) Their education levels
e) Their economic situation
f) Their religious characteristics
g) Their cultural characteristics
h) Their opinion leaders
i) Their favourite group channels
j) Their special personal channels
k) Their daily routines
l) The mass media they attend to
m) The mass media they prefer

If a PR researcher can gather the above information about them, he is in a position atleast to prepare message packages that are likely to attract their attention and are hopefully understandable to them.

The challenge, however, is to find out how they are likely to respond to the stimuli provided by the communicator, how to make the communication package (stimulated response) to get a positive response.

To do that, one has to find out data about their communication behaviour. There is an immense amount of secondary data available in various research studies conducted by the industry from time to time and learned papers. However, nobody ever has the final answers because people vary so much. Hence each communicator must develop his own strategy to tackle this complex task. The central question is how the members of the target public are likely to respond to communicative acts about the campaign. This is like getting a "feed forward" and not a "feedback".

In order to get to the root of the problem, one has to decide what communication barriers will have to be overcome in energizing the members of the target public to:

- Pay attention to what is being said or exposed;
- Reasonably understand what the message is all about;
- Consider to agree with key action propositions;
- Be willing to change their attitude, viewpoint, if called for.

The above can be achieved only if the target public has a sense of personal involvement with the subject of the message or the campaign. In other words, how personally the issue is important for them. The other condition is open-mindedness, i.e. whether the target public is prepared to acquire and consider the information provided to them in the campaign. This will depend on the issue the campaign is trying to influence, and their existing impression about the agency launching the campaign. Thirdly, there is the condition of social constraints. In other words, the target publics would see whether their own social situation lets them get influenced, or whether they take the action, the campaign is urging them to take.

Here we can cite an interesting example about the probably longest run campaign in India on family planning. The target audience was constantly chased through multimedia campaigns to restrict their family. Some of the research studies conducted revealed high exposure and recall of the campaign but the result has been extremely opposite, i.e., population explosion. Why has it happened? As discussed above, it is not just enough to expose the message and aim at comprehension, many other factors, viz.; economic, social and educational, play an equally important role in inducing a change of perception and behaviour of the audience. Communication in fact is an interdisciplinary area encompassing politics, economics, psychology, sociology and anthropology.

Summary

In the chapter we have discussed the trinity, viz., the message, the medium and the audience and their interdependence on each other. The communicator will be at risk, if he emphasizes one at the cost of the other or does not synergise them. For effective communication, the troika is indispensable.

Critical thinking exercise

Carefully study the "Hierarchy of Needs" model propounded by Abraham Maslow. Choose any two social and corporate campaigns to understand the application of the model in communicating to draw the necessary response from the target audience.

Questions

Q.1 What do you understand by "Troika" in PR communication? What are its various elements? Discuss.

Q.2 What are the various mass media? Choose any three and discuss their relative strengths and weaknesses.

Q.3 Discuss various employee communication media and their charachteristics.

Endnotes

[1] *The Economic Times*, 10 January 2009.
[2] *The Business Standard*, *The Financial Express* and *The Economic Times*, 9 January 2009.
[3] *The Economic Times*, 10 January 2009.
[4] S.Watson Dunn, *Public Relations-A Contemporary Approach*, 1986 (Irwin, Harwood III: NY)
[5] Philip Kotler et al, *Social Marketing: Strategies for Changing Public Behaviour*
[6] Lijee Philip and Neha Raghunath, *The Economic Times*, 24 November 2008.

8 Employee Communication

> **Chapter objectives**
> - The definition of Internal audience
> - The Communication needs of the internal Target Audience (TA)
> - Various media to reach out to varying employee echelons
> - Case studies in Internal communication

It is not uncommon to hear managements claiming that employees are its biggest assets. While hire and fire is commonplace in companies, many strategies are employed to retain talent, at the same time. Whether all employees are treated alike and cared for may be a difficult question to answer.

Research in many companies has proved that the management often does not mean what it says. Speaking politically correct rhetoric is the general norm.

The current phase of global economic recession (2008) has witnessed unprecedented layoffs in almost all sectors all over the world. Millions of people have received pink slips (an American term believed to have been coined in the early part of last century. The expression came from the fact that employers put a notice on pink coloured paper terminating the services of the concerned person. The pink slip was slipped in the salary envelope of the employee. Over the years, the colour of paper has become insignificant, but the jargon is widely used globally).

How the termination is worded, how the employees are told, may vary from company to company. Enron when in India had the Damocles' sword hanging on its head about its closure any day. It however, did not hesitate to share the possibility of closure with all its employees. Instead of calling it termination or sacking, they used the term "Separation". The chapter contains the case study in the following pages.

An organization looks like a monolith with common goals and aspirations. Employees are the driving force for any organization. Simple it may seem, but it is not really so. The employees at various levels are divided into various groups and sub groups that are often governed by social and economic considerations, political ideology, gender, education, language, religion and hierarchy, among other things. Effective communication holds the key in cutting across these barriers to some extent. Good organizations spend a lot of effort, time and financial resources to achieve synergy among the groups.

The goal of organizational communication is not only to retain talent but also attract best talent.

In the following paragraphs, we shall look at various aspects of PR in achieving effective employee communication.

Various eras of employee communication

Grunig and Hunt have reckoned the following eras of employee communication:

• The era of entertaining employees (1940s)

In this era, the organizations generally did not share serious issues with the employees, but shared news about employee activities that were beyond work, like promotions, appointments, celebrations, outings of employees etc.,

• The era of informing employees (1950s)

In this period one witnessed the rising expectations of the employees to know about the organizations they worked for and the management's desire to share both the good and not so good issues with employees. This was also an era when one saw the formation of trade unions.

• The era of persuasion (1960s)

In this period, one saw the face of management also changing. More and more companies became public limited companies with shareholders from within and outside the organizations. Managements hence had to communicate with various stakeholders about its decisions and policies persuasively to garner support.

• The era of open communication (Present)

With so much information available to stakeholders from so many sources, it is only prudent on the part of the organizations to pursue open communication.[1]

The basic aim of PR for internal audiences is to create a sense of belonging and pride for the organization.

Goals of employee communication

Various departments like the Human Resource, Marketing, Finance etc. communicate with employees on a day to day basis, but the PR goals of employee communication are broadly as follows:
- To increase employee knowledge of organizational activities
- To enhance favourably employee attitudes towards organization and its various external stakeholders
- To receive employee feedback

- To recognize employee accomplishment in employee communication
- To distribute communication periodically
- To schedule interpersonal communication between management and specific employee group periodically.

Once objectives have been set, appropriate techniques and media are selected to reach out to the internal Target Audience (TA). PR professionals use some or all the media listed below:

Media for Internal Communication

- Indoctrination/Induction training
- Brain storming sessions
- Visioning exercises
- House journals
- Intranet
- Internal television
- Direct mailers
- Tele conferences
- Payslip inserts
- Ideas Box
- Shop floor discussion
- Visits by management
- Clubs and societies

Chapter 6 would detail the role and scope of some of the important media listed above.

Employee communication probably is the only branch of public relations in which the PR practitioner has complete control. Internal communication often requires designing and producing various kinds of media material which may include a whole range of employee magazines, films, audio visuals, instruction materials, safety manuals, corporate identity manuals, bulletin boards etc.

While creating channels of internal communication, a PR practitioner has to weigh the pros and cons of all the media individually and collectively keeping in view the demographic profile of the employees while not losing track of their psychographic profiles. According to expert view, the effectiveness of internal public relations largely depends on the following factors:

- Candid/Openness in management
- Recognition by management of the value and importance of employee communication.

The range of media for internal communications is immense but not all media are used by all the organizations. It depends on the extent of importance an organization gives to Public Relations, locations of the its various projects and the interests the public relations team takes in the activity.

According to Cubertson, the ethos and ideology of an organization determines whether PR would function as a part of the inherent ideology or it would be put to use with a set of strategies that would be applied in specific situations. This may mean departing from the core ideology and values that the organization may have adopted.[2]

Organizations are dynamic. They change from time to time keeping in view the changes in the outside world. PR has an important role to play in bringing about the desired change in the attitude and behaviour of the stakeholders in times of change.

Internal communication in times of change – Implementation to Post Implementation

The public relations team must get to know employees thoroughly both in terms of demographics and psychographics. The communication at various points of time needs to use appropriate media to convey the following:

- Convey urgency for change
- Provide facts about the situation that has necessitated change
- Provide evidence of what you are communicating
- Convey the big picture that your organization is not unique but is touched by the outside world
- Listen to the fears, concerns and doubts of stakeholders
- Express concern about their fears and skepticism
- Restate facts for clarity and apply them to the context
- Involve people in the process of change
- Inspire them that change would be for their progress and that of the organization
- Take feedback on a continuous basis
- Inspire again, based on the insights gathered from the feedback and any new facts that may have emerged
- Create champions of change. People look for champions and leaders in difficult times.

CASE STUDIES

Present the big picture

When it was clear that the Dhabol project was facing problems at the turn of the century in India and could wind up any time, the Enron used an open policy in keeping the employees abreast of all the facts. In order to lessen the stress of the employees, the HR department engaged a headhunter to find suitable jobs of various employees. Curriculum vitaes of those employees who could join its offices elsewhere were forwarded to minimize people's miseries if and when they were served the pink slip. The term used was 'Separation' and not 'Firing' or 'Severance'. Survey by a mainstream media found that the employees had nothing against the management, because it had kept the employees informed of the worst possible scenario, so they accepted change with dignity and without any heartburn.[3]

Create champions

In the mid eighties, Goodyear Tyres, a British company was faced with the problem of growing absenteeism a couple of times in a year, which affected its productivity adversely and thereby the profits. The management found out that as most of the employees who were contract employees, were migrants, most of whom would invariably go back to their villages, twice a year at the time of harvesting. The company employed a number of techniques, including incentives to arrest absenteeism. The PR department came out with an innovative scheme called the "ZERO ABSENTEE CLUB". Employees who did not take any leave were rewarded by way of a visit by the management, presentation of a citation which reflected the name on the roll of honour and a token gift. The experience showed that a couple of hundred employees were on the roll of honour soon. It gave a sense of pride among the employees to be in the Zero Absentee Club. The productivity improved considerably when employees felt involved and cared for.

The top man, whether of the organization or a department, must keep in touch with each person to draw the best performance. People are intelligent enough to be able to distinguish between honest behaviour and 'make believe' behaviour.

CASE STUDIES

Reaching out to employees

At LG the Family Ambassador Programme has been quite a hit. Senior HR executives visit people's homes to find out if there are any glitches at work. On one such occasion, the visiting executive found that the employee used to reach home later than expected by the family. The inquiry revealed that the office bus dropped various employees at certain points. That day due to a strike by auto rickshaw drivers, one of the employees, who was visited by an HR executive had to walk a few kilometers to reach home. Having observed the predicament, he went back to study the bus route vis-à-vis the addresses of various employees. The management took a decision to reroute the bus plan so that no one had to walk more a small distance from the drop point to their respective residences. This small but thoughtful gesture earned the company a great amount of respect. In all probability the management would not have realized it, if people had put up their grievance.

> **When the going gets tough, the tough get going**
>
> At NHPC, the company that operates in very difficult terrain, building hydroelectric projects, the people working at sites are often cut off from the mainstream, the projects being hundreds of kilometers away from the nearest rail or air-head. The nature of the work is also such that it is risky work for an average person, due to the topography and terrain of the place. Visits by the PR team to collect stories of human spirit and grit, especially of the underdog, helped build credibility of internal communication during the initial years of the birth of NHPC. The house journal in fact became a voice of the employees who looked forward to receiving a copy.

Russi Modi, the uncrowned Czar of corporate India in the Nineties visited thousands of employees randomly during his evening walks in the Jamshedpur Township when he headed TISCO.

Some organizations do small acts to achieve fellow feeling among the employees and create an air of being cared for. For instance, in 2008, in cricketing season, HR head of Rediffusion DYR screened the T20 finals between Indian and Pakistan for the entire office staff. Percept has employed a kickboxing expert on board. Employees at Patni Computers organize cricket matches in box cricket for women only.

The KPT Cummins Infosystems Ltd. Football teams reached the semi finals of the 5th Inter IT Football Championship organized by Maharashtra Krida. Talented employees at the Mudra group were sent to West India to watch the World Cup.

There are many more examples including that of public sector Indian Airlines/Air India/SAIL/Indian Railways preparing regional/national level players.

Human capital is of immense value to an organization and PR can play a decisive role in harnessing it for strategic gains.

How PR works internally

PR works at two levels viz. manifest and subtle. It is very important for the PR practitioner to have a genuine and active interest and empathy for people. At the same time, as PR is a top management function, it is important to draw a balance between the two so that one remains credible. Someone has rightly said that PR is akin to atmosphere, which one can't see, but can't do without. Education, training and personal grooming of a PR person go a long way in defining the quality of PR in an organization. Interestingly, PR often is manifest through the actions of the top brass. Hence, it is important for the PR expert to aid and advise the CEO and other top management on various PR issues and angles, especially about media functioning, media interface and crises communication.

PR as said above is a top management function. If the CEO does not care or understand the value of communication, precious little can be achieved in PR. In such circumstances PR is employed as a fire fighting activity put to use in times of crises.

The following considerations are important:
- CEO's skills as a spokesperson for the organization
- Communication infrastructure of the organization to support the CEO
- Is communication an integral part of the organization or brought in when there is a crisis?

CASE STUDIES OF SOME GLOBAL ORGANIZATIONS

GE

Jack Welch (CEO of GE for 20 years 1980-2001), author of the book *Straight from the Gut* established a strong partnership between communication and strategic planning; making communication activity a core organizational value in transforming the company and sustaining its vitality; the role of communication as a 'learning organization'; and the importance of streamlining communication by reducing unnecessary bureaucracy.[4]

Building strong partnership between communication and strategic planning

Welch ensured that he had numerous scheduled and impromptu meetings with 35 top people who reported to him directly and were responsible for explaining and defending their strategic recommendations for their businesses.

Known as 'GE operating system', these meetings had CEOs, role models, and initiative champions from within GE and outside, sharing the intellectual capital and best practices worldwide. These would encompass best practices, customer impact, succession planning, including selection of candidates for leadership training.

Such meetings would generally begin at 8 a.m. and carry on till 10 p.m. These were nicknamed by executives as 'food fights' or 'free for all'.

Making communication activity a core organizational value in transforming the company and sustaining its vitality.

This meant repeating ideas to ensure these were heard broadly via an interpersonal route, through shareholder communication, company's annual report and in interviews with the Press. He motivated senior managers, who in turn motivated people below the line. His senior managers for example after attending leadership conferences with Welch will steer such conferences for their junior officers. This surely had the cascading effect.

All employees for instance were supposed to carry a wallet size card that reads: *"GE leaders... always with unyielding integrity to create a clear, simple, reality based vision... and communicate it to all constituencies"*. This was an indicator for the top GE leaders to express themselves clearly and succinctly

Another such card read: *"GE leaders... always with unyielding integrity have the self confidence to involve everyone and behave in a boundaryless fashion"*. This was an indication of democratization—a free flow of ideas from all directions.

Extending communication more deeply into the organization

"GE leaders... always with unyielding integrity are open to ideas from anywhere... and committed to work-out" said the GE employee value card. 'Work out' meant a forum for brainstorming and decision-making for employees and their bosses. The work outs, according to employees resembled a grueling oral examination with questions and recommendations hurled at managers by their subordinates.

A work out typically included three day sessions where 40-100 employees brainstormed on how to improve their business. The unit boss would set the agenda and then depart. A facilitator and boss's subordinates had a grueling exchange of ideas on various solutions to the discussed problem and when the boss returned on the final day there would be rapid-fire comments and recommendations by the group. Based on the recommendations, decisions were to be arrived at, and if need be a small group would further research the issue for the next such meeting. In about a decade 2,00,000 employees underwent the work out sessions.

This resulted in openness, transparency and respect for people across various echelons and a show of free flow of communication where everyone mattered. The areas of discussions included improving productivity, quality, and customer supplier relationship.

Cut through bureaucracy

Until Welch joined GE, the company was like any big corporation where written documentation was the order of the day. Welch replaced tons of paper with short 'playbooks' that identified important strategies and used these documents as the springboard for strategic discussion with the management. Face to face talk replaced time consuming written procedures. GE today is practically a paperless organization with the exception of a printed annual report.

Welch reduced hierarchical channels from nine to four and six, describing it as 'a big company body in a small-company soul' to operate with the agility and nimbleness of a small entrepreneurial firm.

FedEx

PR function must add significant value to business and fully aligned with those making high impact strategic decisions for the company. At FedEx that works in 200 countries, 24×7 days, the communication function is aimed at working with high speed, high impact and precision.

In Castaway, Tom Hanks played a FedEx efficiency expert who survived a plane crash, returned to the US after years of being marooned at an island and delivered a packet to a customer that survived along with him. That is the efficiency, the company projects. At the company, an annual audit with executives is conducted to find out what they are trying to accomplish and to establish a score card of success. They began 'customer-facing-go-to market' strategies to improve growth and profit.

A multi-talented group of communication professionals has been created that helps solve strategic-level problems that cut across functional areas like marketing, finance, sales, technology and strategy. The CC staff this way, besides the traditional role also can rotate through projects to build broader knowledge of the business and to contribute value-added counsel to those decisions.

Johnson & Johnson (J&J)

J&J has created an excellent synergy between PR and organizational culture. The management found that none of the benchmarking studies about corporate communication could provide a model for the company because of its unique culture. Building consensus rather than imposing one's formal authority and evoking rules characterizes the way work is done even at a very senior level at J&J. Decentralization is of such core value to the company that it is inscribed in one of the rare written statements of the company.

Despite its number of operating companies, J&J has created a climate of understanding and cohesiveness among internal constituencies around a set of values stated in the credo, including the importance of reputation.

Of its one lakh employees, 18,000 are managers at J&J. When a new operating manager joins, the Customer Care (CC) head sends a note asking him 'please stop by next time you're in New Brunswick'. This gives a hint to the new entrant that the CC head has the ear of the CEO and so he can lobby for ideas internally. In the management magazine *Worldwide News Digest*, in place of 'show-and-tell' anecdotal information, now emphasis is placed on stories that affect business development.

Honeywell Aerospace

Change, despite being the only constant, is resisted, because it breaks the status quo and calls for a deviation from the familiar. Employees are very resistant to change, unless they see value in change or are coerced to change. For better results, it is always good to persuade, but before that it is important to listen to the fears and susceptibilities against change.

> Honeywell Aerospace faced with a situation of downfall in their market for reasons beyond its control had to use PR to boost the morale of the employees. The PR department initiated what it called UPWORDS, a process which enables employees to fax or call 800 number for comments or questions, and then the PR group got back to them after checking with senior management for answers. A metrics system was used by the PR to gauge its utility and efficacy of its functions and performance. For instance, if someone from HR said that 'employees believed such and such' then that was countered with metrics that refuted the anecdotal statement if the PR was convinced with facts that it was wrong.

Retaining talented employees is a task by itself. A number of Indian companies are using sports as a means of retaining talent and creating team spirit, problem solving capabilities and leadership qualities among them. It is believed that sports have a universal appeal and bond employees as nothing else.

The Bottom Line

A business can only achieve its best when everyone's energies are pointed in the same direction and are not at cross purposes. Employees need to have a clear picture of the overall direction and ambition of the company and a clear sense of where he or she fits in and how they can contribute to the company. Feedback can be both informal and formal.

A continuous research into employee perceptions about the organization, their job satisfaction and issues that bother them, inspire them and their innovations, goes a long way in making employees feel as a stakeholder.

Idea boxes are an important PR tool. Many organizations keep nice looking boxes at various places in the assembly line/shop floor area and elsewhere, encouraging employees to put their innovative ideas on various areas to bring about change/improvement. Ideas that are picked up by the management are rewarded, and that works as a morale boost for employees.

Informal surveys through discussions, small group interactions, gate meetings can be organized from time to time. Formal surveys either through outside experts or the PR department should also be organized periodically. Organizations that stop listening to dissenting voices don't do well in the long run.

Summary

In this chapter we looked at internal communication; the various stakeholders who comprise internal target audience for PR, various tools to reach out to them. The importance of internal communication was discussed in connecting the management with employees, shareholders and the outside world comprising disparate target audience. We looked at a number of case studies and strategies employed to make PR a strategic partner in achieving organizational goals.

Critical thinking exercise

Please go through the various case studies included in the chapter. Choose any one organization, and do a detailed study through secondary data analysis (through Internet searching) to understand the various policies and strategies adopted by that organization in reaching out to its employees.

Questions

Q.1 What in your view are the various goals of internal communication for an organization?

Q.2 Discuss the various media used for reaching out to employees.

Q.3 Is internal communication in times of change different from communication in normal times? Write your answer giving your argument about the need for change of strategy and process, if required.

Endnotes

[1] B.J. Grunig and T. Hunt, *Managing Public Relations*, 1984 (Holt, Rine Hart & Winston:NY)

[2] Hugh M. Culbertson : "Breadth of Perspective: An Important Concept for PR" in James E. Grunig & Lissa A. Grunig, *PR Research*, Volume 1, ed., 1984 (Holt, Rine Hart & Winston:NY)

[3] *Economic Times*, March 2001

[4] Jack Welch with John A. Byrne, *Straight from the Gut*, 1 ed. 2001 (*Business Plus*)

9 Public Relations Writing

Chapter objectives
- The role, scope and importance of PR writing
- Various kinds of PR writing
- Writing for the media – various genres
- Writing for internal audience
- Hands-on skills on writing for various target audience

Purpose of PR

Traditionally PR aims at building mutual understanding between the organization and its various constituencies. Conventionally human communication can be analyzed at three levels; *knowledge, attitudes and behaviour.*

Analysts believe that as people are exposed to communication they will become knowledgeable (or not); change or (don't change) their attitude towards an object or human, activity and they change or (don't) change their behaviour.

Where does PR writing fit in to the goals of behaviour outcomes?

It needs to be persuasive enough to make people change their attitudes or adopt a behaviour that is desired of them (people paying their taxes honestly, employees working sincerely, people voting for a particular candidate and so on and so forth). PR writers have to be realistic in their expectation of the extent of change of attitude and behaviour as an outcome of their writing. Every piece of PR writing is agenda driven to achieve one or all of the following at different points of time vis-à-vis various publics—to inform, persuade or influence behaviour. So PR writing has to be in a manner and style that suits the various publics viz., media, employees, top management, shareholders, vendors and public opinion makers.

Public Relations requires connecting with a variety of target audience. As we discussed in Chapter 6, PR professionals use various kinds of tools or media that have a better chance of reaching out to the publics. Depending on who the PR is trying to reach, selection of media is made. Most of communication work requires verbal and non-verbal channels. Writing occupies an important place in the day to day functioning of a PR professional, whether he works for a company or a PR firm. A PR person has to write regularly for the media through press releases, press handouts, backgrounders, rejoinders et al.

Besides, a lot of writing and editing work is required for House journals for the internal audience, and other publications like Annual reports, shareholder newsletters etc.

It is not uncommon for PR firms and headhunters to ensure that the person they select for a PR job is well versed in writing. Many a time, journalists with a few years of experience are selected at the cost of PR practitioners, because, it is believed that by selecting a former journalist, it is ensured that his writing skills were good. Besides, he understands deadlines better and has a good understanding of media functioning.

Theoretical underpinnings PR writing

PR, feel analysts, may still be defining its role, scope and relationships, but in no way does it mean that PR does not draw from the solid foundations of theory.[1]

An organization as deliberated elsewhere in the book is like a living organism. It draws sustenance from relationships among various publics. PR works as a conduit between the management and its various publics, also referred to as stakeholders, both internally and externally. The image of an organization to a great extent depends on the nurturing of those relationships in a continuous and sustained manner.

Every piece of communication aims at building a certain desired response from the said public to whom it is addressed. The mechanism of feedback reflects whether that piece of communication was successful or wasted. In fact, critics refer to the manipulative techniques used by PR to change the mindset. As discussed in the chapter on PR Theory, one approach could be press agentry—which calls for one way approach, and the other is a two-way symmetrical communication, in which the stakeholders are regarded as equal partners, who could contribute equally in the process. The systems approach believes that the varying stakeholders may have different approaches but have a common vested interest in the good health of the organization. It is how one draws upon the individual strengths, where the role of PR is seen.

Theories of persuasion aim at the importance of the relationship of an organization with its different stakeholders. It would be based on the ground reality of what these audiences think about the organization. The PR communication therefore, will depend on the existing perceptions of the audience, who the programme is directed towards. If that set of audience does not think positively, then the communication has to look at the various reasons of their belief, and address those concerns. If the target audience is neutral, then the strategy will be suited to wean the audience persuasively to the desired point of view. Similarly if the audience is positively inclined, that needs to be reinforced to make the audience to continue to believe in their existing viewpoint.

The model developed by Grunig and Hunt (1984) clarifies it when it comes to PR writing.

Model	Views of publics	Writing and ethical implications	Desired outcomes
Press agentry / publicity	Publics as targets of one way hyperbole and perhaps questionable truths	Persuasive. Write what works regardless of the ethics of process or outcome.	Behaviour, e.g. voting, purchasing etc.
Public information mode	Publics as consumers of information	Convey the facts honestly. Professional journalism standards.	Informed publics
Two-way/ Asymmetrical Communication	Publics as targets of persuasion based on truth and accuracy	Persuasive/ Informative. Use what you know about the publics to shape organizational communication policy, content, and style.	Publics aligned Behaviourally and /or attitudinally with employer.
Two-way/ Symmetrical communication	Publics as partners in dialogue for mutual benefit	Persuasive/ Informative. Adapt writing to meet needs of both employer and publics.	Behaviour and Attitudes of both employer and client aligned for mutual benefit.

Academics and scholars have referred to the use of rhetoric by communication experts by which truth and situations could be approached.

In olden times, tutors training in the art of persuasive communication were much in demand. The art of speaking was referred to as rhetoric.

Roman Rhetoricians Cicero and Quintilian reckoned rhetoric necessary for good citizenship and governance. They believed that the character of the speaker was important for credibility of his words. In this chapter "Media Tools and Methods" we have included the case study of Delhi Metro, which vindicates the theory.

Aristotle developed three persuasive approaches still in use, especially in politics: ethos, pathos and logos. Ethos reflected the expression of character in the discourse—an appeal to credibility or authority. Pathos is an appeal to the emotions, and logos is the appeal of a logically developed argument.

Chapter 2 may be referred to for a closer understanding of the subject matter. In this chapter we shall look at both kinds of writing, viz. for the employees and the media.

Writing for the media

The PR person is a skilled journalist, but with a difference. A reporter's purpose of filing a story is to inform and educate his audience in as objective a manner as possible. On the other hand a PR person while writing for the media is simultaneously has to advocate his organization's point of view without letting it show. However, if he is not careful, his writing can degenerate into propaganda, the media is not interested in. The media will then surely dump his release. A PR person's writing takes many forms such as:

- News release for general distribution
- Handouts to lead press conferences
- Press notes to individual newspapers, mostly on request, but at times *suo moto*.
- Rejoinders

PR writing must subscribe to the general principles such as openness, providing facts rather than opinions. There are however, specific guidelines applicable to different types of writing.

Simple it may seem to write a news release, but it is not an easy task from the philosophical standpoint. One has to balance two seemingly conflicting considerations, viz., projecting the organization's achievements and at the same time taking care of the news value of the story from the reader's perspective.

On the flip side, media needs information on a continuous basis to fill its columns and bulletins about issues that concern people. What is happening in the business or service sector is also of great interest to the common man. The proliferation of news channels in the last 7-8 years bears testimony to the fact that the audience base for news and news related programmes is expanding by the day.

The media also proactively take up issues which may need clarifications from the organization they are writing about, so press releases are stimulated by media stories.

The global recession of 2008, which has also slipped into 2009, has the stocks of major companies in almost all sectors plummeting. Ideally the organizations would like to keep silent to avoid further damage, but bad news always spreads faster. News bulletins of various channels, especially the business channels are talking only about various scrip and the stock position on a day-to-day basis. Experts of various kinds are invited to "educate" the viewers on sale and purchase of their stocks. Some financial companies however have been going overboard in salvaging the damage through media efforts and also paid advertisement route. The case study of ICICI may be referred to in Chapter 10.

Writing effective news release

A new release is defined as a written or video document sent by an organization about an issue that has reader interest to the media for wider reach.

Media has the following considerations for choosing to use the news release, viz. Immediacy (something that is topical and not old news), proximity (nearness of the event to be of interest to the audience), rarity (something which has not happened before or rarely happened), human interest (anything that touches an emotional chord of the readers/viewers). Releases laced with publicity and aggrandizement are a big "NO" with media houses.

Kinds of press releases

From the academic perspective, the news releases can be classified as under:

Announcement release

A new product launch, the opening of a new factory, joining of the new CEO, diversification, a new HR policy can call for issuing a press release.

One of the oil companies in the public sector recently issued a press release that was covered by a number of mainstream newspapers about its intention to get in to the telephone sector, for which it had applied for license. Another instance was a meeting of the IIT heads with the former UGC (University Grants Commission) Dr. Yashpal about expanding the base of IITs by including medicine and other fields, on the lines of some US institutions and universities like the MIT (Massachusetts Institute of Technology), Harvard and Columbia University.

Created news release

An announcement may not always be attractive enough to catch media attention. Visit by some eminent persons calls for some publicity and there can't be a better way than "create" an occasion to garner some publicity for the organization.

Spot news release

While the announcement and created news release can be planned, the spot news release as the nomenclature suggests often is sudden. Such kinds of releases are in response to a sudden happening like an accident, a sabotage, an unrest, an act of vandalism, death of a prominent person in the organization, or causalities in an accident et al. In cases like this the PR person has to almost work like a reporter in meeting deadlines. He also has to be prepared for media inquiries and media facilitation for visiting the site, if required.

Response news release

The media often have many sources of news and it is not uncommon that news about an organization reaches media from sources other than from the organization itself. At times, it is in the interest of the organization to keep silent till it can.

Special interest groups may be working on some issues which may not be favorable to an organization. Such reports when released to media often create a crisis situation for the concerned organizations. The pesticides in the Colas story in the media was based on the report by an NGO, Centre for Science and Environment. The NGO keeps being in the limelight periodically when it releases its reports. It has also kept up the issue of Yamuna pollution by not only releasing reports to the media, but also organizing events for release of reports/books/videos on the subject that attracted people from far and wide.

If there is anything factual that has been misrepresented, the organization can debate or clarify through news release. There have also been occasions when responding to a media story, organizations have chosen the route of a rejoinder press release and not the letter to the editor route. There have been occasions when media has given that version with post script that it apologizes for misrepresentation or stands by its version, at the same time allowing the readers to have a fair perspective of the organization about which it wrote.

Feature news release

There is more to a newspaper than a reportage about events that happened yesterday. If one carefully dissects various pages of a newspaper, one would find a variety of writings that include features, opinionated articles, question and answers, interviews, advertorials, special supplements, besides editorials etc. Similarly if one were to look at the news channel content, it is not uncommon to find various programmes that are not really news based. For example, Citizens for Earth on CNN-IBN channel cover a whole gamut of developmental issues concerning the human race. PR practitioners can supply feature material on interesting subject matters from within their organizations. It could be on some innovation, new HR initiative, story of human grit and determination etc. Feature material should ideally be supplied exclusively to select publications/news channels, that can expand on the material.

"Bad news" release

There are times when an organization finds itself in a crisis situation. It can be an accident, a sabotage, deaths, industrial unrest, the temptation too often is to keep mum, believing that no one would come to know. Silence generally does not help in a day and age of information explosion. Before the media gets to know from sources other than official, it is a good strategy to volunteer with bad news oneself. When confronted with the media in a situation other than this, organizations seem to take a defensive posture. But when one volunteers information, it often results in two things, first, one is in command, second, media appreciates proactive approach in PR.

In the mid-Nineties, public sector power utility company, the National Thermal Power Corporation (NTPC) set a healthy trend in this regard. Their plant in Kahlgaon in Bihar, while on trial run, met with an accident that killed a few engineers including some Russians who were providing technical support to the company. The PR department prepared the press release, including video shots for the electronic media and issued the "bad" news voluntarily. This resulted in tremendous accolades for the company. In fact, *The Economic Times* wrote an editorial "PR-Coming of Age" appreciating the stand taken by a power utility firm.

Structure of a news release

Once the PR person has been able to identify an issue that has news worthiness for the media, and has worked on the lead, it is easy to start writing the release. Experts believe that no matter whether it is the PR person who writes a news release, or a reporter who writes his dispatch, the format invariably followed is the traditional "inverted pyramid".[2]

The "Inverted pyramid style" entails that the writer presents the most important information early in the press release. By the end of the first paragraph, also known as lead in journalist parlance, the reader should have a clear understanding of the most important information in the document. In the following paragraphs, one can either elaborate on the first and second lead or provide additional information.

News releases also follow the 5W and 1 H formula, viz.

Who?
What?
When?
Where?
Why?
How?

The graphic on the page indicates an inverted pyramid, the upside-down triangle. As indicated, the top or the broad base represents the most important facts. As the base gets narrower, the newsworthiness of the story gets diminished. However it

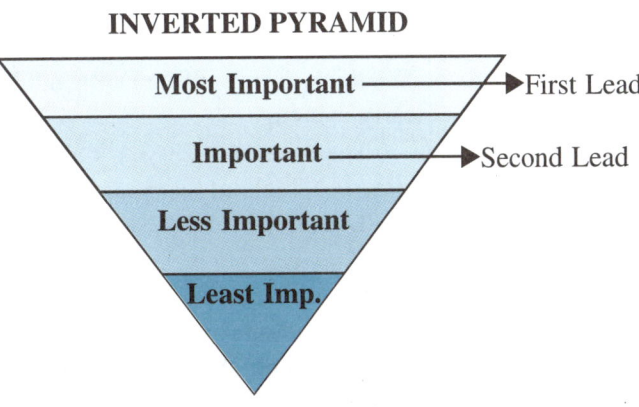

is not uncommon to find that some newspapers may carry the story at the bottom. This can be for two reasons, one, there luckily is no space constraint on that day, two, the news editor finds news worthiness in that information also.

Some organizations devote the last paragraph to writing general information about the organization as a matter of practice in all kinds of press releases they issue, so that the journalist can revisit the basic/updated facts. In case of a new scribe on the beat, this becomes very useful. In the box below, an exercise on the inverted pyramid style of writing a press release is given.

SIMULATION

Available information about an accident

An accident has occurred at the DND flyover connecting Delhi with NOIDA yesterday at 6.00 p.m. Today is Monday, 5th January 2009. The accident was a car accident. One person was killed. The person killed was 28 year old Vijay Singh. He belonged to Patna, Bihar. He worked in the HCL factory located in Noida as project head. He had joined the company two years ago. He had gone to visit a friend in Noida on the day of the accident.

Vijay Singh's car hit a stationery police wagon on patrol duty on the fateful day. The headlights of the wagon were on. The heavy fog that has engulfed the city during the last few days had made visibility extremely poor.

The impact of hitting the stationary wagon was such that the front of the car Vijay Singh was driving was completely smashed and he was thrown out of the car. He landed some 30 feet away on the pavement. Vijay was not wearing his safety belt at the time of the accident. He died of head injuries when his head hit the pavement after being thrown out of the car. The policemen in the petrol wagon rushed him to the Apollo hospital. The doctors declared him dead on arrival.

The inverted style of writing

An HCL engineer died on the spot when his car hit a stationary police wagon on petrol duty at the DND flyover that connects Delhi with NOIDA yesterday evening. The thick fog engulfing Delhi and NCR had made visibility extremely poor since early evening.

The deceased, 28-year-old Vijay Singh who hailed from Patna in Bihar had joined HCL about two years ago as project head. He had gone to meet a friend in NOIDA on the fateful Sunday.

Vijay was not wearing the seat belt at the time of the accident. The impact of ramming his car into the stationary vehicle was so high that he was thrown out of the car, landing some 30 feet away on the divider, hitting his head on the concrete. The petrol vehicle immediately rushed him to the nearby Apollo hospital, where he was declared dead on arrival.

Analysis

In the first lead, all the 5 Ws and one H has been covered. The next two paragraphs elaborate on the first lead providing a complete perspective on the happening.

Some tips on writing effective press releases

It will serve well for the brand value of an organization to have specially designed stationery for the news release. The company's house style in terms of logo, colour scheme and lettering style should be reflected both on the letterhead on which the news release is to be sent and also the envelope that carries the news release. In case a soft copy is sent through the mail, the same strategy needs to be followed. This achieves two positive points for the organization, one, there is instant recall about the organization as soon as the Press release reached the media office, two, it does not get lost in hundreds of news releases that the media houses get everyday.

Always type in double space, leaving a margin of at least 4-5 centimeters on the left hand side. This would allow space to the news desk to put in the editing marks.

Use the inverted pyramid style, ensuring that all the newsworthy facts are contained preferably in the first lead or at most in the first and second leads. In fact the best way to write a news release is to follow the style of stories that appear in newspapers.

Ensure that each paragraph after the first or second lead is self sufficient in covering a point. It is not prudent to carry over the same point to the next paragraph. The media works under tremendous time constraints, therefore when the reporter or a sub-editor takes up a press release, they have no time to sift through news from the sea of information contained in the release. So they either bin the release, or take news from the first few paragraphs, if written professionally.

Don't write long press releases. Ideally a news release should not be more than one page long, but if you can't avoid details, then print it on the overleaf, giving a cue of the last few words on page one. Never staple pages, chances are the pages will not remain together, given the number of hands and desks they travel in a media house.

Write the embargo on the top right hand corner of the first page. For example, if you wish to issue the release, say, on 5th January 2009 for publication on the 6th January 2009, you embargo will read **"For publication on or after 6th January 2009"**. If you have issued the same news release for both print and electronic media, and you wish that the broadcast media uses it in its evening bulletins on the same day of the release, your embargo will read: **" For broadcast/publication on or after 4.00 p.m. of 5th January 2009"**.

If you wish that news appears in newspapers the next day, then it is important that the release reaches various newspaper offices latest by early evening. Different pages in a newspaper have varying "locking" times. The business development news pages often are the early ones to be printed.

At the end of the press release the name of the contact officer who invariably is the PR officer along with the telephone number/mobile number and e-mail id. has to be given. After a news release is issued chances are that some reporter might try to get in touch for more details or a clarification, so it is almost suicidal if the person whose contact number has been given does not answer the call or call back, or leave a message through SMS or voice mail.

Follow up gently with your contact in the media about the receipt of release at their end. It is always a good idea to send the electronic media a visual story, as dry new items are not very relevant to them.

The golden rule is, never remind a scribe if the story is not published. It takes many steps and involves a number of persons for a story to become a news item. It can be killed at any stage, including last minute deletion if a bigger story from another organization had to be accommodated, or due to space constraints.

Handouts

A press handout is generally distributed to invitee reporters to a press conference. A good handout reflects the salient points of the new development that has necessitated the holding of the press conference. Effective PR people provide enough cues in the handout, on which reporters can ask questions.

A handout is written in consultation with the top management team, especially the person who is to address the conference. He must know the thrust and be prepared for any questions that may emerge at the press conference.

Press notes

When a reporter interviews a CEO, sometimes issues may not be dealt with in detail, especially if some jargon or technical input is given. In circumstances such as these the reporter may ask the PR person to provide him with written input, so that the story does not have anything that is out of context or confusing. Smart PR professionals wait for this opportunity, to provide press notes to the concerned reporter which may be more elaborate, explaining company's perspective more lucidly. However, chances are that if it is given to one, the rival reporter complains. Therefore, depending on what he requires, the PR person should be ready to oblige. This works to the advantage of the PR person that he is depended upon by reporters not only for the general news input through the press release, but also for exclusives. The PR person however has to guard against the tendency of obliging one or two reporters. He should be ready to help and assist every reporter who is interested in elaborate press notes for expanding their story. Ultimately, it is in the interest of the organization to have a smart PR person who fulfills the information needs of media when called upon.

Rejoinders

It is a good going if an organization steers clear from rejoinders and denials. Having said that, the PR person has to be ready with them if the situation so demands. Often unethical practices by organizations or allegations of various kinds become PR issues for which rejoinders and, at times, denials need to be issued to the media.

We have Satyam Computer's case of poor corporate governance that snowballed into a major image crisis necessitating the management to use media to be understood. The case study has been included in the chapter on Crisis Communication.

Every newspaper and magazine invariably has a letter to the editor column that reflects public opinion not only from the readers per se but also people who feel wronged by a particular story. Some publications have given up on a daily doze of vox pop. The PR person of the organization generally addresses the letter. The efficacy and usefulness of writing letters to the editor, is debatable. While one school of thought feels that by not responding to a seemingly unfair reportage one is agreeing to what is written, the other school feels that unless the story is totally fictitious which can be denied with facts and figures that are in the public domain, there is no point allowing the readers to go back to the story again after they read the letter which may happen after days of publication of the story.

Writing for employees

Chapters 6 and 8 deal with the aspect of role, scope and need for connecting with the employees and various media to reach out to them effectively. In the following paragraphs we shall discuss on what to write and how to write it, so that it connects people to the overall ethos and culture of the organization.

An organization as we have discussed elsewhere in the book is a place where likeminded people get together to fulfill organizational goals. People who join an organization come with various hopes, expectations and aspirations. It will be a great achievement for an organization, if all feel motivated and satisfied with their work, environment and pay package and the management also feels satisfied with everyone it hires. This is almost impossible to achieve, because human behaviour is dynamic. It changes with time due to various personal and environmental factors. An organization looks like a monolith from the outside, but it is no more than a bundle of complexities. An organization is not made of brick and mortar but thinking people.

It is only natural that people create comfort zones for themselves. The fall out often is that they get grouped based on hierarchies, gender, colour, caste, language, regional diversities, education, political leanings, to name a few. It is not uncommon to see these dynamics working against the progress of an organization. According to Alvie L. Smith, organizations miss out on human capital because they did not give priority to effective communication with employees. To quote him: *"the ugly truth is that employee disloyalty and lack of commitment to organization goals may be costing American businesses more than $50 billion a year. This is probably a conservative figure when you include the cost of absenteeism, labor grievances, production interruptions, poor quality, repair and warranty expenses for fixing poor quality and—highly important—owner disloyalty, loss of rpeat customer sales and credibility. Perhaps most costly of all is inaction by employees who withhold their best efforts and ideas; who cruise along with just passable performance".[3]*

What is true of the USA will not be different in other economies, and India is no exception, where trade unionism and collective bargaining alone has seen thousands of man-days wasted in strikes and absenteeism besides loss to public property.

Printed words

Organizations use a variety of media like letters, brainstorming sessions, gate meetings, open days, inserts, bulletin boards, CCTV, Intranet, video magazines, but printed newsletters or house journals remain the most popular. For the purpose of this chapter, we shall discuss the role and scope of writing for the house journal.

In India most of the public sector organizations have employee journals that come with various periodicities and shapes and sizes. Many large and medium sized organizations in the private sector, especially those who use PR as a strategic communication tool also have house journals. In retrospect, the TATA group is said to be the pioneer in bringing out a house journal for employee communication in the early 1940s.

According to Scot Cutlip et al, following are the broad objectives of employee communication in an organization:

1. To keep the employees informed on the organization's policies, programmes, goals and progress
2. To provide employees the information they need to help them perform their assignments proficiently
3. To encourage employees to maintain and enhance the organization's standards for and commitment to quality improvement, increased efficiency, improved services, and greater social responsibility
4. To recognize employees' achievements and successes[4]

Consider the following before writing:

➢ Who are you writing for and why?
➢ Who are your various stakeholders who need to be informed, inspired and to whom are management's expectations to be communicated?
➢ What messages are needed to maintain positive relationship in normal times?
➢ What messages would be needed to change a negative relationship?
➢ How would you know that the relationship has changed?

A house journal competes with other media like commercial magazines, newspapers etc. for attention. If it is not interesting or is considered biased in favour of the management by some sections of employees, it has a very little chance of being read and respected. A house journal though is a management's tool, but balance needs to be maintained so that each employee feels it reflects his/her voice.

To be a successful writer, it is important to keep the reader's interest in view. Finding interesting subjects to write about in a house journal can be both a joyful and exhilarating experience. Sitting in the corporate chair can't obviously develop good stories. Therefore observing, researching and listening to people is very important before one writes.

Here are some suggestions on what a PR writer can do before he writes for employees:
- Meet employees who have made a difference
- Understand innovations and people behind them
- Visit various places of projects, assembly lines and shop floors
- Understand processes so as to give them a human face.

Some tips on vocabulary
- Know how your audience speak
- Use language they understand
- Choose strong and active words.
- Be careful of the grammar and watch out for the sentence length.

At the end of the day, house journals that are employee oriented, that reflect employee aspirations, that write about "unsung heroes", the underdog, the achievements and success stories of the family members of employees, are rated much higher than those that are the management's mouthpiece.

Periodic feedback also goes a long way in making a house journal an important link among employees of various echelons in an organization.

Summary

In this chapter we have discussed the importance of PR writing in achieving organizational goals. We looked at various media for external communication that need writing skills, like press release, press handouts, press notes, rejoinders et al. We also discussed and deliberated on media for employee communication, especially the house journal that requires good writing skills.

Critical thinking exercise

Visit the website of a large organization that you generally find reflected in the media. Study the press releases issued by them to the media (the organizations generally post their press releases on their websites also) and follow how these were covered by the media in general. Make an analysis.

Questions

Q.1 What are the various genres of press releases? Discuss the purpose behind each kind of press release.

Q.2 Define "Inverted Pyramid" style of writing. What are the steps to be followed while writing a new release in this style?

Q.3 In your view, how is writing for media different from writing for employees. Discuss.

Endnotes

[1] Donald Treadwell & Jill B. Treadwell, *Public Relations Writing*, second ed. 2005 (Response Books: New Delhi) p.237.

[2] Ibid. pp.6-10

[3] Alive L. Smith, "Getting Managers off their Butts into the Communication Game", *Communication World 9*, no. 1 (January 1992) p.35.

[4] Scot M. Cutlip, Allen H. Center and Glen M. Broom, *Effective Public Relations*, seventh ed. 1994 (Prentice Hall: NJ) p.263.

10 PR and Crisis Communication

Chapter objectives
- Definition of crisis
- Various kinds of crises
- Crisis communication plan and process
- Media handling during various kinds of crises

No life—personal, corporate, national or international—can be immune to crisis, yet most of us are taken unawares by a crisis, because most of the crises are unpredictable. All crises pose a severe test. In such test, good planning and sound judgement make all the difference. Public relations plays a special role in times of crisis. Shearlean Duke and Lynne Masland suggest that it is always a good idea to anticipate the worst for one's organization so that one is on guard. This helps being always prepared to deal with critical situations in the best possible manner.[1]

Classification of crises

Hill and Knowlton, a leading PR consultancy in the U.S.A., has categorized crises in the following segments:
a. Actual disasters such as fires, explosions, accidents, earthquakes, floods, famines etc. These can be termed as *exploding crises*.
b. Controversial or scandalous incidents, involving companies, individuals, governments et al. are referred to as *immediate crises*.
c. Anticipated crisis due to premeditated decisions like closure of a plant, discontinuance of a service, retrenchment etc., are classified as *building crisis*.
d. When an organization, a product or a service is under long-term attack from some stakeholders like special interest groups, media, judiciary, consumer group et al, it is called *continuing crisis*.

Cutlip *et al* have categorized crises in three classifications:

Immediate crises: "The most dreaded type" that occur suddenly and unexpectedly, when there is no time for research and planning. Examples like a plan crash, product tampering, fires, earthquakes, bomb scare, workplace shooting by a disgruntled employee or the death of a key officer, are in this category, according to the authors.

Emerging crises: Crises that "allow time for research and planning", but may suddenly erupt after brewing for some time. Employees' dissatisfaction with work environment, pay package, sexual harassment at workplace, substance abuse in colleges or workplace would fall in this category of crises. Here intervention of the competent authority could solve the situation.

Sustained crises: Crises falling in this category persist for months and sometimes years before they surface, despite the fact that the management may be putting its efforts to tackle them. Rumours and speculation that get reported in the media or through grapevine fall within the purview of sustained crises. Misinformation may go on increasing till it snowballs into a major controversy.[2]

An organization in its lifespan may face one or all kinds of crises referred to above.

As we have discussed elsewhere in the book, an organization is made up of people and deals with people, especially those people or publics whose opinions have a direct bearing on its success or failure. Therefore, dealing with publics in times of crisis need special skill and care, hence the role of public relations.

Most organizations have written disaster plans to cope up with various kinds of crises. "In every large organization," says the Dartnel's PR handbook, "the disaster plan is to the Public Relations programme what the fire escape is to a building." This powerful statement sums up the unquestionable role of PR in mitigating and handling crises.

The disaster plan is invariably patterned to fit the organization's own potential exposure to calamity. To illustrate, the disaster plan of a nuclear plant would be very different from that of a steel plant because the potential risk areas would be quite different in the two cases. For instance, in the event of a terrorist strike in a particular city, the police is generally put on "red alert" in other cities, which amounts to gearing up to the immediate possibility of similar strikes in other cities.

Disaster planning, feel experts, is preparing for the worst while hoping for the best. One wishes, it were never necessary to put the disaster plan into action. In a disaster plan, not only are the potential areas of risk identified but programmes are also prepared to be put into action without leaving room for improvisation. The disaster management group is identified so that precious time is saved in getting approvals in a hurry. Many organizations conduct mock exercises, keeping them top secret, to gauge the alertness of those in charge of handling emergencies in coping up with a crisis. This gives the management the chance to review the preparedness and locate gray areas.

No two crises are similar. Even crises of a similar nature have to be dealt with differently depending on the kind of people involved in the crises, the timing of the crises and the circumstances. A checklist may hold good in all types of situations.

In times of crisis, the temptation too often is to cry "sabotage", pass the buck to a "foreign hand" or rush out with an announcement taking an opposite tack, namely a disclaimer. In a crisis situation, the media are insistent and demand quick answers. While realizing their need, one should not mess up with the organization's image. PR needs to share the facts available and supplement them with more facts as one gets them. Fumbling, concocting facts or denying the obvious, rarely helps. Remember, media have other sources of information too. If the PR person does not give timely information, the media may collect it from unauthorized sources, which may prove erroneous. A communication vacuum created by official sources is likely to be filled up by grapevine or by irresponsible information. Then, it becomes a question of credibility. If you dither once, you will never be taken seriously next time and you lose allies in the media for all time to come. The government-controlled/funded media most of the times suffer from a credibility gap for not sharing vital information with the people for whatever reasons—political, national, diplomatic, to name a few. To cite an instance, her security guards gunned down Former Prime Minister Mrs Indira Gandhi in the morning hours of 31 October 1984, but the government-controlled electronic media announced the tragedy only towards the evening, when the whole world already knew about it.

In a crisis, it is imperative to collect available facts immediately and never go beyond them until more have been received. There is no harm telling the media that you are awaiting the latest information. This is better than giving wrong information. In an emergency situation, remember, there is no choice whether to speak to the media or not, because one has to.

Exploding crisis

Let us look at the steps to be taken should an emergency of an exploding nature occur:

1. The first step for the crisis team is to alert security to take charge of the situation and for the public relations persons is to prepare material for the media and arrange interviews or press conferences for the spokesperson, if the situation so warrants. The first information report should contain the following broadly:
   - What is the nature of the emergency?
   - How it occurred (if you know for sure) or a few inferences?
   - Number of casualties, if any, and whether the injured have been removed to hospital?
   - Have families been informed?
   - When are all the facts likely to be available?
2. Identify the spokesperson. The employees must be advised to refrain from speaking for the company to outsiders.
3. Announce a telephone number for public inquiries. A responsible person should attend to the calls.

4. Create a press centre if the situation warrants for continuously feeding the media or when more facts are expected. The information released should be logged to know what information was released to whom at what time. This will help in releasing updated information to the various media. Now that most companies have their websites, they post updated information on the Home page, and news releases on the relevant page created for media, variously known as Media room, Press centre etc. In case there are any queries on the website, address them quickly.

Be careful about pictures. The media in such situations may be interested to sensationalize. You may not be able to avoid that but it is advisable to keep an ample number of bromides ready to supply to the press, if required, and also to place on the website, for downloading by the media. If some press reporters insist on taking pictures, facilities should be provided after ensuring that there is no risk for the media persons in moving around the affected areas.

After the crisis is over, follow up with the press in releasing information about corrective measures taken to avoid recurrence of such incidents. Words of reassurance to different publics, especially the community, should be released. In fact, apt handling of a crisis can turn it into a corporate image-building opportunity. The PR practitioners in the majority of the cases have no control over the crisis. However, should a crisis occur, openness, clarity, precision and empathetic communication in a planned manner can help the affected to appreciate the organization's dilemma and its sincere effort to cope with the crisis, keeping the human interest above everything else.

CASE STUDY

Mumbai siege – a case of exploding crisis (2008)

Ten armed terrorists allegedly from the neighbouring country sneaked in to the financial capital of India, Mumbai on 26 November 2008 and created mayhem for 64 hours, shooting at people indiscriminately, making hundreds of people hostages in two five star hotels and a Jewish family from Israel in their own home, besides shooting at people at a railway station. About 200 hundred people were dead and double the number injured in one of worst terrorist carnage witnessed by the country in its history. The entire world was aghast as it sat glued to their television sets as hundreds of channels beamed the terror theatre live in their homes. The helpless viewers could only pray or clinch their fists in desperation. This also reflected the lack of preparedness on the part of the establishments; both centre and state, as no one seem to be in control of situation at the site at least. There were no instructions to the general public, who could be seen moving around or the media persons camping close to the venue of the siege, whose lives were also in danger. The terrorists could have showered grenades outside. The media came in for severe criticism as they kept telling the tactical and strategic details of the movement of commandoes, which could have helped the terrorists, watching television inside the areas of their capture. However, after a while, some channels showed footage that was 30 minutes old.[3]

In a crisis of this kind and magnitude, there is lesson for those, especially representing the political class to be careful not only about their manifest and subtle intentions, but also how people may perceive them. The Mumbai carnage cost both the Chief minister Vilas Rao Deshmukh and the State Home Minister R R Patil their jobs. The Chief Minister (CM) was almost lynched by media for an act that seemed so insipid and unexpected of a person, in charge of the State. A day after the siege was cleared, he along with his entourage visited the hotel Taj, an exercise in PR, so would anyone infer. However, in his party were two persons that raised eyebrows instantly, namely, Filmmaker Ram Gopal Verma, who has made a number of films on the underworld's nexus in city crimes and film star Ritesh Deshmukh, who is Mr Deshmukh's son. Images appeared in the media immediately criticizing the CM for bringing the filmmaker and his son for a reconnaissance of the place that probably would be plot for Ram Gopal Verma's next film, in which his son would act! No amount of damage control helped, either from the filmmaker or the CM. Media referred the act as "Terror Tourism". While on a piece to camera, the CM tried to justify his stand saying that it was not for publicity as no private channels were invited to cover the occasion. He reasoned that it was only the Doordarshan, the state run TV crew that shot the footage, which was later shared with other channels. What was the logic behind that reasoning, only Mr. Deshmukh could answer? The caption of the interface on the NDTV was: *"Lacking: Sense and Sensibility"*. While giving the interview, it may not be his intention, but his body language did not suggest that he was concerned or felt outraged or hurt given the mayhem the city underwent. He kept smiling and dodging questions. The cameras went on showing repeat actions of some of his gestures, which seemed odd, given the solemnity of time and circumstances. Similarly to a media question, the state Home Minster said, as the city was so big, it was not strange for incidents like the one to have happened. It was not only obnoxious on the part of the person responsible for internal security to say so, he also displayed a complete lack of empathy for those who lost their lives, including 20 personnel from the security agencies that he headed.

"Insensitive, inconsiderate, mindless and cruel...." were some of the words, young people used to describe Indian politicians on their Face book pages, blogs, chat rooms and public space. [4]

The electronic media was also on the receiving end from the viewers through various blogs.

Smallchange, a blog by a song composer reflected on the Mumbai happening thus: "They (meaning the news channels) have to be told how to behave in times like these. Their actions have to be considered criminal conduct if they in any way compromise security operations. And really, if a channel puts a terrorist on air and airs his views in the middle of operations, it should be legally considered a criminal act." There were 850 responses in a day's time. Some also criticized self-promotion by channels during the live coverage, a highly insensitive thing to do. Some journalist went overboard in displaying the emotion too loudly. [5]

Oasis in the desert

In critical times when there is an overflow of adrenalin, it is important that those in charge of communication, both from the media and PR side are sensitive enough to help give a break from the tense atmosphere and make people feel that despite all that was happening, there was still something to smile about, a heroic act, a humane gesture, a healing touch.

As soon as Hotel Taj was cleared of the terrorists, hundreds of media men, covering live, said that from the body language of the security forces, one could make out that the flushing was complete, even before a formal announcement was made by the security personnel. It was a great site to find a few security personnel from various security agencies taking out their cell phones from their pockets and engage in small talks, beaming all through. There was no mistaking that the calls were from or to their harrowed family members and well wishers, who must have heaved a sigh of relief seeing their loved ones alive.[6]

People holding red roses appeared in hundreds from nowhere. Roses were presented to security personnel as they boarded the buses to take them away after their task was over. A soldier feeding the pigeons also made an interesting shot. Public is very sharp when it comes to visual imagery. A channel had a person from the public who criticized the local government for sending mundane BEST buses to take the security personnel back home after they successfully accomplished the task, while some of them sacrificed their lives. He said ruefully that if it were the Cricket team returning from somewhere, it would have been a luxury coach for them, but not for the real heroes who did not bother about their lives so that people could live.

The incident will also serves as a lesson for politicians of various parties. People's apathy was writ large on their faces. Father of Major Sandeep Unnikrisnan from the NSG refused to meet the Kerala Chief Minister who came to offer condolences on the death of their son, only to receive a response " Even a dog will not visit their home, had it not been for Sandeep". Media played on it unceasingly, but the Chief Minster despite being told by the CPM high command to apologize, refused to do so on the same day. [7] He, however changed track the next day and did what was expected of him.

Some Mumbai politicians who have been raising slogans against "outsiders" occupying Mumbai came in for a lot of flak from media and bloggers who made no bones in challenging them on their narrow parochialism. "Who have come to save Mumbai (referring to security forces), would you call them outsiders or Indians?" echoed many voices.

Public opinion swings like a pendulum in a crisis situation despite that it may not always be based on sound reason. It was an outburst of emotion given the critical environment as the Mumbai carnage. In this time and age of interactive communication through the Net, thousands of blogs surfaced and e-mail boxes were overloaded with mails of all kinds. Sample the following that had on its target- the media.

Copy of an e-mail circulated far and wide in India.

Today, three magazines hit the stands.
India Today
Outlook Magazine
The Week

All three of them have the "Mumbai attacks" as the cover story.

However there is a major difference. While India Today and Outlook have jacked up their prices from Rs. 20 to Rs. 25, The Week has increased their price from Rs. 15 to Rs. 20/-. This is a blatant attempt to fleece Indian readers at the expense of the several hundred martyrs who lost their lives!

Hence, we request all patriotic Indians to boycott:
1. India Today & all magazines from the India Today Group
2. Outlook and all magazines from the Outlook Group
3. The Week and all its allied publications.

Let us not purchase these magazines and instead search and read on the Internet.

Please forward this mail to your friends, e-mail addressbookmates, family, colleagues and associates.

Let us lay a wreath over those who sold our country's martyrs for the sake of a few extra bucks.

Yeh Public hai, yeh sab janti haai
Andar Kya Hai Bahar Kya Hai, yeh sab kuch pehchanti hai.........
Forwarded by an unknown Indian...

In contrast to the live telecast of attacks, the situation was very different, about two decades ago, when there was only one television channel, the state-run Doordarshan, that used to telecast news in two bulletins, one in Hindi and one in English in the evenings in a few hours total programme timing. But, the bluff was still called in a matter of hours, when the newspapers published their stories next day. Here is recapitulating on what happened in Uttar Pradesh in 1990. The first time when the Kar Sevaks went to lay the "foundation stone" in Ayodhya on the site of the Babri Masjid on 31 October 1990, people obviously were anxious to know what was happening. In the evening bulletins of Doordarshan, the then Prime Minister Late Vishwanath Pratap Singh appeared to ensure that nothing untoward had happened. He specifically said that some miscreants tried to enter the premises of the mosque, but were shooed away. Right the next morning all newspapers had the pictures of some people atop the mosque, hoisting a saffron flag. The Prime Minister, being the ultimate source of information in a democracy was obviously seen as telling a lie. Did he not know the factual position or he held back the truth so that he could help avoid a possible communal backlash, is a speculative question. If he was not sure, the best course for him should have been, not to give a categorical statement in the interest of credibility. Some fundamental forces razed the Babri Masjid down later on 6 December 1992, when Mr. P V Narsimha Rao was the Prime Minister of India. The unfortunate incident was followed by communal riots in many parts of the country. This was a time when satellite channels had made their inroads into Indian homes, and the coverage from both public and private channels provided people with plurality of views.

Immediate crises

The Watergate scandal in America, the Bofors guns, and more recently the Satyam computers, in India can be cited as examples of immediate crises. In all these cases, ethics were in question. No amount of public relations could have helped in salvaging the situation. Nixon had to leave the U.S. presidency after the scandal was exposed. The Bofors gun case was in the media focus for about 15 years, until Pakistan sent its intruders in the Kargil area in Kashmir in 1999 and the gun supposedly did a good job. Satyam computers case study has been taken up for discussion later in the chapter.

Public opinion often swings from one extreme to the other in a crisis, especially when a scandal or lives of human beings are involved. The swing is not necessarily based on reason. Emotions like anger, lack of trust, propaganda by the contending party could be some of the reasons for surge in public opinion.

CASE STUDY

Lies and politics (1999)

Two politicians from the BJP and alliance parties found themselves in the eye of the storm for their alleged innuendo and sexist remarks against Mrs. Sonia Gandhi, the president of the contending party, viz., Congress in their speeches during the Loksabha election campaigning in August 1999. The reaction was instant from the party. Media provided the multiplier impact and interestingly even those newspapers that were not very positively inclined towards the candidate felt that it was an insult to her as a woman and wrote extensively against the conduct of the concerned members of parliament. The story attracted front-page coverage in most of the dailies. It sure became a crisis for the party. Public opinion seemed to favour the supposed "victim". Various women's groups also got activated, offering sound bytes to media, giving a further credence to the issue. Prime Minister Atal Behari Bajpai was probably the first one in the party to wake up to the sudden image damage, he not only regretted the remarks at a personal level but also exhorted everyone to keep high standards of public morality and be gender sensitive.

The alleged perpetrator, the late Mr. Pramod Mahajan was quick to deny the allegation. He said he was quoted out of context. But when the controversy did not die down and he seemed to lose the argument, he cut short his visit to return to the Capital and addressed a press conference where he showed a copy of the letter supposedly written by *The Hindustan Times* correspondent to his Editor wherein he had written that his story was manipulated at the desk in Delhi. The paper was equally quick to come out with a denial. The editor said that he not only stood by the story but also distributed photocopies of the dispatch of their correspondent who had filed the story.

Wrong representation of facts –a perceived cause for war (1990)

In times of a crisis, the temptation more often is to overdo things or camouflage reality for strategic gains. That is where the credibility of public relations comes under public focus. PR consultancy Hill and Knowlton got embroiled for what was seen by critics as an attempt at the 'manipulation of minds' of opinion makers, a consultancy that it took on behalf of its client "Citizens for a free Kuwait" in 1990, before the Gulf War. The Agency's stance came for critical analysis as critics felt that public relations professionals could manipulate the image "because they know the importance people place on signs and symbols in the culture". The PR strategy, so believed many, catapulted the US into the Gulf War.

On October 10, 1990, a 15-year-old Kuwaiti girl, Nayriah-al-Sabah testified before the US Congress about the atrocities that the Iraqis were committing against Kuwaiti citizens. She specifically mentioned that Iraqis were taking Kuwaiti babies from incubators in area hospitals. Her testimony caught the imagination of the people as her face and tearful disposition was vividly caught by media. It, in fact became the language of the Government's call to arms, as argued by critics. The episode came to be referred to as the "incubator atrocities". Many senators voted for war and cited the story. It came to notice later that Hill & Knowlton was paid $ 10.5 million by a group called the "Citizens for a free Kuwait" which was represented primarily by wealthy members of the Kuwaiti ruling class to manage perceptions of various stakeholders. The aim of the PR strategy was to "Offset unfavourable publicity about Kuwait's form of government as well as its human rights record". It was also revealed that the girl who testified was the daughter of Kuwait's ambassador to the USA. There was even a doubt as to whether the girl was in Kuwait at the time of the alleged atrocities that she testified about. Amnesty International had a difficult time corroborating her allegations. The Kroll Report that came out in 1992 concluded that there had been no mass scale atrocities on babies. It was however, a fact that seven babies died because medical equipment was moved from a hospital.

The PR agency later admitted having coached the girl about the incubator imagery. The agency nonetheless defended its action in the interest of drawing public attention. Thomas J. Mickey in one of his articles questions the use of sign, which may or may not represent reality.[8]

Sometimes organizations find themselves embroiled in a controversy for the alleged unethical or illegal behaviour of its top management or employees, an issue that can snowball into a major controversy, sullying the image of the organization and affecting investors.

In the following paragraphs, two case studies of this nature, though both with varying implications have been taken up for detailed discussion and analysis. One, the fraudulent practices by Mr. B Ramalinga Raju, promoter and CEO of Satyam Computers and Phaneesh Murthy—a high profile employee of competitor Infosys—who received global attention for a sexual harassment case filed against him in a US court.

First the Satyam story.

Satyam Computers- a case of poor corporate governance (2009)

The celebrations of the new year had not even dimmed, when a week later, the afternoon radio bulletins and mainstream and trade channels on 7 January 2009 gave the shocking breaking news as to how the stocks of Satyam Computers took an 80% plunge downwards as soon as its CEO, B Ramalinga Raju resigned and owned up responsibility for the fraud committed over many years, running in to hundreds of crore rupees. Naming it "India's Enron", *The Economic Times* in a banner headline "Satyam – A Big Lie" called it the biggest fraud in India's corporate history (Satyam in Sanskrit means truth, here in this case, the company did not live up to its name, seemed to be the thought behind the paper's headline!).[9]

Sunil Singhania, Executive VP of Reliance MF commented, "This is the worst thing to have happened. It reflects poorly on the corporate governance of the company. From the foreign investors' perspective, the image of corporate India would be dented in a big way".[10]

IT stalwarts like N R Naryanamurthy of Infosys, unsparing on the scandal, commented, "What's happened is shocking. It will have a deep impact on the entire Indian industry. I believe it is in bad taste, but an isolated case. The need of the hour is for the IT sector to walk that extra mile."[11]

Chairman of the regulator body, Securities Exchange of India (SEBI), G B Bhave spoke tough, saying, "It is an event of horrifying magnitude. We are in touch with the Ministry of Company Affairs for coordinated action. We need to learn a few lessons from this. The development will have serious implications for the market."[12]

Later, during the Economic Times Excellence Awards 2008 in Mumbai on 18 January 2009, Prime Minister Manmohan Singh said that the Satyam Computers scandal was a blot on India's corporate image. The government, he said, was determined to unravel the nature of the fraud. To quote him, "The Satyam episode is a blot on our corporate image. It indicates how far malfeasance in one company can inflict suffering on many.... The government is determined to unravel the full nature of the fraud."[13]

The company was guilty of fudging financial figures worth hundreds of crores in its books for years on end to present a rosier picture, when the chief R Raju was led by events that forced him to confess, about which said he wanted to "ease the burden on his conscience", as reflected in his confessionary letter (reproduced later in the chapter).

What this fraud meant in brass tacks?

The accounting books were cooked for years with inflated figures of profit and revenue, exaggerated cash and bank balance, besides an understatement of what was owed and overstatement of what was due to the company.

The statutory auditing firm, multinational, Powerhouse Cooper (PWC) either overlooked fudging of figures or was hand in glove with the management. The CBI after three months' of the unearthing of the scam has named two PWC officers also in its charge sheet.

Satyam founder and former chairman Ramalinga Raju, his brother, Rama Raju, who was managing director, and ex-chief financial officer Vadlamani Srinivas, were arrested in January after founder Raju resigned. Later, two PWC officers were also taken into police custody.

Post scam, there are scores of criminal cases also pending against the company and its CEO in the US courts. Some analysts believed that had he been in the US, he would have attracted a long haul in jail for the laws are very strict against such frauds.

Bare facts about Satyam

Founded in 1987 by the US educated Ramalinga Raju, Satyam Computers soon became one of the top five software services exporter from India. The company was also listed on the NYSE. Some of its competitors from India included, the Tata Consultancy Services and Infosys Technologies as well as global majors such as IBM and Accenture.

Satyam claimed to have 53,000 employees (a fact later refuted by investigating agencies who said thousands of names were fictitious, but their salaries were drawn that filled the personal coffers of the family.).

Satyam specializes in business software and offers back-office outsourcing and consulting. The company at the time of the scam had more than 600 clients, some of the prominent among them being General Electrical, Cisco System and Qantas Airways.

As soon as the fraud was unearthed, the Government of India appointed a new board of directors that retained KPMG Deloitte, an auditing firm, to restate accounts that were overstated for six years.

The rise of Satyam and its promoter B Ramalinga Raju is ascribed in a large measure to the tech savvy ex Chief Minister of Andhra Pradesh, Chandrababu

Naidu, who many believed wanted to create a parallel Infosys' in his state and make his state the IT hub. He was even able to invite Bill Clinton to his state during his presidency. Stories about how R Raju was given preference by the Chief Minister over other industry stalwarts during public functions were a part of the grapevine in those times.

After the Congress came to power, the company was able to maintain cordial relations with it also, garnering many plum contracts in the infrastructure sector. Commenting on the market and the feel, Sumeet Chatterjee of Reuters writes, "At the height of the boom, top software firms Tata Consultancy Services, Infosys Technologies, Wipro and Satyam consistently reported annual 50-percent increases in profits every quarter. Pressure to maintain this pace of growth, please investors and shareholders and justify inflated P/E multiples during a six-year bull run on the stock market have all been cited as reasons why Satyam cooked the books."[14]

How did the fraud take place?

Analysts believe that on the face of it, Satyam did everything by the rulebook. It had an international firm auditing its books, its declaration of accounts were in accordance with Indian and U.S. standards. It had the requisite number of independent directors with good credentials, including a Harvard business school professor and a former federal cabinet secretary.

Ramalinga Raju, in his letter outlining the deception, said no other board member—past or present—was aware of the financial irregularities. Here is the full text of the letter.

Text of B Ramalinga Raju's letter

"It is with deep regret and tremendous burden that I am carrying on my conscience, that I would like to bring the following facts to your notice:

1. The Balance Sheet carries as of September 30, 2008,
    a) Inflated (non-existent) cash and bank balances of Rs 5,040 crore (as against Rs 5,361 crore reflected in the books);
    b) An accrued interest of Rs 376 crore, which is non-existent
    c) An understated liability of Rs 1,230 crore on account of funds arranged by me;
    d) An overstated debtors' position of Rs 490 crore (as against Rs 2,651 reflected in the books);
2. For the September quarter(Q2) we reported a revenue of Rs 2,700 crore and an operating margin of Rs 649 crore(24 per cent of revenue) as against the actual revenues of Rs 2,112 crore and an actual operating margin of Rs 61 crore (3 per cent of revenues). This has resulted in artificial cash and bank balances going up by Rs 588 crore in Q2 alone.

The gap in the balance sheet has arisen purely on account of inflated profits over several years (limited only to Satyam standalone, books of subsidiaries reflecting true performance).

What started as a marginal gap between actual operating profit and the one reflected in the books of accounts continued to grow over the years.

It has attained unmanageable proportions as the size of the company operations grew significantly (annualised revenue run rate of Rs 11,276 crore in the September quarter, 2008, and official reserves of Rs 8,392 crore).

The differential in the real profits and the one reflected in the books was further accentuated by the fact that the company had to carry additional resources and assets to justify a higher level of operations thereby significantly increasing the costs.

Every attempt made to eliminate the gap failed. As the promoters held a small percentage of equity, the concern was that poor performance would result in the takeover, thereby exposing the gap. It was like riding a tiger, not knowing how to get off without being eaten.

The aborted Maytas acquisition deal was the last attempt to fill the fictitious assets with real ones. Maytas' investors were convinced that this is a good divestment opportunity and a strategic fit.

Once Satyam's problem was solved, it was hoped that Maytas' payments can be delayed. But that was not to be. What followed in the last several days is common knowledge.

I would like the board to know:

1. That neither myself, nor the Managing Director (including our spouses) sold any shares in the last eight years - excepting for a small proportion declared and sold for philanthropic purposes.
2. That in the last two years a net amount of Rs 1,230 crore was arranged to Satyam (not reflected in the books of Satyam) to keep the operations going by resorting to pledging all the promoter shares and raising funds from known sources by giving all kinds of assurances (statement enclosed only to the members of the board).

    Significant dividend payments, acquisitions, capital expenditure to provide for growth did not help matters. Every attempt was made to keep the wheel moving and to ensure prompt payment of salaries to the associates. The last straw was the selling of most of the pledged shares by the lenders on account of margin triggers.
3. That neither me nor the managing director took even one rupee/dollar from the company and have not benefited in financial terms on account of the inflated results.
4. None of the board members, past or present, had any knowledge of the situation in which the company is placed.

Even business leaders and senior executives in the company, such as, Ram Mynampati, Subu D, T R Anand, Keshab Panda, Virender Agarwal, A S Murthy, Hari T, S V Krishnan, Vijay Prasad, Manish Mehta, Murli V, Shriram Papani, Kiran Kavale, Joe Lagioia, Ravindra Penumetsa, Jayaraman and Prabhakar Gupta are unaware of the real situation as against the books of accounts. None of my or managing directors' immediate or extended family members has any idea about these issues.

Having put these facts before you, I leave it to the wisdom of the board to take the matters forward. However, I am also taking the liberty to recommend the following steps:

1. A task force has been formed in the last few days to address the situation arising out of the failed Maytas acquisition attempt.

    This consists of some of the most accomplished leaders of Satyam: Subu D, T.R. Anand, Keshab Panda and Virendra Agarwal, representing business functions, and A S Murthy, Hari T and Murali V representing support functions.

    I suggest that Ram Mynampati be made the chairman of this Task Force to immediately address some of the operational matters on hand. Ram can also act as an interim CEO reporting to the board.

2. Merrill Lynch can be entrusted with the task of quickly exploring some merger opportunities.

3. You may have a 'restatement of accounts' prepared by the auditors in light of the facts that I have placed before you.

I have promoted and have been associated with Satyam for well over 20 years now. I have seen it grow from few people to 53,000 people, with 185 Fortune 500 companies with customers and operations in 66 countries. Satyam has established an excellent leadership and competency base at all levels.

I sincerely apologise to all Satyamites and stakeholders, who have made Satyam a special organization, for the current situation. I am confident they will stand by the company in this hour of crisis.

In light of the above, I fervently appeal to the board to hold together to take some important steps. TR Prasad is well placed to mobilise a support from the government at this crucial time.

With the hope that members of the Task Force and the financial advisor, Merrill Lynch (now Bank of America), will stand by the company at this crucial hour, I am marking copies of the statement to them as well.

Under the circumstances, I am tendering the resignation as the chairman of Satyam and shall continue in this position only till such time the current board is expanded. My continuance is just to ensure enhancement of the board over the next several days or as early as possible.

I am now prepared to subject myself to the laws of the land and face the consequences thereof".

(B Ramalinga Raju)

Copies marked to:
1. Chairman SEBI
2. Stock Exchanges.[15]

About $1 billion, or 94 percent of the cash, on the company's books was fictitious. Analysts feel that manipulation of the cash flow may be a reason why the fraud was undetected. "Companies have manipulated P&L (profit and loss) accounts before, but cash flow is the Holy Grail — you don't tamper with it," said Saurabh Mukherjea, an analyst at UK-based research firm Noble Group.[16]

The Central Bureau of Investigation (CBI) issued a statement on 7 April 2009, i.e. after three months of the exposure of scam, filing charges against nine people including Satyam Computer Services' founder and former chairman Ramalinga Raju for alleged involvement in accounting fraud at the outsourcing firm. The charges included criminal conspiracy, cheating, forgery and falsification of accounts. Media quoting CBI sources said that the agency had a feeling that R Raju may not have shared all the frauds in his letter. The agency was contemplating to seek permission from the government to question Raju further and maybe put him on a lie detector.[17]

The crux of the CBI charge sheet indicates the scam money at Rs. 6000 Crores, out of which the family is said to have cornered Rs. 2580 crores. What the family has done with that money, where they have invested it and who were the people who helped them is yet to be unearthed. The Life Insurance Corporation lost Rs 950 crores in the scam, and with that millions of investors their money in LIC mutual funds. Investors like Allahabad Bank, Union Bank of India, Punjab National Bank, Overseas Bank of India and Corporation Bank lost 10 Crores, put together.

Analyzing the crisis

If the one reality was that accounts were manipulated, the other was that truth was also manipulated by the CEO for almost two weeks after the media first got the hint that the institutional shareholders were questioning the wisdom of the board on acquiring the infrastructure firm Maytas. Most thought the problem was internal and would soon be sorted out, as the company went in for damage control, aborting the plan to buy Maytas stakes, but the share price tanked in the meantime. Chairman of Satyam, B Ramalinga Raju promised investors with share buy back, saying, and "please be assured that our intent to acquire Maytas was well within the framework, and these were not compromised in any way. I share your disappointment that the recent developments have caused to us. We have always placed significant value on the interests of our associates, customers and investors. We are in conversation with many of our key stakeholders individually to correct the perceptions". The statement about 'correcting the perceptions' makes one believe that Raju and others did not think at least at that point of time that things would take a different turn altogether. Employees of the company didn't seem to have any clue of the happenings except what probably was coming to them through the media, until R Raju interfaced and mislead them giving false assurance that their interest would be safeguarded.[18]

The Satyam management with an interim CEO Ram Myanampati held a press conference on 8 January 2009 promising their clients and employees that everything would be fine. Myanampati said that the company had taken care of employees' December salary but faced a cash crunch. A helpline was set up for employees to ask about their concerns.[19]

Headhunters interviewed by uTvi, a business channel, said that in just few hours of the unearthing of scandal various portals were inundated with thousands of applications, that reflected the anxiety of the employees.[20]

Some of the representatives of the these firms exhorted the IT industry not to hold the happenings against the employees but come forward in taking them on their rolls without any prejudice.

Next day, media reflected the response of the IT sector. In a box item with caption: "Infy not to hire Satyam employees" the story quoted Infosys Technologies HR, Education & Administration Director T V Mohandas Pai about the decision of their company on this issue thus: "We have asked our recruitment staff not to poach anybody from Satyam. The company is in the middle of a crisis and people will jump ship".[21] The impression sought to be given was that in tough times, one must help a fellow company. This however was in contravention of the stand of its Chief mentor and Non-Executive Chairman Naryanamurthy, who just a day before had said in the context of hiring employees from Satyam, "we will not touch such a tainted company". As reported by the media, Infosys management had also instructed its staff not to entertain any calls or resume of employees from Satyam.

In tough times, especially that involve scandals, it is difficult to garner support from anyone and often one has to sail alone. It remains a huge responsibility on the Satyam management to address the morale of employees.

What are the PR insights?

It is no guarantee that a company that won many awards for excellence in corporate governance, including the Golden Peacock Global Award twice, most recently in 2008 is ethical in its dealings. This also puts a question mark on the award giving organizations, who probably don't do their homework well.

Within days, millions of blogs surfaced on the Net, from among enthusiasts, investors, self-proclaimed analysts and some also sympathizing with the beleaguered CEO remembering him as a great employer! Tracking responses, addressing the concerns is the need of the hour to build back the reputation of the company.

It must be a tough time for the company to address issues raised by various stakeholders including clients, shareholders, and particularly the media. The PR department of Satyam needs to work in close coordination with the new management to respond quickly to the concerns and queries of various stakeholders. In fact, a white paper can be prepared by the company to look at the involvement of internal and external stakeholders including auditors, bankers, and politicians to get to the genesis of the issue and see how confidence can be restored.

Media took potshots at the beleaguered CEO of Satyam, on his life in jail, giving graphic details about the size of the room that he was sharing with other criminals, the toilet that he would be sharing with 40 other inmates and of course the food, not forgetting to write that he came in his Mercedes Benz to the police station for his arrest! It was probably the sadist pleasure they wished to provide to all those who were hurt by his misdemeanour and misdeeds.

Tracking media coverage within India and overseas, especially the US will provide the PR department with an update on issues, views and public opinion on the beleaguered company.

The company's employees obviously were concerned about their future. The sudden turn of events was not only a rude shock to them, but the entire IT fraternity. An IT company's real assets are its human capital. If the company wishes to bounce back, the concerns of their employees need to be addressed. Communicating with them in times of crisis, addressing their fears and apprehensions should be the foremost priority of the new management. After about three weeks, media reports indicated that the employees had formed a union and were demanding their representation on the Board to ensure the interests of the employees are addressed adequately.[22]

While most of the employees avoided talking to media about their state of mind, one newspaper published a picture of the exterior of the jail where R Raju was lodged which had a few placards pledging support to their boss. One of them read: "With you, always". It would hopefully bring, the fallen from grace Ex. CEO some food for thought on the value of trust and sincerity.

After almost a month, the new Board released a video, termed as "Inspirational Video" by media, in which most of the board members assured the employees about the steps taken by the company that would address their concerns. The internal auditing officer also spoke about auditing that was underway to look at the financial health of the company. One of the board members also hoped that the company would be able to borrow money from the banks and other institutions soon to make payments and get over difficult times.[23]

Case of moral turpitude—how did Infosys manage its reputation? (2001-03)

Infosys is one of the most respected companies of India as per several surveys conducted by the media and other rating agencies from time to time. It found itself in a legal and media glare for an act that was allegedly committed by one of its employees.

About the company
A company with 19,000+ employees worldwide, Infosys, provides consulting and IT services to clients globally. The "Phaneesh Murthy Sexual Harassment

Case" as it came to be referred to in the media, was one of its kind faced by the company since its inception. It had the entire IT industry and people in general taking a keen interest due to media coverage in prime time bulletins and mainstream newspapers.

What was the issue?

Phaneesh Murthy, who rose to be the blue-eyed boy of the company joined Infosys in 1992 and was elevated to the board position in May 2000. As per figures reflected in the media, he earned Rs. 1.91 crore annually, which was said to be higher than the salary of even the founder of the company, Mr. N R Narayana Murthy.

In November 2001, Phaneesh Murthy's former Executive Assistant Reka Maximovitch, a Belgian by origin filed a case of sexual harassment against him. After about two months, Murthy informed Nandan Nilekani, the CEO, of a possible sexual harassment case. Both the company and Phaneesh Murthy were served with a legal notice in July 2002. Phaneesh Murthy resigned the same month to fight the case. Soon, however, he set up a consultancy by the name Primentor along with his wife Jaya.

Infosys went in for an out-of-court settlement with Reka Maximovitch to avoid dragging its name in the case for long. The settlement amount was US$ 3 million. Under the terms of settlement the company retained all rights to proceed with legal action against Phaneesh Murthy. Naryanamurthy, Chairman and Chief Mentor of Infosys that time said to the media, "the litigation with the plaintiff is behind us. We have taken further steps to strengthen our internal processes and improve the checks and balances to handle similar situations".[24]

The company is said to have a well-placed policy on sexual harassment at workplace. On a question from the media, its US office sent the following reply on the policy:

"Explaining what constitutes sexual harassment; action an employee can take, if he/she feels that he/she has been harassed; a Governance Resolution Body chaired by Professor Pooja Kaushik of the National Law School and procedure to be followed by GRB, in case of a complaint, etc."[25]

In October 2003, Jennifer Griffith filed a similar sexual harassment case against Phaneesh Murthy and Infosys. The company issued a press release to the media on 24 November 2004, explaining its stand. It said it was not a signatory to the settlement agreement. Phaneesh Murthy and insurers paid the settlement reached at for US $ 8,00,000, fifty-fifty. The company said in its press release: "Infosys refused to make any contribution to the settlement".

Interestingly in the earlier phase of the case, the company seemed a bit sympathetic to Murthy, but changed its stand, after he resigned, started his company and also alleged that Infosys had not settled his accounts against his shares. This is what Narayana Murthy said of him when he resigned in July 2002: "Phaneesh has been an integral part of Infosys' growth in the last 10 years.

Phaneesh has performed outstandingly in sales and marketing and CAPS and we are sorry that he has tendered his resignation in these circumstances. We wish him well for the future." [26]

Infosys remained in the media focus as long as both the cases were under litigation. Despite all the time that has lapsed, media does not forget the episode, so easily. An analyst put it interestingly, "Anytime Phaneesh Murthy is mentioned in the media, there is a token mention of Reka Maximovitch...more akin to the statutory warning on Cigarette packets".[27] As recently as in 2009, when I-Gate, a company where Phaneesh Murthy works, had evinced interest in Satyam; CNBC, a trade channel, while interviewing Murthy had this to say in the introductory remarks: *"Phaneesh Murthy of iGATE says his company is open to buying Satyam Computers Services Ltd. Phaneesh Murthy was the global head sales and marketing at Infosys. He was based in the US and was one of Infosys' highest paid employees and tipped to lead the IT giant. But a sexual harassment case cut his Infosys career short. He was accused of sexual harassment by Reka Maximovitch, a former executive assistant at Infosys in June 2002. The case was settled out of court for $3 million. Phaneesh then joined iGate Corporation"*.[28]

The media, by and large, have portrayed Phaneesh Murthy as a victim and not really a perpetrator, feel some analysts. As soon as he set up his consultancy Primentor, one analyst expressed her surprise that *The Economic Times*, Corporate Dossier could devote almost two pages on his new venture, a feat probably achieved by none in the corporate world. The write up, said the analyst had three parts, in one, it was about Murthy's business plans, in the second, "the wife", she writes, "insisted that she was in love with him, and trusts him more than she trusts herself" and the couple's philosophy about life. Friends and betrayals were included in the third part.[29]

Infosys' strategy to tackle the crisis

As soon as Infosys realized the gravity of the issue, it put its act together. Keeping in touch with the media, posting the developments and press releases on its Website, answering to media queries and sensitizing the employees on its drive named ANSHI (Anti-Sexual Harassment Initiative) were some the actions taken by it. The top management was invariably available for media queries.

What is ANSHI?

ANSHI was an initiative taken up by the top brass of Infosys to inform, educate and spread awareness amongst its employees about sexual harassment. This was done through Notices, In-house journals, Workshops and Seminars. Analysts believe the company also reworked on its Human Resource initiative while the case was under settlement. More women were employed during the period of crisis. After a while, data was issued to the media reflecting more women joining Infosys, making subtly a point that women trusted working in Infosys. (It could be a well thought out HR tactic to hire more women during that period).

Most of the newspapers in the mainstream media carried the story diligently and followed up with an update for months together. Many of them would not miss reflecting on Phaneesh Murthy's qualifications and where he graduated from, i.e., IIT (Chennai) and IIM (A) alumnus. Would he have behaved differently if he was not from these famous institutes or was it expected of him, coming from such coveted learning institutes to behave in a manner, he did, are interesting from the media's perspective of creating certain imagery around the person and the issue.

What are the PR insights?

When faced with a crisis, avoiding or evading does not help. It is important to realize that the crisis has occurred that needs to be managed. Openness, clarity of communication and responsiveness are important in the aftermath of a crisis. Infosys, could have felt a bit embarrassed to be in the eye of a storm for something only one person was allegedly responsible for, but despite that it did not duck. The company on the whole carefully handled the crisis. Most of the press releases and updates can still be found on its website.

Building crisis

A building crisis as the name suggests takes time to build up. Crises of this kind may occur after the management has taken a decision to discontinue a facility, open a plant somewhere, which the community or an Interest group is opposing or closing down a unit, or retrench employees. The following case studies of Tata's and Jet Airways are interesting examples of building crises.

Tata 'Nano' - the Singur Saga (2006-08)

Tata is credited for producing world's smallest and the most economical car.

The car was promised at Rs. 1,00,000 (US$ 2000), attracting global attention. The car was demonstrated at the India International Fair in 2007 creating a near frenzy among Delhi citizens. All roads in the city seemed to go to Pragati Maidan, where the car was exhibited, landing some parts of city in terrible traffic jams as reported by the media.

The media played on the sentiment. It covered stories on how Ratan Tata had once seen a family of four riding a scooter, when he pledged that he would soon produce a car that would be affordable to the common man.

The design and the designers of the car that were kept in a closet until the day the car were introduced to people through the media.

In retrospect

On May 18, 2006, the Tata Group chairman Ratan Tata announced a small car project at Singur, in West Bengal, that for decades has had a Communist government, the CPI (M) in the saddle. The project was announced on the day, Buddhadeb Bhattacharya was sworn in as the Chief Minister.

Just about a week later, Singur, the place where Tata was to set up its factory, witnessed angry demonstrations by farmers over what was said to be a "forcible" acquisition of land for the Tata car project. Critics questioned the wisdom of the state government in acquiring 997 acres (404 hectares) of multi-crop land allegedly through forcible acquisition made under the archaic colonial Land Acquisition Act of 1894. Some felt that even the provisions of this act were not met.

Reacting to farmers' agitation, veteran communist leader and former West Bengal Chief Minister Jyoti Basu criticized Bhattacharya for mishandling the issue pertaining to the acquisition of land for the Tata project.

In July 2006, the protagonist against the setting up of the project, Trinamool Congress chief Mamata Banerjee sowed paddy near the Tata factory site to protest against the "forcible" acquisition of land. The row soon snowballed into a major political issue. The central government mostly kept itself out of the controversy.

The Federation of Indian Chambers of Commerce and Industry (FICCI) warned on 25 August that Singur developments might force the rest of industry players to shift projects to other states.

Mamta roped in Save Narmada activist Medha Patkar in October 2006, who held a meeting of agitating farmers near the Tata Motors factory. The police arrested Medha Patkar for rioting and disturbing the peace of the place.

Singur witnessed many more protests from hundreds of farmers. On December 3, 2006, the protest intensified amidst Banerjee's indefinite hunger strike.

Banerjee broke her 25 day long fast on 28 December 2006, but vowed that the Tatas would have to address the concerns of the local farmers. Ratan Tata said that there was no pulling out of Singur.

As the New Year was ushered in, in January 2007, the Tatas selected its first batch of trainees for the Nano project. When the Tatas commenced work at Singur, local women torched factory fencing. Reacting to the incident, Ratan Tata ascribed it to rivals' doing. (Auto industrialist Rahul Bajaj had also evinced interest in bringing out a small car. The general perception in certain circles was that the entry of Nano would hit the two-wheeler sales). Later, in a talk show on a Hindi news channel, the host asked Rahul Bajaj, if he was behind the rioting, which he vehemently denied, supported by some others. The Indian industry began rallying behind Tata Group at Singur, expressing its concern that continuing protests would tarnish the state's image.

In the meantime the West Bengal Governor played the informal arbitrator during August 2007, but it did not work. In the next few months, the Calcutta High Court decreed that the Singur land acquisition was legal. The Tatas announced Nano roll out by October 2008.

The immediate events, however changed everything, when in May 2007, Trinamool Congress won majority seats in Singur self-governance institutions. Encouraged by the reposing of public faith in her party, Banerjee upped her agitation and demanded that the 400 acres must be returned to farmers.

Exasperated, Ratan Tata announced the departure of the Nano project from West Bengal, if violence at Singur persisted, even if it meant huge losses to the company. Many state chief ministers offered that the project be moved to their state. Tata, at last moved out of Singur and West Bengal in October 2008 and settled for Gujarat.

After moving shop to Gujarat, Chief Minster Narendra Modi at a public function, compared Nano to an orphaned Krishna, abandoned by West Bengal, who would be in good care of Yashodha, the foster mother, meaning Gujarat.

Moving out at that juncture meant a loss of about Rs. 500 Crores to the company. Various vendors also raised claims totaling to Rs. 250 Crores, as reported by the media.

All the while, Ratan Tata, resisted from making any comment on the agitators, led by Mamta Bannerjee. All he would say was that since the lives of the employees were at stake, so Tata motors had no alternative, but to withdraw from the state. However, three weeks later, in an 'Open letter to the citizens of West Bengal' that appeared in a number of newspapers in West Bengal, Ratan Tata minced no words when he openly criticized the Trinamool Congress led by Mamta Banerjee, who he said was supported by vested interests and certain political parties. The letter said, "The land acquired by the State government at Singur and leased to Tata Motors has been, we believe, through a transparent process with fair compensation. The Trinamool Congress's position has been that this land acquisition by the state Government is illegal. In response to a public interest litigation, the Hon'ble Calcutta High Court has ruled out that the land acquisition is totally legal but the same plaintiffs have filed against this judgement in the Supreme Court, which is pending a hearing".

The letter then went on to refer to "constant acts of open aggression on the site, occasional acts of violence, breakage of the compound premier walls, theft of construction material...... intimidation and even physical assault of employees, contract labour and residents of the area".

Mincing no words, the letter alleged that the onus of halting development work in West Bengal rested with none other than the Trinamool Congress.

Pulling out from Singur has not ended Tatas woes. The factory still stands there; the process of returning land to farmers is yet to begin. Experts wonder, if after so much construction work, the land would be ready for tilling any time soon. There have been allegations about the underhand 'deal' of Budhadeb government with the Tata in giving them the land for a song. The deal, it has been alleged by some quarters, has not been transparent. So as a strategy, the company wanted to come out with its version of reality through an open letter.[30] Here is the text of the open letter published in the media:

> **Reproduction**

THE TELEGRAPH

Date: 17.10.08

TATA Motors

OPEN LETTER TO THE CITIZENS OF WEST BENGAL

Over the past three weeks there have been statements by vested interests criticizing the decision taken by Tata motors to move the Nano car project out of Singur claiming that the decision was hasty and politically motivated. I therefore feel compelled to address this letter to the people of West Bengal, to explain how our dreams of contributing to the industrial revival of West Bengal has been shattered by an environment of politically-motivated agitation and the hostility that finally left us with no option but to withdraw the Nano project from West Bengal.

Two years ago, when Tata Motors decided to locate the Nano car project in West Bengal, it reflected the tremendous faith and confidence we had, and still have, in the investor-friendly policies of Mr. Buddhadeb Bhattacharjee's government. All through the two years that we have been constructing the plant at Singur, this feeling of faith and confidence in the vision of objective of the state government has been reinforced. All our interaction with the Chief Minister and the industry minister in particular, as also with several other officers, have been exemplary. We had therefore hoped that this project would reinstate confidence for further investments in West Bengal and would create a large number of jobs for the younger citizens, directly in the company and its suppliers, as also foster a large number of small enterprises in the Singur area which would provide livelihood to the citizens of that area. We had also taken medical and other community services in the Singur region. Our fervent desire has always been to be a good, contributing corporate citizen enhancing the quality of life of the people around the plant.

Unfortunately, the confrontative actions by the Trinamool Congress led by Ms. Mamta Banerjee and supported by vested interests and certain political parties, opposing the acquisition of land by the state government, have caused serious disruption to the progress of the Nano plant. The land acquired by the State Government at Singur and leased to Tata Motors has been, we believe, through a transparent process and fair compensation. The Trinamool Congress's position has been that this land acquisition by the state government is illegal. In response to a Public Interest Litigation, the Hon'ble Calcutta High Court has ruled that the land acquisition is totally legal but the same plaintiffs have filed against this judgement in the Supreme Court, which is pending a hearing.

Throughout the construction of the plant, the Company has had to endure constant acts of open aggression on the site, occasional acts of violence, breakage of the compound perimeter walls, theft of construction material from within the project area, as well as intimidation and even physical assault of employees, contract labour and residents of the area to be absorbed in the project. Country-made bombs have been lobbed into the premises, obstructing the movement of material and personnel into and out of the plant.

Various attempts at finding solutions were thwarted by the Trinamool Congress's consistent demand that land acquired for the Nano plant and/or its integrated vendor park be returned to the segment of the land owners which the Trinamool Congress party claims to represent. Tata Motors has always maintained that this project has been conceived of as an integrated campus of manufacturing facilities and suppliers, so as to maximize integration and minimize logistics and material flow costs. Disruption of this integrated campus would make it extremely difficult for the Company to meet its product price and productivity goals.

On August 22nd, I addressed a Press Conference in Kolkata, generally referring to the hostility and difficult environment we were facing and appealing for a more congenial environment, failing which we would have no option but to consider taking the project out of West Bengal. Unfortunately the response to this appeal was an escalation of the hostilities through a *dharna* on the highway in front of the plant, some more incidents of physical assault and considerable amount of intimidation of personnel working at the site, which finally resulted in the suspension of the completion work on the plant for almost a month. All of you will therefore appreciate that the final and painful decision to move the project out of West Bengal has not been a decision taken in haste, but a decision taken with great regret after a great deal of deliberation and a final assessment that it was unlikely that a sustainable, peaceful environment would develop in which our project could operate.

We are conscious of the disappointment and despondency that may be felt by some of the residents of Singur who may have hoped for an improvement in their quality of life after the plant was operational. We believe the responsibility for this would lie with the Trinamool Congress, which has created the hostile environment that has obliged the Company to move the project from Singur.

In the future, in the state of West Bengal many Tata Motors-type projects may come and go, many political ideologies may come and go, but the future of the state of West Bengal will depend on the path its leaders and citizens take in developing and retaining an environment which will result in the prosperity of the state in the years to come. Many may have forgotten that West Bengal was the major centre for heavy industry and steel fabrication. Agitation and violence drove away many industries around 30 years ago, and it has only been in recent times that the present government has been able to rebuild the confidence of investors to invest in the state.

It is therefore ironic that, at this crucial time and moment of hope for the state, history appears to be repeating itself. Agitation, violence and terror are overtaking the state in the name of the agricultural community, to serve political goals—stalling progress and destroying the newfound confidence in the state, while doing nothing for the rural poor, other than making promises. West Bengal's agriculture was a success story in the 1970s and 1980s but the farm sector's growth has slowed in the recent past. It is self-evident that industrial growth and agricultural growth must happen together in peace and harmony, and not through agitation and activism.

The people of West Bengal—particularly the younger citizens—will need to express their views and aspirations as to what they would like to see West Bengal become in the years ahead. Would they like to support the present Government of Mr. Buddhadeb Bhattacharjee to build a prosperous state with the rule of law, modern infrastructure

> and industrial growth, supporting a harmonious investment in the agricultural sector to give the people in the state a better life? Or would they like to see the state consumed by a destructive political environment of confrontation, agitation, violence and lawlessness? Do they want education and jobs in the industrial and high-tech sectors or does the future generation see their future prosperity achieved on a "stay as we are" basis?
>
> The future destiny of West Bengal lies with its citizens. They will need to decide whether they wish to stand still and let growth take place elsewhere, or move forward with the present Government's progressive policy, so that West Bengal can take its rightful place with other states—sharing in the future prosperity of India.
>
> Ratan Tata

What are the PR lessons?

In a crisis situation many stakeholders get embroiled, who may or may not be involved in the crisis per se. It is important that a list of possible "adversaries" and "supporters" is prepared for strategic intervention by them.

The media needs to be updated on a constant basis to provide the point of view of the organization. In the case of Singur, there in fact were three parties, albeit two on one side, and each roping in "allies" for support. Mamta Banerjee involved veteran crusader Medha Patkar, who is well know nationally and internationally for crusading against development projects that end up helping the rich at the cost of the local population. Celebrated author Arundhati Roy, who had joined Patkar in her Narmada Bachao Andolan, also made headlines on Singur. On the other hand, the industry and friends of Ratan Tata rallied around him and Nano. A generally reticent Ratan Tata, although did not name, but when he said it could be a rival's hand in creating trouble, it was not difficult for people to make a conjecture about the person referred to by him. Many feel, Tata could have been more discreet.

There were analysts, who felt, it did not behove the stature of Ratan Tata to issue an open letter that held only one person and her party responsible for the act. By doing so, he embroiled himself in a political quagmire. While others felt, he had nothing to lose, by doing so. The company lost on time, manpower, and resources and incurred a huge financial loss. So it was a good idea to give back and get the issue off his chest!

The media, by and large, especially national, was sympathetic to the Tata Group.

Continuing crisis

As said earlier there are crises that simmer for sometime, before one can realize their impact. Corrective action by management in some cases can help tide over the problem, while there are other kinds of emergencies like environmental degradation, global warming that need policy intervention and change of behaviour. Crises of these kinds are long drawn and take time to resolve, or subside.

Procter & Gamble (P&G)

Procter and Gamble (P&G), one of the very successful multinational companies, became a victim of wild rumors in the early 1980s that it was in "league with the Satan" and was funding the "Church of Satan". The rumour arose probably from the logo of the company, which had evolved over a century and showed a man in the moon and stars. To deal with the rumor, the company went to the press and also to the courts to stop the wild charges emanating from certain religious groups. But then, in April 1985, P&G gave up the fight and announced that it would remove the logo from its products, thereby avoiding unnecessary controversy.

Often exploding crises like droughts, hunger, diseases, environmental degradation, the depleting ozone cover, the global warming, HIV-AIDS, terrorism can also be categorized in continuing crises that have taken a long to build, over a period of time. Some of these issues have cropped up due to a narrow political vision, religious bigotry, and greed of the rich nations and lifestyle options of people, especially the young generation. It is going to take quite a while before crises of this kind find a solution.

Communication is an important imperative in educating and motivating the target audience for a changed attitude in their own interest.

Following are critical in a crisis situation

A crisis often involves people, emotions, perceptions and opinions. Therefore, it is important that crises managers, keep in view the following:
- Enormity of the disaster/loss of human life
- Perceived abettors and victims
- Perceptions about the crisis
- Media coverage/media stand
- Action plan to deal with the crisis on hand

Two aspects are vital from the Disaster manager's perspective

a) *How does the organization respond to the victims?*
b) *Is it communicating what it is doing, and how shall it rebound?*
   As media acquires centre stage, it is important for the PR manager to understand media needs and their mind. The 24-hour channels can be seen as a problem and also as an opportunity; Internet and Live chat rooms have brought about a paradigm shift in how the organizations need to communicate. In a crisis situation, it is not easy to escape the stereotypes for media and organizations, like "they are going to conceal" (Organization) vs. "they only smell out the bad things" (Media).

Why do organizations behave the way they do and media also behave the way they do? In order to understand that, let's look at the anatomy of both; a typical organization, and media.

Anatomy of an organization:
- Has core competence in one or more areas
- Has worked hard on managing its reputation and is protective about it
- Has many stakeholders to answer to
- Disasters/crises are most dreaded
- Often organizations don't have a media policy
- Despite a general preparedness, the slip often shows
- Organizations tend to be on the defensive in the face of crises

Anatomy of a medium:
- It is in the business of news
- It is in competition with others
- It has certain corporate responsibilities
- It has a reputation to guard and its need for credibility
- Journalists have deadlines to meet
- Reporters are human with rational and emotional sides

It is important that both media and the organization embroiled in a crisis understand their interdependence on each other, not losing sight of the "victims".

What do words and the do?

The readers and viewers according to their understanding, experience, cultural and social milieu deduce visual and textual information. The picture of a little girl afire changed the course of the Vietnam War in the 1960s. The cover story of IPKF in *India Today* had the picture of a dead soldier being devoured by a dog, to symbolize the utter uselessness of getting embroiled in a war that was not our calling. Mumbai Siege by the terrorists on 26 November 2008 and its live coverage was like being in a war theatre.

It is important for the crisis manager to be alert on graphics. This is easier said than done when people carry small digital cameras in their mobiles, but for communicating officially, it is always prudent to keep pictures, video clips ready for use in media proactively and when there is a demand from the media.

What are the lessons for disaster anagers?

- Develop a strategy based on worst-case scenario
- Appreciate the vital importance of preplanning
- The initial critical few moments when a crisis breaks out are very important
- Be alert on graphics
- Know the media and their mind, do journo-tracking

- Isolate the crisis team from daily grind
- Aim at containment and not suppression

Failure in crisis handling happens due to one or all of the following reasons:

- Lack of openness, honesty, or availability of spokesperson in the initial period
- Failure to prepare for the worst case
- Failure to communicate honest, human emotion and concern
- Shortsightedness of organizations in putting long-term goals before short-term goals

Crisis communication involves a tangled web of information. Communication flows from all directions, varying sources, including employees, community activists, unions, opinion makers, national and international organizations, general public and the media. Very often the messages are conflicting in nature. As a crisis communicator, the public relations manager must avoid getting entangled in the web of confusion. The message should avoid jargon and ambivalence. It should be clear and attempt at empathizing with those concerned.

Last but not least, evaluation of crisis handling after the crisis is over will help pinpoint gray areas. One has to be dispassionate in assessment. It is advisable not to rely on the media to know how one did the job. It can be very depressing, because media rarely compliment. Chapters 4 and 9, respectively may be referred to, to understand various kinds of media, their use and how to write for media.

Summary

In this chapter we have defined various kinds of crises and their role in disaster management. We looked at the exploding crises which are sudden and high impact, demanding immediate attention which often involve rescue operations, providing succor to the affected and ensuring that life of the survivors is not in danger. We then moved to discuss crises of an immediate nature that often include scams, scandals and ethical issues. The communication in these kinds of crises has to aim at salvaging damage done to the organization. Building crises that usually take time to grow were discussed. Some of the crises can go on for days, weeks, months and years and these are called continuing crisis. Various case studies, like the Mumbai siege by terrorists, Phaneesh Murthy case of sexual harassment, the pulling out of West Bengal by the Tata Group, Satyam Fraud and many others were discussed to describe the varying strategies adopted by crises managers to tide over difficult times. Planning, preparedness, honest intentions and sharing of information candidly and in a transparent manner with stakeholders, especially the media, often hold the key to a successful management of a crisis.

Critical thinking exercise

Study the Tata Nano case study carefully and work on a crisis communication strategy on behalf of the Trinamool Congress or West Bengal government, keeping in view the circumstances prevailing at that time and in the aftermath of Nano's exit from West Bengal.

Questions

Q.1 Discuss the various classifications of crises.

Q.2 What in your view are the various reasons for failure in handling a crisis? Discuss with relevant cases in point.

Q.3 "Media love crises". Give your viewpoint for or against the statement, building a logical argument.

Q.4 What in your view are the lessons for a Crisis Manager, when dealing with media?

Endnotes

[1] Shearlean Duke and Lynne Masland, "Crisis Communication by the Book", *Public Relations Quarterly*, Fall 2002, pp. 30-35.

[2] Scot M. Cutlip, Allen H. Center and Glen M. Broom, *Effective Public Relations*, seventh ed. 1994, (Prentice-Hall:NJ) pp.366.

[3] NDTV, 27 November 2009

[4] *The Hindustan Times, HT City,* 2 December 2008.

[5] Aaj Tak went on bragging a number of times during the live coverage that the channel was always the first with the news, something that seemed very out of place given the grim situation. Barkha Dutt of NDTV was lampooned by some columnists on her reflecting her emotions too loudly.

[6] CNN-IBN and Times TV, 28 November 2008.

[7] Various channels like Aaj tak, India TV, Times Now, Headlines Today, 28 and 29 November 2008.

[8] The Babri Masjid was demolished by some Hindu zealots on 6 December 2002.

[9] Thomas J. Mickey, *PR Review* [Fall 1997]

[10] Source- Sakshi, NGO (Sample size taken – 2400) http://www.sakshitrust.org/

[11] Sources: Infosys website; Midday.com; various issues of *The Economic Times*; *The Hindustan Times*; *The Business Times*; *The Times of India*; *Business Today*; *Business World*. The study was undertaken by students of Advertising and PR, 2003-04 batch as a part of their learning PR case studies at the Indian Institute of Mass Communication, New Delhi under the supervision of one of the authors who teaches there. The study presented by the students received the first prize at a Public Relations Society of India Conference.

[12] *The Economic Times*, 17 October 2008.

[13] UTI business news, CNN-IBN, Times Now, Aawaz, FM Gold on 7 January and *The Economic Times*, 8 January 2009.

[24] Sources: *The Economic Times*, 17,18, 19 December, *The Times of India*, 18 December, *The Hindu*, 19 December.

[35] *The Economic Times*, 8 January 2009. As per television reporting (Times Now and Headlines Today in the afternoon of 8 January, Mr. Raju is not traceable and might have fled from the country. In the evening bulletin the statement of R Raju's advocate was quoted that his client was very much in India.

[46] *Times of India*, 8 January 2009. The quote along with his picture appeared on the side panel of the newspaper.
[17] *The Times of India*, 8 January 2008
[58] uTvi in 7.30 bulletin titled: "India's Enron" on 8 January 2009

11 PR in Marketing Mix

Chapter objectives
- The role of PR in the overall marketing mix
- PR support in brand building
- The need for synergy between marketing and PR to achieve marketing goals
- Case studies of brands that have used PR strategies and tactics to be successful

The traditional role of PR has been to develop cordial relations between an organization and its various constituencies, besides aiming to 'reconcile and adjust in the public interest those aspects of personal and corporate behaviour which have a social significance' to put it in Harwood I Childs' words.

PR is a top management communication function dealing with public issues encountered by organizations across a wide spectrum. The issues often deal with crises of one kind or the other, from accidents, disasters, sabotage, competition, political loyalty, moral turpitude to family feuds. However in more recent times, PR has suddenly found itself at the centre stage, being invited to lend support and advice on issues that did not traditionally fall within its ambit. Some of the areas that have witnessed greater strategic influence of PR include the following:

- Use of PR for brand building and at the cost of advertising
- Taking PR advice on issues that enhance public support for corporate governance
- Public opinion consolidation by PR on issues concerning war, insurgency and health, especially AIDS.

For the purpose of the present chapter, we shall deal only with PR's now recognized active role in marketing and brand building. There are two schools of thought, one that swears by the value of PR in marketing efforts, while the other feels that it is unnecessarily hyped and not much value addition is achieved in the process.

Marketing is the process through which the needs and desires of customers are assessed and fulfilled. Marketing planning encompasses various tasks like conception, pricing, promotion and distribution of a product. PR is an important tool of promotion in the mix that aims at maintaining cordial relationships with both the internal and external stakeholders.

In a survey conducted through e-mail by the *Advertising Age Journal,* it was found that senior marketers were divided about the role of Public Relations in the overall marketing mix. Against a question on the role of PR in marketing 83% percent felt that PR was effective in creating awareness, 67% felt it provided credibility, 61% felt it educated customers. On the other hand, only 28% felt that PR input helped in prompting trial. Similarly only 22% each felt that PR was able to persuade skeptics or drive sales.

When asked if they saw PR as primarily a strategic or a tactical discipline, 30% said, they perceived it as a tactical discipline, while 35% felt it was a strategic discipline. The remaining were somewhere in between the two options.

On asking how PR firms contributed towards the marketing programmes, 67% cited media contacts, 48% cited creative ideas, 45% said PR was like " arms and legs support" and strategic thinking and only 29% cited PR's role in gathering competitor's and industry insights.

On a question about the role(s) in which PR could be effective, 76% marketing experts saw PR value in supporting marketing, 72% saw it in product launches, while 65% saw PR's effective role in supporting the corporate brand. Surprisingly, fewer at 55% were impressed with PR's role in crisis management and 57% about corporate reputation management.

The survey was distributed to select *Advertising Age* subscribers. Of the more than 130 respondents, 41% described themselves as VP (Marketing), 21% as Chief Marketing Officers, 17% as Presidents or CEOs. The largest respondents at 39% came from consumer goods category, 22% from industrial sector, 9% from health care and 8% from technology.[1]

Philip J. Kitchen and Don J. Shultz talk about the turbulent relationship between marketing and PR with the emergence of a newer discipline called the Marketing PR.[2]

In a Round Table conference organized by *Advertising Age* journal for a special section on PR, a number of marketing and strategy experts were invited to debate and deliberate on the role of PR in marketing. Some interesting viewpoints emerged.

One of the participants in the Conference, David Selby, Chief marketing Officer and senior VP of Potbelly Sandwich Works felt that both PR and marketing were inseparable and needed to be integrated. PR in his view needed to look at long term objectives on programmes undertaken by them. For instance the events in support of a brand did create the necessary buzz and hype, which may also result in media talking about it, but PR, he argued must put a discipline and process in place that can think two or three steps ahead of the immediate need to understand how a brand will be maintained over a period of time.

Jim Speros, Chief Marketing Officer, US, at Ernst & Young almost echoed the same sentiment, when he said that PR input do get media coverage, but what was the return on investment? It was not about how many clips one got, he argued, but about whether the marketing mix in totality resulted in a surge in sales. Sepros was emphatic when he said that whether it was advertising or PR, the state of the art was just not there. He equated the issue of press releases to "flash bulb marketing" without any follow up. Great brands, he argued were built over time with sustained activity.

Andrew Kritzer felt that it was easy for marketers to have control of content in advertisements, but in PR one did not necessarily have any idea what spin was going to be put by media on the information one was providing.[3]

There are PR diehards who feel that PR has been an integral part of brand building for too long to question its efficacy now. Critics of advertising argue that the big bang approach of advertising should be replaced by slow build-up with public relations to have a long-term impact on building strong brands. Public Relations is seen by them as an important part of Integrated Marketing Communication (IMC), which is the coordination and integration of marketing communication tools, avenues and sources within a company into a seamless programme that maximizes the impact on consumers and other end users at an effective minimal cost. The marketing mix comprises the following: product, prize, promotion, distribution, advertising, consumer promotion, personal selling, direct marketing and public relations.

The integrated marketing communication plan begins with the development of a master marketing plan. The plan provides for the coordination of efforts in all components of the marketing mix. The aim of such a plan is to achieve harmony in relaying messages to customers and other publics. An IMC plan broadly would comprise the following tools:

- Advertising tools: using appeals to create effective communication
- Promotional tools: trade promotion, consumer promotion, events, PR mileage and personal selling at this stage, the ad message can be reinforced in trade and consumer promotion.
- Integration tools: Internet marketing in terms of e-commerce activities and other functions that can be performed online.

The IMC ideally should undertake the programme in the following stages:

Stage I: To identify, coordinate, and manage all forms of external communication in order to bring all the company's brands and strategic business units or divisions under one umbrella.

Stage II: The firm's goal must be to extend the scope of communication to encompass everyone touched by the organization. All the external messages must mesh with internal communication with employees. External contacts made through PR events or with advertising agencies must be consistent with what is being said internally.

Stage III: The technology stage when firms treat IMC as an investment and not a departmental function. Companies like FedEx and Hewlett-Packard take these databases and use them to calculate and establish a database.

Oil of Olay is cleverly using various ingredients of IMC in its campaign for 'Spa in a bottle'. The ad campaign, the retail outlet promotion and PR mileage through its brand ambassador former Ms Universe Sushmita Sen carry the common thread throughout. *Times of India* carried a story on Ms Sen when she visited Delhi in the month of August 2008. The picture of the diva sitting pretty on a sofa, with the brand prominently placed on the table was larger than the space devoted to the story. "Being an actor, I use a lot of make-up. Face tons of harsh lights and outdoor activities. I am impatient and couldn't be bothered with layers of treatment for my skin. I am lucky to have this 'spa in a bottle', which takes just about five minutes", she said.[4]

If we look at the history of some great brands, PR has always played a role in brand building but not necessarily in active partnership with brand advertising. Both often worked as islands of isolation, one function handled by the PR department and the other by marketing. The last few decades in the West have witnessed the use of 'third party endorsement' in brand building. The trend became visible in India too, especially during what is known as the era of liberalization in the Nineties of the last century. There are however, some instances in the pre-liberalization period also when companies used PR to launch their products or when they ventured into new territories.

Let's discuss some of the well-researched case studies wherein PR played a big role in brand building in India and other countries.

TUMS

CASE STUDIES

In the US in the early 80s, the antacid market was quite cluttered. Therefore, for a new antacid to be launched, a genuine product differentiation was important. Smithkline briefed its R&D department to evolve a product with a dual benefit. It evolved a calcium based antacid called TUMS with the desire of offering consumers a dual benefit—acidity relief and at the same time calcium for the bones

This way the consumers could be told about taking only one pill for two problems and therefore allay their fears over multiple self medication issues that were emerging.

However, calcium deficiency wasn't a big issue at that point of time in the US. Acidity, on the other hand was a known and established ailment for which people self medicated frequently making antacids a high selling category.

The company realized that the dual benefit would be lost on the consumers unless an education programme around the gravity of calcium deficiency was implemented.

> Therefore, the conventional launch was actually preceded by a huge PR activity around osteoporosis and its debilitating effects. They flushed the media (via doctors, third party stories, media meets of course) with information and educational releases relating to osteoporosis. They made the consumer aware of a big health issue first. When the campaign was launched, people seemed to be waiting for a medicine such as TUMS. TUMS is one of the largest selling medicines in its category today.[5]

Microsoft

According to Carma, a media analysis company, the most reported company in the world today, viz., Microsoft is about three decades old but is considered the second most valuable company after Coca-Cola which was set up in 1886. While one recalls so may Coca-Cola ads, Microsoft ads elicit a poor ad recall. According to analysts, it is PR and the media coverage that has given Microsoft a high brand recall.

CASE STUDIES

In 1995, when software giant Microsoft Corporation came out with its Windows 95, it used PR strategy for the launch. A meticulously coordinated global launch included appearance on the Jay Leno Show, a celebration for 3500 people, a Ferris wheel, hot air balloons, free copies of software for dignitaries across the world and a huge payment for the rights to use the Rolling Stones song "Start me up" as the product launch theme song. After the great PR launch the company spent close to $200 million on advertising to support the introduction. In 1998 the launch of Windows 98 in contrast was a very low-key affair. The company was fighting against law suits for its alleged monopolistic designs. Windows 2000 came about without a whimper, with some standard ads, and hardly any promotion.

The last few years of legal battle has presented the company with a gruesome PR challenge of a huge magnitude. The low point in negative publicity according to analysts came in 1997, when attorneys for Microsoft said in writing to the court "poorly informed lawyers (who) have no vocation for software design". They later regretted having said it. Once it was able to understand the problem, its next step was to evaluate the public persona it was presenting. The public perception of the company was "predatory, hawkish and monopoly seeking". Keeping that in view the Windows 98 campaign's media choice fell on magazines such as *Bon Appetit, The New Yorker* and *Time*. The tone and tenor of ads was friendly and understated. ("Apparently, there are those who do not subscribe to an all Microsoft approach"). The most interesting PR response to the 'publicity hostile' environment according to analysts was when Bill Gates revealed in an ad for Callaway Golf that he was a fairly poor golfer who was really trying hard to get better. This human face of Gates was in contrast with his hawkish image in the legal hearings provided a good contrast.

"Microsoft, which only discovered public relations since feeling the Justice Department's heat, has taken just a small step down this cynical road of dissembling, but a step it still is. And self-destructive at that: phony ''grass-roots'' campaigns reinforce rather than counter Microsoft's troubled image as a power-mad bully that will stop at nothing to snuff out competitors. Bill Gates, golf-playing love muffin, was a phony too, but at least he was good for a laugh", commented Frank Rich in *New York Times*[6].

Every brand according to celebrated authors Al Ries and Laura Ries need an enemy to sustain itself. As Coke has Pepsi, Microsoft has Linux.

Linux is an 'open source' software that is freely available to programmers, who can view the underlying source code and modify it to suit their needs has never used any ad support. The brand, it is said has 99 percent recognition in the technical community. It has made its creator Linus Torvalds, world famous. One realized the brand was so famous when the Microsoft spokesperson lambasted it as 'a cancer that attaches itself in an intellectual property sense to everything it touches'. [7]

Pierre Cardian

CASE STUDIES

Closer home, when Pierre Cardian brand came to India in the early 1990s, a very well thought-out and orchestrated PR strategy was used to launch the product. Mr. Cardian went to meet university students as a part of the event organized for the purpose. The brand was "launched" next day morning by "third party endorsement" in hundreds of mainstream and regional newspapers with picture of Mr. Cardian talking about the brand and his brand differential vis-à-vis competition.[8]

Analgesic Drug

CASE STUDIES

There is a story about an analgesic drug in India that was shifted from its being a prescription drug to "Over The Counter" (OTC) in the 1980s. The doctors did not take kindly to it as it came to them as a surprise. The company suffered a backlash when it was found that most of the doctors began recommending a parallel drug against the one put on the OTC marketing route.

It was a bad strategy to alienate the doctors during this transition. To avoid further backlash of de-recommendations of that drug by doctors, the company put in place a well thought out PR activity with the medical fraternity.

The company flew an expert from the Stanford Medical University (an Indian doctor with international credentials to his name and an established name in his field) to educate doctors about the safety of that drug, which people could buy over the counter for mild fever and pain. They conducted seminars across the country with this expert, meeting doctors and disseminating information about the drug formula.

This way they not only helped the doctors in accepting the drug even after it went commercially on television but also established a better relationship with a very important opinion leader group which could have played havoc with the company's future growth plans[9].

Cooking oil

CASE STUDIES

In the Eighties one of the companies in the private sector used the media route through PR stories on sunflower seeds' potential as a cooking medium at a time when people were used to only Vanaspati, peanut or mustard oil. An environment was created to inform and educate people about the benefits of oil from sunflower seeds. *Business India* carried a cover story on the issue, with articles that quoted oil technologists, dieticians and scientists. Once the stage was set, a multimedia campaign was mounted to introduce 'Sundrop' by ITC.

Branding is how you differentiate your product from competitive products. The goal is to make your product more visible and attain better consumer recall. PR is an incredible way of communicating a brand story via the media that the public trusts. However, going overboard is not recommended.

PR has been used as a proactive choice in brand building or reinforcement as also in bringing back lost confidence in the brand. The Cadbury's imbroglio in 2003 and its build up to regain public confidence built over many decades began from 'project Vishwas' to its charm campaign, bringing in Amitabh Bachchan which had a great PR ingredient.

"Truthfulness, partnership, mutual understanding, team work... 100 years of trust" was the institutional ad using the game of football and children that reinforced the brand equity the TATA's have earned in a century.

Rural markets have great potential for marketing of various products, many companies especially Hindustan Lever Ltd. (HLL) and ITC have gone beyond the traditional marketing route to reach out to the hinterland.

The Hindustan Lever Limited (HLL) Experience

Hindustan Lever Ltd. (HLL) has been one of the successful companies in making definite inroads into the rural heartland of India. Continuous product innovation resulted in producing low unit price packs of products like premium stain removing detergents like *Surf Excel*, beauty soap like *Lux*, talcum powder like *Ponds*, toothpaste like *Pepsodent*, skin cream like *Fair and Lovely*. Like the HLL, other companies have also developed rural-specific products or pack sizes.

Fair & Lovely has received a lot of flak and criticism from feminist groups for promoting fair skin as a key to success. Some of their ad campaigns had to be redone after women's groups complained to authorities against an unfair approach to women in its campaign strategy. The fact however remains that the market turnover of the fairness brand is over Rs. 1000 crores a year. The company as a PR strategy mounted a television serial that felicitated women achievers who were not necessarily fair skinned. Some of those included were super cop Kiran Bedi and Sarvesh, a battered housewife who reinvented herself as a photographer and is a successful photojournalist today.

A number of detergent and personal care products have been keeping aside a part of the profit for social causes that are announced in the ads to encourage people to buy the particular brands as also to reflect their social consciousness.

CASE STUDIES

In 1998-99, HLL launched a major direct consumer contact project titled – Project Bharat, which covered 2.2 crore households. Each house was given a box priced at Rs. 15 which contained a low-unit price pack of shampoo, talcum powder, tooth paste and skin cream, along with educational literature and audio-visual demonstration. According to company sources the project has helped 'eliminate barriers to trials and protect product category and brands'. During the last few years, the company has strengthened its network through mutually beneficial alliances with rural self-help Groups (SHGs). Government offices, NGOs, financial institutions etc. are aligning together to establish SHGs with a view to alleviate poverty through sustainable income-generating activities. The HLL has launched a project called *Shakti* in 2001 under which the SHGs are given the option of distributing company's products as a sustainable income generating activity. There has been tremendous response from the SHGs. As the women were already grouped for micro-credit operations, they saved money from their daily wages or crop sales, they were pitched in by the HLL for what seemed to be an interesting proposition—buying HLL products through some of their savings and then selling it to their friends and neighbours.

In 2002 HLL launched another project with large-scale direct contact, called – *Lifebuoy Swasthya Chetna* (Lifebuoy Health Awareness), which was slated to cover about five crore people in 15,000 villages in ten states. The project according to HLL is intended to generate awareness about good health and hygiene practices and how a simple habit of washing hands with soap is essential to maintain good health.

Handled by O&M Outreach, the integrated communication programme that used multiple contacts which included from communication from child to child, mother to child and contacting students at schools. 450 health development officers and assistants were involved in spreading the message to the target audience. They would conduct the Glow-germ test to show the respondents unseen germs on their hands and how they vanished after hands were washed with Lifebuoy. The agency involved both senior citizens and children to carry forward the campaign: *"Swachch rahenge – swasth rahenge"* (If you are clean; you will remain healthy).

Ogilvy Outreach, the rural marketing arm of ad agency Ogilvy and Mather (O&M), which is in charge of more than 30 brands of HLL is said to have recruited local magicians, dancers and actors to build various brands in rural heartlands of India. In total, 50 teams of 13 performers have been recruited to serve as a link between the brands and rural residents.

HLL's philosophy can be summed up in what Mr. Keki Dadiseth, ex HLL chief said: "Everybody wants brands. And there are a lot more poor people in the world than rich people. To be a global business... you have to participate in all segments". The parent company Unilever has also used PR support for its various brands in the US.

For its shampoo brand Finesse, Unilever worked with the PR firm Edelman during the summer of 2002 to launch the Finesse Hair Evolution Exhibition reflecting the changing hairstyles over the last half a century, since 1950. This also included hair stylists' predictions on hairstyles that would be popular in 2050. As the exhibition toured many cities, local stylists were roped in to give their vision of future styling trends. Local media were instantly attracted to these events, resulting in great success of the campaign.[10]

Brand Axe published a study as the Valentine's Day approached in 2002 on the best dating cities in the USA. This lent immense opportunities to localized PR in such cities.[11]

Providing e-learning in the Indian hinterland

ITC, a private sector company has made definite inroads into the rural hinterland of India, but with a difference. The company came in media focus when it launched e-Chaupals through which computer access was provided to villagers to learn about better ways and innovation in the field of irrigation and related areas. ITC is also planning to start supermarkets in various districts to give rural Indians a choice of various brands.

Indian Farmers Fertilizer Cooperative Ltd. (IFFCO)

A number of companies in the fertilizer sector were set up in the 1960s to give a boost to Indian agriculture during the Green Revolution era. IFFCO, is the number one fertilizer organization in the country with highest production and sales of over 55 lakh tones of fertilizer per annum. IFFCO markets its products through 36,000 cooperative societies spread over 23 states and two union territories. Market can be won by one of the three strategies, viz, a superior product, lower price or personalization. The biggest challenge for various fertilizer companies is to sell a "me too" product at the same price.

> ### CASE STUDIES
>
> IFFCO uses multi-pronged public relations and promotion approach using 'personalization' to reach out to the farmers to create a differential. Some of the strategies include engaging professionals in extension services who work as a link between the organization and various societies. Participation in fairs and *melas* is a continuing activity. In fact the organization looks for opportunities like Cattle fairs and agricultural fairs held in various parts of the country to demonstrate its products, answer queries, distribute literature and at times samples to promote the products.
>
> The organization earmarks certain 'Field Days' in various zones to meet groups of farmers. IFFCO uses audio-visual medium also in such gatherings to show them the scientific basis of the quality of their products. It has recently released a soil testing CD that demonstrates how using right fertilizer and seeds can increase the yield of the farmer from Rs. 2700 per hectare to Rs. 5000 per hectare.
>
> The organization also has a 'Two-Plot' demonstration strategy. Under this scheme, a particular village is adopted and the farmers are asked to make two plots out of their field, hand over one to IFFCO and keep the other one with them to see the difference in yield through the traditional method used by the farmer and the scientific way of improving the yield. Over the years, many villages have been adopted, which have tremendously benefited the sale of company products.
>
> The organization also sends its 'Soil testing' vans which move from one place to another as per their chartered route to help farmers in soil testing. The van also carries products and also has film/video viewing facilities.[12]

There are a number of success stories that include many brands like Amazon.com, Harry Potter, Yahoo, Google which used PR for building very robust brands. Analysts feel that the aggressive approach of advertising needs be replaced by slow build-up using various public relations tools to have long-term impact on building strong brands.

A number of brands according to analysts that are considered ingredient brands can help build brand character of the manifest brand. Intel is one such interesting case in point. Intel ® or Intel Inside ® is seen as a seal of quality, despite its use across some competing brands.

Nike

CASE STUDIES

La Breche Murray, a PR firm once created an opportunity to leverage Nike's participation in both summer and winter Olympic games to gain coverage for its client, Nike. During the summer Olympics, the agency created media hype about a particular shoe that Michael Johnson, the fastest runner in the world at that time, was debuting during the opening competition. A 24 karat gold running shoe, designed by Johnson himself and Nike design experts had the upper sole manufactured with the ingredient brand. No one was expected to wear shoes made of gold, but it created the necessary hype and media coverage for the brand. Again at the time of winter Olympics, the company built the hype for US Speed skaters' wind suits on an ingredient brand. It featured low-friction material that is normally a "hidden" ingredient brand. The product was used in the arm and leg areas to increase the speed of skaters. The agency coordinated an Internet site with Nike, live from Ice Oval that had the ingredient brand company spokesperson explaining the unique combination of technically advanced apparel characteristics.[13]

Subway

CASE STUDIES

Globally the largest sandwich franchise and leader in the crowded quick-serve restaurant category, Subway repositioned itself using the PR route. It signed up Jared Fogle, the celebrity weightloss hero as its brand ambassador. The PR agency positioned SubWay as a leader in addressing the growing obesity issue facing many Americans. It created a multi-layered integrated campaign to kick-off Subway's partnership with the American Heart Association as national sponsor of American heart walks. Its media options included in-store promotion, spokesperson appearance, and targeted media relations. Jared visited schools talking about his battle with weightloss. Promotional opportunities also included events such as the American idol sponsorship and major league Baseball balloting. The company also introduced a number of interesting products alongside. The campaign managed to receive a lot of coverage in top broadcast and print media that included *The Wall Street Journal*, *The Boston Globe*, *USA Today*, *News Week*, and *New York Times*. Stories were also carried in CNN Headlines, Larry King Live, the Jimmy Kimmel show, MS NBC News Live, CNBC's The Squawk Box and Fox & Friends.[14]

VolksWagen's drivers wanted PR campaign

The usual launch includes a social event at a car dealership at a social venue with press and key guests of the industry, where the car may not be an interactive part of the event.

> ### CASE STUDIES
>
> Volks Wagen (VW) used a PR branded approach to help current consumer base evolve from one VW vehicle to another. The strategy was to take the car directly to the public via high-publicity special events with participation of brand loyalists.
>
> "Surferers wanted" gold caravan—the event was both the launch of the local website and of the new golf model. It included a tour of all the beaches in Puerto Rico where the new Golf was displayed with a distinct surfer look. "Beetle caravan"—old Beetle owners participated in a caravan to welcome the new Beetle. The new model led the caravan in a tour all around the San Juan metro area. "Touareg Launch"—the open field location of this launch event offered prospects the opportunity to experience the versatility of VW's new SUV by allowing them to test the vehicle by actually driving it over different terrain—from rough steep hills to paved roads.

In-house models – a great PR triumph

From professional models to sports and film models—the genre of endorsers are no other than people from within the companies—making a great PR statement. When *Hero Honda* ran a corporate campaign, it chose its marketing and sales Director Yoichi Mizutani to feature in the commercial that had him applying *mehndi* on the hand of a lady. Gas Authority of India (GAIL), a public sector undertaking ran a campaign depicting its top brass. In its ad for corporate communicators, the GAIL ad featured its DGM corporate communication along with a team with painted faces exhorting aspirants to join the team of "creative commandos". On Kingfisher flight, owner Vijay Mallaya greets you. On the television he speaks of the virtues of the brand Kingfisher. Years ago, Chrysler's legendary chief Lee Iccocca endorsed the brand challenging, "If you find a better car than this, buy it". Tech companies like Infosys and some BPOs feature young employees in their recruitment advertisements to attract people like themselves. Personal touch and real characters, believe many, lend credibility to ads. The pattern of Infosys vacancy ads has been giving pictures of an employee in varying moods, a little introduction about the employee, then on to the ad text.

> "The 'opportunities-unlimited' face of New India" had the picture of a Sikh youth whose introduction included the following: " Birinder Soni is a B.E. (Mechanical) from Delhi College of Engineering. Currently he is defining the market strategy for a global retailer. His key achievements include working with multi-billion dollar

retail; distribution & CPG companies across the US, Europe and Asia Pacific and helping clients make their supply chain planning and store operations processes more efficient and cost-effective. Not someone to rest on his laurels, he has also anchored Infosys' supplier Collaboration Business solutions". The rest of the ad text invited applications for the post of Domain consultants.

When Reliance Infocomm was launched, Mukesh Ambani appeared in the ad "*Papa ka sapna*". The MDH Masala ads have the family patriarch lending the touch of experience.[15]

Organizing events is an inherent part of public relations activities in the marketing mix. When Lufthansa, the German airliner sponsored world renowned orchestra conductor Zubin Mehta and The Bavarian State Orchestra for a classical Western musical event in New Delhi and Chennai in December 2005, a number of other German firms like Bosch, Siemens, Deutsche Bank became the co-sponsors, besides the TATA consultancy services. The letter sent by General Manager passenger Sales India and Director South Asia which enclosed the invite was addressed to "Dear friends, Dear business partners."[16]

Laura Ries, co-author of book "Fall of advertising; Rise of Public Relations" that brought PR in the big league along with advertising and changed the way PR would be perceived for long, has suggested that all news brands must be launched through PR and not advertising. For doing so, five things need to be addressed according to her:

Change 1: Identify the enemy. Her argument is that in communication, it is important to keep a watch on who is your brands' closest adversary. Having done that, the communication needs to be just the opposite of what the adversary is saying. To make her point she cites the example of Procter & Gamble when it launched a new mouthwash. The company decided that it had to pitch against well established brand Listerine which was a 'bad tasting mouth wash'. So they positioned the scope as the "good tasting mouthwash" making it a strong no. 2 brand. Similarly, when Lowe's was launched, Home Depot was the 'enemy'. It however was messy and male oriented, so Lowe's became the neat, bright and women oriented store, making it a strong no. 2.

She shares that originally the title of the book was "The PR era", but once the enemy was identified, it was changed to " *The Fall of Advertising and the Rise of PR*" creating both an enemy and a huge potential for publicity.

Change: 2 Leak the brand

Her second mantra is to give strategic leaks to appropriate media, who love scoops about what is going to happen in future. Advertising in contrast is formal and launched like a D-day with no inquisitiveness.

Change 3: Tolerate a slow build up

A PR programme in contrast with an advertising campaign has a slow build up. Customers learn about various aspects slowly over a period of time, assimilate it and when the brand is launched, they have enough knowledge about it to take a decision, which often will not be impulsive. She suggests at least six months lead time for the said build up against the big bang approach followed in advertising.

Change 4: Recruit allies

It is important to find ones' natural allies who will lend support to the brand. For their book, the enemy was identified as big advertising conglomerates; the allies obviously would be independent PR firms against the PR subsidiaries of advertising conglomerates. They identified 124 independent PR firms, who were sent advance copies of the book. The media mileage on the book was also sent to them, and the response was tremendous. Many volunteered to send copies of the book to their clients; some promised to invite the authors to address industry meets and so on.

Change 5: Allow for modification of the message

In advertising the brand is positioned in a certain manner, but when media writes about the brand, they have their own understanding of 'reader's/viewer's interest', and different media may pick up varying attributes to highlight, allowing a larger perspective about the brand. Citing the example of Volvo, the author shares that the company went on untiringly on the durability plank of its automobiles for long. The media on the other hand wrote about innovation, especially, the safety attribute, writing about its innovative 3-point lap and shoulder seat belt, the collapsible steering column, the front and rear crumple zone. The company at last understood the dynamics and shifted gears to talk about the safety aspect in its advertising campaigns.[17]

Bollywood using marketing mix in promoting films

Big budget films involving mega stars have also woken up to the use of PR as a build up much before the films hit the cinema halls. Using the small screen across various channels and genres of programmes has been the name of the game during the last five years or so. It is commonplace to find the lead team appearing in Reality shows, entertainment programmes, chat shows as also news channels. *Taare Zameen Par, Singh is King, Yuvraj, Rab ne Banadi Jodi, Ghajini* to name a few have made tremendous use of PR in recent times.

CASE STUDIES

Ghajini

As discussed above, many Indian film producers use various communication tools and strategies for the launch of their films. Aamir Khan has been doing it with quite an élan ever since his period film *Lagaan* was sent for the much coveted Oscar awards. There has been no looking back since then. The usually media reticent Aamir could be seen all over media space as a prelude to the release of *Ghajini*, which went on to make an unprecedented opening in Indian Cinema. As per media reports, the film grossed Rs 170 crores in two weeks.[18]

Aamir Khan is considered one of the smartest marketing strategists by the trade in India, when it comes to his using 360 degree approach to marketing his films. The communication onslaught happened at least 6-8 months ahead of the release of his film, which interestingly was a remake of the South Indian film. Despite the fact that there was no element of surprise as far as the story was concerned, the first thing that caught the attention of generation X was his scarred head. It became a fashion statement, with more and more youngsters supporting it. Remember his goatee in Farhan Akhtar's hugely successful film *Dil Chata Hai* and his dinosaur style of hair in *Taare Zameen Par* (TZP) had youngsters getting hooked on to it. In fact a college in Bangalore banned the *Ghajini* hair style.

Aamir's eight pack body and scarred head look seem to be all over media making people inquisitive about the character and the film. In fact he sported the look for his brand endorsement of a mobile phone also.

Two weeks before the release of the film Aamir turned barber, styling the *Ghajini* cut to youngsters in a Metro. The event attracted huge media coverage in most of the news channels, giving the necessary hype and buzz to his film. A reporter asked, "You have become a marketing god. Tell us how and when do you start planning your marketing strategy?"

The strategy, he said, began as soon as the team understood the core value of the particular film. Each film, he said, had a "unique marketing demand". His team comprises nine members who brainstorm with him with the guiding principle that "cinema is a form of mass communication and we have to tell the audience the core value of the film". Once the film is complete, the team strategise on "how to prepare people for the particular film". The *Ghajini* haircut was also a part of this overall strategy.

"Today marketing is an important part of film making," reasoned Aamir, "you need to create the right atmosphere".

Aamir spoke of two principles that he followed in communicating with the audience:
a) To honestly represent the film so it does not mislead the audience;
b) Not to do anything negative so that it does not harm anyone.

His ultimate aim from his films he said was "to live as much after I am no longer there. Even if someone watches *Lagaan* 200 years later, he should say 'who is that guy, *yaar?*'".

In retrospect, his film *Lagaan* is used as a case study in team building and management in many Business schools. His film TZP again India's entry to Oscar awards, won many critical acclaims from far and wide, especially from among teachers and parents for not only handling the subject so delicately but for widening their vision of parenting.

If we analyze the strategy of *Ghajini* carefully, there was a slow build up through PR using various marketing tools. A good use of imagery was used for visual impact.

Summary

In this chapter we looked at the role and scope of public relations in the overall marketing mix and brand building. We discussed PR as a part of the Integrated Marketing Communication (IMC). The arguments put forth by two schools of thought, one that believes in the inherent role of PR in marketing, and the other that feels PR was short term and was yet to prove the ROI were discussed. A number of case studies from various sectors were taken up to reflect the successful brand building by public relations, such as Microsoft, Unilever, Tums, IFFCO et al. We also discussed Laura Ries' argument on why PR was a better choice than advertising when it came to brand building. A case study of blockbuster film *Ghajini* was discussed to bring home the point on how slow build up through PR using events and media publicity made the audience inquisitive.

Critical thinking exercise

Select any movie involving a well known star cast and a known production house and trace the marketing build up for the film using various promotional media over a period time. Study various reflections in the media including Internet, blogs and the website if any, for the film, to arrive at your point of view.

Questions

Q.1 What is a marketing mix? Discuss its elements.

Q.2 What is the expectation from PR in a marketing mix? Can it build a brand without the help of advertising support. Argue.

Q.3 What is the role of PR in building a brand? Discuss with cases in point.

Endnotes

[1] Paul Holmes in *Advertising Age*, January 24, 2005
[2] Philip J. Kitchen and Don J. Shultz, "Raising the Corporate Umbrella: Corporate Communication in the 21st century", 2001 (Palgrave:NY)
[3] *Advertising Age*, January 24, 2005
[4] *Times of India*, 19 August 2008
[5] Jaishri Jethwaney and Shruti Jain, *Advertising Management*, 2006 (Oxford University Press, ND)
[6] Frank Rich, *The New York Times*, 15 April 1998; www.newyorktimes.com.
[7] Al Ries and Laura Ries, *The Fall of Advertising and Rise of Public Relations*, 2002 (Harper Collins: NY)
[8] Jaishri Jethwaney and Shruti Jain, *Advertising Management*, 2006 (Oxford University Press, ND).
[9] Ibid.
[10] John N. Frank in *PR Week*, August 2, 2004.
[11] Ibid.
[12] Ibid.
[13] www.lareachemurray.com/casestudies
[14] Cerrell Associateshttp://www.worldcomgroup.com/casestudies
[15] Bhanu Pande and Vinod Mahanta, "Double Role: New class of models find favour with Cos", *The Economic Times*, 27 December 2005, p. 5.
[16] Jaishri Jethwaney and Shruti Jain, *Advertising Management*, 2006 (Oxford University Press, ND.
[17] Public Relations Society of America (PRSA website) www.prsany.org
[18] *The Indian Express*, 4 January 2009.

Part II
UNDERSTANDING THE TECHNICAL ASPECTS OF PR

12 Graphics as a Public Relations Tool

Chapter objectives
- Understanding the role of graphic as a PR tool
- Identifying the components of graphics
- Analysing the functions of graphic components
- Learning the significance of design brief
- Explaining layout and design
- Studying the design principle

It is important that PR professionals have an adequate working knowledge about graphics. While a PR professional is not expected to be an expert designer, it is expected that he will have a working knowledge of the relative values of the written message, pictures and layout. If a professional is well versed in the design principle, typesetting complexities, paper quality, production constraints and today's technology, he will be in a better position to brief the designer and get the best results. Most importantly, he would not be taken for a ride!

Choosing the right designer for the job is the responsibility of the PR person. All graphic designers are not specialists in all sorts of work; nor are they equipped with all types of equipment to accomplish the job. Organizations, therefore, depend on ad agencies, or a freelancer, with the PR person acting as a coordinator.

What is Graphic?

Graphic is one of the visual forms used to enhance communication. It has been used ever since man started communicating by carving pictures, to enhance communication.

Man's quest for communication with more people necessitated the duplication of these visual forms, which resulted in the printed word. For many years graphics were confined to printing. Today, we find pictures and letters with spoken messages on television, film or video. The titles of TV serials, special effects in advertisements or animation films are all graphics. They are created by the human hand, but their shapes and styles depend on the tools available during that time. Earlier, conventional tools like brush, pen, ink, etc., were used, now these are available in the most sophisticated form, even in a digitized form in the computer.

Graphic comprises three basic components—*images, letters* and *colours*. These are used in solving the communication need of human beings with appropriate planning termed as layout. Each component of graphics has its unique characteristics that can convey messages independently or when combined with other components.

The Role of Images in Graphic Design

Images are a fast way to represent things through any visual communication medium. Comprehension of a visual message is direct in most cases. Understanding a message from visuals has no geographical or language barrier. An image, besides attracting attention, can explain, entertain, provide information, and create various mood of the message. An image can be photographic, hand drawn or hand painted. It becomes more dynamic in a digitized moving form.

Pictures often face the problem of communication. How can you understand a picture, which appears in the newspaper without a caption? A very good photograph in an advertisement is hardly capable of selling a product without any headline and copy.

Written messages on the other hand are formed by letters of the alphabet which are primarily pictures arranged in a certain order to convey the meaning. Text rendered as image such as headline, caption, blurb etc., allows the communicator to convey things besides the straightforward meaning of the text. Often a written message fails to convey the intended message due to the literacy level of the intended audience. One must learn the language and word symbols of that language to overcome the constraint of the graphic component.

Third component of graphics is colour. It serves a variety of functions. It is one of the components of design that has maximum attraction value. The use of appropriate colours can create the right atmosphere, provide ascent and contest to the design, add sparkle to the page, and direct the reader/ viewer through the message. Negatively, colour however, cannot compensate poorly conceived design and often antagonizes the viewer, and that kills the very purpose of the graphic. Moreover, despite it's power in design, colour has no meaning without a shape or image.

Therefore, only by combining all the three components together can an effective message be created. Layout plays a big role here. Layout is a plan to arrange the words and pictures in colour to create effectiveness. The writer and the designer often need to work together to convey a message. While the copywriter is more concerned with the message content, the graphic designer is more concerned with message presentation. To obtain the best result, a PR person should understand how graphic has to be used for various media formats like printed page, multimedia title, or web page. He should not only learn ways to make art and photographs more effective but also need to know how to crop and size art; the various ways in which typographical composition can be handled, and how to pass along instructions to the printer or the production house so that they obtain the desired result.

It is unlikely that the editor of a small publication, or the public relations professional, or the newspaper editor will be a highly skilled designer who can handle successfully all the various techniques involved in conceiving and preparing a graphic for production. It is rare for all these to be handled by a single professional. But it is absolutely necessary for all PR professionals to understand the graphic design business besides the rules of creating designs and using technology or tools needed in developing and producing a design. The PR person should utilize this knowledge when acting as a designer for his own materials for communication or getting them done by other professionals.

Design firms, small or big, are generally able to undertake various kinds of designing and graphic work. Some offer specialized services like exhibition design, web design or multimedia design, while others may specialize in designing for the print media. There are specializations within print media graphics as well. These specializations are newspaper graphics, corporate identity graphics, advertising graphics and publishing graphics etc. Some organizations, which do not focus on graphic design are publishing houses, computer service companies and manufacturing firms. They hire individual graphic designers or design firms to carry out their work.

The starting point may be identifying the type of materials to be designed and developing a brief for the designer.

What is a design brief?

A design brief is a comprehensive written document for a design project developed in concert with a person representing the business need for design, and, the designer. The document is focused on the desired results of design—not aesthetics. Some prefer the term creative brief. A creative brief is defined by experts as a document used by creative professionals and agencies to develop creative deliverables: visual design, copy, advertising, websites, etc. The document is usually developed by the requester and approved by the creative team of designers, writers, and project managers. In some cases, the project's creative brief may need the creative director's approval before the commencement of the job.

Now begins the aesthetic aspect. It is a subjective element because understanding, comprehension and responding to the design differs from person to person, group to group or from region to region because of varying cultures. Here lies the challenge. How can the design aesthetic influence the larger target group? Professional graphic designers and communication experts have developed some parameters commonly known as *Design principles* based on which design can be created and also appreciated or criticized.

What is Design principle?

A design starts with identifying the elements that are required to be arranged. The elements may be copy block, headline, picture, colour, white space, etc. These are identified by its size, shape, tone, texture and edges. Next, one has to decide on a shape in which these elements will be arranged. This is the shape the viewer will notice first, and go through the others displayed within it.

The next job of the designer is to divide the shape into rectangular grids. Four equal parts tend to make the layout unattractive and unexciting because of the rigid, mathematical division. A layout can be improved by making one of the divisions larger. Many different arrangements of elements may be obtained from such a division. The most pleasing division of space is a set of rectangles of different sizes.

Identifying the elements of design

Design elements are first identified by shapes. Whatever the objects we see around us we perceive them as shapes, each one is enclosed by lines. The shapes may be very regular like square, circle or a rectangle; shapes may be very irregular on the basis of content within it. Innumerable shapes can be obtained in variations and combinations of these basic shapes. Each shape develops an optical weight, which can be felt emotionally. Bigger, filled in and ragged-edged shapes call for more weight than smaller, empty and smooth-edged shapes. The shape may be very distinct or vague. Distinct shapes are easily separable but the vague ones are merged with each other or there are no distinct edges. Some shapes carry information while some others are just for decoration. Photographs, copy blocks and headlines are information-bearing elements; margins, white spaces, borders and colours are, however, decorative ones.

Look of the shape by toning: The relative lightness and darkness of a surface quality is identified as a tone. Whatever we see with our naked eyes is in colour. The degree of lightness and darkness of colour helps us perceive an object in three-dimensional form even on a two-dimensional surface. These qualities of colour are called values of colour. The colour value retains its personality even when it is converted into tones of a single hue.

Tones may be from shining to dull and smooth to rough. A rough surface may be said to have a rough texture.

Proportion by subtle size of shape and tone

When we put two or more elements together, we make a composition. We place them in some order. These compositional forces are measured by proportion. One is larger than another, one is darker than another, and one has a texture that is smoother than another's and so on. On the basis of the proportion, the reader decides which one wants to read first and so on.

Balance around the optical centre

Design elements should be put together not only in proportion, but also in balance. We must place elements on the page in such a way as to make them look comfortable in a particular space, which is achieved by balance. The balance principle is like the principle of gravity. Here, the optical centre acts as the pivot of a weighing machine or as the centre of gravity. The optical centre is the spot that hits the eye first when it encounters a blank page. This is an imaginary point slightly above the geometrical centre.

When two objects of equal weight and volume are put on a balance, they seem to be equally far away from the centre of gravity. Balance in design can be defined as a matter of weight distribution by which elements on a page look settled at their respective position.

Choose between formal and informal balance: Balance can be achieved broadly in two ways—formal or symmetrical, and informal or asymmetrical.

In formal design, space is divided equally from left to right, and elements of equal weight are placed equidistant from the central line. If a single element is to be balanced, that element should he placed at the centre of the space so that the imaginary centre line can divide the element down the middle. Formal balance places all elements in a precise relationship to one another. It gives us the sense of formality that is obvious, in look, familiarity and simplicity. In many cases it is easy to achieve. PR professionals may consider formal balance for a target audience who are by and large conservative and believe that their taste is dignified and sober. Often book covers, company report covers, specialized booklets, etc, are designed formally.

In case of an informal balance, elements of similar but not precisely the same weight are placed in relationship to one another so that there is weight at the bottom of the layout as well as at the top, to the left and to the right, so as to balance the whole.

If a heavy element is placed near the optical centre on the right side of the space, the lighter element should be kept away from the optical centre down the left side, to counterbalance the bigger element. If another element is placed with the left side element, one should visually estimate the total weight of these two elements and then decide where to place them so that the whole looks stable. To understand this particular principle of design take a drawing sheet of size 11"x 16" and identify the optical centre. Collect some matt finished coloured paper, cut it into different shapes and place them around the optical centre of the drawing sheet. Keep on changing their position and try to judge the balance.

Maintain visual consistency: In order to avoid conflict between design elements the design elements of a page should be harmonious. The same principle as in our day to day life—saris matching with blouse, shirt may not go very well with *dhoti*. Here one element should go with another element in terms of tone, shape or design characteristics. If a particular shape is chosen for a design, other elements should be of the same shape to maintain harmony. Likewise, there should be tone, texture

Elements of design around optical center

Symmetrical Balance

Symmetrical Balance (Left heavy)

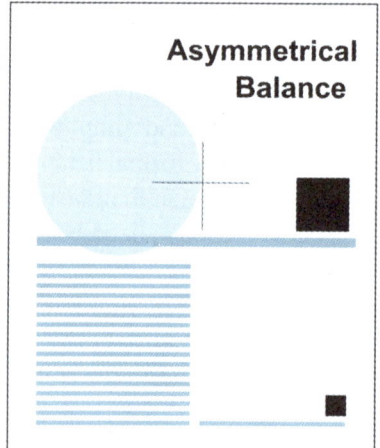
Balance

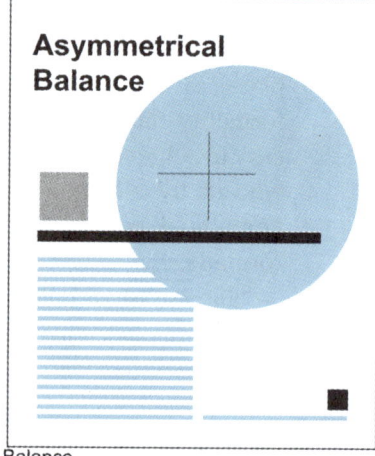
Balance

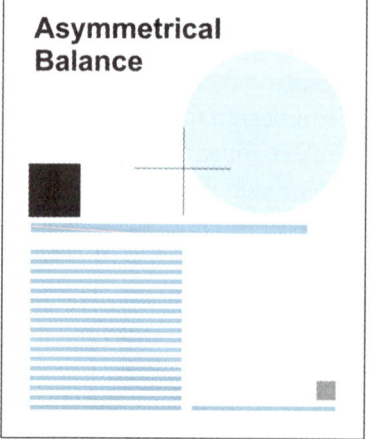
Left heavy

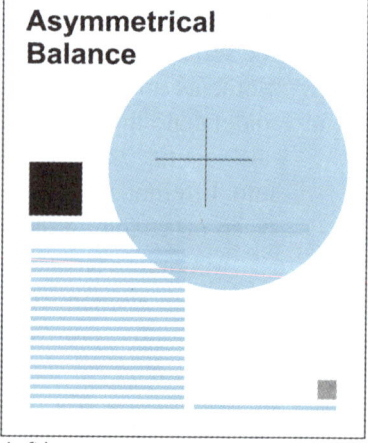
Left heavy

and colour harmony. Typographical harmony means that the type characters including figures, signs and punctuation are of the same style. To achieve type harmony, select one type family and, for variation, use different sizes of the same family including bold and italic faces.

- **Let the reader see at least one element first**

Is it possible to see, hear or read a message at one time? Not really. Obviously, some materials must be stressed more than others. It is called contrast. In graphic design, contrast can be achieved by making one of the items bigger in size, unusual in shape, darker in tone or rough in texture. If lines are running horizontally, and suddenly a small vertical line appears it can create a contrast. On a page designed in black and white, a small coloured element can provide contrast to the page. Other ways of achieving contrast include varying the width of copy block, using a drop letter, occasional blurbs on the page, and so on.

- **Allow the eye of the reader to move on the design**

In moving forms of design, eyes keep on moving as per the movement of the element. But in static form of design, the designer should force the viewer or reader's eye on the page as per his or her requirement. Otherwise some of the elements may be missed out which could be important from the communicator and reader's point of view. Eyes naturally follow in a certain direction. For example while reading text of most of the languages the eyes move left to right. Eyes also move from big to small, dark tone to light tone colour to non-colour. The direction of content of a visual also indicates the movement of eyes.

- **Make your design unified in composition**

The individual elements of the design must relate to each other and to the total design so that they hold together. When we see a loosely printed communication, our eyes cannot find a centre of interest and we bounce around with no place to hold our attention. A design should be so constructed that its elements are combined and comprehended at first glance as a unified composition.

Unity can be achieved in various ways. Some are obvious, such as enclosing everything in a border, or grouping some elements by pushing out the white space and using the same basic shape, tone, typography. Some of the non-obvious ways of maintaining colour or mood throughout are by uniting the elements by imaginary lines, arranging elements on an axis, and inserting lines through the elements.

- **Use colour to create memorable moods**

Warm colours (yellow, orange, red) evoke pleasant, often dynamic, reactions. *Cool colours* (green, blue, purple) evoke a quieter mood, and are considered less outgoing than the warm colours. The "temperature" of colours can also indicate action levels and priorities: warm colours advance from the background and imply a required reaction, while cool colours recede and imply rest or background status. In any hue, single colours, free of dynamic interactions with other colours, are more appealing and memorable when presented against a background of neutral gray.

Layout

Start your design by thumbnail sketches or miniature layouts. These layouts bring forth ideas, save time, prove economical and even help try several approaches. Select the best thumbnail to develop a rough or comprehensive layout.

In graphic design , a comprehensive, usually shortened to "comp", is the page layout of a proposed design as initially presented by the designer to a client, showing the relative positions of text and illustrations before the specific content of those elements has been decided on, as a rough draft of the final layout to build around.

The illustration element may incorporate simulated visuals, clip art, or other found material that gives an idea of what should be visually communicated, before entering into any negotiations concerning the rights to use a specific image for the purpose. Picture agencies may encourage such use free of charge, in the hope that the comp image will end up being used in the final product. Even in the age of rapid desktop publishing software, comps may be developed using hand-rendering techniques and materials to avoid investing too much time on the computer before client approval of the idea, depending on the complexity of the production task. A hand-rendered comp may be useful in helping the client select one to get a design idea but quality may suffer in terms of production requirement.

A creative idea may have been well executed and may well be looking excellent, but unless it fits into the mechanical limitation of the printing process, it will lack effectiveness. Mechanical limitations refer to the adaptability of the content to the machines and substrate that may include a process camera, an electronic scanner, system, printing process and the type of paper.

Persons with considerable knowledge of printing and its limitations must handle the layout for this purpose. The term used for this stage of layout is called the artwork. Conventionally it is drawn on a white paper with black ink outlines for the area that is to be filled with colour and also the area for the illustration. The illustrations are supplied separately to the printer along with the rough layout or comprehensive and the artwork.

These days most of the layouts are done using computers. Here both the line and the halftone elements can be scanned and stored in digital form and the information can be used to create a complete design. The colour monitor of the computer allows the operator or layout person to assess the layout and colour before converting the image into a film positive or negative which is one of the initial requirements for commercial printing.

Summary

PR professionals often use graphics to solve a communication problem. What is graphic? It is a manipulated visual form used to enhance the communication message. Graphic comprises of three basic components—images, letters and colours. Each component of graphic conveys messages independently or in combination with other components. Visual images attract attention, provide information create the various moods of the message. Letters in the form of headline, text, caption, blurb etc. allow the communicator to convey ideas in linear progression besides attracting attention. The use of appropriate colours can create the right atmosphere by providing ascent and contrast to the design and direct the viewer through the message. Arrangement of all the three components in a logical order is called layout, which is vital in developing a design. In order to get a desired result of a design a design brief is a must and that leads to the creation of aesthetic and functional design. Though the professional designers are supposed to create a design based on design principles, PR professionals should also be knowledgeable about it, not only to appreciate or criticize a design but also to participate in designing activities with the professional designer at an advanced level.

Critical thinking exercise

Graphic design involves creative thinking, design skill and technological know how. Prove your worth by suggesting an alternative design of an existing publication. Give your logical explanation in support of the design that will be fit within the technical parameter of production.

Questions

Q.1 Explain graphics. Why is graphic considered one of the important tools of PR professionals? Elaborate your answer mentioning the various forms of graphics.

Q.2 Define layout in context of graphic design. What is the role of a PR person in developing a layout?

Q.3 What is a design brief? Who gives the brief and who utilizes it?

Q.4 Explain design principle is the grammar used to make, appreciate or criticize a design.

References

Bob Gorden and Maggie Gorden, Consultant Editors, *Digital Graphic Design* (UK: Thames & Hudson Ltd 2002)

Arthur T. Turnbull and Russell N.Bairdt, *The Graphics of Communication* (USA: Holt, Rinehart and Winston, 1980)

Ken Smith, Ed., *Handbook of Visual Communication: Theory, Methods and Media* (USA: Lawrence Erlbaum Associates Inc.,2005)

Wikipedia, the free encyclopedia (accessed on December 2006)

Theodore E. Conover, *Graphic Communication Today* (USA: West Publishing Company, 1990).

13 Understanding Type and Printing Processes

Chapter objectives
- Understand the letter form in terms of structure, face, style and function
- Gain knowledge about font, family, readability and legibility
- Learn the use of pica scale for type measurement
- Prepare typesetting and copy for printing
- Learn about various printing processes and their features
- Understand the criteria for selection of a printing process

Printing is a highly technical trade. It is a fast-paced and high-pressure business. On the one hand, printers keep up with the rapid and continuous technological changes, and, on the other, the customer demands greater speed, lesser cost and higher quality. There are various printing processes and type-handling devices, which are available in the market to satisfy the need of various kinds of customers.

A PR practitioner has to undertake an enormous amount of printing work, which includes a newsletter for employee communication, brochures, pamphlets, annual reports, posters, and a variety of promotional literature. Therefore, a basic knowledge of type and printing processes helps him not only in choosing the appropriate type style and a suitable printing process for different jobs but also puts him in a better position to interact with the printer. The following considerations will help:

Understand the letterform

Letter characters existed even thousands of years ago on various surfaces in various forms. Some of the forms like calligraphy and signography are practiced in our day-to-day life. Calligraphy is free hand writing whereas the signographic letterform is drawn, painted and fabricated. Types are the standardized letterform of today.

Know the Type structure

All standardized letters come within a rectangular body and they can be seen within four horizontal parallel lines when arranged in sequence. The vertical distance within the two middle parallel lines is known as x-height. The letters, which extend above the x-height and drop below x-height, are known as ascenders and descenders respectively. Another noticeable character of type design is that the height of the body by which the type image is transferred on to paper is constant but the width varies.

Use *pica scale* for type measurement: Since the body height is the only feature of type that remains constant, types are measured by its body height. To measure it, a special scale known as "pica scale" is used. There are only two units in this measurement system: the point is the smaller unit and pica the bigger. 72 points or 6 picas equal one inch. This means that there are 12 points in a pica.

Type:
Standardized letterform made from mould, stencil or grid

Type face:
Letter image on the body which gives impression on page that is read

Type body:
Type that carries letter image and gives impression on page which has been inked

Type Structure:

Type Measurement

A type is measured by its body, not by its face. The body height is the only features that remains constant, faces are variable.

To get the body height, draw the parallel lines, one from top of the ascender and another from bottom of the descender.

By matching the specimen capital letter you can find that required size of type.

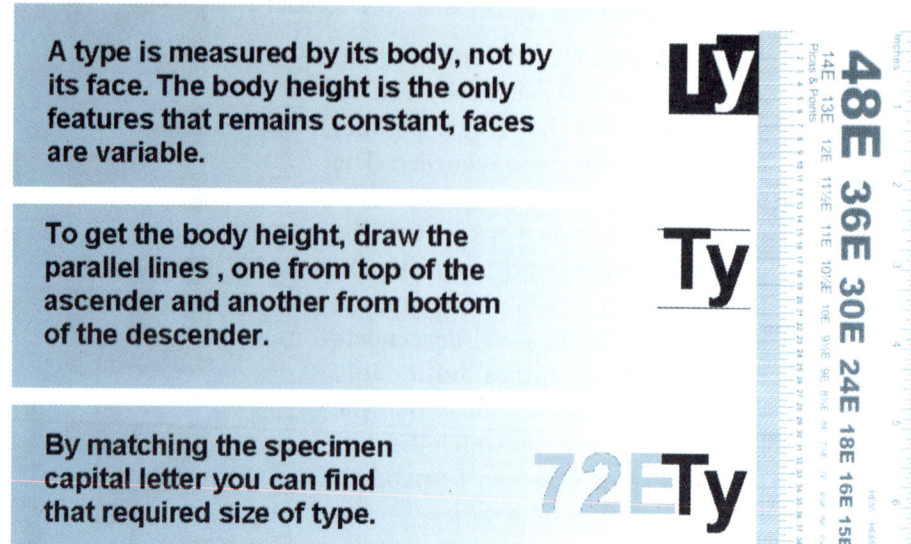

Play with the aesthetics of type

Despite the common features of type design, there are a great variety of typefaces. As there are hundreds of such styles, types are classified in broadly four groups each of which is identified by certain distinct characteristics.

• *Choose classical style for text*

The basic characteristic of this group is: thick and thin strokes within a letter with a short cross line attached to the main strokes of the letter. This cross line is known as serif. Classical Roman faces are considered most legible and widely used in all sorts of publications. It may be due to their thick and thin strokes that create rhythmic pattern, which helps, in faster movement of the eye on type composition. The serif of the faces helps in a horizontal movement. It is also the most familiar type. The font and families which constitute this group are: Caslon, Palatino, Garamond,

Classical
Roman: Thick and thin strokes with serif attached to the main strokes

Family: Palatino, Times Roman

ABCDEFGHIJKLMNOPQR
UVWXYZ&
abcdefghijklmnopqrstuvwxyz
1234567890$

Baskerville, Bodoni, etc. The faces are commonly known as Roman faces and considered basic types.

• Use Lineal style for modern flavour

The next broad category is the lineal group. Lineal typefaces may be with serif or without serif. Without serif lineal faces are called sans serif. The evenness of each stroke including the serif of the Rockwell face makes it a square serif within this group. Lineal faces are monotonic because of their uniform strokes. They are appropriate for children's books, promotional literature and an advertising copy, when text matter is limited. These faces are considered modern because they resemble the modern way of writing like with ballpoint pen, sketch pen etc. Futura, Universe, Helvetica, Avant-Garde, Antique Olive are the families of sans-serif lineal group.

Lineal Sans Serif

Even body without serif

Family: Arial, Avant Garde

ABCDEFGHIJKLMN
OPQRSTUVWXYZ
abcdefghijklmnopqrst
uvwxyz 1234567890

• Give your design a fancy style

As the name implies, the faces of this type group are decorated but do not have any clear-cut characteristics. These faces are designed mainly for display purposes and have extra attention-getting value. They are inappropriate for text composition. Tango, Arnold and Gallia are the families of this group.

Fancy Decorative

Highly decorated faces not having clear cut characteristics

Family: Gallia, Amelia

ABCDEFGHIJKLMN
OPQRSTUVWXYZ&
1234567890$
ABCDEFGHIJKKLMNOPQRSTUVWXYZ
abcdefghijklmnopqrstuvwxyz
1234567890&!?$

• Handwritten style meant for personal touch

This type group has lettering, which looks handwritten. Some of the families of this group are slanted right and have joint letters. Some are straight and have independent letters but maintain the feeling of handwriting by pen or brush. They can create a certain personal touch. Example: invitation card, editorial of a magazine, advertisement copy etc. The families are: Murry Hill, Commercial script, Palace script, Zapf Chancery, etc.

Hand Written

Resembles calligraphy but mechanically developed. Mainly joint letters.

Family: Brush, Commercial

ABCDEFGHIJKLMNOP
RSTUVWXYZ
abcdefghijklmnopqrstuvwxyz
1234567890$&

Differentiate between text, display and poster type

There are three functions of type composition— text, display and poster. The text matter or body copy constitutes the main typographic composition. The designer's ultimate goal is to draw the reader in coordination with the idea of the communicator. Type size 5 to 12 points (8-14 points in the case of *Devanagari*) is considered text matter. These sizes are visually clear and legible at an optimum distance of 10-14 inches from the eye.

Display faces are more than 12 points and up to 72 points. These type sizes are used mainly for heading and subheading. The basic function of this group is to attract attention and summarize the content. Poster types are big, often measured by the area they have occupied. In any case these are more than 72 points in sizes, they appear in a design composition as a visual and the main purpose is to attract attention.

Legibility vs. Readability

Types are meant for reading. Legibility is one of the functions of readability. While reading, some words fall within the eye span and the reader absorbs the meaning of the words at a certain speed and moves on to grasp the subsequent words. This movement of the eye greatly depends on legibility. Therefore, a type composition, which can be read faster, should be considered legible. Often an individual letterform is beautiful and also identifiable but in a composition it is not legible. Decorative and script letters are examples of illegible faces. Letterforms, which are closer to the fundamental shapes of the alphabet, are more legible.

While handling type composition in a design, we should follow some legibility rules. Since our involvement is mainly with the text matter, most of the legibility rules are meant for it.

- ***Never use text composition in capital letter***

Irrespective of the type style, text matter should be set in mixed capital/lower case faces; and capital letters should be used sparingly. In a mixed composition lowercase has more characters per line. The x-height of the face which has more design strokes, creates two parallel lines with occasional breakage of monotonous uniformity by ascenders and descenders. The texture created by lower case letters is pleasing for the reader and increases legibility. In contrast, if all matter is set in capital letter, it creates a uniform parallel and almost uniform white space between lines, impairing legibility.

- ***Use type size as per the intended reader***

Bigger size typefaces are more legible than smaller faces, because the clarity of type design comes from bigger size faces. Larger size type occupies more space and more time is needed to read the copy. At the same time very small faces are also difficult to read. Choose a typeface that is small in point size but large in x-height. Medium weight faces hold out better when used small. Slightly condensed type allows for more characters per line. For children type size should be bigger. An average educated reader can read text comfortably if it is set between 9 to 12 point. Older age group also need bigger type size. Type size also depends on reader's interest. You will not hesitate to go through classified advertisements, which are set in very small type if you are looking for something desperately.

- ***Give due importance to various spacing***

Four types of spacing can be obtained in type\composition: letter spacing, word spacing, line spacing and paragraph spacing. There is natural spacing between letters which is quite adequate for most running text. Extra spacing may be needed to achieve various moods of the type composition. Letter spacing always influences Word spacing. Tight spaced letters need tight word spacing and loose and normal letter spacing asks for loose and normal word spacing.

Like letter spacing, there is also natural line spacing. But most of the time this natural line spacing is not adequate. Line spacing decisions come from the size of the type being used, the style of the face, the line length and the setting of the composition. If the type size is small and the length of the line is big, it needs more spacing between the lines. A type style with small x-height needs less spacing as its ascenders and descenders naturally take care of the white space between the lines.

Paragraph spacing is used to separate a group of lines from the other group. Traditionally, the initial line is indented and no extra space is provided between the paragraphs. This looks uncomfortable sometimes, especially when the last line of a paragraph fills almost the complete measure. Lines without indentation and spaced out composition call for atleast half line spacing. A paragraph with a sub-head needs at least a one-line space at the top.

• Decide the line length based on type size

There are several formulae for determining the length of a line. The most common is that line size should be (in picas) twice the type size (in points) being used. That is, if the type size is 8 points, or I 0 points, the line length should be 16 or 20 picas. Small size type requires short line length and bigger type requires a longer line.

• Set the alignment on natural reading criteria

The manipulation of space by type is the format of a typesetting. The most common setting format is, "justified", where the type lines are aligned both left and right. It is considered the most legible format because of a uniform line length. The reader's eye moves from left to right uniformly.

The next most legible format is left flush and right ragged. Here also the reader's eye movement is fairly uniform as in both sides aligned, or justified format. The additional advantage of this format is that there are no hyphenated words at the end of a line.

Two other setting formats are (1) ragged left and (2) centred. These two formats should be avoided for long copy because they reduce reading speed. The reader takes time to find the beginning of the next line because of the uneven starting point.

• Choose only medium weight for text

Types come in various weights— bold, medium, light and so on. Bold is the darkest, medium is less dark, and light is the least dark. The weight of type adds tone and texture to the type composition.

Long copy set in light and bold is tiring for the reader's eye. Both of these faces are common for short copy, especially when emphasis and variations are needed. Medium weight faces are most legible and, therefore, used in almost all printed publications.

Like light and bold faces, italics (slanted) faces are also used for variation or emphasis. These are normally not used for long copy as these faces are not quite as easy to read as normal (upright) faces.

• Avoid mixed style to maintain visual consistency

These are not used in typographic design, especially for test. Modern typographers call this the rule of typographic harmony. This harmony is achieved by using one family of type throughout, in one design.

• Don't tire the eye by reverse type

This means white (or light) letters against a dark background. The legibility of this arrangement of type is less because white letters on a dark background shrink optically.

Therefore, long copy should not be set in reverse, or on tint, or colour.

- **Avoid text type in colour**

This also appears to sink into the page and reduces legibility. Since contrast and clarity are the main factors of legibility, care should be taken by using bold and bigger size type. Never use long copy in colour.

Handling the Display faces

The purpose of this category of faces is to invite the reader to notice the design and to apprise him of the message in a very short and subtle form. Handling the type in this situation is the same for designer and writer. Due to absence of set type style rule for display faces, these are used freely. But in many places Lineal and Traditional faces are widely accepted. Don't hesitate to make use of slightly fancy style in some places to create an appropriate mood.

In display, an irregular line length is preferable to justified (both sides aligned). It may be centred, left flush or right flush or free set according to the nature of the job and the designer's task. Centred settings are very formal and go well with formal design and justified body copy.

Left flush is an all-purpose display setting. It looks less formal and creates contrast even when set in the same family of text copy. Left ragged setting is comparatively dull. It is often used to balance other elements. Free setting is the most dynamic composition used mainly in advertising or type format, which serves the purpose of advertising. Headlines with wide white spaces are more legible than those surrounded by other visual elements. To attract the attention of the reader bold and big headlines are preferable.

Preparation *of* copesetting

The original manuscript should be typed or keyed in if you have a personal computer, preferably in double space so that if there are any corrections these can be made above the line without disturbing the readability of the script. The idea is to provide a clean copy to the typesetter. The typesetter or the operator is likely to make more errors or repeat lines in the case of closely spaced type matter or a shabbily corrected/edited manuscript.

Once the manuscript is ready it should be marked *for* typesetting. If the copy is entered in the word processing system of a personal computer it needs some basic information. The typesetter too will not be able to compose a single line of copy unless the following information is there:

- Type size in points
- Fonts or family (example: Helvetica, Caslon, Times)
- Space between lines in points
- Width, weight and posture

- Mixed letters or capital letters
- Line length in picas
- Space formats (justified, left aligned, or centred)
- Special instructions (like indentation, drop letters, spacing, etc.)

In the case of display type, markings should be on the line and *for* body copy, margins may be used *for* copy marking purposes. The designer marks the copy on the layout itself. It is preferable to mark on the overlay of the artwork in order to maintain neatness.

Typesetting

Nowadays composing, that is typesetting, is no longer the job of a low paid compositor. The art director and designer who prepare the Camera-Ready Copy (CRC) for the offset process often handle it. Modern typesetting machines are friendlier for creative people than *for* mechanical compositors.

Until recently, hot metal composing was the dominant typesetting method. It is now diminishing in importance. Cold composing, in which no molten metal is involved, is replacing it. It is much cleaner and proves cheaper in several respects. It does not require the investment of large amounts of money for type as was needed for hot metal typesetting. The greatest advantage of cold typesetting is that it is compatible with modern methods of printing.

The two hot metal mechanical typesetting methods (Mono and Lino) which once brought about a revolution in the printing industry and maintained their position for more than a century, are now considered obsolete because the high speed letterpress is out of use. However, hand setting, a manual method, is still in demand in our country as some kinds of job work are more economically done in the letterpress process of printing.

The latest technology is cold typesetting. As in hot metal typesetting, cold typesetting methods can be categorized as manual and mechanical. The manual method consists of composing individual letters in the desired typefaces and pasting them together to form complete words. This is mainly used for headlines and short copy because in long copy it is laborious and time consuming. Strike on lettering of manual typewriters is another type of copy in this category.

The mechanical typesetting method of cold composing mainly consists of electronic typewriters, phototypesetting and DTP (Desktop Publishing) system.

Electronic typewriter copy has reproducible quality and some of it has justification and font changing facilities too.

Until recently phototypesetting meant a process of getting type impression on photographic paper or film flashing a light through a film negative just as in photography. Now phototypesetting has turned into digitized image setting which provides high resolution output on film or bromide paper of typographic images. This system not only produces types, but also graphics created by the personal computer. It can take commands from its own input devices and also accepts inputs from other digitized phototypesetting or DTP systems. As a result; test, tints, patterns, line art, halftones, etc., produced by appropriate software can be obtained as laser image output of high resolution.

The next stage after composing is to prepare the artwork. In this, all the elements of design— the text, the graphics, etc.— have to be placed exactly in the places in which they are needed in the finished product.

Printing

There are a variety of ways to reproduce your work, from your office printer, a copy shop, a small print shop, to a large commercial press. The process you choose depends on your project. Since it is good to understand the advantages and disadvantages of each level of printing, and exactly when to choose each one, this chapter provides with some details on this topic to satisfy the need of various kinds of customers. To choose the right kind of printing process for a particular type of job depends on the PR person's knowledge of the print trade and detailed understanding of the project.

Before you begin to create your print project take note of the following:

1. What kind of job is it? The answer to this question will come from the physical properties of the piece to be printed. This may be a book, booklet, brochure, office stationery, flyer or annual report of the company and their approximate size, number of pages, number of colour etc.

2. How many copies are needed? In most cases it is an arbitrary decision or based on rough estimation of target readers. Sometimes the number of copies is decided by printing economy. For example, if you only print 600 copies of a coloured brochure at a commercial print shop it may cost you Rs.12, 000 or Rs. 20 per copy. But if you print 1,000 copies it may cost Rs.13,000 or Rs 13 per copy. Will you not go for 1,000 copies thinking the rest of the copies may be utilized without any extra cost? The number of finished pieces is sometimes called the "print run".

3. When is the job needed? Each print job requires a certain time to print. The print buyer fixes the time or the deadline with the print shop. It can be a year, a month, a week, weekend or immediately. Some jobs may be very flexible. Deadline is beneficial for both print buyer and printer. As a PR person you can plan other parts of your project so that everything will be ready on time. The printer on the other hand will be able to schedule the other jobs and your job will be delivered on due date.

4. What quality is in demand? Each printed piece needs certain quality depending on the function it will perform. Promotional literature requires a much more superior look than a newsletter to be distributed among the internal employees of the organization. If you don't have money to waste, you will not print a circular letter in multicolour. When photostat copies are sufficient to distribute the class notes among students, should one go for a laser printout. Cost and

number of copies are also determining factors of quality. Often quality is compromised due to cost.

5. How many colours? It is a very tricky thing in print trade. The numbers of colours you see on a printed page are not necessarily those many colours used while printing. In most cases they were printed by a combination of four colour inks— Cyan, Magenta, Yellow and Black— (CMYK) that are mixed in different proportions at the time of printing, creating an impression of various colours on the page. Some of the pages are printed with solid or pre-mixed colours and their tints are used to get a desired effect. They are called processes and spot colour printing respectively. In some situations both techniques are used.

6. What kind of substrate? Substrate refers to all kinds of materials on which your job can be printed. Besides paper, it may be cloth, plastic, foil, etc. When printing on T-shirts for an event management show, printing will be on cloth; when a folder needs to be distributed among the participants of a workshop, materials of the folder may be plastic or rexin. In case of paper, there are wide varieties available. Some are versatile, while others are suitable for printing for specific types of jobs.

7. What about artwork? It is a technical term for layout meant for the printer. Who is preparing it? Due to the computer savvy environment, nowadays most of the artwork is done at the end of the print buyer. If the job is to be photostatted, the artwork is to be made on the computer and printouts can be taken on a laser printer. The artwork is a bit tricky if it is meant for commercial printing.

8. What is the budget? As always cost is one of the major factors for any commercial project. How much money you can spend lets you know your budget for the project. You may not be able to take the services of Thomson Press (One of the top commercial presses of India) for printing your office stationery. At the same time for the printing of multicolour time bound Annual Reports of your company, you cannot rely on local print shops. Budget may be low or high, you must know your own limitation and also the limitations of the service provider.

All the printing methods available in our country can do some kind of job or other. Each one has got some unique features and can handle certain kinds of jobs efficiently. At the same time they also have number of limitations. Here we are discussing some processes. Let us divide them into three groups for easy comprehension.

Copy Printing

There are printing machines available in the market, which can duplicate the job instantly. Electrostating or photocopiers may be most common for today's fast speed communication business. These machines utilize the principle of static electricity, employing photosensitive materials that may be electrically charged in the form of a desired image and then caused to attract dry ink known as "toners" that prints on paper or other substrate.

There are various copiers available in the market with their own features that can be handled by a casual user. These copies can be used not only as a printed output but also for instant imaging for a graphic artist. These machines can enlarge, reduce and crop an image to a desired size. The printers find these machines very handy for stapling, collating and even gluing the pages. Colour photocopiers, though a bit costly, can be used for various purposes when minimum copies are required and prove very cost-effective if compared with coloured photography or scanned image output. Colour photocopy is also very handy on OHP (Over Head Projector) sheet for use in presentations or as teaching aids.

Some copiers can be connected with computers so that images created and manipulated in the computer can be transferred to the copier and the output can be obtained instantly.

Desktop printing

As per the nomenclature, people generally believe that it is a small outputting device, which is kept on a table or desk. But it can be as big as the size of a room or as small as a briefcase or even the size of a photocopier. Whatever may be the size, it is hooked to a personal computer in which the image to be printed is stored in order to get the copy. No matter what kind of desktop printer one uses, one must know some general things to handle a print document easily.

Printing quality: It is determined by resolution. The number of dots per inch or dpi identifies its quality. The more dots per inch, the higher the resolution and better the quality. So a printer that prints at 1200 dpi is higher quality than one than prints at 600 dpi.

Paper size: Most desktop printers can carry some standard sizes of paper—either A4 or A3 size, whose dimensions are 210x297 mm and 297x 420mm respectively. Decision of size of paper largely depends on the content to be accommodated, set up of the page elements, artwork and printer's paper tray. Remember, hardly any desktop printer can print edge to edge, which means it can apply ink from toner right up to the edge of the paper.

Speed: How many pages per minute the printer can output largely depends on processing of the document inside the printer and printing on paper by ink. If you give print command of a ten-page document separately for each page, it will take longer time than giving the command for ten pages at a time. For the same reason ten copies of a one page document print command should be given for ten pages, at a time. This makes the process faster as the initial page is processed and then printed and the rest of the copies are duplicated quickly.

Cost of consumable: Paper and ink are the two major consumables for a desktop printer. Various types of paper are used for different quality outputs. You may get an almost photograph like output, but for that a special paper is needed which is costly. Since the cost of each output is the same for any amount of copies, you may avoid going for a larger print run. Ink is bit expensive for a desktop printer, though there is a tendency to use duplicate ink to keep the print cost lower, you may not get quality for printing photographs or large area in dense colour.

Font: Some of the printers have an inbuilt library of typefaces to produce true to the character of the file sent to it for printing. Here the printer with the library has the choice of getting the font itself or downloading it from the computer. The only benefit of having fonts in the printer is that it speeds up the printing process.

PostScript Printers: Printers are also identified as dumb and intelligent or PostScript and non–PostScript. An intelligent printer understands postscript language, a special programming language created by Adobe System, Inc., that describes the appearance of a printed page. Though PostScript printers are more expensive in comparison to non-PostScript, output of both font and graphics from these printers is equally good.

Desktop digital printing has probably the greatest impact in the modern printing industry. In the evolution of print production, it has stepped in from a craft-based to technology-based business especially when copies are needed immediately. Since the copies are reproduced directly from computer memory, bypassing the steps of making film and plate, it reduces the lead time needed for printing and changing the image on each revolution of the press. Thereby, it has altered the publishing procedure from 'print and distribute' to 'distribute and print'. Two types of digital technology is involved in desktop printing—inkjet and laser.

Inkjet Printers:

A machine most favoured among the graphic artists and designers as it can give truly layout print inexpensively, is not really popular as back room office printing in professional institutions. The reasons are not far to seek. It does not give typographical printing sharp and clean as it uses liquid ink that spreads a bit just after printing. Therefore, inkjet printer is a poor choice for printing long documents with a lot of text. The colour image also looks washed out with loss of details.

Many people like them due to the cost factor of the machine. Instead of investing a large amount of money in buying a laser printer, inkjet printers can be used for printing for classroom projects of students, letters for correspondents, preparing bills etc. Since inkjet printers are non-impact process, it can print almost any surface regardless of surface texture and pressure resistance. Sophisticated inkjet printers give very good look of colours. One can choose the printers in creating charts graphs and illustration with text. Even a photo quality image can be obtained using glossy paper specially made for this purpose. The printer is very handy for its lightweight that it can be carried to any place keeping it in a brief case. Thinking for making some presentation on OHP sheets in colour? Go for inkjet printer, but use only specially made textured OHP sheet available for this purpose.

All inkjet printers are not restricted to desktop printing. New-age technology can print huge pieces on materials other than paper like canvas, nylon-reinforced vinyl etc. mainly used for outdoor signage. These machines are not economical for day to day work. In case of any need it is better to get your job done from a service bureau or print shop.

In inkjet printers digitized computer information directs the outputting device to force or spray individual tiny drops of liquid ink, which are given an electrical charger, from an opening through a small air gap to a printing surface.

Inkjet printers create colours on paper based on the same principle of process colour printing by four colours—cyan, magenta, yellow and black. These colours are sprayed from the cartridge in various proportions to create different colours. Some printers use two cartridges—one with three colours; cyan, magenta and yellow, and the other, black. Some printers are armed with four separate cartridges for each of the colours. It has got extra advantages, besides getting better print in black, it is easier to replace just one cartridge. Some inkjet printers use even more than four, colour cartridges. This extra ink enables the printer to produce more subtle colours especially when one colour is blended with another.

Laser Printers:

It works almost like a photocopier with the principle of electricity that positive and negative attract whereas positive-positive or negative-negative repel. Here, laser light passes through a finely tuned optical system and strikes on a light sensitive negatively charged rotating drum. It scans the surface of the drum as a computer activates it. Wherever it strikes, it neutralizes the spot and dots are formed at the points on the drum. A series of dots create the image to be printed. A negatively charged roller containing powdered ink, known as toner, is used to form the image, when it rolls over the drum. The neutralized area of the drum adheres to the powder from the toner, whereas the negatively charged area repels the ink. The paper receives a positive charge as it enters the printer and dots formed on the drum are transferred to paper. The heated rollers fuse the dots on the paper, creating a permanent image. It is because of this that freshly printed laser printout is warm.

Laser printers are largely associated with desktop publishing due its ability to print for typeset text along with visuals and graphics even for very small runs, presentation purposes or for group discussions etc. But the quality of production depends on the density of dots. The more the dots, the more superb the quality. A printer that uses 300 dots per inch (dpi) is considered a low-resolution printer. Laser is used for printing house journals, booklets, folders, etc. where high-quality production is not the prime aim. A range of 300 to 600 dpi is considered good resolution suitable for fine-quality printing. High-resolution images, i.e. between 1200 and 1600 dots and above are used for camera-ready copy or mechanicals for commercial printing. Low and good resolution printouts can be obtained from a Desktop Publishing system on various types of paper, and high-resolution imagery from an image-setting system on bromide or direct on film.

There are some disadvantages of this printing. It is because of these that many buyers continue to use conventional type of printing processes and utilize laser printers as a peripheral device. These include cost of consumables, especially toner which is many times higher than a set of process colours needed to print a job by offset process. It is also a slow process for a high run job. Most of the desktop digital printers can print only up to A3 size paper. Though the quality of colour print is impressive in many cases, it is much inferior when compared with inkjet printers while reproducing photographs, especially on inkjet's special glossy paper.

Colour laser printers use four different toners of cyan, magenta, yellow and black to create a cooler image. Due to the cost of toner and quality of paper needed to print a colour image, the unit cost of production is a bit higher which may prevent from opting for multiple copies. However, there are high-end multi-user applications that can justify the cost, such as printers with fax, copy and print facility. Some of the printers can now print on both sides, as well as collate and staple.

High resolution cost-effective multiple copies output is obtained on paper by a regular print shop that uses a high-end computerized film outputting device, image-setter.

Why is the output of a desktop laser printer not considered as professional as that of an image-setter? The simple reason is that the capability of creating number of dots (dpi) of an image-setter is much higher than that of a laser printer and the image is very sharp and clean on film or photographic paper (bromide), the substrate used for outputting. Dots transferred on plain paper by laser printer often don't print evenly due to the texture of paper and ink of toner may be peeled or spilt off on paper.

Commercial Printing

Due to the obvious limitations of quality matching quantity, large print run job is done by major printing processes like flexography, offset, gravure and silk-screen.

Flexography

It is one method of printing by which words and images can be printed onto foil, plastic film, corrugated board, paper, paperboard, cellophane, or even fabric. In fact, since the flexographic process can be used to print on such a wide variety of materials, it is often the best graphic arts reproduction process for package printing.

Flexography is related to the oldest printing process, Letterpress, because both flexography and letterpress print from a raised image. In its original form, letterpress used individual metal characters called *types* and a mechanical press. The type was combined to form words and sentences and tightly arranged on the flat surface of the press. Then the raised areas were covered with ink. The message was formed when paper was pressed against the flat metal type.

Flexography prints from a flexible printing plate that is wrapped around a rotating cylinder. The plate is usually made of natural or synthetic rubber or a photosensitive plastic material called photopolymer. It is usually attached to the plate cylinder with double-sided sticky tape.

Of late, flexographic printing has become even more popular because of its environmental conditions: unlike the oil-based inks used in the other types of printing, flexography uses water-based inks or non-solvent inks that are environmentally friendly.

Offset lithography

This is the most popular among various genres of printing kind and suitable for printing various kinds of quality literature. Unlike other type of printing, offset lithography involves printing from flat surfaces. It works on the principle that oil and water do not mix. The printing plate holds ink because the image is treated so that it is received to oil based ink but not to water.

In any form of printing, at least two surfaces are needed—one to carry the images and the other to give pressure against those images. But in the case of offset printing, three surfaces are used. The additional surface receives the inked image from the image carrier surface and then sets it off on paper. That is why it is called offset. As photography is the key to the modern make-ready procedure, it is also called photo-offset.

Offset printing requires an elaborate make-ready procedure. Whatever is to be printed has to be pasted on paper. This is commonly known as artwork. Visuals and types are pasted on the position exactly as they are to appear in the final printed job. Type and other solid coloured elements are considered line artwork from which line negatives are made. Continuous tone illustrations like photographs are generally submitted separately so that the camera can shoot them through a screen and make a second negative which is then stripped into position with the line negative. Recent developments in scanners and typesetting have produced machines that can scan pictures and typeset verbal copy in a digital form. Information of all these can be stored and used, as described above, with electronic devices, to create a complete page from which film negative or positive are made. Remember, film for printing should be that of the size of the image to be printed. The other steps are: transfer of film image on aluminum plate which is grained to hold water. There is a choice between surface plate PS or pre-sensitized and CtP or Computer to Plate depending on quality requirement and print run. Surface plate is the chipset plate but not suitable for quality halftone job and can on limited number of copies.

PS plates are readymade plates, ideal for most kinds of jobs. CtP technology is the new entrant in offset printing, which has eliminated one of the most important steps of plate making—film. The technology has gained popularity because of its high quality, but restricted to big printing houses because of high cost of plate-setter—the plate-exposing machine.

The offset press is the most important modern method in printing because of its ability to print near-natural quality of fine screen halftones. It can, besides, be printed on less expensive paper, whereas halftones in letterpress require art paper. The printing plate for offset is inexpensive and it can be easily curved to fit around the cylinder. It also occupies less storage space.

The preparation of copy of the offset process is mainly photographic or image-assembly which goes well with modern reproduction methods. Offset presses are generally rotary, which makes for faster printing speed. They can also print on large size paper and on materials other than paper, like tin, plastic, etc. Its compatibility with computer-oriented typesetting made this process much more popular.

Silk Screen

It is a print making technique that creates a sharp-edged image using a stencil. It is also called screen-printing because here forcing ink through a stencil, a screen or a mesh of silk fabric does printing. Nowadays, silk cloth is replaced by nylon, dacron, and wire screens. A screen is made of a piece of porous, finely woven fabric stretched over a frame of aluminum or wood. Areas of the screen are blocked off with a non-permeable material to form a stencil, which is a negative of the image to be printed; that is, ink or colour can be forced through them by a rubber squeeze. Thus, the images are obtained by depositing ink on paper placed under the frame.

This process can print any number of colours, but a separate screen is needed for each colour. For accurate registration in a multi-colour job, it is better to have all the stencils made on screens of equal size and at corresponding places on the screens.

There are several ways to create a stencil for screen printing. The manual method is to create it by hand in the desired shape, either by cutting the design from a non-porous material and attaching it to the bottom of the screen, or by painting a negative image directly on the screen with a filler material which becomes impermeable when it dries.

The commercially used method is photographic by which an image can be reproduced with a high level of detail, and can be reused for tens of thousands of copies. A photo stencil can be prepared either by transferring the image indirectly using film positives and pre-sensitised five-star film or exposing the light-sensitive emulsion directly. The ease of producing transparent overlays from any black-and-white image makes this the most convenient method for communicators who are not familiar with other print-making techniques.

Though the process is by and large manual and slow, it is used commercially because of its unique advantages. It is a simple and in many cases a very cost-effective method. The process is popular among the communicators because of its ability to transfer images onto almost any surface, whether flat or odd shaped. It may also use any colour, like opaque, transparent, glossy and fluorescent. The main charm of the printed image is that it looks like the original because of its high relief quality and brilliant colours. This is the only process where overprinting by light colours is possible. The materials involved are simple, inexpensive and easy to handle. One can enter the silk screen-printing business with very little capital.

However, there are some limitations in this process too. Most of its operations are manual, thus it is a slow process. It is difficult to achieve fine details and mechanical characteristics like halftones and process colour. Because of the thick ink, drying after printing takes time. However, the availability of many faster drying types of ink nowadays has solved this problem considerably. Because of its widespread use many printing presses are going for automation that enhance the speed of printing, even then it is much slower than other process like flexography and offset.

Summary

Printing begins with type composition. The use of type requires both skill and imagination. In order to understand this graphic component one should study physical structure, aesthetic and function of type.

Physical structure consists of type body, body structure, typeface and font. Points—are units of a special scale known as pica scale, measure type. Typefaces are available in thousands of design variations. Each one has its own style to contribute to the aesthetic aspect of type composition. The main function of the type composition is readability. Legibility or clarity of letters is one of the readability conditions in design. These days most of the typesetting is done in a desktop environment. Here, text copy and visuals combine to make a complete page for printing.

There are several printing processes available with various features to meet the requirements of both printers and print buyers. They are categorised as—desktop printing or on demand printing and commercial printing. The offset process is the most common for any commercial job. Whatever may be the printing process, selection criteria of a process depends on the type of job, print order, quality needed, time for printing, number of colours, substrate and budget for the project.

Critical thinking exercise

Pick-up two facing pages of an article published in a magazine. Identify text and display type faces used in the article and mention the instructions were given to make the pages for printing. Imagine the article is on Save Your Environment which should be distributed free of cost among 2000 school children. Suggest a printing process that will be economical but maintained the quality to impress the children.

Questions

Q.1 Explain standard letterform and its structure.

Q.2 What do you understand by type aesthetics? Give your views on its impact in communicating a message

Q.3 Compare between legibility and readability of type composition.

Q.4 What action to be taken to enhance legibility of text type composition?

Q.5 What are the points should be kept in mind while preparing a text copy for typesetting?

Q.6 There are various printing processes available in the market. What criterion determines the selection of particular printing process?

Q.7 Write the characteristics of copy printing, desktop printing and commercial printing. Mention the types of job can be printed by each category of printing.

References

J. Michael Admas and Penny Ann Dolin, *Printing Technology* 5E (USA: Delmer Thomson Learning, 2002)

Sean Morrison, *A Guide to Type Design* (New Jersey: Prentice-Hall, 1986).

Kate Clair and Cynthia Busic-Snyder, *A Typographic Workbook,* Second Edition (New Jersey: John Wiley &Sons, Inc., 2005)

John Kane, *A Type Primer* (New Jersey: Prentice Hall Inc., 2003)

N. N Sarkar, *Art and Print Production* (New Delhi: Oxford University Press, 2008)

Elizabeth W. Adler, *Print That Works* (California: Bull Publishing Company, 1991).

Helmut Kipplan, *Handbook of Print Media* (Germany: Springer-Verllay, Berlin, Heidelberg, 2001)

National Institute of Industrial Research, *The Complete Book on Printing Technology* (Delhi, Asia Pacific Business Press Inc.2005)

Sandee Cohen, and Robin Williams, *The Non-Designer's Scan and Print Book,* (USA: Peachpit Press,1999)

Hilary Ashwoth, Ed., *The Business in Graphic Design: A Professional's Handbook* (Ontario: The Association of Registered Graphic Designer's of Ontario, 2004)

14 Printed Literature

Chapter Objectives

- Understaning the role and scope of printed literature in PR activities
- Learning the physical form of brochure and leaflet, their functions and design process
- Learning the use of newsletters as official periodicals
- Handling the distribution of these literatures

In a publicity mix, organizations select media vide which they can exert control in terms of producing their literature, selecting the specific target audience and sending copies to them directly.

One needs a publication that outlines the company's special service or when one wants to publicise and explain the group's viewpoint in collaboration with a foreign investor. One may also need a publication listing a range of products with their special features and prices. There may be some self-answering publications, or one that can accommodate more information to satisfy customers.

In all these situations, a well-funded publicity blitz does not do well. The message is lost in a cluttered up or distorted situation by the time it is absorbed by the bulk of the audience. Printed literature like brochures, leaflets and newsletters play an effective role here.

Brochure

The physical forms of a brochure range from a single or two-fold sheet to an elaborate publication printed on glossy paper with lots of information.

Corporations find that this form of literature has several advantages that other media cannot offer. An advertiser can take full advantage of the directness and intimacy of the medium by developing a mailing list of the target audience. Due to increasing media cost, a personalized approach to marketing is becoming popular these days. The formats of brochures are flexible; the designer tailors the piece according to the need and convenience of the target audience. A brochure can stimulate replies when an order form with no-postage necessary envelope is included in it. The target audience can get everything in a brochure to take a decision in favour of the product or service.

The primary task of the corporate is to get the brochure picked up, opened and read. It involves making decisions regarding the form and format of the brochure. The forms of the brochure range from single-fold paper to a three-dimensional object. To many advertisers, the best form of a brochure is a folder. Some also call it a pamphlet, where a few loose sheets are used to deal with a topical subject.

The format refers to:

(1) The overall size of the piece;

(2) The style of sizing, shaping and toning of design elements;

(3) The headline and copy block pattern and their placement;

(4) Illustrations and techniques and their use;

(5) Use of other non-information-bearing elements like border, colour and other graphic devices; and

(6) Folding style, and opening and closing style.

Begin designing a brochure by cutting and folding paper, preferably in actual size. To avoid wasting time, try complicated folding in a miniature form. The possibilities of folding are unlimited, still you will find some of the common folding styles good enough for your work. The unusually folded brochure may show your creative talent, but remember it must come out from a standard size paper and fit into a standard size envelope for distribution and mailing. The folding of papers provides panels or sheets in equal sizes. Each panel may be complete in itself in what it says. Or the panels may combine to make one big panel and when they are opened out, make a large spread.

Whatever the folding style may be, one question should always be answered: what is the sequence of the panels or how can you remember the pages when they are folded?

Take a regular six-page folder. The cover of the folder is on the last inside page. As you open the folder, you get first the inside page and then the third outside page—they become one unit. For the purpose of sequence of information, these pages may be treated as No.1 and No.2. Display the elements of design on this spread as well, following the design principle that the heading on the left panel should counterbalance the illustration on the right panel, or that the subheadings and graphs on the left page creates a harmonious unity with the copy block and illustration of the next page.

On opening the last fold, you get the spread of all the three inside pages. Now the sequence is No.1, 2 and 3 for left, middle and right respectively. So the information sequence and design unit is complete in itself. The left panel is common for both the two page and the three-page units. Take care in providing information on the left outside page, as on opening the fold it is separated from the panel of the inside spread. It is preferable to allow the reader to read it in isolation.

The last page of the folder is the middle panel of the outside spread. This panel is read only when the recipient wants to take action on the information provided in the brochure or takes a decision to throw it out or preserve it for further enquiry. This panel is normally used for the address of the advertiser or some additional information, which is not directly related to the topic being promoted in the brochure. For example, a publisher may list some of his publications on this page of the brochure, which is meant for promoting a particular book. If the brochure is used as a self-mailer, this page can be used for mailing purposes by including the printing of the postage stamp area and providing lines for the recipient's address.

Multifold brochures are much more complicated than regular fold brochures in terms of creating the sequence of information. The best way is to hook the reader is to have a strong or individualistic cover that guides him in opening the folds. Divide the content in groups, which are independent in themselves but maintain a relationship with the other pages and the overall mood of the brochure.

Design Approach:

The first step in designing is cutting and folding of paper. To proceed further, what you need most here is adequate briefing. There are two approaches for a brochure design:
1. Only the written content.
2. Written content of the topic and the organization along with both visual and verbal copy.

In the first method, design is restricted a bit by the length of the copy, the sequence and also the type of visuals and their content. But you find it comfortable, as you need not run around any longer to collect the appropriate copy and visuals.

First design the cover. Find out a short description from the copy or develop one from the brief. Display it on the cover in an appropriate type style. If you plan a cover illustration, select one from the existing lot, which gives the complete mood of the topic. Colour, graphics, slogans, etc., if used creatively, add aesthetic value to the cover of the brochure.

For inside pages, find out the headline of each unit of the topic that summarizes the whole theme of the brochure. Evolve a distinctive shape in terms of headlines and their surroundings.

Copy block-formatting is another creative task. A particular style of column width, line alignment, spacing, etc., of the copy block can, if combined with the heading, present a topic or point to be made. All these also create a rhythm when aligned with the elements. These are vital in going through the brochure.

Be wary of monotony. Take the help of blurbs, boxes, graphics and pictures of suitable sizes to ward off monotony.

Design some of the pages free of literature—ideally, the last few pages or the one, which is read last. We may call these pages action pages. You may provide an application form, a reply coupon box panel with suggestions or instructions for further inquiries, etc.

While developing a design on a brief provided only as a written statement, visualise the complete brochure. After such visualisation, lay out the design elements, including the possible copy area. Fill the visual parts with illustrations roughly drawn or just paste simulated pictures. The copy area is indicated by parallel lines or simulated type.

Leaflet

The leaflet is a form of advertisement on a loose sheet. This direct promotional piece is normally used for local issues like announcing events or organizing a drive like for cleanliness or for saving water, or asking students to join a study centre or announcing free gifts with purchases of a new product, etc.

Designing a leaflet is a challenging job, as many copies of this form of literature find a place in the wastepaper basket. When the public is flooded with professional and unprofessional literature, naturally it is the professional one, which stands out.

In order to give a leaflet a professional look, write and design it as a promotion in its own right. Decide on a handy size. Divide the space into suitable grids, leaving adequate margins on all the sides. Reach as many people as possible by making the headline or picture big. There should be a promise or benefits for them. Use a sub-headline for the readers who have no time to read the copy in small letters. But you can tempt them into looking for things of their interest. If you succeed in generating enough interest, some of them will definitely read all the interesting bits, and then take action. Leaflets are used as handouts and rely on inexpensive methods of distribution instead of a ready mailing list. The marketplace, the main crossings of roads and gatherings for an event, are, some of the common distribution places.

Use the visual devices creatively. In case you fail to find an appropriate photograph or feel that it is too expensive to procure one, you may bank upon various techniques of graphics such as various styles of letters and their arrangement, usual and unusual graphic shapes, charts, graphs, tinted panels, starbursts, white spaces, etc. The desktop system offers you all the above techniques that are accurate, fast and less expensive *vis-a-vis* the conventional ones.

As always, tailor the techniques according to the target. Leaflets for general awareness like health programmes or dangers of pollution should be simple enough for everyone to understand the message. Never try to accommodate more than one idea in one leaflet. Give the leaflet the visual look of a press advertisement, which can stand out in a clutter.

Leaflets which are to carry complete messages— like the benefits of filing the income-tax returns or opposition to the remarks of a political leader on a local issue— should provide a framework for action or at least persuade you to take the idea with you to discuss with others at home. This type of leaflet often serves as a supplement for an advertisement published in the mass media or a meeting or a workshop held on the subject. Let typography play a major role in its design. The selling of new products also is a matter for a supplementary leaflet. It is prepared only to catch the local or specific target group. The necessary facts and specific benefits are highlighted in its design. Sunbursts and oversized type, work well in its design.

The message for a new public school, an evening branch of a bank or the weekly *pravachan* of a religious organization may be compared to institutional advertisements. Therefore, design its leaflet form by talking more about the organization and its credibility. A sober and formal layout should be appropriate for its design style. Besides headings, use a tint panel or a few box items for variation.

The ultimate goal of a leaflet is getting a direct response, so indicate clearly: whom to contact, the contact place with telephone or any other contact numbers, suggestions for discussion, with whom one should discuss, whom to pass it on to, how to reply, how to buy, where to go for further information, etc. Throughout the design, call your readers' attention to the reply elements at strategic places.

Distribution:

The printed literature of any form reaches the target audience directly. There may be several methods to reach the members of the audience. It is a management task to select the right method to get the printed piece into the right hands.

What is your role or that of other creative people in this step of the process? Yes, there are a lot of things to do. The distribution method affects the design and vice versa. In fact, the management executives should work in active coordination with you. It is in their interest that you be briefed about this step or the method of distribution well before you have developed a format.

The commonest distribution method is mailing the copies. When a piece comes by mail, it receives a moment of the recipient's undivided attention. You can cash in on this moment and hold his attention by using interesting visuals, headings or other graphic devices.

Postal regulations are another important aspect of direct piece distribution. You must know how, according to them, a piece can fold. Also the permissible size of the card for business reply, minimum sizes permissible for envelopes and so on. All these details have a direct bearing on the design format.

The recipient's convenience is your major concern. So also is the convenience of those responsible for distribution. Whether your piece should be stuffed into an envelope/package or sent as a self-mailer depends on the nature of the piece and the characteristics of the recipient. For some, the envelope is a barrier, barring the priority to open it immediately. On the other hand, a self-mailer can generate immediate interest and save the cost of the envelope. An envelope generally does offer some protection against your piece being torn, bent or dirtied. It also gives to your piece, privacy and allows you to send additional enclosures.

The success of distribution through mail largely depends on your mailing list. You can select your target audience carefully and tailor the piece specifically to them. You can plan to reach them at their convenience. Make sure that your mailing list is up-to-date, otherwise your whole effort will go up in smoke.

Some direct pieces are distributed at the sales or distribution counter of the organization. People come and collect the pieces in bulk or one each. This kind of distribution requires some publicity through other media. Many people collect the direct piece not for its own sake but for additional information of some product or service they are interested in or simply for fun. There IS a possibility of some pieces landing up in wrong hands.

Another distribution method is sending the copies by hand to the place where the target audience is located. The distribution manager should be well aware of the members of the audience in relation to their movements. That is where they go daily, weekly or monthly and so on. For example, students go to school five days a week, one goes for vacation once a year, housewives go for shopping twice a week.

Some direct pieces may be sent along with something else in print. A flyer may be sandwiched between newspaper pages, a brochure with a letter, a leaflet with a bill, a reply card in a magazine, etc.

A direct piece publication can be highly expensive when considered on a cost per contact basis. A well-planned distribution system often gives a low ratio of cost per inquiry or even cost per sale.

Newsletter

The newsletter is also a sort of a magazine. Since its aims and objectives are confined to communicating specific messages, prepared by a group or organization, to a particular set of publics periodically, a different nomenclature is used for it. The two words, "news" and "letter", indicate that it carries information or news which is being sent to the likes of you or me, in the format of a letter. Therefore, the physical appearance of this periodical often comes closer to a personal letter.

Thanks to the new image revolution, the newsletter is out of the old established style and is placed comfortably somewhere between the newspaper, the magazine and promotional literature. Therefore, instead of developing a separate design style, the newsletter follows now all the techniques of these forms of printed literature. For example, the masthead can be with letterhead style, the column grid as in a magazine, the headlines as in a newspaper, and the pictorial placement as in promotional literature.

A newsletter is one of the important tools of public relations. It serves as a catalyst between the management and the employees, or between the company as a whole and the external publics. Through it, the management tells the staff about the development of the company and their contribution to it, which boosts their morale. The staff also creates a demand through the newsletter for welfare and also shows that it belongs to the management along with other categories of staff. Therefore, it is considered a two way communication tool. Large companies or organizations dealing with specialized markets, often publish more than one newsletter in order to satisfy the readers of specific and distinct interests. A newsletter is, therefore, a forum to express the thoughts and vision of the management, the employees and others who are interested in the fortunes of the company. It is a sure vehicle to foster oneness in the organization and to bind the readers together to strive for a common goal.

A newsletter covers a wide number of topics to satisfy different target groups. Some newsletters are exclusively meant for select target audiences. If a newsletter is meant for in-house staff, and the resources are limited, its appearance may come closer to that of a conventional letter. It will have a masthead on the top as in a regular letterhead plus the text; a simple typewritten copy. This may be all. It may sound too simple, yet its readers find a personal touch in it.

A specialised target audience may be the marketing and sales people of the company. They need technical details and information about the products that are being marketed. This type of newsletter also attempts to build brand loyalty, publishes articles on merchandising ideas, and makes an effort to increase cooperation between the merchandisers and the manufacturer by explaining and interpreting the company's policies. It may look like a catalogue or brochure and may be termed a company bulletin, a trade bulletin or a sales bulletin, a dealers' journal, etc.

If a newsletter covers primarily news items, it often takes the shape of a regular newspaper mainly in a tabloid form. In such cases, the format of the newsletter resembles that of popular tabloids.

The newsletter takes on an interesting shape when it is meant for a target audience available at a particular location like a factory, a club, a health centre, etc. Since it is for community reading, the size is big enough for display on notice boards, walls or any other convenient place for reading. Such newsletters are often called wall-newspapers. The production cost of this type of newsletter is very low, as only a few copies are needed for display at select locations. A typed, photocopied and even handwritten copy is good enough for such newsletters. Its size may vary from broadsheet to tabloid, depending on the news and information that is to be conveyed.

The publishers of a newsletter, in general, consider its design a peripheral matter. From a designer's point of view also, a newsletter is a rather uncomplicated printed form of communication. Since each newsletter has a captive audience and no other newsletter competes with it, many designers become complacent. As a result, we come across too many ugly, amateurish newsletters. Yes, the designer of a newsletter, who may perhaps be the editor himself or a hired professional, works under several constraints, such as typesetting method, printing process and paper quality, besides the limited amount of money allotted for these purposes. But if you are an imaginative designer you can make the newsletter design attractive, easy to read, memorable and effective even if you have to use only the printed text. This you can achieve in a variety of ways, such as typography, box items, headings, subheadings, blurbs, graphics, etc.

There is a close relationship between a magazine design and a newsletter design. The size, format, masthead and grid sheet all follow the magazine design. But choosing the type style and graphics and photographs and their placement on the page can make newsletters distinctive, separating them from magazines and other publications as a class by itself.

Design:

Always place the masthead at the top and make sure that it does not occupy more than one-sixth of the page. Most newsletters start the editorial content on the front page itself. Let the column grid on the first page be different from that of the inside pages. A wider column grid or even a single column is preferable. One narrow column and a wider column also make the page have a characteristic of its own. The first page may carry the contents. Make them distinctive by surrounding them with white space, a border or a tint block. Select the first heading's type style and size cautiously, lest the headline and the masthead should get mixed up. The typewriter type style with a left aligned and right ragged format for text copy gives to the newsletter the look of a regular letter. Choose the text type style from lineal Sans-Serif or Modern Roman faces in case of mechanical typesetting. This will make the page clean and uncomplicated.

In general, newsletter articles are short. These should be accompanied by short headlines, small in size but bold enough to stand out. Occasional lines and boxes can also separate one article from another. Several subheads, occasional blurbs or an introduction may break up pages with a long running text in a different type style that not only summarizes the contents but also creates a vigorous graphic texture.

In order to stress the simplicity of the newsletter, limit the graphic elements, photographs, etc. In case these are to be used, take care of their size and placement so that they do not look too much like a magazine's illustrations.

As for the back page, give it special treatment. Have a regular feature, which is particularly fun to look at. It may be a cartoon, a special service of your company, an interesting off-beat photograph or a quiz. The back page should also take care of the mailing address space, if it is meant for circulation by post. Many organizations send it as mail to people's homes by simply wrapping and stapling it. Design the back page after consulting postal authorities about their requirements.

Production:

An electronic typewriter and a duplicating machine are sufficient for some newsletters, but others can make wide use of computers and modern offset printing.

Among the duplicating processes, the office Photostat machine is good enough for a short run job. It can give output quickly and instantly, from a master copy that makes the newsletter inexpensive.

In-house printing with a table top or small offset machine provides fast and inexpensive printouts. Elaborate make-ready system is not needed for printing. Simply type the text on a low-cost Paper Master and heat it up to make the image firm and a bit raised, and wrap it around the cylinder of the machine for printing.

This Master can take the image from the artwork as well as when the image is transferred on to it by Photostatting. The image can also be obtained directly on the Master from the laser printer.

Since most parts of the newsletter that come from the quick print shop are in black and white, you can print the masthead in colour in bulk at one time on one of the major printing machines and supply this masthead printed paper to the printer for every issue. The rest of the matter can be printed in black and white when needed. This will give the newsletter a touch of colour and also save a great deal of money.

Newsletters are generally very thin. Stapling at the top corner or at the side is sufficient to hold the pages together. Centre stitching or simply one or two folds to a sheet, can make a newsletter.

Desktop Publishing has become very popular in today's newsletter production. It can do almost anything that is needed to print a newsletter. It allows the arrangement of the text in a manner that comes close to the requirement of typesetting. The time-consuming paste-up process is completely eliminated in page formatting. The system provides a printout on inexpensive paper by laser. This printout can be used as a master copy or artwork for printing by any of the processes discussed above.

Summary

To promote an organization's various activities, PR persons use several printed literatures. Some of the common forms of such literature are; brochures, leaflets and newsletters. These are sent to the prospects directly either by mail or through some other inexpensive distribution systems. Production and distribution of these literatures are within the control of the firm. A brochure format ranges from a single fold paper to a three dimensional object like a sample product attached to it. They may also be in the form of multi-page centre-stitched booklet. The leaflet is a single sheet advertisement printed on both sides meant for promoting local issues. Newsletters are official periodicals. Its format varies from that of simple letterhead to a newspaper, or brochure. The literature is meant to function as a catalyst between the management and the employees. The management of the organization takes care of distribution of these literatures. They must take the help of a designer in developing the format for ease in distribution and convenience of the recipients.

Critical thinking exercise

You are involved in developing multi-page image building brochure of your company using one of the success stories. Write the points to be written by the copy writer and an appropriate brief for the designer. Provide adequate support materials like published content related to the topic, photographs, diagrams etc. to these professionals.

Questions

1. What are the types of printed literatures that sent directly to the target audience free of cost? Mention the characteristics of content carry these literatures of an organization.
2. Identify any one of the forms of printed literatures, discussed its form, format and design process.
3. What are the methods to be adapted in distribution of printed literatures?

References

Elizabeth W. Adler, *Print That Works* (California: Bull Publishing Company, 1991).
Theodore E. Conover, *Graphic Communication Today* (USA: West Publishing Company, 1990).
Roy Paul Nelson, *Publication Design* (USA: Wm e Brown Publishers, 1991).
N.N Sarkar, *Art and Print Production* (New Delhi: Oxford University Press, 2008).

15 Web page Design

Chapter Objectives
- To define web page designing and understand the functioning of the Internet along with its requirement
- To gain knowledge of connectivity between pages
- Learn the use of hypertext markup language for text, graphics and animation
- Design web pages based on medium's distinct characteristics
- To know about various software available for web page editing and production

What is Web page design?

All of us who pursue communication or aspire to be communicators have some notion of what web designing is. Even those not involved in the communication profession can talk about it. However, not many may be able to define it. Jakob Nielsen writes that there are two basic approaches to design: the artistic idea of expressing oneself and the engineering idea of solving a problem for customer. As per Thomas A Powell—beyond visuals and technology considerations, many point to the creation and organization of content in websites as the most important aspect of web design.

Wikipedia provides the academic definition: "Web design is a process of conceptualization, planning, modeling, and execution of electronic media content delivery via Internet in the form of technologies (such as markup languages) suitable for interpretation and display by a web browser or other web-based graphical user interfaces (GUIs)".

Whatever may be the definition, web page designing needs an artistic perspective plus computer skills. The last decade or so have seen a spurt in the interactive media.

In today's world, one can't think of an organization that does not have its website. In fact organizations have been using their website as a great Public Relations tool for connecting with its various stake-holders. In many organizations, the PR department is put in charge of maintaining the website.

What is Internet?

The Internet is a collection of computer networks that connects millions of computers around the world. It is also called the "Network of Networks". Simply put, many computer networks are linked together and they exchange data among themselves. Through the Internet, one can gain access to the vast stores of information on these computers.

If there is any medium, which has shrunk the world, it is undoubtedly the Internet. The Internet, which is also known as the 'Information Superhighway' is accessible to anyone who has connectivity to this big network.

What is a Network?

When two or more computers share and exchange data, it is called a network. A simple networking between computers is through wires and cables which is LAN (Local Area Network). But networking between computers is also possible through WAN (Wide Area Network) using satellite or wireless technology.

Requirements for the Internet

To log on to the Internet, one needs the following:

Computer: This is the basic requirement to view web pages. The faster the computer, the easier it is to download graphic and multimedia files (those that contain sound, animation and video).

Modem (Modulator/Demodulator): This is required to dial up to the Internet Service Provider (ISP). This is also used to change the analogue data into digital data and vice-versa because the computer only understands digital language.

Connection: A telephone line is another requirement through one can connect to the Internet if one has a dial-up access. But one can also access the Internet through satellite. In India, one has VSNL, Satyam Online, Mantra Online and others, who are the ISPs (Internet Service Providers).

TCP/IP: This stands for Transmission Control Protocol/Internet Protocol. It is the required standard that all computers must follow to understand and interpret data among themselves.

Browsing Software: A software needs to be installed in the computer because through this, one can view various text, graphics etc. in a website. The most common browsing software are Netscape Navigator and Internet Explorer which come bundled with one of the operating systems of a computer (WINDOWS).

With an Internet connection and browsing software like Microsoft Internet Explorer or Netscape Navigator, one can find and view information about anything on the Web. After dialing the ISP, the provider connects the user to the main backbone of the Internet which is in the USA. The Internet backbone is nothing but the place where all the major networks are connected together. Nobody owns the Internet. The web servers are only registered with the InterNIC (Integrated Network

Information Centre), which is in the USA which in a way is the controlling body of the Internet. The only requirement is the information about the account name and password from the Internet Service Provider.

Internet Address

An Internet address, sometimes called URL or Uniform Resource Locator typically starts with a protocol name, followed by the name of the organization that maintains the site. The suffix identifies the kind of organization it is.

For example, the address http://www.iimc.edu/ provides the following information.

http: This Web server uses the http: protocol.
www   This site is on the World Wide Web.
iimc   The Web server at Indian Institute of Mass Communication.
edu   This is an educational institution.

Generally, commercial site addresses end with .com, and government site addresses end with .gov and organization as .org. If the address points to a specific page, additional information — a port name, the directory in which the page is located, and the name of the page file — is included. Web pages authored by using HTML (Hypertext Markup Language) often end with an .htm or .html extension. When a web page is being viewed, the page's address appears in the Address bar in the browser.

What is E-Mail ?

An e-mail is the short form of Electronic Mail. After the popularity of e-mail, the traditional mail is called snail mail in web language because e-mail is fast. It can reach the other computer in another part of the world in seconds and it is accurate. It rarely ever gets delayed or lost. When you send an e-mail to another person, it gets stored in the server of the E-mail Service Provider (in our case the ISP) and you have to retrieve it from there. You can send pictures, movies, sound files, etc. attached with your letter.

Website

A website is an electronic page or various pages complete with text, sound, colour, graphics, pictorial images with or without animation, movies, etc. Putting up a website means creating an address in cyberspace, where one can have an instantaneous two-way interaction with those interested in doing business with one. Since the Internet opens an entirely cost-effective opportunity to reach the global market, it has become almost essential for all corporate organizations to have their own websites. Their presence on the Internet through their own websites gives an opportunity to provide a complete picture about the company, the services offered, the products or product catalogue, advertisements, corporate information, employment opportunities and so on.

The website acts as the window to the world by providing a radically simpler and easier way of access to the business from anywhere in the world by a simple click of the mouse. Millions of users of the Internet can have easy access to the site and know about the products and services offered. This enables business to reach a wider and larger customer base without the need for any additional physical infrastructure. It can register all business inquiries and pass these on to the user instantaneously. One can cater to the customers and have prospects all through the year as the website is open 24×7. It enables the user to learn more about the customers and prospective clients because of its interactivity. One can provide better and timely customer support by directly answering customer queries on the net. Because of its cost-effectiveness, the user can provide support and services directly from the site. It adds prestige to your business and demonstrates your commitment to use the best of technologies for your business.

Mere designing and hosting the website is not enough. Like any good advertisement, the website too, needs to be placed in the right medium to achieve the right exposure — a fact, most ordinary website designers fail to recognize. This probably is the single biggest pitfall — not knowing how to market the site, you require the services of a specialist. Ironically, the websites have to advertise in the established media like direct literature, outdoor and television to inform the prospective users about themselves, at least in the initial stages.

Creating a Web page

To build a coherent web or entrant site, an overall organizational plan for the site is required. In the end, though, the project comes down to making the web pages. All the pages need to be converted to HTML (Hyper Text Markup Language) in order to be put on the web. The existing documents can be converted to HTML. This can be done easily either in a simple text editor or by using one of the many available web-publishing tools. First of all, a blank page is to be created after which the basic content can be added, usually text.

Basic Formatting:

Once the text is in place, it is formatted to give your site a glossy and consistent look. Some basic colour decisions about the page's background, text, unvisited links and visited links are also taken at this stage. If the pages are created from a standard template, one can make sitewise colour-scheme decisions in the template and need not have to repeat them for each document. Text formatting on the web is still generally limited compared to the state-of-the-art in the world of word processing, at least without any gimmicky tricks. One can assign heading levels, separate sections of text, make tables, add emphasis to selections, make block quotations, and so on.

Linking Pages Together:

The essence of a website is that the individual pages are connected with hyperlinks. Links can be inserted into a document and then the pages can be created to which it is being linked. Links are like flipping the pages of a book. All the pages can be created without links, and the links can be added afterwards. The latter approach works better with many web-publishing programmes that can make and track links automatically if the documents linked to, already exist. External links can also be added from any of your pages to other sites on the web or other resources on the Internet. Before getting on to creating a web page, it is a good idea to surf the net to see the variety of web pages available.

Web Editing Tools

The web editing software can be evaluated on the basis of their raw-HTML or WYSIWYG (What You See Is What You Get) approach, and on how well they handle the tasks like text formatting and lists, images, links, tables, forms, frames, multimedia objects and previewing the page or showing HTML.

HTML editors, such as WebEdit for Windows or Bare Bones for the Macintosh (with HTML add-ins) actually have shortcuts for most basic tags, including formatting, pictures, links tables and frames. A rudimentary WYSIWYG editor such as Microsoft Word has toolbar buttons and dialogue boxes to automate formatting and ease the insertion of image, links, tables and forms (at least the front end part of forms), if not frames or multimedia objects, and it can show the underlying HTML.

Building a Website

Web editors are all well and good for the laborious task of creating web documents, but they don't necessarily help out much with the ultimate projects of building a coherent site out of its constituent pages. Sure they might check the links as they exist now, on the computer, but it takes a special programme to help remotely control a site on the server, updating changed pages regularly and moving pages around without having to manually retype all the links to those pages. These programmes are more than web editors since they help out with the site management. They are called web-publishing programmes.

Designing the Pages

Designing of a web page has got a lot of similarities with traditionally designed printed pages. Therefore, designers of web pages can take many cues from the print publication to give viewers a sense of place, visual stimulation and ease of navigation.

Grid:

Start designing the page by dividing the viewing area in grids as you do to layout pages for newspapers, magazines or even promotional literature. Grids are always helpful in determining the size of graphics and text block that help viewers go through the page in proper sequence. Designers take the decision easily in placing the text and graphics in relation to other elements. It is however, not possible to translate a print page into a web page. The average monitor size is different from the standard paper size in proportion. Moreover, web pages are viewed by scrolling the browser window where text may flow, wrap and stop for reviewing. Long scrolling is tiring and often detract from page sequence. Create systematic clickable icons on the page that will not only help the viewer locate desired information but also break the monotony of the page.

Storyboard:

The term for web page layout is storyboard. Like movies, animation, and multimedia presentation, storyboarding helps in visualizing the page layouts of each page, as well as to get an idea of the three-dimensional navigation and relations throughout the site.

Storyboard can be drawn on paper or on prototype screen in HTML or in one of the graphics programmes. The pages can be laid out or linked to other areas in different ways. Make the storyboard and its structure in a logical and useable manner. Create a title page of a story with brief contents or blurbs, make each one clickable that brings the viewer into the next account of the story in further detail. There may be a number of photographs in your story. Make the title page with a series of thumbnails of those photos keeping only one reasonably big in proportion to others for the purpose of attraction and to give an idea about the story. The layout of the image area and the text or other graphics should be purposefully linked to one another to give viewers the choice of how to access the site's information.

Image:

Wherever possible, images should be added to the web page, to make them more pleasing to the eye and to help communicate more clearly. Insertion of an image is very easy with most web editors and it is not too difficult even in raw-HTML. But it occupies a lot of computer space that keeps one waiting for long durations to appear on the screen. Images should be talking so as to enhance the content even if the site is not about art and photography.

Place the pictures logically, may be on the centre or right- or left-aligned on the page. Knowledge of your graphic syntax may come very handy. Images can be cropped, retouched and even changed in an image-manipulation programme like Photoshop, Photopaint, Image Editor etc. Converting the edge of the image vignette, combining pictures to make a collage or superimposing icons on the pictures is a matter of computer command. They may look great on these programmes, but check them in whatever browser you are using before you put them on your site.

Format:

Pictures on web have to be in GIF (Graphic Interchange Format) or JPEG (Joint Photographers Expert Group) formats. The images developed on other formats like PICT (Picture), BMP (Bitmap), TIFF (Tagged Image File Format) can also be used but they have to be converted to the above formats for the purpose of compression. The image files should be made smaller for efficient online transfer and viewing. The uniqueness of JPEG format is that despite loss of resolution in compression, its visual effect remains absolutely normal on a monitor or screen. As the file size becomes smaller, it is easily manageable thereby facilitating comfortable handling on the Internet for transferring files. But this kind of compression is not fit for print publishing since the details of the picture will be lost when the film output is taken from the image setter.

For printing, a TIFF file is ideal since it contains all the details and the minutest part of any graphic. But for compressing the files in printing, we can use LZW (Lempel-Ziv-Welch) compression. This compression was named after the three persons who invented it.

In web page design the key to create a good graphic is to make an image small. Small does not mean the physical size of the picture, it is just to reduce the kilobyte of the image.

Icon:

In web design, simple and cute icons are preferable to descriptive text. Definitely icons represent topics and sections of the site visually that convey the message instantly. But beware of its originality and individuality, otherwise they will look ugly and cluttered annoying the browser.

Frame:

Make use of Netscape frames to attract immediate attention. Frames can contain ordinary HTML mark-up, are scrollable, and can even hold clickable images or image maps. While interacting with one frame, the contents of the other frames remain on screen.

Type:

Typographical content is the most crucial form of communication tool in any media, including websites. These days, one may argue for its popularity, for its ability to display graphic, moving animation and sound effect. But nothing has replaced text.

Selection of type and its format can almost follow the same rules as that of print communication. Line length, type size, spacing (word, letter, lines), setting, format, colour, etc. all have the same effect on the viewer/reader as they read the printed page. However, one thing should be kept in mind—when one forces the reader to read a long column, and then scroll down to read it, one may loose the beginning of the next column or may miss some portion of the text that was off the screen. This may happen when you are reading a textual publication like a newspaper on the web.

Typographical contents of web page are different from ordinary text format of computer. These are developed by simple mark-up codes called HTML tags. These codes are typed right into a document they control the formatting and layout for the finished document and specify links with others.

You may need your text in colour which may be specified by RGB colour code in the HTML document. You can use as many as 256 colours including white.

Colour:

Web page colours are translucent, in any circumstances. They are bright and each one is capable of getting attention which is not desirable from a communication point of view because they have a tendency to cancel each other. The viewer's eye will move from one place to another very fast, without rest, or paying attention to a particular element or elements. Therefore, the proportion in terms of space it has occupied and value and saturation of the hue are the keys in selection of colour for a web page.

To engage viewers in a page, separate the information bearing colour and decorative colour. The colour of text, pictures, and others that carry information may be placed in contrast, to stand out on the page. The decorative or non-information bearing colour, like background, borders, graphic shapes, etc. may be used creating mood, meaning or just to help the information bearing elements to stand out. Here too, colour for communication discussed in the context of printed pages may be kept in mind as a guiding principle.

While planning the page in colour, use only browser safe colour, otherwise the viewer's monitor may not be able to display the colour. The colour that will be displayed, will look spotty or rough, called dithered colour. There are some default colours as well which may help you to make a page faster and are often good for contrast. But it is monotonous, and may get it mixed up with other sites. So, always depend on your own creative colour scheme.

Publishing a Site

Publishing a site requires more than just the tools for transferring the files. A host is needed to make your files public. Once a host is found for the site to be published, the site needs to be promoted to make sure that the intended audience knows it is there and what is available to entice them to drop by like useful files to download, helpful advice, free information etc. Finally, you've got to dig in for the long haul and be prepared to update the site, keep it fresh and occasionally revise its layout and its colours.

Finding a Host

The final question about the home page is where to put it. Many Internet service providers and some of the online services offer free space on their web servers, up to some quota of disk space (generally five megabytes) to all their customers. If the e-mail provider does not offer access to a web server, some other host is to be found for your site to go online. There are also some free home-page hosting sites. These may require inclusion of their advertisements on your page.

Some providers will ask the user to send them the files via e-mail. Others will suggest the use of FTP (File Transfer Protocol), a fast way of exchanging data to upload your files to them. They assign the URL for that particular home page, often in the format *http://www.their.name.com/~your-username,* but other variations are possible as well.

Once the page and other associated files and linked pages are out there on the provider's website, anyone can visit that website.

Production of a Website

The text, graphics, illustrations, animations, audio and video are all converted into HTML language in order to be put onto the web. Since all the websites in the WWW follow the Hyper Text Transfer Protocol (HTTP), the pages need to be formatted in HTML.

A hyper text page means that a particular page has further links added to it. In other words, one can go to other linked pages from that page by following a hyper link. Since most of the web pages in the WWW have hyper-links, one needs to create the web pages in HTML.

At first look, HTML resembles any other computer language or programme and that will scare away many a designer! But there is good news. There are specialized software which convert the normal text, graphics, animation, etc. to HTML. What one needs is good design sense, good graphics and illustrations. Even simple animations can be created with the use of these software.

The most commonly used software to make web pages are Microsoft FrontPage, Claris HomePage, Adobe PageMill and Adobe SiteMill. Of these four, Microsoft FrontPage is the most popular and user friendly software in the market. With its help, one can create a nice web page with graphics, animations and upload it onto a web server.

Microsoft FrontPage for Windows is one of the world's leading desktop web design programmes, that allows users to produce professional looking websites without necessarily knowing HTML. The programme makes extensive use of wizards and themes which decrease site development time. Now, let us look at some of the features of FrontPage. FrontPage Editor is a combination of word processing and text styling, graphics integration and sizing, page layout, hyperlinking of elements to each other internally and externally, grouping and linking of web pages into a website, publishing of FrontPage webs on Intranet or the Internet, graphics programme, file linking device and element stylist this is essentially a TCP/IP file transfer programme. This is essentially a Windows-level file management programme but it also manages files remotely over Intranet and the Internet.

FrontPage has an extensive repertoire of the latest Web enhancements to animate pictures including interactive forms, search capabilities, sound, movies, virtual reality and many more. But they are proprietary to FrontPage, and many of them only work when the web pages are published on a Web server which has Microsoft FrontPage extensions installed to support them.

If the web pages are intended for publication on web servers that do not have the Microsoft FrontPage extensions installed, the FrontPage bells and whistles should be left out, and the pages should either have the ordinary, bulk standard coding version of the techniques included, or they should not be used at all.

Images can be used for more than decoration and illustration. Images can also be used for hyperlink buttons and other interactive graphics. Images can have hyperlink-areas or "hot-spots" drawn on top of them in any shape, transparently or opaquely. When a number of hyperlink-areas are drawn on top of an image, the image becomes an image map, which is used for navigating a whole site. FrontPage comes with a library of clip art and commonly used buttons, icons, background patterns, etc. Background images, wallpaper, watermarks, and colours can be put on the web pages. Text can be given styling and colouring. "Curly quotes" and bullets and other special characters can be used to give pages a finished and professional typographic look.

Tables can be used for organizing information as in ordinary documents, but which have even greater use in controlling the layout of Web pages. Table layouts can be used for the headers of all the pages, with each element in a different cell, in order to put separate elements side-by-side which is not possible with tabs. Frames are special divisions of the Web page into different areas which are independent pages in their own right, and which can have multiple functions, doing such things as having a table of contents that can remain on the left side of the screen; while the right hand pane, or frame, has scrolling text from different items on the TOC (Table Of Contents). Dynamic downloads of programmed applications, called applets, to client computers, to run effects such as complex animations on the client computer itself. These include Active-X, Microsoft's proprietary system, Java, the Sun proprietary system, special proprietary plug-ins such as Quick-Time for viewing video clips and Real Audio for sounds, Microsoft PowerPoint Animation, Secure Sockets Layer (SSL) support — encryption for credit card money transfer, etc. Image animation is possible through external automated plug-ins like animated GIF images.

FrontPage comprises two main programmes named Explorer and Editor. The Explorer is the hyperlink, file display, file management and file transfer utility. The Editor is the page creation utility that combines word processing, text styling, graphics integration, element hyperlinking, and page layout.

FrontPage works with other programmes. It is designed to be used with a browser like Netscape or Internet Explorer to preview pages exactly as they will be seen on the Internet. The browser is kept running in the background while you edit pages in front page. You can preview pages in the browser at any time. To bring the browser to the front at any time, click on the icon in the Microsoft Windows taskbar at the bottom of the screen.

Since it is already mentioned that FrontPage does not require knowledge of HTML, it is obvious that elements are created, edited, placed, moved around and laid out in a WYSIWYG interface. The effect is not perfect and a browser is to be used for an exact preview. The programme creates all the HTML code for the user and embeds it seamlessly.

FrontPage works like and interfaces with many other Microsoft programmes and most functions are similar to those of Word, Publisher, etc. FrontPage can import and translate files of many types: .DOC, .TXT, .RTF, .XLS, etc.

Summary

Web design is a process creating web pages for presenting information and disseminating it through Internet. The Internet is a collection of computer networks that connects millions of computers around the world. In order to access Internet some of the computer hardware and software are required. Designing a web page involves artistic flair, technical knowledge and most importantly the connectivity between the pages that is converting the pages to Hyper Text Markup Language (HTML). Handling text graphics and colour is almost similar to any visual communication but special attention is to be given to the navigational aspect. Before initiating a website for a company or individual one should go through the various advantages the Internet offers, and also scrutinize the disadvantages it has. Finding a host to upload the site and make the site popular by publicity is the final task of web page design.

Critical thinking exercise

A team of professionals has created a website for your company. Look for a host to publish your site and prepare a proposal to make your site popular.

Questions

Q.1 What is Internet? What are the requirements to access Internet?

Q.2 Explain website and web page.

Q.3 Describe the steps involved in designing a web page.

References

Crystal Waters, *Web Concept and Design* (USA: New Riders Publishing, 1996)

Jacob Nielsen, *Designing Web Usability* (USA: New Riders Publishing, 2000)

Ned Snell, *Teach Yourself to Create Web Pages* (Delhi: Techmedia, 2000)

Joe Kraynak and Joe Habraken, *Internet 6 in 1* (New Delhi: Prentice-Hall of India,1999)

Thomas A. Powell, *Web Design: The Complete Reference* (New Delhi, Tata McGraw-Hill Publishing Co. Ltd. 2000)

Ann Navarro, *Effective Web Design* (New Delhi: BPB Publication, 2001)

16 Understanding Multimedia

Chapter Objectives

- Defining multimedia and its functions
- Understanding interactive and non-interactive multimedia
- Explain aesthetics and technicalities of each media content
- Know the various software available for developing a project
- Understand the assembly of pages using authoring tools

The term multimedia is used to describe different things in different situations at different times. Traditionally many of the static content like paintings painted or structured by 3D materials, oil colour, adhesive was called multimedia; printed publications containing pictures, text, and graphics is also multimedia; live performance with background light and sound effects is also multimedia.

As the world witnessed progress in human communication in the last three decades in comparison to the last century, there is a paradigm shift in the definition of multimedia. Now it is often identified as multimedia technology or new media for information dissemination combined with entertainment and education. Whatever may be its application, multimedia is media that utilizes a combination of different content forms. In today's context multimedia includes a combination of text, audio, still image, audio and video content form. All these contents communicate ideas or disseminate information either separately or in combination.

Various categories

Multimedia may be broadly divide into two categories: Non-interactive or linear and interactive or non-linear. In non-interactive programmes, the audience just watch the show as it proceeds from beginning to end in a sequential manner, there is no navigation control of the viewer as in the case of cinema. Broadcast and presentation multimedia may also form part of this category. In interactive content the user participates in every stage of proceedings as the programme advances as used in computer games, CD-Rom titles, computer based training, touch screen kiosks etc.

Within these categories some are meant for entertainment, some for education, and others to provide information. Cinema and computer games are for entertainment; CD Rom title and presentations for education; and broadcast and touch screen kiosks for information. All these multimedia applications are not restricted to its respective areas. Multimedia is now widely used in various areas like advertising, engineering, medicine, mathematics, business, and scientific research. Multimedia presentations can be live or recorded. A recorded presentation may allow interactivity via a navigation system. A live multimedia presentation may allow interactivity via an interaction with the presenter or performer.

What is Interactive?

Interactive means that the user does not receive the information passively. The user controls the information, deciding which of the various avenues to access and explore, jump forward, backward or move from one to another at will.

What is a CD Rom?

The full form is Compact Disc Read Only Memory. It first appeared in mid 1980s to meet the need for high capacity storage medium of digital multimedia data. A CD Rom looks the same as audio CDs originally developed by Sony and Phillips of Netherlands, but the information they carry now is of much greater variety. It can not only store digital audio, but also a whole range of graphic images, digital video and various other forms of computer related information. It is cheap, durable and efficient enough to give error free data retrieval. To read the data stored in a CD Rom one needs a CD drive. Today almost all computers have built-in CD drives and most software applications are always packed in a CD-Rom.

What is Hypermedia?

In multimedia context, it is a well defined structural arrangement of information of multimedia content pertaining to a topic with relevant linkage in between them. When all the text based content is interlinked it is called hypertext. The contents linked other than text is hypergraphics. A typical hypergraphic system contains some or all graphic based information of a project, suitably interlinked with all other portions of the project, by means of relevant hyperlinks between them.

What is hyperlink?

An element in an electronic document, some portion of text, image or picture are distinguished from other normal portion either by some coloured outline or some other suitable mechanism that links to another place in the same document or to an entirely different document. Typically, you click on the hyperlink to follow the link. Hyperlinks are the most essential ingredient of all hypermedia, including the World Wide Web.

Interactive multimedia titles are divided in three categories: Reference, Education and Entertainment.

Reference:

Reference is the oldest use of a multimedia CD Rom. Traditional reference books such as encyclopedias provide information in a comprehensive source, atlases take a tour of the world through thousands of maps, dictionaries provide the meaning of a word simply by clicking on it. Directories and biographies are most popular on one CD Rom. One complete set of Encyclopedia Britannica (32 vols.) is available on one CD Rom.

> MTNL is bringing out a periodically updated phone directory on CD Rom to facilitate customer convenience. The CD Rom telephone directory of MTNL gives the customer fast and convenient search facilities right on his customer screen. The CD ROM directory not only enables users to search phone numbers of specific persons or organizations, but also give full address of the said person or organization.

Education:

Multimedia has enormous potential from the point of view of self-based learning and it can serve as an independent complementary tool for enhancing the learning process. In the present scenario of school education, the primary source of teaching is the text book: sometimes supplementary reading material is available for certain subjects, apart from, of course, the reference books. On the other hand, in the so called K12 level (from kindergarten to standard 12), requirement for multimedia educational material is non-trivial. Here the perceived benefit is that students can supplement their intra-mural learning with materials which bring them experience with real life situations by which they would be able to better understand the text book and class room education.

Pre-school/early learning (alphabet, rhymes, concepts like opposites, joining dots etc) as well as curriculum-based subjects like mathematics, science, history etc. Language learning is fun with multimedia because of its interactive capability. It can take the responses from the learner, evaluate them, if there is an error, point it out, in terms of pronunciation and gesture and can explain how the answer is wrong. Educational software promotes learning through interactive exercises and games. All these can be done by the students at their own place.

Entertainment:

- *Puzzle Games:* Puzzle games have fun in finding solutions to perplexing predicaments. Example: Purple Place
- *3-D action games:* Prince Of Persia, Hitman, Blood Money, Harry Potter and The Goblet of Fire, in which the players can make the casts act or perform as per his or her will.
- *Cartoon Entertainment:* Movies like Alibaba, Disney's Donald and Company take the player to a fantasy world.

- *Interactive Movie:* Gameplay consists of a running "movie" with several different storylines that the user can follow by making choices during the viewing, although occasionally an action/arcade sequence may be included. Interactive Movies are best suited for novice gamers looking for entertainment without too much effort. Examples: any Multipath movie; Infocomics; Star Trek: Borg, etc.
- *Multimedia Music:* The CD Rom offers ripping, encoding, decoding music tracks, allows downloading facility of features details of each individual programme. Example: Live-7.1 developed by Ableton.

Design and Development

- ### Research and Analysis:

Like any other media communication, the designing of a multimedia project begins with research or collecting information in relation with the topic being handled. Talking to the subject expert maybe your first choice. In absence of a subject expert their published articles, written books and video interviews may be of great help. These days another easy source is the Internet from which even a pool of global information can be obtained. The information may be in the form of visuals, text or audio input. All the collected information may not be required for the project. Now in order to pick-up the right content for the project, the content should be filtered. The entire material has to be collected, then edited or structured. A database is made where all the salient things are visible on screen or page details are hidden behind the hot spot or live words.

Before getting into the process of actually developing a structure one should understand the difference between multimedia and other media, mainly print and audio visual. This distinction is important because the medium for which a developer conceptualizes may determine how he or she approaches the subject. For example, in print you explain or tell your audience by words, which become the primary concern of the writer. In audio visual the approach is to show and listen by visuals and sound. But in multimedia it is all the above two plus navigation facility that offers great independence to users. For a multimedia developer it is a navigation map. A navigation map is a well structured route or path created to go through various portions of the project without being lost in an unwanted location and wasting time or finding it difficult to come out from there. A navigation map is similar to the storyboard, except that it doesn't provide details as to the contents of individual pages. It is basically a diagrammatic presentation of pages with clear functional and graphical continuity between various components and subsections of the multimedia production. The initial or homepage of any multimedia production should always be a landmark, able to be accessed from anywhere within a multimedia piece.

260 Public Relations Management

Linear Structure

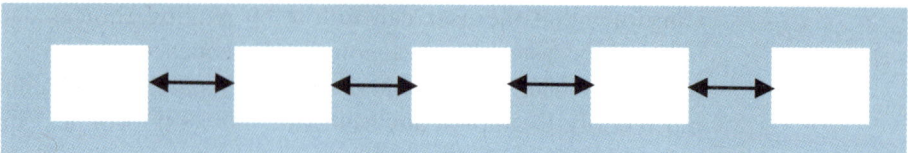

Non-Linear Structure:

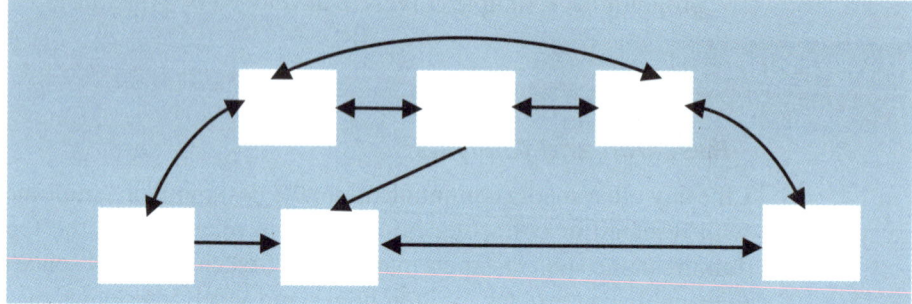

Hierarchical Structure

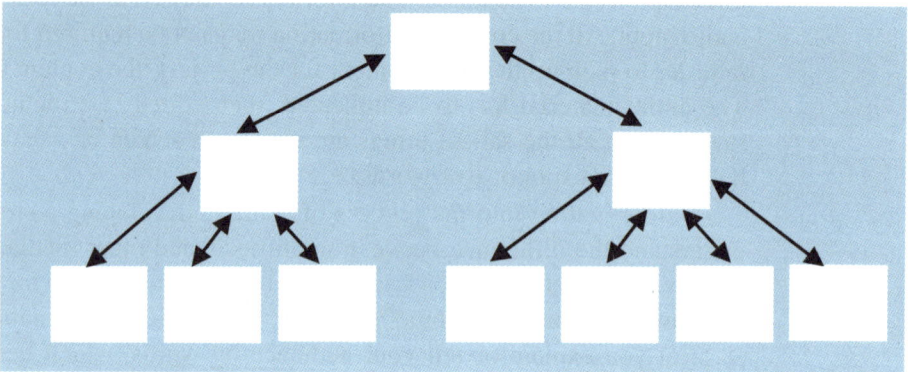

Composite Structure

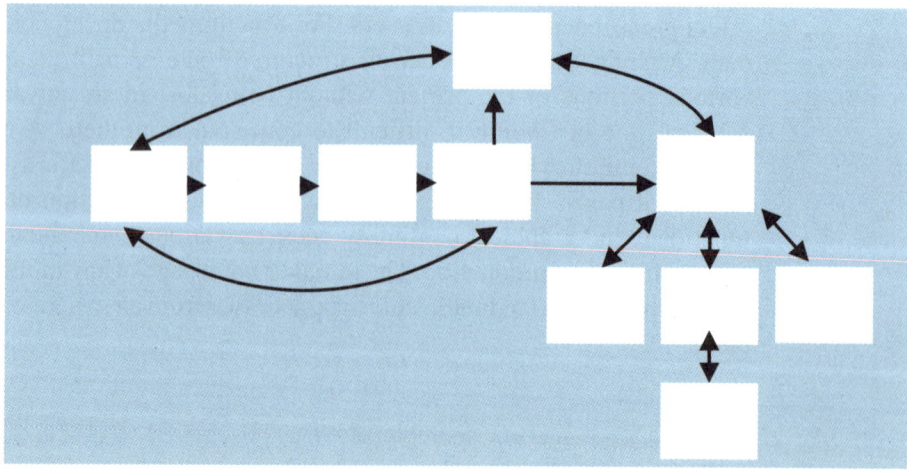

Kinds of navigation maps:

- *Linear Structure:*

It is the sequential navigation process accessed by a user. Here a user moves freely in between pages step by step, either one step forward or backward. Sites best suited to a linear structure are: corporate presentation, educational programme for school children, live lecture supported by various slides.

- *Hierarchical Structure:*

It is similar to the staffing pattern of an official hierarchy, often attributed to the branches of a tree. To move from top to bottom, one must move down one branch at a time with more branches being available the lower one goes. The structure is shaped by a natural logic and is most suitable for educational programmes.

- *Non-Linear Structure:*

Users can navigate freely through the content of the project, unbound by predetermined routes.

- *Composite Structure:*

For the most part users can navigate freely (as in the non-linear structure), but are occasionally constrained to a linear or hierarchical structure for some of the material.

Design

Whatever may be the structure, each page of a project needs to be designed with text, audio, video, graphics and animation in either a combination of all or of more than one.

Text of a multimedia project is normally short and precise, but its importance cannot be ignored due to the fact that in many cases, text is the major component to explain the details of the content specially for reference multimedia. In general, text is used for title, as navigation items, display of information, as caption.

Like printed literature, multimedia text is also meant for reading and its legibility should be given adequate importance. Here legibility rules are slightly different than that of printed text. The main reason is that text is read against a translucent or lighted screen. Irregular sequence of pages and viewing distance may be other reasons. More than often, text is displayed on a background picture. Content of the picture and colour tend to reduce the legibility of text, especially smaller font size.

Here also typographical content is divided into two categories—title and running text. In both cases selection of the font involves creative judgement and function of the page.

Running text:

If you have a long text, then the best advice is to rewrite it and make it shorter or to place it in chunks of smaller typographical pages. Scrolling is an option for long text for a non-linear structure project but remember it is difficult to read much and for long on a computer screen. Most of the rules for the use of text in terms of number of words per line, spacing, setting format etc. in a multimedia page are more or less the same as that of a printed page. Due to different viewing distance of pages in different situations or projection, choice of type size is often a bit flexible.

Text for titles:

These are display matter different from headlines of printed pages for two reasons. One, often text is displayed on the page out of context, may be as part of a list of topics for navigation aid of the user. Two, even if the title is displayed within related context it is difficult to get enough information that can be seen at a glance and learn more from the surrounding data. Therefore, a page title should be short, simple and visible in clarity. In general, the user will find it easy to understand your title if it is explained by 40 to 60 words.

Take care of the following points for the selection of text for the multimedia project:

- *Appropriate font:*

As always, lineal sans serif and classical style are appropriate for most of the multimedia title. Titles for corporate image building, children's educational programmes, telephone directory, encyclopedia etc look modern, simple and accessible in a lineal sans serif style. Classical serif type may be used for news related topics, historical and archaeological programmes which are related to the past or are conventional and traditional. Fancy styles are also appropriate in some situations. Use of fancy style for handicrafts, jewelry, interior decoration, folk art and music, etc may create the mood of the topic. Even simple text can be made to look fancy by using drop shadow, 3D effect, textured etc and many cases looks appropriate. If the multimedia title is combined with animation, text can be made interesting by using various effects of animation like fly, dissolve, spin, float etc.

While selecting text, another point should be taken care of, that is the jaggis or steps like pixels around the curve of the letters, which is apparent for larger font sizes. Removal of this shortcoming is a must for multimedia text. The process is known is anti-aliasing. Anti-aliasing is a technique which causes the edges of objects to be rendered smooth by placing pixels at the edges that carry different hues of the same colour as the object. Some of the image editing software offer this facility.

Colour:

In print, more the colour, more the cost. But multimedia pages are not restricted by this. Therefore, colour can be used freely for multimedia titles. The only restriction of colour is the capacity of the text. Remember text suffers from illegibility more often than not due to extravagant use of colour.

Contrast is the main criteria for text colour. Maximum contrast can be obtained by using black letters against a white background, which is the thumb rule for printed text. Multimedia title would be uninteresting if one followed the same rule.

Therefore, use colour but keep it as contrasting as possible. Legibility reduces if one uses red text on a green background, black on brown, blue on grey etc. Although contrast ratio is the same in case of reverse letters, but the scheme throws people off a title and slows their reading slightly, especially for running text.

Text handling software

All the above mentioned text attributes are solely dependent on the software being chosen. A number of them are available for this purpose. Microsoft Word may be the best for content development as it allows one to check spelling and grammar of the language and can placed or exported to other programmes easily. Image editing programmes like Adobe Photoshop, Corel Photo Paint, Paint Shop Pro are ideal for various special effects. For 3D texts and text animation, packages like 3D Studio, Liveware 3D, 3D modeling are the most suitable. Multimedia based authoring system that makes the content design and hyperlink with other pages is Macromedia Director.

Graphics

Multimedia graphics create a lot of drama in a page besides attracting attention, providing information and creating an environment. Here graphics include photographs, drawing, charts, graphs, maps etc. All the graphics to be used in the multimedia project are created in the computer or taken into a computer by scanning or from a digital camera. Some of the pictures can be downloaded from the Internet and CDs or from software programmes that carry clip art. In all these situations images either 2D or 3D illusion are in digital form. Since the computer screen is 2D most of the multimedia graphic images are in 2D form. 3D can be used to show something in virtual reality or to visualize physical objects that need to be understood in their solid form. Examples might include: Games, Trade shows, Engineering or Architectural models.

For the purpose of multimedia projects there are two kinds of graphics: Interface and Content.

Interface:

The traditional graphic design seeks to make the object or application physically attractive, the goal of user interface design is to make the user's interaction as simple and efficient as possible, in terms of accomplishing user goals. Thematic or non-thematic pictures are manipulated in different special effects, combined with buttons as iconic menu just like the menu bar of the Windows software programme. These iconic menus developed from the familiarity people have with the properties these symbol represent. For example, a pair of scissors is for cut, a floppy for save or dustbin for trash. These are almost standarised for most software programmes. But interface graphics are much more than the menubar icon and each one is unique in itself and are normally designed for specific purposes by specialists. That is the reason all multimedia projects are visually different from each other.

Interface graphics are often confused with hypergraphics. Hypergraphics are the portion of an image or an icon meant for linkage to the other portion of the project. It is highlighted by clicking the image and takes the user on to the other pages that helps free navigation. Function of the hypergraphics is almost similar to that of hypertext.

Content:

There is an unlimited scope of creativity in development of content graphics. Various effects of computer software applied creatively make the pages exciting. Before choosing any effect for the pictures for a multimedia projects, one should understand two basic types of computer images: Vector and Bitmap. Both kinds of images have some merits and demerits.

Vector images:

The mathematically defined curves and line segments of a computer image is called vector. Since the vector image creates objects like rectangle and circle, it is also called object-oriented graphics. Illustrations made in a vector programme occupy a fraction of a space in the computer memory and can be scaled or modified to virtually any size without any loss of detail. Some of the programmes that create vector images are Illustrator, FreeHand, MacDraw, CorelDraw etc.

Bitmap images:

These images are made up of a whole lot of tiny dots, called pixels. Here painting like illusion of continuous tone is created by pixels, thus called paint-oriented graphics. Like half-tone images, more the pixels, the sharper the image on the computer screen. The computer stores this file by recording the exact placement and colour of each pixel. The computer has no idea that it is a circle, only that it is a collection of little squares. Number of pixels of the image determines the size of the file. The problem arises when you try enlarging a raster image. Because the resolution is set, when the image is scaled, in reality, the pixels are enlarged, which results in a jagged or pixelated image.

Illustrations can be created in bitmap images on programmes like Photoshop, CorelPaint, PixelPaint, PhotoSuit, etc.

In general, working with vector graphics requires lesser artistic skill than working with bitmapped graphics but realistic pictures like a human faces or a landscape cannot be created by it. In creating a bitmapped graphic, the mouse and other pointing devices are used just as an artist uses a pencil, pen, or brush. However, one may face difficulties in combining scanned drawn images with bitmapped ones.

File Formats

Image files are saved, stored, opened and transported in specific formats before the final imaging. Understanding of these formats helps in choosing the right format for the right kind of image being handled.

Native Format:

The native file format is the default file format used by a specific software application. PHD, CDR, AI are the native formats of Photoshop, CorelDraw and Illustrator respectively. The native file format of an application is proprietary and these types of files are not meant to be transferred to other applications. Therefore images of native format should be converted to any of the following formats.

For easy storage and transportation of image information, files may be saved in a compressed format. ZIP and JPEG are two commonly used formats in multimedia image content development. While compressing the file one must take care of image resolution. Resolution of an image means quality or the degree of details of an image. It is always on the basis of expected enlargement or projection of a page.

Image Editing:

Image editing involves selection of right content, elimination of unwanted elements, compensation for technical defects and scaling and cropping to fit the pictures in a design. A large picture is better than a small one in order to have the desired impact, but sometimes the resolution of the available image and file space may create problems. There may be a need to have small versions of images to create thumbnails. Though the resizing command makes the picture small enough, it often results in losing details and the picture becomes too crowded to be meaningful when combined with other pictures.

Technical defects refers to a picture's shortcomings in terms of being overcast, a lack of contrast, too low resolution, etc. Hundreds of special or image altering effects like vignette, feathering, posterize and montage can be applied on images to enhance the mood of the image.

Since no picture comes to a multimedia developer in a size as per the requirement of the page, in most cases pictures have to be reduced or enlarged and this process is known as scaling. Make sure the picture is not distorted while scaling. Cropping is the elimination of part of the content of the picture. It should be done carefully in such a way that no important content of the picture fall within the crop area.

Some of the task of editing on computer is quite simple, and some, a bit complicated, requiring artistic vision and software knowledge. Therefore, before jumping into a multimedia project, learn some of the software thoroughly. Recommended software are Photoshop, Corel, Photo Paint, Paint Shop Pro in 2D environment, and 3D studio and Lightwave 3D in 3D environment.

Audio

From the user's point of view graphics are better when sound is imposed. Speech can be used to offer a community or help without obscuring information on the screen. Sounds can also be used to provide a sense of place or mood. Music is probably the most obvious choice for creating a mood. A speaker's face instead of a video clip and his recorded voice provide a sense of the speaker's personality. Non-speech sound can be used as an extra dimension in the user interface to inform the user about the background event. Example: entrance of title on a page or credits at the end, dropping an object on the floor, flying sound for something disappearing from the scene, and an active sound on clicking the hypergraphics.

What is Sound?

As per elementary physics, sound is created when an object vibrates. The vibrations cause change in air pressure called sound wave. It enters our ears by causing vibrations of small bones in the eardrum. These vibrations then cause nerve impulses to be sent to the brain where they are interpreted as sound.

Recording of sound:

Sound is recorded in two ways: By means of analog signal and digital conversion. Analog recording is done when sound waves strike a microphone, they are converted to an electrical signal which is then etched onto a magnetic tape.

Analog sound can be presented visually which looks like a wave. The wave height indicates the volume, distance between the cycles is wavelength and the number of cycles per second that our ears interprets, is frequency.

Digital recording differs from analog recording in that the "picture" of the sound is created by measuring the voltage changes coming from the microphone and assigning numbers to each measurement. The term "sampling" is used to describe the process of measuring an electrical signal's voltage thousands of times per second at a given level of precision (resolution).

Sounds that are used in developing a multimedia project are necessarily digital. Remember, your eardrum cannot process digital information. It can only hear an analog sound waveform. Digital audio is merely a representation of this analog waveform.

Advantages of digital sound

The biggest advantage of any digital system is the ability to store, retrieve and transmit signals without any loss of quality. Digital sound is non-destructive during editing and processing. It has immunity to noise and distortion while in the digital state and has a long shelf life (around fifty years). Editing; that is, cutting, pasting and other manipulation of special effects, like echo, is easy with digital signals.

Hardware and software requirement

To begin working with multimedia sound you will need a multimedia computer with sound input and output hardware. Every Apple Macintosh in production today comes with all the necessary hardware and software one will need to begin. For some PCs running Windows, however, it may be necessary to buy a sound card and have it properly installed by a technician.

Audio software can be divided into two groups. One group is meant for playback, that controls one or more multimedia devices or files, like audio CD, Wave Sound or MIDI audio files. The second group is meant for audio editing and creation. The Wave studio is one such programmes that allows cutting, copying and various other editing operations. There are a host of software available today, some of which can even be downloaded free of charge from the Internet. But professional software must be purchased based on their capabilities and the computer platform one is working with.

What is MIDI? The full form of MIDI is Musical Instrument Digital Interface. It is a hardware and software standard that, among other things, allows users to record a complete description of a lengthy musical performance using only a small amount of disk space. Standard MIDI Files can be played back using the sound synthesis hardware of a Mac or PC.

Video

For long, moving images have provided a real life feeling in film and Television. Now these have become an integral part of multimedia and web in the form of video clips. But due to some technical limitations these are not as popular as film and television. That is why video has to serve as a supplement to text and images more often than to provide the main content of a project.

However video clips are incorporated in a multimedia project for several reasons. Explaining cultural functions, religious rituals, dance performance in a much more impressive fashion than writing pages or showing static visuals. Videos are a good medium for product demos like a new brand of mobile phone, providing users an impression of a speaker's personality; live lectures, or the event that has a certain sequence.

A major problem with most videos for multimedia is that each clip has to be shot exclusively for the project which often proves to be a costly proposition. If something is available on the Internet, their production values are much too low while others may be copyright protected. Editing of individual content of a video clip is often difficult. In most cases editors use hard cuts between shots as a result of which images lack transitional effects like dissolve or wipe. Digital video clips occupy a lot of computer memory space and the ability to display the number of frames display on screen per second in most of the motion videos are in quarter screen which may not have the same effect as a full screen experience. In order to get smooth viewing of video pictures, played back digital video file should be at 25-30 frames per second.

Video Technology

Video technology is based on either analog or digital. Analog is synonymous to the word analogous, which means similar or equivalent. Since the video pictures simulate real life on screen they are a continuous flow of picture by electronic signal. In general, humans experience the world analogically. Vision, for example, is an analog experience because we perceive infinitely smooth gradations of shapes and colour. Most analog events, however, can be simulated digitally. Look at the photograph on a computer screen, it appears as continuous tone, but the image is basically made up of small pixels or dots.

Digital Video is a video, the signal of which is captured in a format which is recognized by a computer. This means its signal is read with the same binary coding (0,1) as most computer applications. More importantly, digital video promises to eliminate many of the problems associated with analog video including signal path degradation and generation loss. It also blends video and audio signals more "seamlessly" than standard analog video.

Video editing tips

- The editing, cutting, mixing, sequencing, etc. of the analog video clips should be done on original images. Their conversion in digital format would look good despite compression of files at low resolution and frame rates.
- Close-up shots are preferable to wide shots. Wide shots have too much detail and make no sense at low resolution.
- Use talking heads only if the video clip truly adds to the user's experience. Shoot this type of image against a simple monochromatic background whenever possible. This will make small video images easier to understand and will increase the efficiency of compression.
- Avoid too much camera movement. Video shoots from one position reduces the difference between frames and facilitates compression without losing image quality.
- It may be exciting to have zooming and panning in your video clip. However these can cause low frame rate leading to viewing difficulty and confusing interpretation.
- Don't use the transitional effects offered by video editing software, such as, dissolves or elaborate wipes, because they will not compress efficiently and will not play smoothly on projection.
- Don't be playful with video clips by using it as interface design. It should be used only to enhance the content.

Animation

Moving images have an overpowering effect on human vision. Animation plays an important role in a multimedia project that goes from vision to mind. In most cases, the weight of an animation file is more than that of a video clip, because often fun and gimmicks are attached to it.

What is animation?

An animation is a sequence of images played or moved at a speed that gives an illusion of smooth moving analog images simulating motion picture. An animation consists of number frames of images that are artificially created through drawing or some other simulation method.

There are many different types of animation that are used in our present day world. The two main ones are Cell animation and computer animation. Both of them have several sub types. Each one has its own distinct uniqueness.

Cell animation is originally drawn on 2D format. Later the 3D (three-dimensional) animation is created using clay modeling. In 3D animation 3D figures are made out of clay like materials that are made to move slightly on a 3D set and frame by frame pictures are then taken of it.

These figures move around among objects to provide a sense of perspective. Animations can also focus on relative size, speed of an object, or how it moves in relation to other objects.

The use of computers has brought about a new way of approaching animations. It started when computer experts saw the possibility of computers as a way of developing wonderfully good pictures that would have taken a lot more effort to produce or would even be impossible to produce otherwise.

Computer animation is very much the same as cell-based animation, where each frame in the animation is created by computer programming which is slightly different from the one preceding it. Here simple use of 3D also gives the pictures a view not only from the front, but also from different angles and positions (e.g. top view or side view). Some of them can even be rotated to show all the sides of the object.

2D Animation software:

In two dimensional environments, *Autodesk Animator Studio* works on a Windows platform. Designed for 2D classical animation and animated backgrounds, the Animator Studio with its various inks, brushes and other features makes it easy to join everything—painting, sound, video and tools—for professional presentations of various qualities.

Adobe Flash is another example of multimedia software created by Macromedia and currently developed and distributed by Adobe Systems. Since its introduction in 1996, Flash has become a popular method of adding animation and interactivity to web pages. Flash is commonly used to create animation, advertisements, and various web page components, to integrate video into web pages. Flash can manipulate vector and raster graphics and supports bi-directional streaming of audio and video.

The benefits of Flash: The files are usually compatible with Windows and Macintosh. Flash is flexible enough to add simple player controls (e.g. Pause, Replay) and more complex interactivity. Flash can be used for illustration on both still illustrations and animations can be in the same style. Flash software combines ease-of-use with a wealth of powerful animation. It allows you to use templates or create your own designs.

Toon Boom Studio software offers true animation features designed to facilitate the creation of any style of animation, including traditional frame-by-frame animation, keyframe animation, cut-out, photo animation and live-action cartoon. Toon Boom Studio Express helps you learn the traditional animation work flow and get started on producing your masterpiece. It is ideal for individuals looking for an all-in-one animation software that facilitates drawing digitally, scanning hand-drawn animations or seamlessly importing existing artwork.

3D Animation software:

Developing three dimensional animations involve several steps of modeling, lighting, material application, key framing and rendering. *Autodesk 3ds Max* is popular in this group. The 3D system software creates the models simply by lines, curves and shapes, down in 3D space that simulate life after appropriate rendering; a jargon that refers to the process of finally applying light, material attributes and animation to a particular 3D scene frame by frame.

Other high-end software

Java: In the past Java was a popular tool used to develop interactive animations. Unfortunately, it remains difficult to programme an application compatible on both Windows and Macintosh. The software is used for creating, editing, compressing, optimizing, animating, and working with Web graphics.

Maya: This is a programme used by major film studios to create realistic 3D objects and scenes. As of now, exporting final animations is extremely CPU intensive and time consuming.

Softimage|3D: It was a high-end 3D graphics application developed by *Softimage, Co.*, a subsidiary of *Avid Technology, Inc.*, which was used predominantly in the film, gaming and advertising industries for the production of 3D animation. It has been superseded by *Softimage|XSI.*

Authoring

This stage of multimedia project works like print media page assembly in which all the components of a page created in different programmes are integrated to make a final layout or artwork that goes for production. Here also some dedicated software are used that accept all the elements needed in a project under production. The programme allows to place the elements at their respective places guided by the story board made for the project. It is then manipulated by the software's own features like making realistic simulations, and adding immersive interaction to the project.

Multimedia authoring sometimes refers to multimedia programming. Whatever the term we may use, it is basically a process of developing a multimedia project using various system level commands to handle various media files and integrate them.

There are several authoring tools utilized in developing a project. Some tools are meant for arranging content as individual frames with sound, music and animation etc. Some are time based that allow various media elements sequentially in a particular time line. Whereas some are icon based that indicate the flow of information sequentially in the form of icons.

All these tools are capable of handling the media to be used in a project, and contain a lot of copyright free media clips, mapping or story boarding features to plan the structure of the project. They also provide media embedding features that support other media despite their varying environment.

There are several authoring programmes available in the market wherein each one has its own methods of working, but most of them have the above-mentioned features. The most commonly used authoring programme is Macromedia's *Director*.

Summary

Multimedia is a technology engaging a variety of media, including text, still image, audio, video and animation content; in order to communicate ideas, disseminate information or provide entertainment either separately or in combination of any two or more media. Multimedia may be broadly divided into two categories: Non-interactive, where the audience just watches the show as it proceeds in sequence, and Interactive, where the user participates in every stage of the proceedings. Multimedia projects begin with research or collecting information in relation with the topic being handled, followed by a navigation map that leads to develop a structure containing various pages. All the pages of a project are then designed with text, audio, video, graphics and animation that are linked to each other for navigation. Handling each of the multimedia components requires dedicated software, of which some are multifunctional and some are content specific. Assembly of all the pages is known as authoring of the content. There are several authoring tools utilized in developing a project.

Critical thinking exercise

A real state developer wants to project itself and ethical company by informing and educating its staff, workers, suppliers and shareholders through a multimedia project. Prepare detailed plan inclusive of research, navigation map and various components to be used in the project.

Questions

Q.1 Define multimedia in various communication contexts.

Q.2 Compare between non-interactive and interactive multimedia.

Q.3 Discuss interactive multimedia in relation to reference, education and entertainment.

Q.4 What is a navigation map? Prepare a navigation map for an interactive multimedia project using a structure most suitable for the project.

Q.5 Multimedia project contains text, graphics, audio, video and animation. How are these handled independently and in combination while designing?

Q.6 Mention the basic software available for developing each component of multimedia. Discuss their features in brief.

Q.7 Explain multimedia authoring using one of the programmes available for the purpose.

References

S. Gokul, *Multimedia Magic* (New Delhi: BPB Publication,1998)

Arena Design Team, *Web Animation* (Mumbai: Aptech Limited, 2005)

Sunita Pant Bansal, "CD Rom Publishing" (New Delhi: Paper Presented at the 16th Condensed Course for Publishing Professionals, 2003)

http://www.mobygames.com/genre/sheet/interactive-movie (accessed on October 2008)

Dr. Steve Anderson, *Multimedia on Internet* [http:/ www.usu.edu/sanderson/multinet (accessed on October 2008)]

http://animation.about.com/od/referencematerials (accessed on October 2008)

Vasuki Belavadi, *Video Production* (New Delhi: Oxford University Press, 2008)

17 Corporate Identity for Image Build-up

Chapter Objectives
- Understand the concept of corporate identity and its role in image building
- Know the role of management and creative professionals in developing the physical forms of the identity
- Analyze the design brief, research and creative concepts
- Describe the creative process of an identity mark
- Handle the implementation of a corporate identity programme

What is Corporate Identity?

Corporate identity is defined as the character and image of an organization, reflecting the culture that is presented to its various publics, including the organization's name and logo or how a particular business is perceived by its customers and the rest of the marketplace.

Who needs a Corporate Identity?

In order to promote or improve an organization's corporate culture, identify marks that facilitate the attainment of objectives of various groups. Most notable are the companies that have their own identity running through all their products and merchandise like Hindustan Unilever Limited.

Educational institutions, insurance companies, hospitals and hotels offer services to the people and form a strong service group. Some organizations like the Public Relations Society of India, the Association of Advertising Professionals or the All India Federation of Master Printers are group associations of professionals who work together for promoting and developing the aims and objectives of their organization instead of selling a particular product. The ISI mark or Agmark of the Bureau of Indian Standards promise a guarantee of standard for the product and also validate the identity of the Bureau as a certification group.

A political group can also have a distinct corporate identity. In a country like ours where there are so many political parties each one has a symbol, like the Congress (I) has a hand, the BJP, lotus flower and BSP an elephant, which reflect their philosophy and ethos. In a large society, members of a minority tend to develop a corporate identity where they feel a special bond with any other member of that minority even though they might not have met the person before. Identity is needed for the majority cultural group as well. Their identity is used to promote, strengthen and encourage activists in teaching the language of their origin. Such identity formation is carried on by the practice of rituals and social customs, discouraging marriage outside a particular group, etc. Professional groups may be of doctors, lawyers, painters, etc who maintain a particular culture among themselves have also set identities. Even an individual may need an identity mark.

How is Corporate Identity viewed?

Corporate identity represents two characteristics, viz. the intangible and tangible. The intangible qualities of an organization are just like the personality of a human being which can be felt only by an interaction, involvement and eagerness to know the person. An organization can be perceived as modern, traditional, international or conservative. Organizations build an image of being reliable, efficient, authoritative etc. and reflect the internal values and norms of the organization. Tangible qualities are the manifestation of graphic shapes in the form of logos, uniform, colour, lettering style etc. which are visible on various application areas of the company. Combination of these two qualities develop an image of a corporate brand that acts as a guarantee to the product or service being used by the target audience.

Corporate Visual Identity

Management aspect:

First, it should provide an organization with visibility and recognition by appropriate planned development and maintenance to know the existence of the company using signage system. Second, it should symbolize an organization by corporate colour and shapes used in developing the identity mark which will contribute to its image/reputation among stakeholders. Third, it should express the structure of the organization by decorating the interiors that will present a visual coherence as well as the relation between divisions or units. Fourth, the internal function of corporate visual identity through uniform or other communication materials like newsletters, business card, letterhead, notepad etc. It relates to the employees' identification with the organization.

Design aspect:

The starting point of building the visual identity of an organization is developing a logo. Most people think creating an identity mark or logo is a simple job that any skilled designer can do without much effort. But developing a logo requires more than graphic skill. It is because the logo is expected to express a lot with minimum graphic elements. A logo is like an advertisement of the company or a product in miniature. Therefore all the rules of an ad campaign should be followed. These include (1) developing a design brief, (2) gathering information about the clients' requirements, (3) developing creative concepts, (4) presenting solutions and justifying them, and (5) implementing the chosen solution.

Design brief:

A design brief is a written document outlining in complete detail, the business objectives and corresponding design strategies for a design project. There is a saying that 'client is the boss.' Whatever he or she says is right. This concept should be ignored while taking a brief from the client. Make the person your friend by displaying positive attitude and make it seem like the beginning of a long term relationship. Listen to clients patiently and try to understand their expectations. Identify the problem area and ask questions for clarification. Be analytical and see things from the end users' or beneficiaries' perspective. Many a times clients may overlook this aspect in the proposed solution. But always maintain a balance between their and your point of view and give them a feeling that you understand their need.

The design brief will include a brief history of the company, possible expansion plans and new areas of activities focusing on the plan of the company for the development and sale of products or services, its marketing segment and competitors, consumer attitudes towards the company, etc. In case of the necessity to redesign the existing identity, a brief should include the company's policy towards the continuation of the visual image or for overhauling the complete image.

Gathering information:

Before beginning to work on the design, you must undertake an information gathering process to understand the business. You will get sufficient information on questioning him about this matter. The idea of a design solution will emerge from your interaction with your client. In many situations the client may have some limitations. You must explore your own source. It may be your own scrapbook or reference materials from books and catalogues. Collection of some of competitor's visual identity and a knowledge of their activity may also help a great deal. Surfing various websites is one of the good ways of information gathering.

Creative concept:

The logical starting point of a creative concept is organizing a brainstorming session. It is generally a discussion among a group of people in which each individual throws up ideas that stimulate the subconscious minds of the others. Ideas beget ideas. A brainstorming session encourages the members to come out with better and more effective ideas. The individual imagination is then shared by the group and there emerges a composite idea to solve the problem design. The team would be able to create a custom logo for the client based on the client organization's objectives and target customers.

A series of questions on the proposed logo may help generate several alternative ideas. The probable questions are:
- Is the mark aesthetically pleasing?
- Can the mark stand out among others with its shapes, form, and colour?
- Is it simple enough for recognition and to recall?
- Can it be associated with the organization's activities and its target audience?
- Is it visible on any item in any size without losing its graphic details?
- Is it contemporary and will not be outdated in the near future?
- Is it flexible enough to be adapted to various media and surfaces?
- Is the design original to get legal protection?

Answer to all the above questions would hopefully lead to develop some lines and shapes. Remember, each line and shape used in identity mark design can create a mood and a meaning in a design. It is because most logo designs are developed with minimal graphic elements. There is very little scope to explain a company's activity by using visual and verbal copy.

Physical form of lines can be straight or curved, heavy or light, smooth or rough, continuous or broken. In case of mood and meaning, if horizontal, a feeling of calm and speed — the calm of the sea, the speed of arrow — is created. A vertical line, on the other hand suggests strength — the strength of a pillar or that of the stem of a tree.

Straight lines give a sense of direction. Similarly broken lines give the feeling of low speed or pause between movement. Straight horizontal lines lead the eye from left to right, whereas vertical rules take the eye downwards. The straight vertical lines give the feeling of firmness but if it is slanted, loses its strength and may begin to fall. Curved lines suggest the grace of a creeper, the movement of water, the growth of a plant which rises from the ground in the form of vertical curved lines and of opposition — a line divides space into two parts which come in opposition to each other. Lines are used forcefully, casually or mechanically to create a mood or express a personality. This is so, because they are abstractions of objects and figures that create the mood and the personality.

The shapes may be square, circle, triangle or any combination of these. Logo designers use these shapes as coded communication and represent or express certain qualities, attributes, or characteristics.

Symbolically, a circle can stand for perfection, wholeness, or a boundary (protective or confining); circling round something can be a way of honouring or blessing it. The circle is a universal sign because of the ancient Indian philosophy of cyclic movement. It is patterned on the shape of the earth, the moon, the sun and the wheel. A wrong answer is always marked by a circle which means zero. A portion of visual or verbal copy marked by a circle indicates a restriction on the area for attention. It conveys several ideas in different cultures. It symbolizes life and death to some; onward march of human life to others. It is an ancient and universal symbol of unity, wholeness, infinity, the goddess, and female power. To earth-centered religions throughout history as well as to many contemporary pagans, it represents the feminine spirit or force, the cosmos or a spiritualized Mother Earth, and a sacred space.

Triangle: The objectivity of this sign represents the pyramid, the tree and the mountain. In subjective connotation, a triangle shows three aspects of a single figure. A triangle in a red colour outlines a warning, danger and caution. It suggests direction in placing the apex in a pointing position. Triangles are associated with the number three. Pointing upwards, it symbolizes fire, male power and counterfeit view of God.

Several alternatives may be tried on a tracing pad by a sketch-pen or HB pencil but the best one will emerge only on getting satisfactory answers to the above questions. Computers these days help us try several options much faster and accurately. Typography skill is another important requisite for a logo designer. Selection of the appropriate type for a particular application from thousands of typefaces requires knowledge and love for typefaces. Physical manipulation of typefaces is maximum in logo design and requires both skill and imagination.

Most designers of identity marks follow the basic principles of design, i.e., line tone, shape and balance.

The creative concept also includes colour. The use of colour for an identity mark is different from other two-dimensional designs like books, folders or advertisements. This is because most logos are reproduced as line art on various kinds of surfaces and surroundings. Though black and its tones are the safest colour for logo design, primary and vivid colours are the first choice of the designer if colours other than black are to be used. Bata's bright red, Hindustan Unilever's blue, and Kodak's yellow, red and black combinations are quite eye-catching and enjoy great recall. Subtle gradation tones and shades of colours are also not uncommon in logo design. The effectiveness of these colours will depend on what combinations have been used and the designer should be sure that the colour he has specified comes back as it is from the printer. Logos and marks developed in colour should work well even if converted into black and white.

Skillfully used line, shape, and colour helps the designer to develop an identity mark of a character of its own. It may be termed as style. Style makes the mark standout from others. Obviously the design style should go well with the organizations' function/activities or the product line. Style may be signature, geometric, pictorial, folk, national, international and so on. Examples of signature are: Kirloskar, Parrys, Johnson and Johnson, Godrej etc. The signature style evolved from the signature or the name of the entrepreneurs who had initiated the business. Geometric style is used in the logo of All India Federation of Master Printers, in the form of registration mark which is vital in multicolour printing. Nestle's birds on nest, Leo Toys' lion, are some of the examples of pictorial style. Use of national bird in Film Festival logo makes the mark national whereas VSNL's two arrows moving in opposite directions around a globe imply the international nature of its activities.

Some identity marks are developed by graphic shape, that is, manipulation of picture, line shape, letterform and colour. Some of them have a direct association to the product, brand name or organization and some have indirect or abstract associations. Some of them have no association at all and that is simply an arbitrary graphic shape. The 'U' shape, the first letter of the Unilever logo filled with 25 different icons representing every aspect of their business which has its presence in areas like nutrition, hygiene, personal care, food and drinks, etc., fulfilling their basic mission "add vitality to life", and the benefits Unilever brings to consumers is an example of direct association. A solid circle with a key hole is the logo of State Bank of India indirectly associating with the bank's commitment to the customer that their money has been kept in safe custody. Diversified activities of Imperial Tobacco company are represented by a triangle within which two solid arrows are drawn in an inward direction and the initial letters of the company name, give it a distinct image but suggestive meaning. All areas of the business form a united whole and display an upward trend. There is no better example of an arbitrary mark than the Family Planning red triangle, which has no manifest meaning, no association, but it draws great recall value and distinct visibility at any place among all kinds of audience.

Selling the Design

You must sell your design to your client like any other commodity. Sell is a dirty word for some creative professionals. But in a highly competitive environment when clients have so many options one must stand out and impress the prospective buyer, one must do the same as others do: presentation

The presentation of your design solution may be as simple as taking some printout of your design on a desktop printer or as elaborate as the presentation of an advertisement campaign especially if it is for a complete identity programmer. Simple presentation does not mean inviting the client to choose one from the alternatives that have been prepared.

Prepare a summary of the whole process starting from design brief to design execution. This may include company profile, expansion plan, list of competitors and their area of operations. Take a print out of three alternative logos you have prepared. Select the best from your point of view. Make a three fold or eight page folder of A4 side using coloured pastel paper alternatively a pamphlet with a pocket in which eight loose sheets can be kept. The first page of the folder or the pamphlet may be used as a cover with project and presenter name. One page may be used for presenting the alternative logos, next page for five different sizes of the selected logo. This is just to judge the design's clarity in different sizes. Third page can be utilized for the summary of the presentation. The rest of the pages should be devoted for some application areas to see the logo at work.

Now show your design to your client who has gradually developed his or her opinion. Upon receiving your initial logo design concepts, the client would let you know which of the logo designs he/she likes the most. Be prepared to make further alterations, if necessary, to those designs until the client is satisfied with the final design. The design team should work with the client every step of the process to ensure full satisfaction to you and your client.

For the presentation of the complete identity programme, a PowerPoint presentation will be ideal. It is because a lot of money is invested to build a company's or product image. In most cases it is assigned to an established design firm or an agency specialized in this area. The complete identity programme would differ from company to company. In general, it includes logo/ brand name, colour, slogan, type style, stationary items, signage system etc.

Develop a set of slides listing only relevant points of your proposal. You should come well prepared for presentation so that you are in a position to explain your work and answer client queries. This may include copy of original design brief, originals or copy of all previous design work prepared for the same project. Remember, the client is an important person and his or her time is valuable. You must bring an executive summary at the presentation which should be brief and precise. In this format of your presentation you can impress your client by making the prototype of your application both in 2D or 3D format. It is understandable that many of the 3D formats are so large or voluminous that it is difficult to carry them to the place of presentation. Alternately, you may click the photograph of those application areas and place the logo at the appropriate position. Image editing software like Photoshop will be helpful for this task. Some companies may insist on the adoption of a house style. It means that the logo should go well with type style, graphic shapes, and colour used in different formats of application area. A handout of selected slides or printout of logos and other elements of house identity may allow the client to review your presentation better.

Implementing the Identity Programme

Once the design proposal is approved, it should be implemented in the company's different application areas and image building programme. Many organizations use it as and when they need it without maintaining much of a standard. For example, in the same organization one department may be using the logo on top centre of their letterhead and another on the top right. Even the colour of the logo may differ from department to department. Some organizations are very conscious about their visual image and try to maintain a harmonious visual relation among their application areas. In order to avoid any distortion of the design solution the design team and organization's management, mainly public relations personnel, should work in coordination. The first step is to develop an Identity Manual in which all design solutions should be presented in an easy to understand manner. It is basically a guidebook for the implementer in which all the details of design solution have been indicated. (Some pages of NTPC identity manual are reproduced here). The implementers should correctly adhere to the guidelines laid down in the manual.

280 Public Relations Management

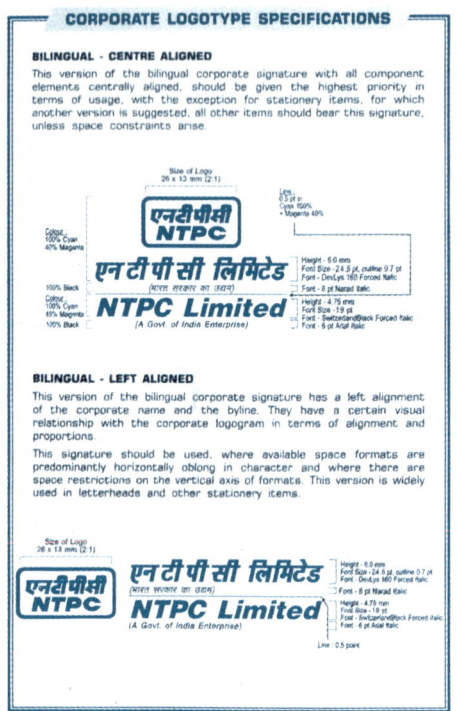

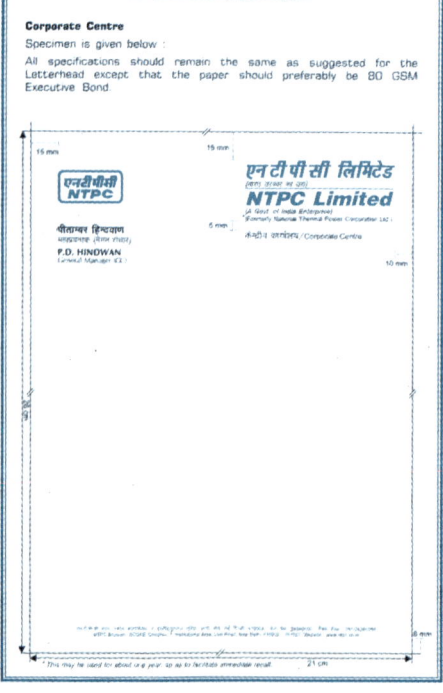

The implementers of the programme may be printers who are doing the print job, like stationery, house journal, and annual report etc., a film maker making a corporate film or TV commercial; fabricators, who are engaged in developing the signage system, exhibition panels, decor etc.; or computer professionals who are developing advertisements of tender notices, business proposal or website for the company. Whosoever may be the implementer the company's PR persons, the purchasing and marketing departments and of course the top management should supervise the work. In order to check the distortion and wrongful application of the design, all the departments should work in full cooperation.

The implementation work may not end here, especially when a company wants to create a new image or a new logo is to be introduced. The company should launch an elaborate publicity programme when a new identity is sought to be established both for the external and internal publics, including staff and employees. This may include an ad campaign focused on the logo and a booklet or special issue of the newsletter of the company for internal publics.

The new logo can be of a new company or an existing company's new area of operations either holding a majority of shares or serving as an umbrella organization. Some companies want to change their identity as their value and philosophy has changed over a period of time. Some organizations retain some of the elements of the previous mark to maintain a sense of continuity. Others have had to change their established identity out of compulsion, such as, government controlled organizations. In case the original logo carries only Roman alphabets, the logo has to be bilingual, in combination with Hindi (Devanagari alphabets), official language of the Government. The following are some of the examples of new logos, redesigned logos and bilingual logos.

Hindustan Lever Ltd (HLL)

One of India's best known fast moving consumer goods company with popular brands like Liril, Lux, Brooke Bond, Kissan, Lakme and Kwality Wall's has got a new corporate identity and logo, changing its name Hindustan Lever Limited to Hindustan Unilever Ltd. Its new logo is symbolic to the Firm's mission of 'Adding Vitality to Life'. The new identity would  hopefully help the company confidently position themselves in every aspect of their business. The group believes that the new name provides the optimum balance between maintaining the heritage of the company and the synergies of global alignment with the corporate name of Unilever. The new logo tells the story of Unilever and vitality using 25 different icons representing Unilever and its brands, the idea of vitality and the benefits the company brings to consumers.

Meanings of some of the icons: The sun is the primary natural resource. All life begins with the sun—the ultimate symbol of vitality; the heart represents love, care and health—feeling good; the shirt represents fresh laundry— looking good; a bird is a symbol of freedom signifying relief from daily chores—getting more out of life; lips stand for beauty, looking good and taste.

Vodafone

The company's identity emphasized on the colour rather than the shape of a drop within a circle. They say 'Now it is red'. In 2006, Hutch took over Orange and painted the country pink and now Vodafone has gone ahead and painted it red. The Hutch mascot, was a pug dog that depicted the reach of the network, in that the dog followed everywhere. The mascot remains the same but the tag line with it has now changed to Vodafone's "willing to help you".

Recently there were charges of cruelty to the pug used in the advertisement. The charges had been leveled by the Animal Welfare Board of India (AWBI). In its notice sent to Vodafone April 25, 2008 AWBI said: "The pet dog was made to run, gallop and chase the school van for a long time on a public road. Thereby, the dog was made to undergo severe pain and suffering due to the exhaustion caused by chasing (the bus)."

A spokesman of mobile telephony denied charges based on the clarification given by the officials of Nirvana Films, which had made the ad for Vodafone. They said: "The AWBI is unaware of modern techniques of filmmaking. No single shot of a television commercial lasts more than 15 seconds at the most. Therefore, to suggest that the dog suffered due to exhaustion by chasing a bus is taking things a bit too far."

Reliance

After the split between the two brothers of Reliance group, the Anil Dhirubhai Ambani Group has come out with a new group logo without any visual association with the original logo of Reliance.

According to company sources, the logo consists of the word Reliance in capital letters in an entirely new font along with the line—Anil Dhirubhai Ambani Group.

A combination of blue and red colours is meant to convey solidity and the alphabet 'A' in the Reliance name has been converted into two arrows arching upwards.

The new logo had to reflect the group's business interests from telecommunications to entertainment, urban infrastructure to financial services, and energy to a new area such as healthcare. The need, therefore, was to evolve a logo that did not reflect any one specific product category.

Fever 104

The FM Channel Fever104 was launched on October 30, 2006 with a big bang, advertising it on the first two pages of *The Hindustan Times*. The front page of the advertisement looked like a regular newspaper page with musical notations similar to various fonts. There was no logo on the page, only the headline on the solus position of the page giving the theme of the advertisement. It wanted to create music fever among the young target group. It was a simple logo bold enough to stand out, showing a compact disk on which the Channel's name was written in outline letters. The letter V is manipulated to form an aerial with graphic sound waves on top, directly associating with the organization's activities. It's punch line says 'Less talk, more music'. Fever expanded its base to all the metros of the country giving due importance to regional music. The stations continue to uphold the Fever brand, and communicates and represents values such as vivaciousness, wittiness and fun. However, the new elements are in line with the evolving tastes and preferences of the listeners.

The channel will now have a good mix of regional music and conversation, interspersed with Hindi music and English interaction. One of the executives of the channel justified the change by adding, "If one looks back, one realizes that seven-eight years ago, Hindi as a language was in a similar position as that of, say, Kannada today. Earlier, Hindi was looked down upon as a secondary language, but the business arithmetic at work has turned the table in favour of the language. Today, Bollywood music rules the roost, cutting across age and class. Similarly, Kannada, too, is going to be a favourite with our target audience."

Indian

Indian Airlines, the domestic carrier in public sector underwent changes in its corporate identity several times, the last one in 2006. After independence it was a corporation and carried the logo of the two wings of a bird against the backdrop of the sun, combined with the three letters "IAC" (Indian Airlines Corporation), directly related with the company. In early 1980s it changed its trade name from Indian Airlines Corporation to Indian Airlines and so the logo continued with "IA", two stylized lineal letters graphically shaped into looking like the runway of an airport.

Now the Indian Airlines is simply "Indian". The new logo is a graphical image of a partial wheel inspired by the wheel of Konark Sun Temple. It abstractly gives the feeling of openness and vastness, and symbolizes the timeless motion. The new identity accompanied by the word "Indian" both in Devanagari and Roman emanates from its core value of being the epitome of Indian hospitality. The current design retains the type font and colour of the earlier mark to maintain continuity.

Simulation

In the following paragraphs two hypothetical examples, various steps of Corporate Identity Presentation are articulated.

Heritage Tea

Summary of the Identity Project

Company Profile: HERITAGE TEA is a modern tea emporium that offers a wide selection of the finest quality teas available in India. We are dedicated to leading the rediscovery of a "proper cup of tea" and sharing our passion for teas with tea lovers everywhere.

At Heritage we are passionate about one of the world's favorite drinks—tea. From picking the leaves from the best tea bushes and blending those leaves to create the perfect taste, to vacuum packing the tea and locking in the freshness. Every part in the Heritage process is dedicated to making sure you experience a perfect tea-drinking moment in every cup.

Marketing Plan: The company plans to have many tie-ups in South India and also with cafes selling our tea. Currently coffee is more famous in south India and a majority of the population there drinks coffee. We plan to target those people through our extensive marketing, and we will try to convince them to switch to our tea, thereby creating a huge unexplored market for our company.

Competitors: Tata Tea, Taj Mahal, Lipton, Red Label

Logo Logic

The logo consists of three elements:
1. Company Name: The logo is combined with company name 'HERITAGE' so that the customers can easily remember the company when they see the logo.
2. Leaf: It is directly associated with tealeaves.
3. Crown: The crown goes well with the name of the company that gives the company a royal look.

Colour Logic

Company name in Black. It is a colour of sophistication that signifies the company's image and also black stands out most in almost all circumstances.

Leaf in Green: It is the natural colour of tea leaves.

Crown in brown: The colour has the association with richness and heritage.

Coffeestop

Summary of the Identity Project

Company: Coffeestop is a chain of restaurants which primarily serve prepared coffee and other hot beverages.

From a cultural standpoint, Coffeestop restaurants largely serve as centres of social interaction: the coffeehouse provides people a place to congregate, talk, write, read, entertain one another, or pass the time, whether individually or in small groups. Coffee has been drunk in India since the 17th century, but it's consumption was largely confined to the southern part of the country.

Market: Coffeestop had its humble beginning in Chennai in 1982. Now it has an annual turnover of Rs 400 crores from 250 outlets mostly in metros with a large workforce. As the city culture is spreading to small towns, company is planning to open a large number of outlets in suburbs and small towns.

Expansion: Meanwhile, as part of its expansion plans, Coffeestop is tapping the home brew market and planning to launch a Coffeestop House Blend, a premium blend of Italian coffee. It has also made forays into branded merchandising that would include caps, coasters, CDs and cups, mugs, T shirt, etc.

Competitors: Barista, Café Coffee Day, Coffee House

Logo logic

Image: A stylized graphic shape of cup is chosen to identify the company's basic activities. The cup is the unchanged coffee drinking pot from Victorian era to modern microwave days. It is simple enough to remember and can be adopted on any surface in any size.

Colour: The logo is in two colour- brown and dark olive green. Green is the unroasted colour of coffee beans which turns into brown after roasting and goes to grinding and brewing. Dark olive green also signifies sophistication that clearly says that Coffeestop is for people a class apart.

Type font: Single font Arial is used in two different sizes with weight variations. Arial is one of the modern typestyles known for its uniform strokes that is not only going well with the shape of the image but also the company's intended identity as modern. Type weight and toning of some letters have created subtleness in the design.

Summary

Corporate identity represents both the intangible and tangible qualities of an organization. When a company or organization is perceived as modern, traditional, international or conservative etc., it can be termed as intangible, whereas graphic shape, logos, colour etc. that build the image of an organization are tangible. The combination of these two qualities develops the image of a corporate brand. The management of an organization is represented by PR persons. They work with creative professionals in designing various elements. It may start with a design brief explaining the company's present activities and future plan, gathering information to understand the business. Physical forms of the identity are then developed based on the creative concept evolved by the team. These are then presented before the top management for necessary amendments or approval. The chosen solution—made of various physical forms of the identity—are then implemented as the identity programme using various application areas identified by the company.

Critical thinking exercise

Identify one of the existing companies or create a new name for an imaginary company. Write down the profile of the company in terms of present activities, future expansion plan and competitor if there is any. Also mention the type of image it wants create among its audience. Redesign or create a new logo on computer. Prepare a PowerPoint presentation of your work explaining the various steps taken in developing the design

Questions

Q.1 Define corporate identity and discuss its need in developing the image of a company.

Q.2 How is a corporate identity developed? Write your answer mentioning the role and management and designer in this task.

Q.3 What are the points to be considered while selecting a good logo for an organization?

Q.4 Presentation of a visual solution of any form of communication is an important activity of Public Relations. How is it done for corporate identity?

Q.5 What is the role of PR Department of an organistion in popularizing the redesigned visual identity?

References

http://en.wikipedia.org/wiki/Corporate_identity accessed on October 2008

N.N Sarkar, *Art and Print Production* (New Delhi: Oxford University Press, 2008)

Jaishri Jethwaney and Shruti Jain, *Advertising Management* (New Delhi: Oxford University Press,2007)

Indian Symbology, "Proceedings of the Seminar on Indian Symbology" (Bombay: Industrial Design Centre, IIT, 1987).

Frank J. Romano and Richard M. Romano, *Encyclopedia of Graphic Communications* (USA: Prentice Hall PTR, 1998).

A Correspondent, "Logos Not Mere Symbols" (New Delhi; *Economic Times*, January 25, 1992)

Henry Dreyfuss, *Symbol Sourcebook* (New York: McGraw-Hill Book Company, 1972)

Satish Sud, "Logic of Logo: Corporate Identity" (New Delhi: *Economic Times*, January 25, 1992)

Faber Biren, *The Symbolism of Colour* (New Jersey: Citadel Press,1988)

Part III
UNDERSTANDING LEGALITIES AND PROFESSIONAL REQUIREMENTS

18 Public Relations – Laws and Ethics

Chapter Objectives
- Various laws concerning the profession of PR
- Code of ethics propounded by professional bodies

Public relations practitioners deal with a wide variety of publics. They have communication obligations to fulfill for which they utilize various kinds of mass media. While there are no specific laws to govern the profession of PR *per se*, but the mass media laws concerning the profession of journalism by and large are applied in PR practice. As the profession of PR requires an immense amount of writing for various stakeholders, so it is prudent that the practitioner has a thorough knowledge and understanding about the application of various laws.

In the following paragraphs we shall have a closer look at the aspects, viz., laws and ethics.

Defamation

Under the Indian Constitution, the fundamental right to free speech (Article 19) is subject to "reasonable restrictions". What is reasonable is subjective and the interpretation may vary from time to time depending upon the prevailing circumstances. The law of defamation widely made use of against the mass media occupies an important place in the Indian legal system. There are two independent components to this law, each of which operates independently of the other; the Criminal law of Defamation is contained in the Indian Penal Code, 1860, and the Civil law of Defamation in the Common Law. The Civil Law of Defamation is less clearly defined. It is to be found, not in any statutes, but in that age-old repository of legal wisdom, the Common Law of England—which continues to be followed in India with minor modifications to suit local situations.

Defining Defamation

Defamation is defined as wrong done by one person to another's reputation by words, signs, or visible representation. It is different from wrongful acts which injure reputation including assault involving disgrace, unlawful arrest or attachment, malicious prosecution or breach of contract like breach of promise of marriage, or a banker dishonouring his customer's cheque inspite of his having money in his account, and on the other, from words which cause damage to a person's property or business and not to his reputation.

The word defamation is a generic one and libel and slander are 'particular forms of it'. Let's define these two separately:

Libel

Any false statement about a person printed or broadcast and which brings upon the person hatred, contempt or inflicts mental torture or has an adverse impact on his occupation or business constitutes libel.

There have been many instances in the past when "aggrieved" persons and parties have sued newspapers, magazines and television channels for libel. PR professionals by the very nature of their profession have to write for various publics and this mundane activity may cost someone his job, if the practitioner is ignorant about the legal implications.

A PR practitioner once wrote a farewell note for a retiring officer in the house journal that she edited. A copy was sent to him, after which she received a complimentary letter from the gentleman, appreciating what she wrote about him. However, out of the blue, after about four-five months, she received a typed letter from the same gentleman threatening to sue her in the court of law, for what he thought was a libelous description of him in the said article, which said "Mr..... drew contrasts. He was the most loved and hated person simultaneously". He thought that by writing that he was 'hated', she had diminished his chances of re-employment, which he was seriously considering. The letter came as a total shock to her. It was clear that he was quoting the line out of context. At the same time, if he sued her, she would have to undergo the torture of going to another city to fight the case. The letter he had written earlier after receiving a copy of the house journal came to her rescue. She immediately discussed the issue with the legal wing of the company where she worked. They made a suitable reply in the legal jargon and sent him and that was the last she heard of the gentleman. The moral of the anecdote is that never take anything lightly. If in doubt, consult the rule book, a competent authority or experts. It is not worth hurting someone unwittingly or getting oneself in trouble.

Public relations aimed at creating a positive image also helps in building bridges, hence normally there should not be a problem, but it is worth taking precautions. In political PR however, where mud slinging is used as a matter of strategy, one needs to be careful. Most libel cases, in fact, happen because the writer or the publisher became careless. Libel, however, has three defences, viz., **truth, fair comment, criticism and privilege**. If the writer can prove that what he has written is true with documentary proof, he can fight the libel suit to his advantage. For example, if the writer called someone a criminal and he faced a suit, than he must prove through documentary evidence that indeed the man was convicted in a criminal case in a court of law. Similarly, while criticizing or commenting on someone's work, it has to be restricted to the work of the person and without malice. Celebrated author Khushwant Singh's preview of his biography in a publication earned the ire of Ms Maneka Gandhi. She felt some remarks about her in the book were libelous. She moved the Court urging it to order the author to expunge those references from the book before it hit the stands. The honourable Court gave the judgement in her favour and the author was asked to edit the book accordingly, which he did.

On the other, there are some documents of an official nature, which are immune to libel action. If quoted from such documents, libel action can be avoided under privilege. Sir Elton John, famous gay singer lost a defamation case in December 2008 against *Guardian* for publishing a spoof column on his AIDS charity dinner; which he felt was defamatory.

The column in verbatim

A peek at the diary of ...Elton John

What a few days it's been. First I sang Happy Birthday to my dear, dear friend Nelson Mandela—I like to think I'm one of the few people privileged enough to call him Madiba—at a party specially organized to provide white celebrities with a chance to be photographed cuddling him, wearing that patronizingly awestruck smile they all have. It says: "I love you, you adorable, apartheid-fighting teddy bear."

The next night I welcomed the exact same crowd to my place for my annual White Tie & Tiaras ball. Lulu, Kelly Osbourne, Agyness Deyn, Richard Desmond, Liz Hurley, Bill Clinton—I met most of them 10 minutes ago, but we have something very special and magical in common: we're all members of the entertainment industry. You can't manufacture a connection like that. Naturally, everyone could afford just to hand over the money if they gave that much of a toss about Aids research—as could the sponsors. But we like to give guests a preposterously lavish evening, because they're the kind of people who wouldn't turn up for anything less. They fork out small fortunes for new dresses and so on, the sponsors blow hundreds of thousands on creating what convention demands we call a "magical world", and everyone wears immensely smug "My diamonds are by Chopard" grins in the newspapers and OK!. Once we've subtracted all these costs, the leftovers go to my foundation. I call this care-o-nomics".

As seen by Marina Hyde

Sir Elton described the "A Peek At The Diary Of......." Column, published on 5 July 2008 as having a "gratuitously offensive, nasty and snide tone"

The newspaper defended its position arguing that it was a satirical piece of comment rather than a factual account.

The interim judgement hearing decreed "the words complained of ..... could not be understood by a reasonable reader of the Guardian weekend section as containing the serious allegation pleaded."

Commenting on the judgement, the Guardian reported: "In a groundbreaking libel decision, the judge said that "irony" and "teasing" do not amount to defamation. The ruling offers protection to writers of satirical articles clearly not meant to be taken seriously and was welcomed last night by media lawyers and journalists."

The judgement meant that Sir Elton, who had sought damages and apology was ordered to pay the costs. He however had the option to go to the Court against the judgement.

In retrospect, Sir Elton's £3,000 a head White Tie and Tiara Ball in June was able to raise £10 million from a celebrity auction that had the virtual who is who attending it, including former US President Bill Clinton, Elizabeth Hurley, Jemina Khan and Uma Truman. As per media reports, an unidentified bidder paid £6, 50,000 for dinner with Bill Clinton at Gordon Ramsay's New York restaurant.

Slander

Slander is very much like libel, except that it is verbal or spoken. It can occur in a broadcast, in a speech or in an informal conversation. It becomes slander, when a third party hears it. However, if someone wants to "fix" a person, it is not difficult for him to produce false witnesses. Parliamentarians in India enjoy the privilege of immunity on what they speak within the House. Reporting such comments also enjoy immunity from legal action provided these are accurate. But the same privilege is not available while reporting the proceedings of the state legislatures. Interestingly, however, in an age when parliament and state assemblies are covered live on television, people have witnessed, the hurling of chairs and shoes, not to speak of abuses – so does it really make a difference!

Defamation of a Corporation

The reputation of a human being differs from that of a company or a body of persons. A company, for instance, can't be accused of murder or immorality and can't sue for any such imputation. It can however complain of words in disparagement of its corporate property, business and reputation. It would be libelous, if someone said or published that the company was a bad paymaster or did not pay its contractors on time, if that were not true. Similarly a political body, professional association or social club may be able to sue when it suffers in public esteem by attacks on its corporate life or activities. For instance, if there was an allegation by someone or media that a political body promoted sedition or reputed social club was promoting immorality it would amount to defamation, if the allegation can't be sustained.

In an insightful article: "Defamation litigation – a Survivor's Kit", Subramanian Swamy, former Law minister has provided strategies from the rule book to be followed in the face of a litigation. Here is the first person account of how Mr. Swamy handled the defamation cases against him.

"I once received a summon from a Delhi Court because I had called a BJP leader, V.K. Malhotra, "an ignoramus." The remark was made by me during the Lok Sabha proceedings, but lifted by a sub-editor and inserted in a column I wrote for the magazine.

Under the law, I had to prove that it was true — or face imprisonment. Now, how does one prove that a person is an ignoramus in a court of law? Add to that the harassment I would have to suffer of travelling to court at least 10 times a year for at least five years to attend the case or face a warrant for my production in court. Or I would have to engage a lawyer who would charge me a hefty sum. All this for a mild rebuke of a political leader? The editor of the magazine decided he could not stomach it, so he apologised for printing the remark. I was left holding the bag.

However, I fought the case and won. Mr. Malhotra was directed to pay me Rs. 8,000 as compensation for my petrol bills, which he paid with some reluctance. Now how did I do it

I pulled out of my survival kit the first tool of defence: in a defamation case, the aggrieved person must prove "publication," which means Mr. Malhotra would have to prove first that I had, in the original text given to the magazine, written what was printed. The onus was on him to produce the original. Now which magazine keeps the original? He failed to produce it and I won.

In a 1997 press conference, I made some charges against Chief Minister M. Karunanidhi. He used Section 199 of the Criminal Procedure Code to get the Public Prosecutor to file a defamation case. This meant the contest in court was between me and the State, and not between me and the Chief Minister personally. Thus the Government would spend the money out of the public exchequer and use Government counsel to prosecute me, a totally unequal contest and wholly unfair (even if legal).

If Section 199 had not been there, the Chief Minister would have personally been the complainant and I would have had the right to cross-examine him. Now which busy politician would like that? Hence, I pulled out the second tool in my survival kit. I filed an application before the judge making the point that the alleged defamation related to the personal conduct of the Chief Minister and not to anything he did in the course of public duty. I argued that Section 199 would not apply. Thereafter, the State Public Prosecutor quickly lost interest in the case. Had the judge rejected my prayer, I would have gone in appeal to the Supreme Court and got Section 199 struck down. But alas, I could not.

In 1988 another Chief Minister, Ramakrishna Hegde, filed a suit against me under tort law for Rs.2 crore damages for my allegation that he was tapping telephones and using his office to benefit a relative in land deals. Although ultimately, the Kuldip Singh Commission and a parliamentary committee studying the Telegraph Act upheld my contentions, I would have had a problem had the court decided the case before these inquiry reports came out.

So I pulled out the third tool in my survival kit, namely the U.S. Supreme Court case laws, the most famous of which was *The New York Times* case decided in 1964. Contrary to popular impression, U.S. case laws on fundamental rights are applicable to India following a Supreme Court judgement in an *Indian Express* case in 1959.

Furthermore, since 1994, these U.S. case laws have become substantially a part of Indian law, thanks to Justice Jeevan Reddy's judgement in the *Nakkeeran* case.

> The principle in these case laws, restricted to public persons suing for damages, is wonderfully protective of free speech: if a person in public life, including one in government, feels aggrieved by a defamatory statement, then that person must first prove in court that the defamatory statement is not only false, but that the maker of the statement knew it to be false. That is, it must be proved by the defamed plaintiff to be a reckless disregard of the truth by the defamer defendant. This principle thus reversed the traditional onus on the defamer to prove his or her allegation, and placed the burden of proof on the defamed.
>
> This reversal of burden of proof is just, essentially because a public person has the opportunity to go before the media and rebut the defamation in a way aggrieved private persons cannot do. If criticism and allegations against a public person have to be proved in a court of law, what is likely to happen is that public spirited individuals will be discouraged and thus dissuaded from making the criticism. This is what the U.S. Supreme Court in the famous *New York Times* case characterised as a "chilling effect" on public debate; it held this to be bad for democracy.
>
> Hence the need to balance the protection of reputation in law with the democratic need for transparency and vibrant public debate. The U.S. Supreme Court admirably set the balance for freedom and democracy.
>
> Today, with developing case laws, defamation litigation has become a toothless tiger for politicians to use against the media. There are enough dental tools in my survival kit to ensure this. [1]

It is uncommon especially in India for a bureaucrat to slam a defamation threat to a politician, but it happened in 2008. A 1994 batch IPS officer Paresh Saxena sent a legal notice to Bihar Minster Bhola Singh warning him of a defamation suit if he did not tender an apology for humiliating him at a public function. According to the notice, Sing**h** 'badly insulted and demoralised' the officer by using 'offending, libelous and defamatory' language at a function for not presenting a bouquet to the minister. The notice quoted the minister as saying *'Shasan hum karte hain, adhikari nahi'*.[2]

According to an ANI report, a number of celebrities were suing media for defamation, making London the defamation capital of world celebrities. Media experts believe that one reason for the greater willingness among celebrities to go to court when they are harshly treated in the press is the increasing influence of the celebrity lawyer over the star's agent. While an agent may argue in favour of "all publicity is good publicity", the lawyer can now offer the client a chance of a libel victory with the payoffs. [3]

Invasion of privacy

There is no statutory enactment expressly guaranteeing a general right of privacy to Indian citizens, but elements of this right as traditionally contained in Common Law are recognized by courts in India. In addition two pieces of legislation recognize this right viz., The Children's Act, 1960, and The Hindu Marriage Act, 1955, which impose similar restrictions on publication of reports concerning, proceedings under the Act. The Code of Criminal Procedure, 1973, also permits restrictions to be imposed on the publication of reports concerning certain proceedings, i.e. rape trials. In the last decade or so, no issue has been as much in focus as the issue of invasion of privacy.

The tragic death of Princess Diana was ascribed by many to the invasion of privacy. Her brother said publicly at her burial mass that the hands of the media were indeed bloodied by her death.

Photographer Gallilo was so obsessed with the life of Jackie Kennedy that he followed her with his camera wherever she went. So sick was she that she sued Gallilo for invading her privacy. He pleaded innocence in the court of law. He argued that Mrs. Kennedy, wife of slain American President John F Kennedy was a public figure, and he had every right to shoot her because that was his livelihood. In a landmark judgement, the Court allowed him to continue with his professional job but from a distance of some meters!

In more recent times, photo journalist Jamie Fawcett who was chasing Hollywood actress Nicole Kidman lost a defamation case against an Australian newspaper that said he wanted to "wreak havoc" on actress Nicole Kidman's private life with the court agreeing he was a "cowboy." The New South Wales State Supreme Court ruled that the article saying photographer Jamie Fawcett was a "cowboy" who once dubbed himself the "Prince of Paparazzi" and who was determined "to wreak havoc on Kidman's private life," was not defamatory.[4]

During the hearing, Kidman told the court that Fawcett chased her car across Sydney in 2005 at speeds, which made her crouch on the back seat, tearful and frightened of crashing. The Hollywood star said Fawcett's car and another vehicle drove "dangerously, mounting concrete traffic barriers and driving through red traffic lights in the pursuit."

Judge Simpson justified keeping in view the nature of Fawcett job who made his living from taking and selling candid photographs ... of famous people. He, she argued, had made a goal of obtaining photographs of Ms Kidman for which he had waited all day, unrewarded, for a photograph of her. So, he was clearly motivated to obtain such a photograph, and he recognized that his remaining opportunities on that evening were very limited indeed," she said. Therefore, she said, "the evidence amply demonstrates that Mr. Fawcett's conduct was 'intrusive' and 'threatening'."[5]

Indian media, especially the news channels of late has been drawing flak for coverage of crime, especially when they covered the Arushi murder case in 2008. The media sensationalism and their invasion to privacy received a comment from chief Justice K G Balakishnan when he said, "journalism must not encroach upon people's right to privacy". This he said while inaugurating a workshop on reporting at the Bombay High Court. "Privacy of the person," he commented, "must be protected. Sometimes, damaging information is revealed during the investigation. It adversely affects people's right to a fair trial". The Chief Justice said that sometimes, the media gave so much information on the victim, especially of sexual assault, that it was not difficult to know who the person was, even if the name was concealed. He however said, that newspapers can't be as drab as government gazettes, so a "tinge of sensationalism is necessary". Commenting on the lack of editorial control on live coverage in the electronic media, he lamented, "in a paper, it is possible to edit material, but on television, when a reporter's version is directly broadcast, there is no editorial control".[6]

The PR practitioners working in hospital public information need to be very careful. The privacy of patients and their medical records have to be maintained scrupulously. In medico-legal cases, care and sensitivity is necessary. In case the media insists on taking an interview or photograph of such patients, it is important that necessary permissions in writing are taken from the patient and guardian, in case of children. Hidden camera/recorder techniques should never be allowed. Not only are these illegal but unethical as well. The emergence of AIDS has posed difficult ethical problems confronting the media. The syndrome has aroused acute public curiosity and anxiety. Because of the social stigma attached to it, it is only prudent that both media and people in charge of public information safeguard the identity of people living with HIV and AIDS. Similarly, in giving a statement about the condition of a patient, the doctor should never offer prognosis. In the case of the death of a prominent person, the hospital has the responsibility to inform the next of the kin before releasing information to the media.

Copyright

The copyright act grants the copyright owner the exclusive right to publish, print, or reproduce an original literary, musical, or artistic work for a certain number of years. The copyright also extends to illustrations, plays, musical works, motion pictures, sound recordings, graphics, sculptures, pantomimes and dances. The aim of a copyright is to secure for the creator of the material all the benefits accruing from the creation. The law provides exclusive right for life of the creator and 50 years beyond for those who own the copyright. The year 1992 marked the end of embargo on the works of Nobel Laureate Rabinranath Tagore. The copyright is vested with Vishwa Bharti. The organization lobbied and was able to secure an extension of ten years of copyright for them from the Government. This meant extension for others as well. Post 2002, Tagore's works are in the public domain for use and adaptation.

In the case of the National Council of Education Research and Training (NCERT) that publishes books for school children, the copyright rests with it. Until recently only seven states in India were using NCERT textbooks in their schools. Five more states were included for extension of copyright to these states, Bringing the total number of schools covered by NCERT books to 13,727 secondary schools. With this, 31.3% of 8,736 CBSE- affiliated senior secondary schools in India and abroad have been covered. The 12 states include the following: Andhra Pradesh, Sikkim, Uttranchal, Himachal Pradesh, Delhi, Jharkhand, Bihar, Chattisgarh, Haryana, Kerala, Punjab and Goa.[7]

The invention of Photostat machines in a way has played havoc with books, especially textbooks. But then it is very difficult to catch the culprits. The PR practitioners need to be careful not to reproduce material in their publications or audio and video clips beyond what the act stipulates. Fair use for purpose of criticism, comment, news reporting, teaching, scholarship, or research does not amount to infringement.

Imitating the voice or mannerisms of well-known personalities and artists, for commercial purposes is also tantamount to violating the right. Famous Hollywood actress Audrey Hepburn sued a fishing company which imitated her voice in a radio commercial. This practice is not uncommon in India, especially the imitated voice of celebrities like Late Ajit, Amitabh Bachchan, Shahrukh Khan and among the politicians, Mr. Lalu Prasad Yadav.

The Indian Performing Right Society ltd. (IPRS) and Phonographic Performance Ltd. (PPL) issued an ad before the festive season in December 2008 which exhorted the people who organized parties to take the license before playing any music which was copyrighted. The ad read: " Good Food, Wine, Dance, but no Music!!!" the ad was addressed to "Event Organizers/Hotels/Restaurants, X'Mas week and new year night party goers" who were warned that " playing music in public without obtaining the license from PPL and IPRS was an offence under the copyright Act 1957. Noncompliance with the requirement was tantamount to violation of the copyright Act, which was a cognizable and non-bailable offence, which would attract penalty up to Rs. 2.00 lakhs and 3 years of imprisonment. The ad then went on to warn: "More important, your party may be stopped by the police. The ad ended with: "Issued in public Interest by The Indian Music Industry". The organization published the ad in many newspapers just before X'Mas on 25 December 2008. Warning the event managers and the public at large is a sign of companies asserting about their rights. The copyright violation has been going on unabated in India for decades, at times due to ignorance of the law. The warning through a mass media ad may bring in the necessary caution among violators.

Some acts relating to Advertising

Most PR practitioners use advertising as a tool of communication. There are certain laws and enactments that are directed specifically at the industry, which determine both the broad framework within which the industry is allowed to operate and the content of its output. Some of these include the following:

Public Morals and Public Policy: Section 292 and 293 of the Indian Penal Code, 1860, prohibits the dissemination of any obscene matter. The Indian Post Office Act, 1898, imposes a similar prohibition on the transmission of obscene matter through the post. The Customs Act, 1962, allows the detention and seizure of any obscene matter sought to be imported to the country.

The Young Persons [harmful Publication] Act, 1956, prohibits the dissemination of publication deemed to be harmful to persons under the age of twenty years.

The Indecent Representation of Women [Prohibition] Act, 1986, prohibits the depiction of women in an indecent or derogatory manner in the mass media.

The Children Act, 1960, prohibits the disclosure of the name and address and other particulars of any child involved in certain proceedings.

The Emblems and Names [Prevention of Improper Use] Act, 1950, forbids the use by any private party of certain names, emblems, etc.

The Prevention of Insults to the National Honour Act, 1971, forbids the bringing into contempt of the national flag or the Constitution of India in any manner.

The Indian Penal Code, 1860, prohibits the publication of any matter connected with unauthorized lotteries, while the Indian Post Office Act, 1998, imposes a similar prohibition on the transmission by post of such matter.

The Drugs and Magic Remedies [Objectionable Advertisements] Act, 1954, prohibits advertisements for products and services claiming to cure certain medical conditions.

The Indian Penal Code, 1869, prohibits, the publication of appeals using national symbols for furthering the prospects of any candidate at an election.

The Prize Competition Act, 1978, prohibits the publication of matter with unauthorized prize competitions, while the Prize Chits and Money Circulation Schemes [Banning] Act, 1978, imposes a similar prohibition in respect of chits and money circulation schemes. The provisions of law imposing limitations on message/content in the media apply *mutatis mutandis* to advertising as well, with such modifications as the context may require. It is in the interest of the practitioners to have copies of these acts handy for reference and at the same time keep an eye on various judgements, which appear in the media. Ignorance of law does not provide any protection to the defaulters.

PR Ethics

When we talk about ethics in a profession, what is generally at the back of minds is, the fear of lack of ethics or the confusion about what is ethical and what is not.

Ethics in any profession is governed by two factors:
- A code of professional ethics developed by a professional body.
- Conscience and grooming of a PR practitioner as a human being.

The code of ethics in Public Relations originally known as the "Code of Athens" made in 1965 has been adopted by the Public Relations Societies in various countries. The PR code is inspired by the Universal Declaration of Human Rights of Man adopted by the United Nations Organization [UNO] on December 10, 1948. Some of the highlights of the code include:
1. To encourage free circulation of information.
2. To deserve the confidence of all those one comes in contact with.

3. To demonstrate exemplary conduct in public private behaviour.
4. To respect and uphold the dignity of human person.
5. To recognize the right of parties involved to explain their point of view.

The PR persons **must not**:

- Subordinate truth to any other considerations.
- Disseminate information not factually correct.
- Lend assistance to any enterprise which might harm the morality, honesty, dignity of the human race.
- The use of such words that make receivers act irrationally.

Quoting John F. Kennedy who once said: 'all businessmen are sons of bitches'. [His comment to reporters came during a 1962 steel strike], Paul Fireman, Chief Executive and Chairman of Reebok International while addressing ethics executives from over 20 countries said that since his company became involved in advocating human rights and labour practices, its business had thrived overseas. Horror stories about children in third world countries working as child labour could become rarer; felt Fireman, only if US shops could become more sensitive to cultural differences. The day Coke made its re-entry in India, in the early 90s, when rival Pepsi was well entrenched, it looked odd, but on one of the pages a mainstream newspaper had the Coke ad, while the business page carried a box item report about child labour in a Coke factory. Even though the timing was coincidental, it damaged the reputation of the company which was making a cautious entry in the country from where it was asked to leave lock, stock and barrel in 1977.

Medical profession is generally termed a "Noble" profession by common people. Pharma companies, however, go out of the way to lure doctors to recommend their drugs. Hospitals in the private sector look and practice like corporate behemoths. With medical insurance gaining ground, it is not uncommon that some of these hospitals in league with insurance agents squeeze both the patients and the companies.

Mainstream newspaper, *The Times of India* in a front page story "Is your doc. being bribed to suggest medicines?" wrote that many pharma companies were doling out goodies which clearly was a case of conflict of interest, but who cared! Doctors, it is alleged are given various kinds of coupons to earn freebies. For instance if drug X was prescribed by a doctor to 10 patients, he/she would be entitled for a platinum coupon, a gold coupon, if brand Y was prescribed to 25. The more coupons a medico got, more were his chances of winning various prizes that may include a car, frost free refrigerator, TV sets, digital camera and silver coins.

For instance in one case, 100 doctors who topped the prescribers' charts from cities like Ahmedabad, Chennai, Alwar, Belgaum, Ambala and Agra participated in a lucky draw were awarded publicly by Gujarat based Torrent Pharmaceutical. The same company took other doctors to Turkey as a part of an international symposium on metabolic medicines. The same company took a group of Sri Lankan doctors to a safari in Kenya for "education" as reported by the publication.

Interestingly, the story points out that these were not allegations, but the information was available on the company's website. The promotion offer is worded: "Torrent has once again raised the bar in offering a perfect combination of knowledge sharing and hospitality in the pharma industry". [8]

If we were to analyze the above case study, it's clear that the company does not think there is any ethical issue involved in such promotions, which is quite surprising! Pharma companies set aside budgets worth crores of rupees to entertain doctors in what are generally termed as education symposia. These are organized in five star hotels and are attended by thousands of doctors regularly.

Diagnostic equipment centres openly share a "cut" with doctors who refer patients to them. Doctors frequently send patients for MRI and CT scan diagnosis. It is not uncommon to see dozens of such diagnostic centres mushrooming around large government hospitals which may not have the facilities but the doctors do recommend such tests to patients.

In India such promotions continue unabated. It is expected that there will be self regulations on the part of various pharma companies and the ethics of doctors. The Indian Drug Manufacturing Association (IDMA) and Organization of Pharmaceutical Producers of India (OPPI) on paper have a code of ethics for marketing practices along with receiving and examining complaints, but nothing really happens. Some people in IDMA and OPPI feel that in the absence of penal powers, the associations could do precious little. Government regulations, however, could help address the menace.

Many countries have brought in legislation to stop these unethical marketing practices. The penalties are also stiff. According to the report, over 25 medical centres in the USA and Europe including the Harvard Medical School, University of California and the Stanford School of Medicine have put in place strong policies that include zero tolerance for company gifts and free meals. Some of the cases against practitioners in other countries may help address the issue in India.

In September 2007 in the USA, five Arthtotics companies accounting for nearly 95 per cent of hip and knee surgical implants in the USA had to pay $310 million in penalty for paying surgeons thousands of dollars per year as consulting contracts and sending them on lavish trips and expensive perks to get them to choose their products.

Bristol-Myers Aquibb Company had to pay $515 million in January 2007 as penalty on the proven charge of paying illegal remuneration to physicians and healthcare providers in the form of consulting fees and travel to luxurious resorts in return of promoting BMS drugs.

Neuro-surgeon Patrick Chan had to shell out a penalty of $1.5 million in January 2008 for taking hefty kickbacks from medical suppliers.

Bio-tech firm Cephalon had to pay $425 million on charges of spending millions of dollars of grants to continue medical education programmes to promote off-label use of its drugs. It also gave illegal kickbacks to physicians.

Often ethical issues and concerns, especially when reported in the media become PR issues for the company as the image of the company is at stake. There is however little PR can do to salvage the damage for unethical practices.

This is a dilemma the PR professionals generally find themselves in. The issue of ethics has to be seen more deeply than just looking at a professional code. A person's value system and his beliefs are very important in making him what he turns out to be as a professional. The code may be like a beam of light to steer him through the haze, but his beliefs make him the real professional. Ethics is not an issue governed from outside, but one lives with it.

Summary

In this chapter we discussed that there are no specific laws governing the profession of PR. However the various laws that concern the field of journalism are also relevant to PR. Laws of defamation, invasion to privacy and law of copyright were discussed in detail. A number of case studies were discussed to make understanding about application of laws easier.

The chapter also looked at PR ethics. Some salient features of the Code of Ethics adopted by the Public Relations Society of India were also included.

Laws and ethics in fact go hand in hand. Most of the time legal issues become image issues, especially when made public.

Critical thinking exercise

Study the various laws and code of ethics and case studies reflected in the chapter carefully. Follow trends in the media about companies that have got embroiled due to unethical practices (For example, Satyam Computers, 2009).

Questions

Q.1 Describe the similarities and differences between libel and slander?

Q.2 What do you understand by the term "invasion to privacy"? Discuss with examples.

Q.3 What is the role of a professional code of ethics? Give salient features of PRSI Code of Professional Ethics.

Endnotes

[1] http://www.hindu.com/2004/09/21/
[2] Friday, 31 October 2008 | http://www.nerve.in/news:253500177192
[3] http://www.andhranews.net/Intl/2008/October/13/
[4] http://www.reuters.com
[5] http://www.reuters.com
[6] *The Times Of India*, 20 October 2008
[7] *The Times of India, Education Times,* 12 January 2009
[8] *The Times Of India*, 15 December 2008

19 PR: An Agenda for Tomorrow

PR is all about publics and perceptions. It relates to issues and works as a barometer of changing trends. When we talk of the agenda for tomorrow, it boils down to understanding what issues are we anticipating to concern societies and nations and industry and what responses are we seeking from Public Relations? In the new millennium, not only have the problems from the last century sneaked in, some have even got reinforced. Let's look at the state of various challenges staring in our faces.

Societal

At the societal level, the world has witnessed deteriorating values. Economic pressures among others have reduced families to nuclear units. Progressive disintegration of the institution of marriage is increasing the number of single parent homes, drug use, the scourge of HIV and AIDS, the impatience of the growing inspirational class, crisis of identity specially among the youth, religious fanaticism, racism, parochialism, terrorism—to name a few problems—are facing the human race. With issues getting entangled and more complex, we may never be able to get to the root of the causes of some problems. Some of the maladies however demand immediate redressal. The potentially worst carnage of the last century, the Acquired Immune Deficiency Syndrome (AIDS) to some extent seem in control in the new millennium as more and more people are informed, but the availability of Anti-retroval drugs is yet to be within the access of all those living with HIV or AIDS. Despite almost two decades of its existence, there is still stigma attached to the syndrome. People living with HIV and AIDS are forced to live on the fringes, especially in traditional and superstitious societies making the task of informing, educating and communicating; challenging, if not impossible to achieve.

The issues relating to HIV and AIDS are not the responsibility of the governments alone. The whole society has to wake up to the challenge. To illustrate the point, in the Indian context one of the high risk groups for AIDS is industrial workers, especially migrant labour from villages, who leave their families behind and come back home once in a couple of years. Their life styles have exposed them, and in turn their spouses and unborn children, to the possibility of acquiring AIDS. It is the responsibility of the corporate sector to inform and educate the workers about the issue through various channels. Bharat Petroleum Corporation (Ltd) a public sector enterprise, for example has initiated a programme on educating its workers and others on drugabuse. Apollo tyres runs an extensive programme for truckers on HIV and AIDS.

Similarly, the youth must be educated about the causes and the preventive measures, by the universities. The sex workers and drug users, among others, have to be educated about the precautions in their self-interest also. Someone has rightly said: "Until now the problems of mankind have been one of nature. From now on they will be ones of human nature."

If only women were treated equally and had a voice, the world would be a better place to live in. For centuries, women who comprise half the human race have been subjected to untold atrocities, discrimination, sexual harassment at the workplace, domestic violence and a general marginalization. The efforts of many crusaders, feminists and advocacy groups have resulted in bringing the issue in focus. Many research studies have reflected the media in stereotyping woman as an unequal and a submissive partner at home and at work. Gender sensitization is an area that needs to be taken up seriously at all levels, governmental and non-governmental.

From professional communicators, specially those involved in formulating strategies and those in creative writing and visualization, society will demand that they set their gender perspectives right. Projecting women as sex symbols in advertisements has earned the ire of many right-thinking people and such issues have become PR issues.

The United Nations has been designating various years to focus attention on issues concerning the human race. However, large scale efforts have to be made by national governments and donor organizations including international bodies, to solve the problems of hunger, inequality, diseases, wars, terrorism, devastation, increasing chasms among nations on various social, political, economic and governance issues.

Communication will be imperative in reaching out to not only to decision makers but those whose lives are affected. Public relations practitioners will surely be put to the test while creating communication strategies and right media channels to reach out to a disparate audience.

The occurrence of 9/11 in the USA, the various terrorist attacks in various countries, especially South Asian countries, the 26/11 attack on Mumbai and the unending Israel-Palestine issue that has seen scores of innocent people dying, is a grim reminder about what the perpetrators of violence are capable of. Some nations that have becomes hubs of terrorism have to realize that the onslaught on the neighbouring states would not spare their own people from the very forces the states have created and nurtured.

More than war, it is terrorism that the UN has to address more closely. A consensus is required to be built on rogue states, which need to be isolated diplomatically.

Media unfortunately becomes an active player as information disseminator in the drama of terrorism. Media has to realize that it is being stage-managed by violent groups to create an environment of fear through words and visual imagery that result in bruising the psyche of the common man for a long time. The Mumbai siege by Pakistani terrorists in November 2008 was covered live non-stop by dozens of news channels for 64 hours, an act which has received a lot of flak from many quarters. It is believed that the live coverage helped the terrorists in strategizing their acts keeping in view the movement of security forces.

The 9/11 attacks also reflected the preparedness of the terrorist groups to the extent that they kept a gap of 20 minutes between hitting two towers, so that the media could reach in the meantime and cover the razing of the second Tower live.

The choice of date, i.e., September11 was also not without planning. (In the USA, the month is referred before the date, hence 9/11). 911 is the emergency number in the USA. The terrorist group succeeded in creating an "emergency" resulting also in an imagery that will be difficult to erase from the minds of the people at large and the fact that the security agencies of the most powerful nation had no inkling that an act so dastardly, using their own aircrafts could happen on their soil.

The Media will have to do a lot of introspection and come out with a code of conduct as to how to cover terrorism so that they are not guilty of unwittingly lending support to the forces that are antisocial and inhuman.

Economic

At the economic level, globalization has been the corporate *mantra* since the early nineties. With increasing foreign investments, collaborations and tie-ups, not only have the products to match international standards, communication has to respond to varying "publics" keeping in view the local culture, ethos, and prejudices. Gurcharan Das, argues, *"Globalisation does not mean imposing homogeneous solutions in a pluralistic world. It means having a global vision and strategy, but it also means cultivating roots and individual identities. It means housing local insights, but it also means re-employing communicable ideas in new geographies around the world".*[1]

Redefining the concept of lending in Bangladesh, Muhammad Yunus, Nobel Laureate challenges, "Let's now ask banks who is credit worthy: the rich who do not pay back or the poor who do?"[2]

CK Prahlad, the former Professor at IIM (A) in India now a Professor of Corporate Strategy at the ROSS School of Business speaks about the fall of dominant logic. He suggests that in order to create a future, we need to unlearn the past.

Dominant logic, he argues, is the result of a pattern of socialisation, most of the people are susceptible to. To quote him, "there was a time when the general belief was that the developed markets are the source of innovation and the benefits of their innovation may flow over time to emerging economies like India. That the opposite could be true, that the world could be more equitable and that innovation could flow from the emerging markets to developed markets was never seriously considered. Why is the obvious sometimes so hard to recognize? Is it because of the tyranny of the dominant logic?" Supporting his argument he gives the example of emerging economies becoming the laboratory of new business models. In India, where a large number of people live in abject poverty, there is also a young class of consumers who want world class goods and services at low prices. The challenge is to figure out how to do it. Prahlad talks about "disruptive innovations" that would take into account the size of the market. He gives the example of disruptive products like Re.1 shampoo sachet that revolutionized the market especially in the rural hinterland; $30 mobile phones, $30 cataract operations at an eye hospital, and $2000 Nano from Tatas.[3]

There are umpteen examples, not to forget McDonalds' pricing strategy in India that is unmatchable, Rs. 10/- an ice cream scoop and Rs. 20/- a burger.

Consumerism is fast picking up the world over. Industry can no longer take the consumer for a ride. The emergence of consumer forums, quick redressal at consumer courts and the intervention of the media has made a major difference. Public relations will have to work as a close ally of marketing and advertising departments to meet the challenge.

Political

On the political front, if we witnessed the unification of Germany, the disintegration of the USSR, was also a stark reality—a logical culmination of people's desire for an open system and a vote against regimentation. The growing ethnic violence against one's own brethren, group rivalries and racial hatred has led to widespread death and destruction. Military intervention to combat violence, and reaching out to innocent victims with help and succour, have given an additional role and responsibility to governments, non-governmental and international bodies

On the one hand, technology and the media have helped shrink the world, on the other, the increasing chasm in the thinking of nations needs more openness and effective communication to build bridges of understanding. "Today the encompassing issue is", writes Peter Jackson, editor of *PR Reporter*, "whether humanity will eradicate itself through nuclear weapons, chemical warfare, or perhaps genetic mis-engineering. Of the disciplines available for dealing with this ultimate problem, the one that is directly relevant here is the science and art we know as Public Relations".

Environmental

Growing environmental degradation and its repercussions have put to test the wisdom of many a government and international funding organization who in the name of development have probably irreparably damaged some areas.

Environmentalists and many advocacy groups have launched quite an impressive public relations campaign to mobilize public opinion against some such projects.

A gripping British television documentary by John Pilgar, *War by Other Means* graphically depicts the devastation in the Philippines to the rain forests and other arable land caused by building projects funded by the International Monetary Fund (IMF) and the World Bank (WB). In its new World Development Report, the Bank acknowledges other horrible results in Brazil, Indonesia and Sri Lanka.

In India, the Sardar Sarovar hydroelectric project was completed despite the hue and cry raised by thousands of people who lost their home and hearth and the efforts put in by advocacy organizations. Whether or not to fund projects that pave the way for "development" at the cost of the people who live on the fringes is an area that needs a revised policy consideration in funding by organizations like the World Bank.

The Green Movement and environment-friendly products are the latest concepts catching on. Public relations will find itself at the centre stage of these issues in the years to come.

Is the scenario only grim, or is there something to cheer about? There obviously is a lot to cheer about. The last two decades have seen most of the changes driven by technology. The new millennium has reinforced the trends of the Nineties – the increasing access to the world wide web, the social networking sites, access to mobile phones, the blogsphere have helped create a flat world, where nationalities, geographies have lost their separate identities. Public opinion is formed on issues that concern the human race cutting across narrow boundaries of nationalism.

The triumph of Barack Obama in the USA is seen as a victory of not a person or a political ideology but of hope and aspirations of millions of people all over the world who have lived for generations in an unequal world divided by colour and race, among other things.

Are PR professional equipped to take on the challenge?

Are the public relations practitioners equipped to respond to the issues, some of which are referred to above? Let us see the tools available to them.

Information technology has taken giant strides in the last couple of decades. Electronic techniques help transmit large amounts of information over long distances in no time. This was not possible a few years ago. Satellite communication has complemented electronic technology by making information cost-effective and has helped bring the nations close together. Today the world is networked with the Internet—a medium that ensures non-regimentation. The Internet is an ocean and the opportunities immense. The third transmission technology is fiber optics—tiny threads of glass, one-sixteenth the width of a human hair—which have the capability of carrying several thousand vocal conversations, or TV pictures, or computer streams of information over long distances, even under sea, is the in thing. The fourth screen, the mobile telephone has revolutionized the life of people, especially those who were not touched by the information revolution of the last century, people living in the hinterlands. The technology is being increasingly used for accessing information, for communication and business opportunities. The Indian Farmers and Fertilizers Corporation (IFFCO) in alliance with a service provider has made the access of mobile phone voice over alerts to an average farmer in thousands of villages. The voice over alerts informs them about various fairs and *haats* for sale and purchase of agriculture produce on a day to day basis. Community radio opportunities in some Indian villages also take up discussion on price of agricultural produce so that farmers get the best value for their produce. These technologies, complemented by innovations in printing technology, colour reproduction, use of computer graphics, desktop publishing, and use of computers for research have given tremendous opportunities to public relations practitioners. Many believe that the changes in future will be all technology-driven. Does technology force a change in society or vice versa, however, is a moot point.

The media scene has taken a 180-degree turn. If anything has helped in fulfilling the dream of the world turning into a global village, it is undoubtedly satellite media. In the Indian context, one finds a proliferation of satellite channels since the beginning of nineties. Today an average home has hundreds of channels to choose from. It is estimated that the cumulative programming per day works out at more than 3000 hours. This also brings about opportunities for public relations practitioners to make use of the media to remain proactively in focus.

Can mass communication be a substitute for interpersonal communication and folk media, especially in the context of Indian society? The answer is, both have to complement each other. With a spurt in technology on the one hand, and the multifarious challenges, it is increasingly felt that a modern organization can no longer use the tools in isolation from different forces at work. Advertising, public relations, promotion, information, market research, direct and indirect marketing, rural media and Internet and telemarketing all need integrated communication. After all, the main objective is reaching out to different publics for selling a product, service or an idea. Everyone needs a climate of understanding and a human approach.

With the world turning into a virtual cauldron of simmering problems, societies, nations and the human race as a whole, need a humane approach and a healing touch. And it is hoped that Public Relations that is symmetrical and non-manipulative, would find its true identity and recognition in doing the needful.

Endnotes

[1] Gurcharan Das, Ex. Vice-President of Procter and Gamble in *The Harvard Business Review*, April 1993
[2] *The Indian Express*, 12 April 2009.
[3] CK Prahlad, *Economic Times*, CD, in "Guru Guide", quoting his address on the opening address at the strategy management society conference at Indian School of Business at Hyderabad, January 9, 2009.

Glossary

A size paper: Series of finished trimmed sizes in ISO International paper sizes range. A0 (841 x 11 89mm) is the first size and is one square meter in area

Account: A client of a public relations or advertising agency

Advertising: Presenting persuasive material to the public via paid space or broadcast time to promote a product, idea or service

Analog pictures: Continuous flow of pictures on computer screen, film or video produced by varying electrical voltage, as opposed to digital, which refers to numerical values

Animation: A motion picture production from drawings, each successive drawing showing a very slight change of position so that a series of them give the effect of definite movement

Artwork: Line drawing, a photograph and a continuous-tone or halftone illustration, for the purpose of reproduction is called artwork. Abbreviation of artwork is art

Audio Visual Communication: Communication by means of electronic devices, which usually involves screen and visual images, as opposed to printed material

Audit Bureau of Circulation: The organization sponsored by publishers, agencies, and advertisers to secure accurate circulation statements

Bit map image: These images are formed by rectangular grid of small squares, known as pixel. Each pixel contains data that describes whether it is black, white, or a level of colour

Bleed: Running an art to the edge of a page. The effect is produced by printing a bit on an inch of an inch of an image beyond the desired dimension and then trimming the sheet to obtain the bleed

Blurb: A brief paragraph of verbal copy written as promotional text for a book jacket or highlighting the essence of an article or some parts of it, in a magazine or book

Brainstorming: The creative process of a group thinking about and articulating ideas on a given subject or problem, generally recorded for future evaluation and use

Broadcast: The disseminations of programmes or messages through radio or television

Brochure: Usually refers to a printed piece containing six or more pages

Byline: Name of the writer positioned under the headline at the beginning of the story

Cable TV: Distant and interference-free images received on a TV screen by means of wires rather than by means of an antenna receiving signals from a broadcast station

Camera-ready copy: The complete page or a publication assembled with text and graphics and ready to be photographed as the first step in the process of making plates, for offset printing

Character kerning: Adjusting space between two adjacent letters so that one is positioned within the space

Client: The organization or person who retains an outside agency for specialised services

Closed Circuit TV: Live video-tape or film material transmitted by cable for private viewing on a TV monitor

Colour registration: Placement of printing formes, plates or negatives in such a way so that they will print in a correct position over another forme or plate, as in colour printing

Communication: The art of transmitting information, ideas and attitudes from one person to another through verbal and/or visual symbols. Requires sender, message and receiver

Content Analysis: The technique of reading publications/advertisements/messages to find references to an organization or an idea, then coding and analysing the content to determine trends and opinions

Contingency Plan: A written plan prepared in advance to be put into effect only if certain specified events occur

Continuous tone: An illustration or photograph — whether black-and-white or colour — that consists of many shades between the lightest and the darkest tones, and which is not broken up into dots

Copy-editing: It can be defined as working over copy and preparing it for publication by improving the clarity and correctness of exposition specifically instructing the printer on matters concerning typesetting

Corporate Colour: Colour(s) authorised for use in the corporate logo

Corporate Communication: The entire range of public relations activities of a corporation as a whole, rather than activities designed for its individual segments.

Corporate Typeface: Approved typeface for use in the corporate identity programme

Created Event: An event or occasion created by public relations personnel to attract news coverage

Cropping of image: Eliminating part of a photographer illustration by trimming its edges to make it fit in a given space or removing its unnecessary parts

Data: Raw facts or observations; factual material used as a basis for discussion or decision-making

Deadline: The day and hour by which news copy must be in the hands of the editor of a newspaper or broadcast/telecast producer

Deep-etch plate: Special offset plate made from film positive for long-run and high quality fobs

Direct Mail: The promotion of ideas, products or services by letters or advertising sent to a carefully selected list of people

Disclaimer: Generally, a statement to qualify or disown responsibility for a statement ascribed to the source, in printed material

Editorial: An expression of the views and opinions of the management of a publication or broadcasting operation

Embargo: The warning about publication of a news release on a specified date, usually appears at the top of the first page of the news release or statement

Employee Communication: The two-way transmission of information to and from management and employees through various media, letters, newsletters, magazines, etc

Evaluation: Measurement of success or failure of a programme or a concept

Exclusive: A news story offered by a public relations practitioner to a single newspaper, broadcast or television station

Exposure: The extent to which the target audience becomes aware of a person, activity, theme or organization by the efforts of PR or advertising

Feature Article: A newspaper or magazine article which discusses and interprets an event or trends as opposed to spot reporting

Film Strip: A visual aid consisting of a short strip of film on which individually projected pictures are printed, generally sychronised with a sound track or audio tape

Financial Public Relations: The efforts of a publicly held company to communicate with shareholders, security analysts, institutional investors, stock exchanges, etc

Format: The size, make-up and general appearance of a publication

Fourth Estate: Generally identified with the Press. Derived from England where the Lords Temporal (House of Lords), the Lord Spiritual (the Clergy) and the House of Commons occupy the three "estates of the realm". Looking at the clout the press enjoyed it was recognised that the press was the Fourth Estate

Gatekeepers: A jargon used for people or groups who filter information in a communication network. Also referred to as opinion leaders, they accept or reject a message before it reaches the public. Gatekeepers exert great influence. In a newspaper or periodical, the term refers to the person (News Editor, Chief Sub- editor) who decides what news is to be used and what not

Ghost Writer: The term is used for a writer who is engaged to prepare material that will be attributed to another person. PR persons are also ghost writers

Going Public: The process by which a company issues and sells stock to the public, thus converting it to a public limited company

Grapevine: A slang used for information passed among employees that has not been officially circulated by the company

Grid sheet: Spaced vertical and horizontal guidelines for making layouts

Hard copy: The material sent to a typesetter in typed or hand-written form, for conversion into typset material

House Journal: A company publication aimed at its employees and/or other target groups. It can be internal, external, or a combination of the two. Also known as house magazine, house organ or newsletter

Image: The impression that the public has of a company

Image assembly: Alternate term of stripping, cutting out and placing in position, particularly with reference to arranging a photographic negative on a masking paper for a plate

Imagesetter: A high-resolution outputing device produces image on photographic paper or film which is used by the printer to make plate for printing

In-depth Interview: A lengthy technique requiring skill that gauges both conscious and unconscious perceptions and motivations

Information bearing element: Illustration, type, colour background, etc. that bear information in a design where as white space, pattern, colour background, etc. are decorative elements

Institutional Advertising: Paid advertising that promotes the company and its ideas or policies rather than its products and services

Interviewer: The individual who asks respondents the questions specified in a questionnaire for a survey

Laser Printer: A printer that uses laser technology to project an intense light beam with a very narrow band width to create the charge on the printer drum that picks up the toner and transfers it to the paper

Leaflet: A printed piece, usually with four to six folds, for inexpensive distribution

Letterform: The design elements that comprise the identity of individual letter characters

Libel: Printing or broadcasting a false or defamatory statement that injures a person's feelings or reputation

Line art: Black and white original, which can be reproduced without breaking into dots

Logo: A graphic symbol or combination of symbols and stylised letters, forming an acronym

Makeready: Copy or machine preparation of graphic materials production

Management: The people charged with the responsibility of determining organizational or corporate policies and planning and directing its operations

Mass Media: A medium of communication directed at and reaching a wide variety of people rather than a specified group

Media: The mass communication outlets available for the transmission of messages. The media include newspapers, magazines, radio, television, etc

Media Relations: The relationship between the company and all the various media of communication, including print and electronic

Mileage: A slang, used to refer to the number of column inches obtained in the print media on a given subject being publicised

Muckrakers: A term used for journalists who seek out and expose scandals or supposed scandals with unworthy motives

News Conference: A gathering of members of the news media, both print and broadcast, to cover an announcement usually too complicated to convey in any other manner

News Release: A written communication usually containing information of a timely nature sent to all news media

Open House: An occasion when a company invites its employees, customers, suppliers, or neighbours to visit the factory. Senior managers generally circulate among the guests

Opinion Polls: Research based on the theory of probability, generally conducted with questionnaires to ascertain the attitudes and opinions of a particular section of the community, public

Pamphlet: Almost synonymous with booklet or brochure

Press Conference: Same as news conference

Press Junket: A facility visit for media representatives in which transportation accommodation and other facilities are provided so they can view a special event or visit a site for reporting

Press Kit: Usually a docket containing background material, photographs, illustrations and news releases distributed at a news conference as source materials, for the news media.

Prestige Advertising: Advertising that tends to build an image or reputation rather than sell a specific product or service. It is in fact another term for institutional advertising

Proactive PR: Suo moto public relations anticipating events, circumstances, or situations, often through the execution of contingency plans; basically planned as aggressive public relations

Process Camera: A large camera used for graphic arts photography, such as shooting negatives and positives as a prelude to plate making, colour separation, or screening continuous-tone images into halftones

Proof: An impression of composed type in ink for making corrections

Propaganda: Originally ment to spread a belief, propagate an idea, now used to denote the promoting of true or false ideas, to make converts

Publics: Any group of people bond together by a common interest which a public relations programme seeks to influence; for example stockholders, customers, legislators, media employees, etc. The need to define publics is a primary responsibility of PR operations

Public Affairs: Usually refers to an organization's relations with government and legislative bodies

Public Relations: Planned, organised and sustained programme to develop public confidence and increase understanding towards an organization

Public Service Advertising: Advertising with a message in the public interest

Publicity: Information about an individual organization, event, issue or product disseminated through various media of mass communication to attract attention and influence opinion

Reactive PR: A policy of responding to a given set of circumstances, situations or events after the fact. Basically defensive PR

Reinforcement: To strengthen the attitudes and opinions of those who already tend to agree with or are committed to a given cause

Resolution: The number of dots per inch (dpi) used to represent an alphanumeric character or a graphics image

Respondent: The individual who is questioned and who responds to survey questions

Rumour: A widely circulated, unverified and usually inaccurate story from an unknown source

Sample: A portion of the total population involved in a survey. Although relatively small, if scientifically drawn, this portion is representative of the total population involved

Satellite: A communication satellite by means of which messages are relayed to and from earth stations

Slides: A visual aid making use of pictures projected on to a screen

Sound Slide: Visual illustrations projected on a screen simultaneously with a record or sound tape

Source: A person with useful information to communicate and who is contacted by the media

Special Event: A situation or happening designed to influence opinion, such as an anniversary, reception, grand opening, sporting event, product introduction, etc

Synergism: The action of two elements that when mixed have a greater impact than the sum of the two acting independently

System: An operating system of computer. It includes multitasking and an improved user interface

Targets: Any primary group/audience to be reached with a message — like teachers, farmers, scientists, employees, shareholders et al

Thermography: Thermography is a raised finishing process that uses special non-drying inks on letterpress presses. Before the ink gets dry, the surface is dusted with raisin powder then it passes under a heater which fuses the ink and the powdered compound causing these areas to swell

Trade Mark: A work or design used on an article of merchandise to identify it as the product of a particular manufacture like the Tatas, Hindustan Lever, Steel Authority of India, Bharat Heavy Electricals, etc

Type font: One complete set of characters in the same face, style and size, including all of the letters of the alphabet, punctuation, and symbols

Vector graphics: Also called object-oriented graphics, are made up of mathematically defined curves and line segments called vector

Index

26/11, 63, 185, 186, 303, 304
9/11, 18, 63, 109, 303, 304

A
Aaj Tak, 61
Aamir Khan, 203
Abhilaksh Rekhi, 97
Abhishek Bachchan, 67
Abraham Maslow, 122, 123
Aditya Birla, 7
AG Krishnamurthy, 11
AIDS/HIV, 10, 19, 123, 124, 184, 189, 291, 296, 302, 303
Air Deccan, 67
Air India, 139
Ajit, 297
All India Radio (AIR), 61, 97, 98
AL Jazeera, 17
Al Ries, 10, 194
Alvie L. Smith, 155
Amitabh Bachchan, 195, 297
Andrew Kritzer, 191
Anil Dhirubhai Ambani Group, 282
Animal Welfare Board of India (AWBI), 282
Arundhati Roy, 183
Arushi murder case, 295
Ashiwariya Rai, 67

B
BJP, 274
BSP, 274

Barack Obama, 306
Beijing, 61
Berlin, 18
Bharat Petroleum Corporation (Ltd), 302
Bhopal, 30
Bill Clinton, 292
"Bindas Bol", 124
Britain, 16, 17
Budweiser, 18

C
Cadbury, 20, 195
Carl Burton, 32
Cellular Mobile Telephone Service (CMTS), 62
Chief Justice K G Balakishnan, 295
China, 30
Cipla, 19
CK Prahlad, 304
Coca-Cola, 18, 108, 150, 193, 299
Congress (I), 76, 274
Corporate Identity for Image Build-up, 273-285
  corporate identity programme, 279-281
    Corporate visual identity, 274-278
      Creative concept, 275-278
      Design aspect, 274-275
      Design brief, 275
    Gathering information, 275
    Management aspect, 274
  Hindustan Lever Ltd (HLL), 281-282
  reliance, 282
  simulation: coffeestop and heritage tea 284-285
  vodafone, 282

D
David Selby, 190
Deepak Parekh, 121
Defining Public Relations, 3-24
  Care management, 19-23
  Corporate governance, 12-14
  Crisis communication, 18-19
  Defining PR, 4-6
  lessons for PR professionals, 23-24
  media watch, 14-15
  PR and propaganda, 4
  PR and public opinion, 6-9
    core values and competencies of organization, 6-7
    stakeholders/publics, 7
    communication needs of various publics, 7-8
    scanning environment 8
    cost-effective media 8
  PR in brand building, 10-12
  PR-global trends, challenges and opportunities, 9-10

public opinion consolidation, 16-18
Delhi Metro, 148
Delhi Milk Scheme, 108
Don J. Shultz, 190
Doordarshan, 95

E
Edward Burney, 26, 28
Edward J Robinson, 26
Electronic Mail, 247
Elizabeth Hurley, 292
Employee Communication, 134-144
   How PR works internally, 139-140
   Internal communication in times of change -137
   Media for internal communication, 136-137
      Era of entertaining employees (1940s), 135
      Era of informing employees (1950s), 135
      Era of open communication (Present), 135
      Era of persuasion (1960s), 135
Erik Kiirschbaum, 18
Ernie Pyle, 16

F
Farhan Akhtar, 203
FICCI Powerhouse Cooper (FICCI-PWC), 56, 59
Ford Motors, 76
France, 17, 18
Franklin D. Roosevelt, 76

G
General Electrical (GE), 12
Gas Authority of India (GAIL), 200

George C. Homans, 31
Georg Simmel, 32
George W Bush, 17, 60
Germany, 17, 18
Google, 65, 198
   Layout, 214
   Graphic design, 208-209
   Design brief, 209-213
      colour to create memorable moods, 213
   design principle- 210
      Elements of design, 210
      optical centre, 211
Greg Leichty, 29
Gulf War, 95, 127

H
Harwood I. Childs, 5, 189
HDFC Bank, 121
Hero Honda, 200
Hindustan Lever Ltd. (HLL), 195, 196, 281-282
Hugh M. Culbertson, 26
Hypertext Markup Language, (HTML), 247, 248, 249, 250, 251, 252, 253, 255

I
IBM, 12
ICICI, 149
IPKF, 185
ITC, 108, 195, 197
Indian Farmers and Fertilizers Corporation (IFFCO), 198, 204, 307
India, 3, 11, 12, 13, 14, 15, 30, 31, 55, 56, 59, 61, 95, 97, 108, 109, 124, 134, 139, 156, 166, 203, 284, 297, 299, 301, 304, 305, 306
Indian Airlines, 139, 283
Indian Drug Manufacturing Association (IDMA), 300

Indian Performing Right Society ltd. (IPRS), 297
Indian Railways, 139
Indira Gandhi, 161
Infosys, 13, 121
Integrated Marketing Communication (IMC), 191, 204
Intel, 198
International Monetary Fund (IMF), 306
International Public Relations Association (IPRA), 14, 15
Iraq, 16, 17, 18

J
Jakob Nielsen, 245
James E. Grunig, 27
Jamie Fawcett, 295
Jamshedpur, 139
Jemina Khan, 292
Janelle Barlow, 76
Janis Forman, 13
Jet Airline, 74, 125
Jim Speros, 190, 191
John F. Kennedy, 76, 295, 299
Joy C Gorden, 4
J. Walter Thompson, 73

K
Karan Thapar, 69
Karl Marx, 32
Kashmir, 166
Khushwant Singh, 291
Kingfisher, 200
Kiran Bedi, 196

L
Lalu Prasad Yadav, 297
L A Coser, 32
Larissa Grunig, 29
Laura Ries, 10, 194, 201, 204

Ledbetter Ivy Lee, 26, 28
Local Area Network, (LAN), 246
Lufthansa, 201
Lun zi pai bei system, 30
Lynne Masland, 159

M

MDH, 201
MMS, 64
Mahatma Gandhi, 6
Mahinder Singh Dhoni, 67
Mamta Banerjee, 183
Maneka Gandhi, 14, 291
Mantra Online, 246
Marlboro, 18
Marshal McLuhan, 100, 109, 125
Martin Nobon, 94
Martin Turner, 17
Matrix, 70
McDonald, 14, 305
Medha Patkar, 183
Media and PR, 55-71
Media scene, 56-59
    Internet, 64-66
      Cyber crimes, 64
      Future television, 65
      Power of people, 65
      Social networking sites, 66
    convergence, 63-64
    Media and politics, 69
    Media and social responsibility, 67
    Media fragmentation, 61
    New media, 62
      Cell revolution, 62
    Print media, 60
    Trends in print media, 60
    programme content, 59
    Radio, 61-62
    Reality shows, 67-68
      Beating trumpets, 68
      Paid communication, 68
    Trivialization of issues, concerns and human matters, 60-61
      Bollywood, 61, 2002, 203
Mercedes Benz, 14
Micheal Nauman, 4
Microsoft Corporation, 193, 194, 204
Muhammad Yunus, 304
Mukesh Ambani, 201

N

NDTV, 61, 67
Narmada Bachao Andolan, 183
Naryana Murthy, 13
National Council of Education Research and Training (NCERT), 296
National Rural Employment Guarantee Act (NREGA), 97
National Thermal Power Corporation (NTPC), 103, 151, 279, 280
New Delhi, 3, 107, 201
New York, 30, 99, 292
Nicole Kidman, 295

O

Organization of Pharmaceutical Producers of India (OPPI), 300

P

Pakistan, 13, 139, 166
Paul Argenti, 13
Pentagon, 16
Pepsi, 12, 194, 299
Pervez Musharaf, 67
Peter Blan, 32
Peter M. Blau, 31
Philip J. Kitchen, 190
"Phir Milenge", 124
Phaneesh Murthy 186
Pooja Bhatt, 124
Phonographic Performance Ltd. (PPL), 297
Crisis Communication, 159-186
    Emerging crises, 160
    Immediate crises, 159-160-166-183
    Sustained crises, 160-161
    Continuing crises, 183
    Exploding crisis, 161-166
    Failure in crisis handling 186
    Procter & gamble (P&G), 184
    Disaster managers, 185-186
PR lessons 183
    Marketing Mix, 189-204
      Analgesic drug, 194-195
      Cooking oil, 195
      e-learning, 197
      Hindustan Unilever limited (HUL) 196-197
      Indian farmers fertilizer cooperative ltd. (IFFCO), 198
      In-house models 200-202
      Microsoft, 193-194
      Nike, 199
      Pierre Cardian, 194
      Subway, 199
      Tums, 192
      Volkswagen- 200
PR Process, 72-89
    Communication, 78-79
      Monitoring and evaluation, 79
    planning, 77-78
      Channel-media preparation, 78
      Message-package production, 78
      Problem definition, 75-77
        Formal research methods, 77
        Informal research techniques, 75-77

Personal contact, 75
Media content analysis, 77
Field reports, 76
Focus groups, 77
Gatekeepers, 75-76
Mail analysis, 76
Strategy, 74-75
Creative strategy, 75
Media strategy, 74-75
PR Tools 91-119
  Internal environment, 92
  Corporate face 92-93
    External media, 93-99
      Mass media, 93-99
        Film/video, 98-99
        Outdoor, 99
        Press, 94-95, 110
        Radio, 97-98
        Television, 95-97
  media characteristics, 108-110
  Media for external communication, 104-108
  Annual reports, 104-105
  Brochure, 105
  Direct mail, 106
  Exhibitions, 106-107
  Open days, 107-108
  Publicity and promotional literature, 106
  Printed literature, 105
  Special events, 108
Media relations, 114-116
  Hospitality, 115
    Press briefings, 115
    Press conference, 114
    Press tours/facility visits, 115-116
  Print media, 110-114
    Cinema, 112
    employee communication, 113-114
    Local/ regional newspapers, 110
    Magazines, 111
    Mobile phones and sms, 113
    New media; Internet, 112
    Outdoor (posters, billboards/hoarding), 112
    Radio, 111
    Television, 111
  Selective media, 99-104
    Bulletin boards, 103-104
    Closed-circuit television, 102-103
    Clubs and societies, 104
    House journal, 101-102
    Idea boxes, 103
    Induction literature/ information kiosks, 101
    Shop-floor discussions, 103
    Visits by management, 104
Press Information Bureau (PIB), 95
Printed Literature, 235-243
  Brochure, 235-238
    Design approach, 237-238
  Leaflet, 238-240
    Distribution, 239-240
  Newsletter, 240-243
    Design, 242
    Production, 242-243
Project Vishwas, 195
  Corporate visioning, 48-49
    Creating corporate identity, 49
    Horizontal information flow, 47
    Informal information flow, 47
    PR communication, 47-48
    vertical/upward flow of communication, 47
  Media relations, 50
  finance, 52-53
  Law, 51
  Marketing, 50-51
  Personnel, HRD, industrial relations, 51-52
  Production, 53
Princess Diana, 295
Public Relations Consultants Association of India (PRCAI), 15
Laws and Ethics, 289-301
  Defamation, 289-290
  Libel, 290-292
  Slander, 292
  Defamation of corporation, 292-294
  Invasion of privacy, 294-296
  Copyright, 296-297
  Prethics, 298-301
Public Relations Society of India (PRSI), 15
Public Relations Theory, 26-42
  J M Grunig's model of symmetrical public relations, 28-31
    Autonomy, 29
    Conflict resolution, 29
    Equality, 29
    Holism, 28
    Innovations, 29
    Interdependence, 28
    Interest group liberalism, 29-31
    Moving equilibrium, 28
    Open system, 28
  Organizational theories, 31-33
    Conflict theory, 32
    Exchange theory, 31-32
    Structural- functional theory, 32-33
    Symbolic interactionism, 31
Public relations writing, 145-157
  Handouts, 154
  Kinds of press releases, 149-151
    "bad news" release, 150-151
    announcement release, 149

created news release, 149
feature news release, 150
response news release, 150
spot news release, 149
Press notes, 154
Printed words, 156-157
Rejoinders, 154-155
  effective press releases, 153-154
  structure of a news release, 151-152
  theoretical underpinnings, 145-148
  writing effective news release, 149
  writing for employees, 155-156
  writing for the media, 148-149
P.V. Narsimha Rao, 3

R
R Raju, 121
Rabinranath Tagore, 296
Ralf Dahrendorf, 32
Ratan Tata, 127, 183
Ray Eldon, 78
Red Cross, 18
Reliance Infocomm, 201
Rex F. Harlow, Dr. 5
Richard Ice, 30
Richard M. Emerson, 31
Robert Merton, 32
Russi Mody, 127, 139

S
Salman Khan, 67
Satish Gujral, 6
Satyam Computers, 12, 74, 121, 129, 155, 166
Satyam Online, 246
Scot Cutlip et al, 156
Shabana Azmi, 124

Shahrukh Khan, 297
Shanghai, 30
Shearlean Duke, 159
Shiela Dikshit, 76
Singur, 183
Sir Elton John, 291, 292
Sonia Gandhi, 67
South Africa, 19
Steel Authority of India, (SAIL), 103, 139
Subramanian Swamy, 292
Sushmita Sen, 192
S.Watson Dunn, 121

T
TISCO, 127, 139
TATA group, 74, 107, 156, 186, 195, 201, 305
Talcott Parson, 32
Telecom Regulatory Authority of India (TRAI), 62
Television Rating Points (TRPs), 61
Tony Blaire, 17
Trade Fair Authority of India (TFAI), 107
Troika of Communication Message, Medium and Audience, 120-132
  Audience, 130-132
  Designing messages, 121-125
    Themes, 122-125
  Media, 126-127
  Media attributes, 127-128
  Media objectives, 128-1030
    Special promotionals, 130
    Strategy, 129
  Message, 120-121
  message package options, 126
    audio visuals, 126
    films, 126
    print, 126
    radio, 126,

    television, 126
    video, 126
Tsunami, 63

U
USA, 3, 4, 11, 13, 14, 15, 16, 17, 18, 19, 30, 64, 109, 124, 149, 156, 159, 166, 190, 246, 247, 299, 300, 303, 304, 306
Uma Truman, 292
UN, 10, 298, 303
Understanding Multimedia, 256-271
  Animation, 268-270
    what is animation?, 268-269
    2d animation software, 269-270
    3d animation software, 270
    Other high-end software, 270
  Audio, 265-267
    Advantages of digital sound, 266
    Hardware and software requirement, 266-267
    Recording of sound, 266
    What is sound?, 266
  Authoring, 270
  Design, 261-263
    Running text, 261-262
    Text for titles, 262-263
      appropriate font, 262
      colour, 262-263
  Design and development, 259-261
    Kinds of navigation maps, 261
      linear structure, 261
      hierarchical structure, 261
      non-linear structure, 261
      composite structure, 261
    research and analysis, 259-260

file formats, 264-265
  image editing, 265
  native format, 265
graphics, 263-234
various categories, 256-257
  what is interactive?, 257
video, 267-268
  video technology, 267-267
  video editing tips, 268
    text handling software, 263
cd rom?, 257
hypermedia?, 257-259
  education, 258
  entertainment, 259-260
  hyperlink, 257
Type and Printing Processes, 216-233
  commercial printing, 230-232
    flexography, 230
    offset lithography, 231
    silk screen, 232
  copy printing, 226-227
  desktop printing, 227-230
    inkjet printers, 228-229
    laser printers, 229-230
  differentiate between text, display and poster type, 220
  display faces, 223
  type structure, 217-218
  legibility vs. readability, 220-223
  preparation *of* copesetting, 223-224
  printing, 225-226
  typesetting, 224-225
  letterform, 216

V

VSNL, 246, 277
Vietnam War, 16, 185
Vijay Mallaya, 200
V.P. Singh, 6

W

Watergate scandal, 166
Weapons of Mass Destruction (WMDs), 16
Web page Design, 245-255
  building a website, 249
  creating a web page, 248-249
    basic formatting, 248
    linking pages together, 249
  designing the pages, 249-252
    colour, 252
    e-mail, 247
    format, 251
    frame, 251
    grid, 250
    icon, 251
    image, 250
    internet, 246
    storyboard, 250
    type, 251-252
  internet address, 247
  production of a website, 253-255
  publishing a site, 252-253
    finding a host, 252-253
  web editing tools, 249
  website, 247-248
    requirements for the internet, 246
    what is network?, 246
    what is web page design?, 245
West Bengal, 74, 127, 186, 187
Wide Area Network, (WAN), 246
Wilbur Schramm, 75
World Trade Organization (WTO), 19
World War II, 16

Y

YV Networks (Regulation) Act 1995, 59
Yahoo, 65, 198
Yamuna River, 42, 150
Yoichi Mizutani, 200

Z

Zubin Mehta, 201